A CELEBRATION OF MAINE CHILDREN'S BOOKS

A Celebration of Maine Children's Books

by Lynn Plourde *&* Paul Knowles

THE UNIVERSITY OF MAINE PRESS

ORONO, MAINE 1998

05 04 03 02 01 00 99 98   1 2 3 4 5

ISBN: 0-89101-093-9

The paper used in this publication meets the minimum requirements of the American National Standard for Information Sciences—Permanence of Paper for Printed Library Materials, ansi z39.48-1984.

Printed and bound in the United States of America. Book design by Michael Alpert.

Acknowledgements for permission to reproduce book-covers and illustrations can be found on page 333.

To all Maine children,
especially our own Maine children—Lucas, Seth, and Kylee

CONTENTS

CHAPTER BOOKS 95

ANTHOLOGIES, SHORT STORIES, AND COLLECTIONS   153

POETRY   165

ACTIVITY BOOKS   289

INTRODUCTION

A *Celebration of Maine Children's Books* is a guide to what we feel are the best current Maine children's books. More than 400 books were considered for this guide, with 185 selected for inclusion. We chose books that were written about a Maine topic, set in Maine, or created as a result of the author's or illustrator's experiences in Maine. All selected books were in print as of the fall of 1997; a few books have recently gone out-of-print (as indicated in the individual accounts), but they are likely to still be available at libraries, some local bookstores, or on-line retailers.

This book is divided into eight sections:

> Alphabet, Counting, and Concept Books;
> Picture Books;
> Chapter Books;
> Anthologies, Short Stories, and Collections;
> Biographies, Autobiographies, and Journals;
> Informational Books;
> Poetry;
> Activity Books.

Each section is arranged alphabetically by author, with the exception of the biographies section which is arranged alphabetically by the subject of the biography.

The accounts of individual books consist of bibliographical information, a summary of the book, learning activities based on the book, and author/illustrator information. The information about authors and illustrators was gathered from written questionnaires, personal interviews, publisher brochures, book flaps, and reference sources.

At the end of *A Celebration of Maine Children's Books*, readers will find various lists and indexes, including addresses of authors, illustrators, and publishers.

Maine has an abundance of quality children's books. This heritage reflects the great affection that Maine citizens of all ages have for their state. Enjoy the celebration.

–Lynn Plourde and Paul Knowles

ALPHABET, COUNTING, AND CONCEPT BOOKS

ISLAND ALPHABET:
AN ABC OF MAINE ISLANDS

AUTHOR / ILLUSTRATOR: Kelly Paul Briggs
AGE LEVEL / LENGTH: 4-10 years / 32 pages
PUBLISHER / COPYRIGHT DATE: Down East Books / 1995
FORMAT / ISBN: Hardcover / 0892723696

Island Alphabet: An ABC of Maine Islands is an abecedary that works on several levels. Younger "readers" will enjoy listening to the short rhyme for each Maine island represented in the book, and they will enjoy looking for each letter of the alphabet in the illustrations. Older readers will focus on the interesting facts written in small print on each page. For example, on the "U" page, information about Upper Goose Island focuses on the largest great blue heron rookery located in New England. And the "S" page tells about Seal's Island's fire of 1978, which burned much of the island, and the current project by the National Audubon Society in which volunteers hand dig nesting burrows for puffins.

Author/illustrator Kelly Paul Briggs has created a unique alphabet book that adults, as well as children, will enjoy. Her illustrations are soft, delicate, and detailed; and her additional facts about each island are interesting and seem to challenge the reader to search for information about the stories behind additional Maine islands.

LEARNING ACTIVITIES

1. After reading *Island Alphabet: An ABC of Maine Islands* several times, play a guessing game with the book. Either show one of the illustrations while covering the text beneath it, or read one of the rhyming poems aloud while leaving the actual name of the island blank, or read a fact or two at the bottom of a page (without saying the name of the island). Then challenge others to remember and guess the actual name of the island shown in the illustration or referred to in the rhyme or the factual information. Take turns challenging each other with this guessing game as you refer to different islands in the book.

2. Using a Maine map or atlas, try to locate each of the Maine islands referred to in the book. Some pages give hints by telling what the island is located near (e.g., "offshore from the mouth of the St. George River," "nearby Islesboro and Seven Hundred Acre Island").

3. Select one letter of the alphabet. Use maps and Maine reference books to find as many other Maine islands as you can which begin with your selected letter. For example, for the letter "F," in addition to Fisherman Island, which is mentioned in the book, there are also Friendship Island, Franklin Island, Freese Island, Fiddle Head Island, and Flint Island. Or for the letter "T," in addition to Teal Island, included in *Island Alphabet,* there

are also Toms Island, Turtle Island, Tinker Island, Tumbler Island, Two Bush Island, and Trafton Island. Try to learn information about these islands and make a booklet about them—draw illustrations, create a rhyme about each one, and write one or more facts about each island.

ABOUT THE AUTHOR/ILLUSTRATOR

Island Alphabet: An ABC of Maine Islands is Kelly Paul Briggs' first book. Both sides of her family, going back seven generations, are from Maine. Briggs, a freelance illustrator and calligrapher, currently lives in Camden, Maine, with her husband and two children. For hobbies, she enjoys skiing, horseback riding, and collecting shells.

As a child, Briggs spent many summers sailing to the islands in Penobscot Bay; her father took the five children in their family boat for island picnics every weekend. As an adult, Briggs happily returned to visit the islands which were "home" to her. She has also spent two summers on Mosquito Island, caring for sheep and the island's stone house.

For this book, Briggs drew with Rotring artist's colors and pen. It took her twenty to thirty hours to complete each detailed illustration. When working, Briggs claims that she is in "a trance for days."

THE ALPHABET SYMPHONY

AUTHOR / PHOTO-ILLUSTRATOR: Bruce McMillan
AGE LEVEL / LENGTH: 4-8 years / 32 pages
PUBLISHER / COPYRIGHT DATE: Greenwillow (available from Apple Island Books) / 1977
FORMAT / ISBN: Hardcover / 0688801129

This alphabet book has no words, only letters of the alphabet and instruments. Photo-illustrator Bruce McMillan photographed the Portland Symphony Orchestra during rehearsals. McMillan shows the letters of the alphabet with black-and-white photos of different instruments in the orchestra. For example, the slide on a trombone looks like the letter "H" and the design on a cello looks like the letter "S." At the end of the book, McMillan names each instrument included in the book along with a full-view photograph of the instrument.

LEARNING ACTIVITIES

1. Look through *The Alphabet Symphony* and try to locate each letter of the alphabet in each photo. Then go back though the book, including the inside cover photo, to see if you can find even more letters of the alphabet. How many can you find in all?

2. As you look at each page of *The Alphabet Symphony*, try to guess the name of the instrument shown in each photograph. Then check to see if your guesses were correct using the key in the back of the book. If possible, arrange to visit a local middle school or high school band or orchestra. Look at their instruments. Can you see any letters in them? Use *The Alphabet Symphony* as a guide.

3. Try a different alphabet search. Choose a category of objects such as toys, foods, tools, trees, or clothes. Then study objects within that category and try to find as many letters of the alphabet as possible. For example, with toys, the grip on a wagon might look like the letter "D," or the handle on a jack-in-the-box might look like the letter "J," or the underneath of a top might look like the letter "V." Draw pictures to show the letters you found within your category and make a booklet from them. From your category, entitle your booklet (e.g., "Alphabet Toys" or "Food Letters").

ABOUT THE AUTHOR/PHOTO-ILLUSTRATOR

Born in Massachusetts, Bruce McMillan was raised in Bangor and Kennebunk, Maine. McMillan graduated from the University of Maine and worked as both a broadcasting producer/director and as a caretaker of McGee Island. While island-living, he decided to polish his writing skills. He has since combined writing and photography to create more than forty children's books, including *Nights of the Pufflings*, *The Baby Zoo*, *Fire Engine Shapes*, *Wild Flamingos*, *My Horse of the North*, and *Salmon Summer*. McMillan also speaks at conferences and to school children throughout North America, and he teaches writing courses at the University of Southern Maine and the University of New Hampshire. He lives with his wife in a home he built himself in Shapleigh, Maine.

Bruce McMillan credits his father with his early interest in photography. His father gave him his first camera at the age of five and his first professional camera at the age of nine. McMillan learned photography by "doing." Even as a child, McMillan tried taking creative photos—"one of a burning Christmas candle from above!" In high school, he took photos for his school newspaper and yearbook. McMillan claims that he takes many "bad" pictures, but the key to his success is shooting thousands of photos, if necessary, in order to get the few "perfect photographs" that he uses to illustrate his books. McMillan also takes great pride in designing his own books which often include playful borders like the colorful jelly beans in *Jelly Beans for Sale*.

"Parts of me are in all my books," claims McMillan. Some of his books reflect his training in biology, some his love of the sea, and all derive from his "Maine roots."

COUNTING WILDFLOWERS

AUTHOR / PHOTO-ILLUSTRATOR: Bruce McMillan
AGE LEVEL / LENGTH: 3-7 years / 28 pages
PUBLISHER / COPYRIGHT DATE: Lothrop, Lee & Shepard (hardcover); Mulberry, division of William Morrow & Co. (paperback) / 1986
FORMAT / ISBN: Hardcover / 0688028594; Paperback / 0688140270; Library binding / 0688028608

This simple counting book encourages youngsters to look for wildflowers and to count "nature's objects." The book illustrates numbers from 1 to 20, using photographs of wildflowers. Each page has a large photo of the appropriate number of wildflowers, as well as the written number, and a colored dot diagram that represents the flower on the page. For example, the page with the Black-Eyed Susans shows orange dots with black circles at the center. Wildflowers include the woodlily, black knapweed, chickweed, and spiderwort. The scientific name for each flower, the places where they grow, and the times of year they bloom are listed in the back of the book. McMillan photographed most of the flowers in their natural settings near his home in Shapleigh, Maine.

LEARNING ACTIVITIES

1. Go on a *Counting Wildflowers* hunt. Find as many wildflowers as possible using the book as a guide. If you find wildflowers other than those described in *Counting Wildflowers*, use reference books to discover their names, or consult a local gardener or horticulturist. Keep a list of the wildflowers you find, and draw a picture of each flower.

2. Create a counting book following the format of *Counting Wildflowers*. Draw pictures or take photographs of vegetables, fruits, toys, or pets. On each page of your book, write numbers and create colored dot diagrams, as Bruce McMillan did.

3. Play a memory game. After reading *Counting Wildflowers* several times with friends, close the book and test your memories. For example, which flower was used for the number eleven? If no one knows, the one asking the question can give verbal hints, such as "It has two words in its name and its initials are MC (Maltese cross)." Continue with more questions, such as: What color is the common tansy? Which number did the true forget-me-nots represent? How many sundrops were there?

ABOUT THE AUTHOR/PHOTO-ILLUSTRATOR

See information about Bruce McMillan on page 5.

GROWING COLORS

AUTHOR / PHOTO-ILLUSTRATOR: Bruce McMillan
AGE LEVEL / LENGTH: 2-6 years / 32 pages
PUBLISHER / COPYRIGHT DATE: Lothrop, Lee & Shepard (hardcover); Mulberry, a division of William Morrow & Co. (paperback) / 1988
FORMAT / ISBN: Hardcover / 0688078443; Paperback / 0688131123; Library binding / 0688078451

Growing Colors features large and bright close-up color photographs of fruits and vegetables. Each color in the book is paired with a fruit or vegetable (e.g., red–raspberries; orange– carrots; yellow–summer squash). A smaller photo on the opposite page provides a wide-angle view of each fruit or vegetable in its natural setting (on a bush, underground and barely peeking above the soil, on a vine, etc.), with the color-word printed in large correspondingly-colored letters. All fruits and vegetables shown were grown on farms and in gardens in York County, Maine, and in neighboring Rochester, New Hampshire.

Growing Colors is a great way for young children to learn their colors. Older children will enjoy studying the many kinds of fruits and vegetables pictured, including unusual ones such as purple beans and brown peppers.

LEARNING ACTIVITIES

1. Collect some of the fruits and vegetables found in *Growing Colors*, then have a tasting party. Talk about the different tastes (e.g., The cantaloupe looks juicy; does it taste juicy? How do raw peas taste? How do cooked peas taste?).

2. Work together with friends to create your own color book using a new theme, such as flowers, drinks, or ice cream flavors. Brainstorm to think of a variety of objects from your selected theme. Then illustrate each colored object on a separate page. Combine all the pages to make a booklet.

3. Have a discussion about nutrition. How many servings of fruits and vegetables are recommended daily? Keep a simple picture log of all the fruits and vegetables you eat every day for a week.

ABOUT THE AUTHOR/PHOTO-ILLUSTRATOR

See information about Bruce McMillan on page 5.

A CARIBOU ALPHABET

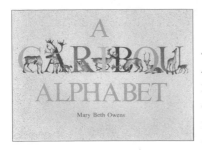

AUTHOR / ILLUSTRATOR: Mary Beth Owens
AGE LEVEL / LENGTH: 4-8 years / 32 pages
PUBLISHER / COPYRIGHT DATE: Tilbury House (hardcover); Farrar, Straus, & Giroux (paperback) / 1988
FORMAT / ISBN: Hardcover / 0937966258; Paperback / 0374410437

In *A Caribou Alphabet* the reader is immersed in the world of caribou. Many Mainers today are not familiar with this animal. Caribou have not lived in the state since the early 1900s, but an effort was made in the 1980s to transplant caribou from Newfoundland, Canada, to Maine. In spite of much hard work, the transplant effort was not successful.

This book follows a traditional alphabet book format. Each page shows a letter of the alphabet, with a picture and brief line of text providing a fact related to the caribou (I— When maddened by *insects*, a herd can stampede; X—By Micmac called *xalibu*, "pawer of snow," etc.). Consecutive phrases rhyme.

At the end of the book readers will find a compendium by Mark McCullough, who served as the director of the Maine caribou transplant project. The compendium lists every alphabetical word from the book, giving additional facts, such as the weight of caribou (calves, cows, and bulls), what caribou eat, and how they grow and migrate. This appendix is very detailed, yet it is easy to read and will interest both children and adults.

LEARNING ACTIVITIES

1. After reading *A Caribou Alphabet* several times, try to remember the special word that goes with each letter of the alphabet. What was the word for the letter B? For M? Check the book to see if your guesses were correct. How many words could you remember?

2. Take turns asking and answering questions about the book, such as:

   —How much does a caribou bull weigh? (200-650 pounds)
   —How many miles do caribou travel to get from their summer feeding ground to their winter feeding ground? (over 1,000 miles)

3. Select another Maine animal (moose, chickadee, lobster, etc.), research it, and write an alphabet book about that animal. Share your book with friends or family.

ABOUT THE AUTHOR/ILLUSTRATOR

Mary Beth Owens moved to Maine in the 1970s. She says that she was attracted by the land, people, and climate of Maine. Foremost, Owens considers herself a children's book illustrator. Her books usually start with images and concepts, which she then illustrates. The writing, which Owens calls minimal, flows from the illustrations. Owens is also the author/illustrator of *Counting Cranes,* and the illustrator of *Prize in the Snow* (see page 35) by Bill Easterling, as well as the illustrator of two books by Ethel Pochocki—*Rosebud and Red Flannel* (see page 92) and *A Penny for a Hundred* (see page 77).

Mary Beth Owens currently lives in Walpole, Maine, with her golden retriever which "takes *her* for walks in the woods everyday." Owens says that her two great loves are animals and music. She serves as a guide for the Audubon Society's winter walks. She also works with a local children's choir and teaches art lessons to children at her home.

When reflecting upon her work, Owens says that *A Caribou Alphabet* is her favorite book. She says that she "fell in love with the caribou and felt mysteriously connected to them." She wishes that the caribou transplant project could have been successful, but she believes everyone involved "gave it their all." When illustrating books that she has also written, such as *A Caribou Alphabet,* Owens uses watercolors with a dry brush technique so that there is less blurring and bleeding at the edges of the illustrations. For the books she has illustrated but not authored, she uses a more traditional watercolor style.

ABC'S OF MAINE

AUTHOR / ILLUSTRATOR: Harry W. Smith
AGE LEVEL / LENGTH: 3-7 years / 60 pages
PUBLISHER / COPYRIGHT DATE: Down East Books /
1980
FORMAT / ISBN: Paperback / 0892720700

ABC's of Maine pairs a drawing of a Maine scene with a short two-or-three-word phrase for each letter of the alphabet; for example: O—Osprey Overhead.

A two-page appendix provides further information for each phrase (e.g., what Acadia is and where it is located, special characteristics of osprey). The bold letter and simple phrase on each page make this book appropriate for young children who are learning the alphabet. Older children can also learn from it by studying the vocabulary words (e.g., luminous, osprey, rivals).

LEARNING ACTIVITIES

1. Before reading the book, make a list of possible Maine items that could go with each letter of the alphabet. For example, for the letter "A," ideas might be apples, Atlantic Ocean, and Augusta. See if any of the words are actually used in the book.

2. Use any page in the book as a story starter. Tell or write a story with that page as the beginning. Research the topic using nonfiction books if you wish to write a factual story, or create a fictional story about the Maine word and picture you select. Share your story with friends.

3. Use this book as a model for creating your own alphabet book. Follow a similar format to create an alphabet book about your town, county, or region of the state. Maine animals and foods are other possibilities for alphabet books.

ABOUT THE AUTHOR/ILLUSTRATOR

In 1972, Harry Smith moved from Indiana to Camden, Maine, in order to be near the sea. He and his wife bought an old sea captain's house located on the side of Mt. Battie, overlooking the village and the ocean. Smith has studied art at St. John's Academy, Washington University, and the Chicago Academy of Fine Arts. Currently, Smith works out of his own studio as a master miniaturist, author, illustrator, goldsmith, and sculptor. He has had one-man shows throughout the United States.

When creating *ABC's of Maine*, Smith wished "to teach the abc's in a manner that was not only colorful but educational. I felt kids would learn faster if they could associate the letters with things that were around them every day, in their own state." Smith is also the author and illustrator of four other books, including *The Art of Making Furniture in Miniature* and *Windjammers of the Maine Coast*.

COUNTING OUR WAY TO MAINE

AUTHOR / ILLUSTRATOR: Maggie Smith
AGE LEVEL / LENGTH: 3-7 years / 32 pages
PUBLISHER / COPYRIGHT DATE: Orchard Books / 1995
FORMAT / ISBN: Hardcover / 0531068846; Library binding / 0531087344

In *Counting Our Way to Maine*, a family heads to Maine for a summer vacation. They pack one baby, two dogs, three bicycles, and so on. As the family's vacation continues, the numbers in the book increase and the reader can see some of the family's special Maine experiences—twelve lobster pots, fifteen boxes of blueberries, eighteen mosquito bites!

The text for Maggie Smith's story is appropriately simple for young children; but her cartoonish, colorful illustrations are filled with humorous details which older children and adults will enjoy. This book works best as a "lap book" for an adult and child to share one-on-one, so that both may enjoy the detailed illustrations and also be close enough to locate all of the small objects (nineteen clams, twenty fireflies).

LEARNING ACTIVITIES

1. Before reading this book, try to guess all the "Maine" objects that might appear in this vacation book about Maine. Could someone see a moose on a vacation to Maine? Or skyscrapers? What about pine trees? Write down or draw pictures of all your guesses. Then after reading *Counting Our Way to Maine*, compare your list of guesses with the actual objects in the book. Which Maine objects from the book did you guess correctly? Do you think some of your objects might have worked just as well in this book? Why or why not?

2. Share this book with a friend and try to find all the objects in each picture, but have a special rule: no pointing. You can*not* point to the objects you find, but rather you must tell where each object is located. For example, you might say, "I see one sand castle on top of the mother's legs," "I see a second sand castle in front of the baby," "I see a third sand castle between two flip flops," and so on. Continue describing where you see each object until you and your friend find every object on each page of the book.

3. Create your own counting book. For example, you might create a book about "Counting Our Way to Grammy's House," or "Counting Our Way to School," or "Counting Our Way to Baxter State Park." Include objects in your book that you would actually see on the way to your selected location. Make certain that each page has the number written correctly and the appropriate number of objects drawn for that number. When your book is finished, share it with a friend and challenge your friend to locate all the featured objects on each page.

ABOUT THE AUTHOR/ILLUSTRATOR

Maggie Smith was born in Boston in 1965. From the time she was four years old, she has vacationed in Maine during the summer because her family "deemed it the only destination worthy of summer vacations." Her illustrations for the book are done with watercolor gouache, pastel pencils, and pencil and ink line. While Smith was a fine arts major at Washington University in Saint Louis, she worked on crafts and textile design. She has written and illustrated other picture books, including *My Grandma's Chair* and *Argo, You Lucky Dog*.

Smith currently lives in a small apartment in New York City. She hopes someday to have more space for her work so that she can pursue her interests of fabric painting and dollmaking—supplies for which she has "collected at many top-notch Maine yard sales!"

PICTURE BOOKS

MUD MAKES ME DANCE IN THE SPRING
I WEAR LONG GREEN HAIR IN THE SUMMER
WIND SPINS ME AROUND IN THE FALL
I SLIDE INTO THE WHITE OF WINTER

I SLIDE INTO THE WHITE OF WINTER

Charlotte Agell

AUTHOR / ILLUSTRATOR: Charlotte Agell

AGE LEVEL / LENGTH: 3-7 years / 32 pages

PUBLISHER / COPYRIGHT DATE: Tilbury House, Publishers / 1994

FORMAT / ISBN: Hardcover / 0884481123 (Mud Makes Me Dance in the Spring); 0884481131 (I Wear Long Green Hair in the Summer); 088448114X (Wind Spins Me Around in the Fall); 0884481158 (I Slide into the White of Winter)

Brunswick author Charlotte Agell has written a set of seasonal books:

> *Mud Makes Me Dance in the Spring;*
> *I Wear Long Green Hair in the Summer;*
> *Wind Spins Me Around in the Fall;*
> *I Slide into the White of Winter.*

These small-format, brightly-colored books are perfect for little hands and little hearts. Agell captures each season from a child's perspective. In the spring, there's mud, swinging, hummingbirds, planting, dandelion greens, and more. In the summer, the little girl in the book goes to the beach with her father and has "peanut butter and jam and sand sandwiches" and wears seaweed for hair. In the fall, the girl plays in the leaves and visits a pumpkin farm. And in the winter, the same little girl has steamy breath like "dragons in the winter," goes belly sliding on the snow, makes snow angels, and enjoys oranges and hot chocolate for a winter picnic. The set of books as a whole gives young readers a clear picture of the differences in Maine's four seasons. Each book may also be enjoyed by itself for its playfulness and celebration of both the individual season and family life.

LEARNING ACTIVITIES

1. Charlotte Agell's seasonal books are very personal in some ways. She shares what must have been special to her family, such as getting a haircut outside in the spring or sharing one cup of hot chocolate on a winter picnic. Think of some of your own family's experiences and rituals during one of the seasons. Write down words and draw illustrations to make your own personalized season book.

2. Play a guessing game with these four books. Take turns with friends or family acting out a section from one of the books. You might pretend to be digging dandelion greens, or doing a headstand in the ocean, or losing your boot in a snowdrift. Everyone else must guess which book or season the action is from and then try to guess the actual activity portrayed. Continue with more role-playing and guessing.

3. In these books, author/illustrator Charlotte Agell shows close family relations. In the summer book, she has a little girl and her father share a day at the beach, just the two of them; and in the fall book, she shows the girl's close relationship with a special aunt. The dedications to the books appear to be to Agell's family members. What about your family? Write or tell a story about a special member of your family.

ABOUT THE AUTHOR/ILLUSTRATOR

When asked about her Maine connections, Charlotte Agell claims that they started when she was a child:

> When I was a Swedish child living in Montreal, I wrote a story about a fictional town called Halibut, Maine. I can't remember much about the story except that the young protagonist led a bleak and romantic life. Although I wouldn't necessarily use those two adjectives to characterize my life, I sometimes feel as though I wrote myself into Maine right there and then. I did not actually come to Maine until 1977, when I arrived from my Hong Kong high school to go to Bowdoin College. I have been living here in Maine happily ever since.

Agell currently lives in Brunswick, Maine, with her husband and two children. She loves baking and reading.

Charlotte Agell is the author/illustrator of numerous children's books, including *The Sailor's Book*, *Dancing Feet*, and *To the Island* (see page 168). When talking about her "Maine" children's books, Agell describes her seasonal series, including *Mud Makes Me Dance in the Spring*, as her fictional autobiography, with the pictured backyard being her "old Gardiner backyard, quince bush, hawthorn tree, and all" and the summer beach actually being Popham Beach. As for her book *I Swam with a Seal* (see page 167), which features Maine animals, Agell states that the book grew out of an experience she had swimming with a seal in the ocean near Harpswell. Agell's illustrations are done with ink, watercolor, and Berol Prisma Color Stick.

A POSSIBLE TREE

AUTHOR: Josephine Haskell Aldridge / ILLUSTRATOR: Daniel San Souci
AGE LEVEL / LENGTH: 4-8 years / 32 pages
PUBLISHER / COPYRIGHT DATE: Simon & Schuster Books for Young Readers / 1993
FORMAT / ISBN: Hardcover / 0027004074

A Possible Tree tells the story of a crooked, old fir tree. People laugh at the tree. It's not tall and straight enough for the woodsmen, and it has a funny shape, making it look "like

Christmas wreaths all over." Yet, there's something special about the tree. It's a safe haven for animals. A raccoon hides from a hunter in the top branches of the tree. A blue jay rests and preens on one of its branches. A squirrel family lies on the tree's thick needles and eats the seeds hidden in the cones. An injured fox recuperates under a low branch of the tree. An owl, rabbits, and a coon dog join the tree's menagerie.

Then on Christmas Eve, the humans return and look at the tree in wonder. As they view the hodgepodge collection of animals nestled in the crooked fir tree, they ask, "Who would believe this was possible?" A *Possible Tree* is a beautiful Christmas book. Author Josephine Haskell Aldridge's text is simple and poetic. Daniel San Souci's watercolor illustrations capture the beauty of an unusual Christmas celebration.

LEARNING ACTIVITIES

1. Discuss the title of this book. Why do you think it was called A *Possible Tree?* Do you think this title was the best one for this book? Why or why not? Look at several other books and discuss their titles. How do you decide what titles you want for your own stories? Is it easy or difficult for you? Do you think of a title before you start writing or afterwards? Would you ever change a title to one of your stories? Why or why not?

2. Learn more about fir trees by reading nonfiction books or talking to a nature expert. What different kinds of firs are there? How tall can firs grow? What uses are there for fir trees? Write a short report about what you learn.

3. Turn A *Possible Tree* into a play and act it out for schoolmates, friends, or family. Create scenery for the play. Add dialogue to the story. Should the characters be costumed people or puppets?

ABOUT THE AUTHOR

Josephine Haskell Aldridge was born in New York City in 1925. Her father's ancestors came to Maine in 1720, and her father bought a saltwater farm in 1906, in Phippsburg, near the fishing village of West Point, Maine. Aldridge spent summers on the farm as a child and has lived there as an adult for thirty-five years. Aldridge's late husband, Richard Aldridge, was a well-known New England poet; and her father, Ernest Haskell, was a distinguished artist. Some of his works are in the art collection at Bowdoin College.

Aldridge began her career as an illustrator, but then she switched to writing. She is the author of four children's books, including A *Penny for a Periwinkle* and *Fisherman's Luck.* She claims that her books "germinated over a full dishpan or an ironing board or a broom" while caring for four children. Aldridge still lives in Phippsburg. Due to ill health, she is not able to respond to letters from young fans; but she "loves" reading letters sent to her in care of her publisher, Simon & Schuster.

ABOUT THE ILLUSTRATOR

Daniel San Souci is the illustrator of more than thirty children's books, including two "Maine" ones: *A Possible Tree* and *Jigsaw Jackson* (see page 20). As a child, San Souci was encouraged to draw by his parents. His father, who could draw well, taught him when he was young; and later he took painting classes in the evening through an adult education program. San Souci went on to study art at the California College of Arts and Crafts in Oakland. Several years later, he collaborated with his brother Robert San Souci, an award-winning author, on a children's book entitled *The Legend of Scarface: A Blackfeet Indian Legend* which won numerous awards, including the "*New York Times* Best Illustrated Book of the Year." Currently, San Souci lives in the Oakland Hills, overlooking San Francisco Bay.

Watercolors is the chosen medium for San Souci. He claims that his work has been inspired by Winslow Homer, Andrew Wyeth, and Edward Hopper. For each book that he illustrates, San Souci experiments with different papers and develops a unique palette striving to create a fresh look.

COCOA ICE

> AUTHOR: Diana Appelbaum / ILLUSTRATOR: Holly Meade
> AGE LEVEL / LENGTH: 5-10 years / 56 pages
> PUBLISHER / COPYRIGHT DATE: Orchard Books / 1997
> FORMAT / ISBN: Hardcover / 0531300404; Library binding / 0531330400

In the late 1800s, Maine harvested ice from its rivers while Santo Domingo harvested chocolate from its cacao trees. Schooner ships sailed the Atlantic, bringing the ice south, the chocolate north; this trade resulted in two treats: cocoa ice and chocolate ice cream. In the first half of this picture book, young readers glimpse the life of a Dominican girl—how her family turns cocoa beans into chocolate, how it goes diving for conchs, and how it trades coconuts, bananas, and cocoa beans from their hollowed out canoe with sailors on the large schooners. The second half of the book shares the story of a girl who lives near the Kennebec River in Maine—how her father cuts ice from the river, with a crew of 50 men, storing it in an icehouse for safe-keeping until shipping season, how he rides a horse-drawn wagon (equipped with runners) up the icy river to the falls, and how he sends her sailor-uncle off in a schooner to trade their sawdust- and hay-covered ice for treats from Santo Domingo. The uncle also trades mementos between the two girls: a conch shell and a balsam bag.

Cocoa Ice weaves historically-based facts into an interesting story. The complexities, uncertainties, and details of ice harvesting are clearly explained through the text and illustrations. For example, one two-page spread shows large, horse-pulled saws crisscrossing the river while the story states: "Back and forth they go, grooving and cutting until the river looks like a giant checkerboard, only—all the squares are white." Appelbaum and Meade have created a distinctive Maine children's book—one that informs as well as entertains, as it shows the impact of Maine beyond its own boundaries.

LEARNING ACTIVITIES

1. *Cocoa Ice* tells how Maine in the late 1800s traded ice harvested from its rivers for goods from the south. Learn the story behind modern-day Maine trade. What Maine products are traded or sold in other parts of the world—blueberries, potatoes, shoes, etc.? Select one such product and learn the story of its place in a global economy. Where is it sold? How is it marketed or advertised? How is it shipped? What special laws or rules apply to its sale outside of the country? Check nonfiction books and interview sales or marketing representatives (by phone, by mail, or in person) for your selected Maine product. Write a summary or give an oral report describing what you learned.

2. Learn more about ice harvesting in Maine. When did it begin? When did it end? Where was ice harvested in Maine? How was it harvested? Who could claim rights to harvesting ice in a specific area? What were the dangers and pitfalls of ice harvesting? Check with your local historical society or at a Maine museum to learn the answers to these questions. Write a report about ice harvesting.

3. Help to make some homemade chocolate ice cream. You'll need to find a recipe and someone with an ice cream maker. Gather the ingredients, follow your recipe, and enjoy! Instead of making homemade chocolate ice cream, you might arrange a visit to a commercial ice cream producer to view how they make chocolate ice cream.

ABOUT THE AUTHOR

Diana Appelbaum wrote *Giants in the Land* (see page 232), her first children's book, while researching the history of New England's environment. Appelbaum grew up in Old Lyme, Connecticut, and graduated from Barnard College. As a child, Appelbaum enjoyed visits to Castine, Maine, to see her cousin who was the commandant of Maine Maritime Academy. As an adult, Appelbaum still enjoys summer visits to Maine with her own children; they have camped, hiked, and canoed on the Penobscot River, and visited relatives in Falmouth and on Peak's Island. Appelbaum currently lives in Newton, Massachusetts, with her husband and three children.

Cocoa Ice is her fourth picture book. She is also the author of *Thanksgiving: An American Holiday* and *The Glorious Fourth*.

ABOUT THE ILLUSTRATOR

Holly Meade lives in New Hampshire. She is the illustrator of the Caldecott Honor Book, *Hush! A Thai Lullaby*, as well as *Small Green Snake*. To create *Cocoa Ice*, Meade used cut paper and gouache illustrations. She describes the illustrations as "an exciting challenge" since she had to mix a warm palette for the tropics and a cool palette for Maine.

JIGSAW JACKSON

AUTHOR: David F. Birchman / ILLUSTRATOR: Daniel San Souci
AGE LEVEL / LENGTH: 5-10 years / 32 pages
PUBLISHER / COPYRIGHT DATE: Lothrop, Lee & Shepard (a division of William Morrow & Co.) / 1996
FORMAT / ISBN: Hardcover / 0688116329; Library binding / 0688116337

Jigsaw Jackson is an original tall tale about a young potato farmer from Saponac, Maine (Yes, there really is such a Maine town. Hint: look at Grand Falls Township in Penobscot County.) Actually, the farmer's name is J. Jupiter Jackson, and at the beginning of the story he's never even heard of jigsaw puzzles. He's passing the winter season by playing checkers with the plow horse, reading stories to the chickens and barn mice, and listening to opera records with his mynah bird. But Maine winters can be long. And so when Sean McShaker (the world's greatest jigsaw-puzzle maker) offers Jackson a chance to join him on the road putting jigsaw puzzles together, Jackson agrees so long as he's back by potato-planting time.

It just so happens that Jackson is a whiz at putting together jigsaw puzzles. He can put together a ten thousand piece puzzle in fifteen minutes (his secret: "join the pieces that fit together and don't join the pieces that don't fit together"). Jigsaw Jackson travels the country with Sean McShaker, performing greater and greater jigsaw feats, and becoming a national hero. Everyone seems happy except for the animals Jackson has left behind on his farm. They send telegrams, make phone calls, and track Jackson down in New York City, begging him to return home. Jigsaw Jackson performs one final jigsaw feat before the President and Congress, but something goes terribly wrong; and Jackson realizes that there's no place like home after all. Jackson happily returns to Saponac, his pets, and the continuing Maine winter.

Author David F. Birchman and illustrator Daniel San Souci have teamed up to create a read-aloud, laugh-aloud tale. *Jigsaw Jackson* is filled with clever words, delightful characters, and numerous visual jokes.

LEARNING ACTIVITIES

1. Have your own jigsaw challenge. Invite a friend or relative to have a puzzle-making race with you. You should each have your own jigsaw puzzle with the same number of pieces. Then race to see who can complete their puzzle faster (It may take you longer than 15 minutes—more likely, parts of several days—so don't get discouraged!). After your race, discuss strategies. Did you put the border together first? Did you sort pieces— how so? Keep helpful strategies in mind the next time you make a jigsaw puzzle. Rather than working independently, you might prefer making a puzzle with several friends or relatives. In that case, estimate the total time you believe it will take you to complete the puzzle altogether; then race to try and beat your predicted time.

2. Learn about the history of jigsaw puzzles. When was the first one created? Who invented jigsaw puzzles? How were early puzzles made? How has puzzle-making changed over the years? Write a report summarizing what you learn.

3. Maine winters can seem a bit long (that's an understatement!). How do Mainers pass the time in the winter? Take a survey of at least twenty Mainers to learn what they do to help pass the time in winter. Survey people from different age groups. Make a graph to show the results of your survey. Did you find differences between age groups?

ABOUT THE AUTHOR

David F. Birchman grew up in the 1950s on a small farm outside Battle Ground, Washington. He spent much time as a child curled up behind the woodstove with a good book. His definition of a good book included anything illustrated by N. C. Wyeth or Howard Pyle, Carl Sandburg's *Rootabaga Stories*, and a story about Paul Bunyan by Louis Untermeyer. Birchman claims that these stories strongly influenced his own writing. As a writer, Birchman says that he works slowly and "half by ear;" he believes that a successful children's story must have "a strong internal rhythm that carries the reader along."

Birchman created *Jigsaw Jackson* after reading an article about the history of jigsaw puzzles in *Smithsonian* magazine. For the story, the author needed a modest, unassuming hero—"someone inclined to hide his shining talent under a bushel basket." And so a humble potato farmer from Maine seemed like a natural choice. When deciding where in Maine to set his story, Birchman simply pulled out a Maine map and randomly pointed. And that's how the small town of Saponac came to be featured in *Jigsaw Jackson*. Birchman is also the author of several other children's books including *The Raggly Scraggly No-Soap No-Scrub Girl*, *Brother Billy Bronto's Bygone Blues Band*, and *A Green Horn Blowing*.

Currently, Birchman lives in Thousand Oaks, California, with his wife, two children, and "one out-of-tune piano, three fat old cats, and a cranky parrot."

ABOUT THE ILLUSTRATOR

See information about Daniel San Souci on page 18.

THE LITTLE FIR TREE

AUTHOR: Margaret Wise Brown / ILLUSTRATOR: Barbara Cooney
AGE LEVEL / LENGTH: 4-8 years / 32 pages
PUBLISHER / COPYRIGHT DATE: HarperCollins Children's Books / 1954
FORMAT / ISBN: Paperback / 0064430839 (recently out of print); Library
binding / 0690040164

A little fir tree sits by itself in a field. It feels lonely, far from the big trees in the forest. One day a man appears, carefully digs up the little tree, and takes it through the forest to his home. The tree is a special surprise for the man's little boy, who is lame and in bed and has never been outside. The tree is decorated for Christmas and stays in the house until spring, when it is carefully returned to its place in the field.

As the tree and the boy grow, they continue to be reunited each Christmas. But one year, the boy's father does not come for the tree. The tree stands alone, feeling abandoned, until it has its own special Christmas surprise.

LEARNING ACTIVITIES

1. Maine grows many Christmas trees, a great number of which are shipped out of state. Visit a Christmas tree farm. See and learn how the trees are grown and cared for, and how and when they are shipped to other locales.

2. The boy in *The Little Fir Tree* is described as lame, a term that is rarely used today. There are many reasons why a person might not be able to walk, such as cerebral palsy or muscular dystrophy. Through the special education department in your school system, arrange to meet a child who has difficulty walking. How does that child deal with his/her disability? What exercises or equipment must that child use to help with walking?

3. Barbara Cooney began illustrating books in 1940. Her illustrations have changed over the years. Compare the pictures in *The Little Fir Tree* with those in more recent books like *Island Boy*, *Hattie and the Wild Waves*, and *Emily*. How are the illustrations similar and different? Can you tell the books were created by the same illustrator? Which illustrations do you like better—the older ones or the most recent ones? Why?

ABOUT THE AUTHOR

Margaret Wise Brown (1910-1952) worked as an editor, translator, poet, songwriter, and children's book author during her short life. She was prolific, authoring more than 100 children's books under her own name and three different pen names: Golden Mac-Donald, Juniper Sage, and Timothy Hay. Brown was a pioneer of concept books for preschoolers, including the *Noisy* books and her classic, *Goodnight Moon*. Brown was reported to write a story in 15 to 20 minutes on whatever was available (e.g., old envelopes, grocery bills), but then to take up to two years testing the book on children and polishing it until she felt it was right.

Many of Brown's children's books included animals and wilderness settings, which were inspired by her abundance of childhood pets, and her time spent in Vinalhaven, Maine, as an adult. Brown spent from May to October of each year in an isolated, granite-cutter's house at Wharf's Quarry, Vinalhaven. The house could only be reached by boat or plane and had no bathroom, electricity, or phone. Her life on Vinalhaven served as the inspiration for her 1947 Caldecott-winning book, *The Little Island* (see page 24).

ABOUT THE ILLUSTRATOR

Barbara Cooney was born in Brooklyn, New York, and spent her summers as a child on the Maine coast. Cooney's mother, an artist, encouraged her early on. After graduating with an art degree from Smith College in 1938, Cooney decided that children's book illustrating would be a job suited to her desire for artistic freedom and creativity. In 1940, she illustrated her first book, *Ake and His World*, by the Swedish poet Bertil Malmberg. More than five decades later, she is still creating children's books, including her recent *Eleanor* (about Eleanor Roosevelt), which she wrote and illustrated.

Cooney has received the Caldecott Medal twice—in 1958 for *Chanticleer and the Fox*, and in 1979 for *Ox-Cart Man*, written by Donald Hall. During the first two decades of her career, Cooney used scratchboard. Since then, she has also illustrated books with pen-and-ink, collage, and watercolors. Most recently, she has worked almost exclusively in acrylics on silk.

Cooney lives in Damariscotta, Maine, with her husband, a retired country doctor, in a house overlooking the sea. Her interests include gardening and swimming. She has four grown children and three grandsons. Cooney's love of the ocean has led her to illustrate several books set by the sea. Her books are known for their historical accuracy and attention to detail. Cooney writes, "Of all the books I have done, *Miss Rumphius* and *Island Boy* are the closest to my heart." She has illustrated a total of 109 books, eighteen of which she has also authored.

THE LITTLE ISLAND

AUTHOR: Margaret Wise Brown (using the pen name, Golden MacDonald) /
ILLUSTRATOR: Leonard Weisgard
AGE LEVEL / LENGTH: 5-8 years / 48 pages
PUBLISHER / COPYRIGHT DATE: Bantam Doubleday Dell Books for Young Readers / 1946
FORMAT / ISBN: Paperback / 044040830X
AWARDS: Caldecott Medal, 1947

Children today can best enjoy *The Little Island* by Margaret Wise Brown when they put it into historical perspective. *The Little Island* was a remarkable book for its time, as shown by the fact that it won the Caldecott Medal for picture book illustration in 1947. Brown's quiet, poetic text tells young readers about the changes that come to a Maine island throughout each of the four seasons; and Weisgard's illustrations were described as "brilliant and exciting" by book reviewers in the 1940s.

The Little Island also shows a small black kitten visiting the island. The kitten imagines himself being like the little island, but rather "a little fur island." However, the kitten sees himself connected to the rest of the world as he touches and stands on land. The kitten doubts the island's connection to the rest of the world until he learns the island's secret—that below the ocean "all land is one land." The message of oneness with nature continues as the book ends with the words:

> And it was good to be like a little island.
> A part of the world
> and a world of its own
> all surrounded by the bright blue sea.

LEARNING ACTIVITIES

1. When writing this book, author Margaret Wise Brown used a pen name, Golden MacDonald. Brown wrote under a different name so that it wouldn't seem like she had quite so many books published (She published more than 100 children's books during her short career). Brown chose the name Golden MacDonald from someone she knew, an elderly Maine handyman. If you were to choose a pen name for your writings, what name would you choose? Why? Could you create a pen name for yourself that combined a favorite hobby and your street name? Or a name that used your middle name and the name of one of your ancestors?

2. *The Little Island* was the Caldecott-winning book in 1947. The Caldecott Medal is given annually to the children's book with the best illustrations that was published in the United States during the previous year. Ask a librarian to help you find two Caldecott Medal books in addition to *The Little Island*. Try to find two books published in different decades. That is, *The Little Island* was published in the 1940s, and so you might read a Caldecott book from the 1960s and another from the 1980s. After reading the two other books, compare them with *The Little Island*. Which of the three Caldecott Medal winners was your favorite? Why? How did the illustrations in the three books differ from each other?

3. *The Little Island* is poetic as it describes how a small Maine island changes during each of the four seasons. Write a poem that tells how your yard changes during the four seasons. Don't try to make your words rhyme, but rather try to make word pictures in your poem. For example, "The snow makes a tiny white mountain on my swing seat," or "I make crunchy jumps into the fiery pile of leaves," or "Robins on my lawn eat spaghetti worms."

ABOUT THE AUTHOR

See information about Margaret Wise Brown on page 23.

ABOUT THE ILLUSTRATOR

Leonard Weisgard is the author and illustrator of more than 180 children's books. His fifty-plus year career began in 1937 with his first book, *Suki, the Siamese Pussy*. He was also the illustrator of two Caldecott Honor Books, *Little Lost Lamb* and *Rain Drop Splash*. In 1947, he won the Caldecott Medal in recognition of his illustrations for Margaret Wise Brown's *The Little Island*. In his Caldecott acceptance speech for the book, Weisgard explained that the pictures "grew right up out of the water." He described how he visited the little island off the Maine coast (near Vinalhaven) and experienced its mists, sunrises, swimming seals, changing clouds, and more. And then he tried to store all those memories and incorporate them in the book. Weisgard claims that he learned much about children's books from Margaret Wise Brown. He collaborated with Brown on twenty-five books, including several of the "Noisy" books. He visited Brown frequently and featured her terrier named Smoke in several of their books.

Weisgard was born in New Haven, Connecticut, in 1916. He grew up in England. He studied graphic arts at the Pratt Institute and the New School of Social Research in New York. Weisgard remembers many "dreary" pictures in books when he was a child, and he was determined to create brighter books which would be more inviting to children. Weisgard has been a resident of Denmark since 1970.

GLUSKABE AND THE FOUR WISHES

AUTHOR: traditional legend, retold by Joseph Bruchac /
ILLUSTRATOR: Christine Nyburg Shrader
AGE LEVEL / LENGTH: 6-10 years / 32 pages
PUBLISHER / COPYRIGHT DATE: Cobblehill Books/Dutton (Penguin USA) / 1995
FORMAT / ISBN: Hardcover / 0525651640

In this Abenaki legend, author Joseph Bruchac retells the story of how Gluskabe, the helper of the Great-Spirit, came to grant the wishes of four Abenaki men. As Bruchac states in his introductory note, this tale is the combination of four different written versions of the legend combined with oral tellings that he has heard over the years. The result is a story which both entertains and teaches.

The four men struggle on their difficult journey to Gluskabe's island through fog, wind, and rough seas. Finally, they arrive on Gluskabe's island and each asks for a wish. One man wishes for numerous possessions, another wishes to be taller than other men, another asks for a long life, and the last asks for the ability to be a good hunter so that he may feed his people. Gluskabe gives each man a pouch with answers to their wishes and asks them not to open the pouches until they return home. But on the journey home, the first three men are anxious and peek into their pouches. Each of their wishes are fulfilled but in unexpected ways. The last man waits and opens his pouch when he arrives back at his lodge. When he opens his pouch, he finds nothing inside, but "a great understanding" suddenly fills him, and he becomes one of the best hunters in the land. His unselfish wish has been granted by Gluskabe.

LEARNING ACTIVITIES

1. Talk with your family members and learn about a story from your immediate family's past or one that has been passed down about your ancestors. It might be a story of a big event, such as a wedding or a flood; it might be a story of how your ancestors came to settle in a specific area of Maine; it might be a story about a family mystery. Talk with different family members in order to hear several versions of the family story. Then combine the versions into one written story. How will you decide which parts to include? How can you make the story seem as if it is from one perspective, told by one storyteller? Afterwards, share your written story with family members and learn what they think about it.

2. Have a "what if" discussion about *Gluskabe and the Four Wishes*. What do you think would have happened if each of the first three men had waited and opened their pouches when they arrived back home? Do you think their wishes would have been granted in the same ways or different ways? What if all four men had asked for unselfish wishes—do you think their wishes would have come true? What if you could ask a wish of Gluskabe? What would your wish be? How do you think it would have been granted?

3. Find the double-page spread in *Gluskabe and the Four Wishes* which has no words and shows the fourth man listening to the voices of the animals. Write your own words for this page. What do you think the voices would say to the man? What would the mountain lion say? The bear? The deer?

ABOUT THE AUTHOR

Joseph Bruchac was raised by his grandparents in the small town of Greenfield Center, New York. He credits his grandmother, who had a law degree, with filling the house with books and encouraging his love of reading. His grandfather was of Abanaki Indian descent and taught him to respect nature. Bruchac helped out at his grandparent's little general store and enjoyed listening to the stories told by the local farmers and lumber-jacks who visited the store.

Bruchac attended Cornell and Syracuse University and received a doctorate from Union Graduate School. He has had poetry and adult novels published, and he is a sought-after storyteller. His first children's book, a collection of Iroquois stories, was published in 1975. He is the author of many Native American short story collections and picture books including *Thirteen Moons on Turtle's Back* (co-authored with Jonathan London), *Fox Song, Between Earth and Sky*, and *Lasting Echoes*. He also has co-authored *Keepers of the Earth: Native American Stories and Environmental Activities for Children* and its sequels, which are volumes targeted toward parents and educators and which include stories, crafts, and scientific experiments to share with children. Many of Bruchac's books for children retell stories from his Abenaki heritage.

On his Maine connections, Bruchac says that he has visited with the Penobscot and Passamaquoddy tribes in the state many times. He has worked with Wayne Newell, a Passamaquoddy who has promoted bilingual programs. He has also taught writing work-shops to prisoners at the Maine State Prison in Thomaston. In addition, the subject of Bruchac's book of poetry, *Remembering the Dawn*, was a Passamaquoddy native from the Pleasant Point Reservation (*Remembering the Dawn* is now out of print).

Bruchac still lives in Greenfield Center, New York, in the same house where he was raised. He has combined the family's living space with his grandparents' former general store to include space for The Greenfield Review Press, an independent publishing house founded by Bruchac and his wife. Bruchac continues to work on children's books, all using his central themes of listening to and respecting one another and the earth.

ABOUT THE ILLUSTRATOR

Christine Nyburg Shrader is an artist from a coastal island off Washington State. After working as the co-owner of a Seattle financial planning business for ten years,

Shrader decided upon a career change and pursued an art degree at Seattle's School of Visual Concepts. Her artwork has been shown at several art shows in the Northwest. *Gluskabe and the Four Wishes* is her first children's book. She illustrated it using pastels on printmaking paper. Shrader enjoys working with pastels because "she likes the intensity of color, high drama, and variable texture" which she can achieve with them.

ISLAND BOY

AUTHOR / ILLUSTRATOR: Barbara Cooney
AGE LEVEL / LENGTH: 6-10 years / 36 pages
PUBLISHER / COPYRIGHT DATE: Viking Books (hardcover); Puffin Books (paperback); Audio Bookshelf (audio book, with two Cooney books taped) / 1988
FORMAT / ISBN: Hardcover / 067081749X; Paperback / 0140507566; Audio Book / 1883332206

Island Boy tells the story of Matthais, who grows up on Tibbetts Island, off the coast of Maine. Here Matthais learns to read, tames a baby seagull, and catches lobsters. But when his older brothers and sisters leave the island "to see the world," Matthais leaves too. He first works as a cabin boy and later as the master of a great ship which travels around the world. After many years of traveling, Matthais realizes "where his heart lies." He marries a school teacher and settles down on Tibbetts Island. Matthais and his wife raise three daughters.

Later, after his wife dies, Matthais continues to live on the island with his widowed daughter and his grandson, little Matthais. The three generation family supports itself by raising vegetables and livestock to sell to the "people from away" on the mainland. They lead a quiet, happy life. One day old Matthais leaves for the mainland on a windy day. He runs into trouble on this trip and dies. People from near and far attend Matthais' funeral, and they bury him on a "handsome day" under his favorite "red astrakhan tree" on the island.

Barbara Cooney tells a simple and noble tale of a man wedded to his own Maine island. *Island Boy* is a book that is meant to be read slowly, so as to savor the warm, detailed illustrations that show so much and the equally warm, detailed words which say so much. Barbara Cooney calls *Island Boy* her "love song to the coast of Maine," and says that it was inspired by the real life of John Gilley of Baker's Island.

LEARNING ACTIVITIES

1. Use the map on the inside front and back covers of *Island Boy* to develop basic map and geography skills. Use a penny or another small object as a pretend boat and make it go from Tibbetts Island to Egg Rock, Green Harbor, Granitesville, etc. while telling what

direction you travel. You also may play a game with the map using compass directions. For example, if you are on Egg Rock and you head due east, where will you end up? If you are on Cranberry Island and you head northeast, what place do you come to? Compare this map with a real map of the Maine coast. How are they similar and different?

2. Look for new vocabulary words in *Island Boy*. Do you know the meaning of "wafting"? What are "rusticators"? How is the game fox-and-geese played? Find as many new vocabulary words as you can. Learn the meaning of these words and write an *Island Boy* glossary with the definitions of the words.

3. Approximately at what time in history do you believe this book is set? Is it a modern story? Was it set in the late 1800s? Mid 1900s? When? Make a guess at the time-frame of the book; then give a short speech explaining why you selected the time you did. Make certain to consider hints in both the words and the illustrations. Think about the types of clothing, transportation, pastimes, occupations, etc.

ABOUT THE AUTHOR/ILLUSTRATOR

See information about Barbara Cooney on page 23.

MISS RUMPHIUS

AUTHOR / ILLUSTRATOR: Barbara Cooney
AGE LEVEL / LENGTH: 5-10 years / 32 pages
PUBLISHER / COPYRIGHT DATE: Viking Books (hardcover); Puffin Books (paperback); Audio Bookshelf (audio book, with two Cooney books taped) / 1982
FORMAT / ISBN: Hardcover / 0670479586; Paperback / 0140950265; Audio Book / 1883332206
AWARDS: American Book Award; Lupine Award

In this book, Barbara Cooncy creates a strong, independent, and inspiring main character, Miss Alice Rumphius. Miss Rumphius decides as a child that when she grows up she will visit faraway places and live by the sea. Her grandfather advises her that she must do a third thing: "something to make the world more beautiful." Young Alice is not certain how she will accomplish this, but she promises her grandfather that she will try her best.

When Miss Rumphius grows up, she fulfills her wishes. She visits many far away places with cockatoos and camels. And after a time, she returns to live by the sea. But she also wonders how she can make the world more beautiful. After being ill one year, she finds the answer to this question. While she was sick, the beautiful lupine flowers she had planted began to spread; their seeds were carried by the wind and the birds. Now Miss Rumphius knows how to make the world more beautiful. She plants "five bushels" of lupine seeds and becomes known as the Lupine Lady as her flowers magically blossom and spread to cover the town.

Barbara Cooney's *Miss Rumphius* is a modern-day classic. It is a simple, beautiful tale that dares young readers to find their own way "to make the world more beautiful."

LEARNING ACTIVITIES

1. Learn about lupines. Plant some and watch how they grow. Try to make drawings of lupines after studying them closely. Research the flower's history, its favored climate, its varieties/colors, etc. Write a summary of what you learn.

2. Declare a make-the-world-more-beautiful week. Invite friends, family, and classmates to try for one week to make the world a more beautiful place. At the end of the week, have everyone report (orally or in writing) on how they made the world more beautiful.

3. Research the life and work of author/illustrator Barbara Cooney. Study her children's books. Read biographical information about her. Combine this information to create a picture book or a biographical booklet about her.

ABOUT THE AUTHOR/ILLUSTRATOR

See information about Barbara Cooney on page 23.

A GARDEN OF WHALES

AUTHOR: Maggie Steincrohn Davis / ILLUSTRATOR: Jennifer Barrett O'Connell
AGE LEVEL / LENGTH: 4-8 years / 32 pages
PUBLISHER / COPYRIGHT DATE: Firefly Books Ltd. / 1993
FORMAT / ISBN: Hardcover / 0944475361; Paperback / 0944475353

A Garden of Whales is a lyrical fantasy about whales. A young boy sits in his bathtub dreaming of whales. He dreams that he is swimming with the whales. As his dream continues, he discovers that the whales are in danger. He tries to save them, but he is unable to do so. Then in an attempt to bring back the extinct whales, the boy calls in a flotilla of tubs filled with children. The children watch as tears from whale-shaped clouds rain into their secret garden. New whales blossom and grow in the garden and are returned to the sea by the children in a joyous celebration.

Author Maggie Steincrohn Davis uses repetition to create a musical quality for her text: "In the sea, in the sea, the Whales sang to me. They breathed and their breath was the breath of the sea." Jennifer Barrett O'Connell's illustrations show the beauty and wonder of whales. In addition, her palette of bright colors helps to foster the feel of fantasy in the book. As the back of *A Garden of Whales* explains, a portion of the proceeds from the book will go to the Earth Island Institute to help with its efforts to help conserve, preserve, and restore the global environment.

LEARNING ACTIVITIES

1. Create cut-outs or clay models to act out the book, *A Garden of Whales*. Have a group of friends or classmates act out the story using the cut-outs or models as it is read aloud by a narrator. You may wish to present the story to an audience and charge a small admission which you can then donate to your favorite environmental organization.

2. Reread *A Garden of Whales* several times and look for the ways that the author makes her story sound like a poem, almost a song. Does she use repetition? In what ways? Do her words rhyme? Do her words follow a pattern? Does she use alliteration (repetition of beginning sounds)? Where?

3. This book is a fantasy, a world of make-believe. How can you tell it is a fantasy? What words tell you so? Which illustrations tell you so? Write your own short fantasy about another Maine animal (e.g., deer, chickadee, puffin). Draw illustrations to go with your story if you wish.

ABOUT THE AUTHOR

Maggie Steincrohn Davis has lived in Maine for nearly ten years and claims that "from the first day Maine felt like her heart's home." She has been writing for nearly thirty years and is the author of more than ten books, including the children's books, *Glory! To the Flowers* (see page 32) and *Something Magic* (a picture book inspired by trips to Isle au Haut; see page 91).

Davis lives in Blue Hill, Maine, where she runs her own publishing company, Heartsong Books. As a publisher, she tries to use local illustrators and printers, and to publish books that share a message of "the interconnectedness of all life." As a writer, Davis claims that she writes in sections which she later pieces together as she did puzzles when she was a child. Davis describes her background as "varied" including stints as a teacher, editor, mediator, counselor, herbalist, homeopath, and cafe owner. Davis and her husband share a "Brady Bunch" of six children. And she claims to need no hobbies or vacations from her work since her writing, publishing, gardens, and community work bring her such joy.

ABOUT THE ILLUSTRATOR

As a child, Jennifer Barrett O'Connell spent many hours in her room drawing. She graduated from the Philadelphia College of Art and has worked as an illustrator and designer since 1982. She has illustrated three children's books, including *Promise Not to Tell* and *Imagine That!* She lives in Bethesda, Maryland, with her husband and two children.

GLORY! TO THE FLOWERS

AUTHOR: Maggie Steincrohn Davis / ILLUSTRATOR: Cara Raymaker
AGE LEVEL / LENGTH: 4-10 years / 32 pages
PUBLISHER / COPYRIGHT DATE: Heartsong Books / 1995
FORMAT / ISBN: Paperback / 0963881329

Glory! To the Flowers is an unusual picture book. It doesn't tell a story, but rather it is a party on pages—a celebration of flowers. The words of author Maggie Steincrohn Davis read like a song:

> We sway with the flowers, duet with the flowers.
> ZingZinga K'Ling. Z'li. Z'lo.
> Each one is part of our family, we know.
> Anywhere's home where the flowers grow.

And the drawings of fourteen-year-old illustrator Cara Raymaker burst off the pages with their wild patterns and brilliant colors. It's impossible to read this book without a smile.

Glory! To the Flowers speaks of the joy of flowers found in puddles, on mountain sides, and in windowsill flats. The book sends a message to young readers that just as we live and grow, so do flowers; we are both part of nature, more alike than different.

LEARNING ACTIVITIES

1. Have a "conversation" with some flowers. Choose any flowers—wildflowers, budding house plants, vegetable blossoms, or others. Spend some time sitting quietly with the flower. Watch it, study it, enjoy it. What do you notice about the flower? How does it make you feel? Can you see or feel it growing? Afterward, write words about your experience. You might write a poem, a song, or whatever comes to mind.

2. Study the illustrations of artist Cara Raymaker. How does she portray different flowers? Are her drawings accurate for the violet, bee balm, yarrow, etc.? What moods does Raymaker create with her illustrations? If you were the illustrator for this book, how would you have chosen to illustrate it? Try your hand at creating a piece of flower artwork. Feel free to use sculpture, collage, or any other medium.

3. Select and study a flower that grows in Maine. It might be a wildflower or one that is cultivated. Read nonfiction books and interview flower gardeners or horticulturists to learn about your selected flower—where it grows, its size, its colors, its uses. Write a report about what you learn.

ABOUT THE AUTHOR

See information about Maggie Steincrohn Davis on page 31.

ABOUT THE ILLUSTRATOR

Cara Raymaker was fourteen years of age when she illustrated *Glory! To the Flowers*. She lives in Ellsworth, Maine. She has also illustrated a book featuring young writers called *Writers of the Future*. Raymaker collaborated closely with author Maggie Steincrohn Davis on *Glory! To the Flowers*. In fact, she did some of the work in Davis' cabin surrounded by flowers. She describes her work on the book as feeling "like a dance."

BLAZING BEAR

AUTHOR: Sis Boulos Deans / ILLUSTRATOR: Nantz Comyns
AGE LEVEL / LENGTH: 8-12 years / 56 pages
PUBLISHER / COPYRIGHT DATE: Windswept House Publishers / 1992
FORMAT / ISBN: Paperback / 0932433944

Blazing Bear tells the fictional story of a Norridgewock Indian (from the Kennebec Tribe of the Abenaki Nation) who helps his son, Fleeting Deer, to accept the difficult transition from boyhood to manhood by relating his own coming-of-age experiences. As the fall hunting season approaches, Fleeting Deer feels left out since his two older brothers are old enough to join the hunting party, but he is not. Blazing Bear tells his son about the time when he also was considered too young to hunt and was left behind by his father and brother to help care for his baby sister. But as Blazing Bear watched over his baby sister, he found that he needed more courage than the hunters did. He had to save his baby sister from a bear. Through determination and quick thinking, Blazing Bear managed to scare off the bear, save his sister, and make the transition from boyhood to manhood.

Blazing Bear is a picture book with more story than pictures. Sis Deans' tale is detailed and believable; its universal coming-of-age theme rings true. There are only five full-color pages of illustrations within the text-pages; yet Comyns' bright watercolors seem to burst off the page and help to reflect important imagery from the story. In addition, the back of the book includes a chart showing the different Maine Abenaki Tribes, a bibliography, a map of the Kennebec River, and a helpful glossary of terms, such as cradleboard, Guarding Spirit, and poultice.

LEARNING ACTIVITIES

1. The first time you read *Blazing Bear*, do not look words up in the glossary; instead, try to guess their meaning from the story's context. Afterwards, read the story a second time while checking the meaning of asterisked words in the glossary. How accurate were your guesses? Which words did you guess correctly? Why? Which were incorrect? Why? Did you need to know the meaning of every word in order to understand the story as a whole?

2. Reread *Blazing Bear*. Select a scene from the book that was not illustrated by artist, Nantz Comyns. Then create your own illustration, collage, or sculpture to depict the scene you chose.

3. Turn *Blazing Bear* into a play. Rewrite it as a script with character parts and a narrator part if you wish. Create simple scenery for the story. Rehearse the play and present it before an audience of peers or parents.

ABOUT THE AUTHOR

Sis Boulos Deans was born and raised in Portland, Maine. She currently lives on a small farm in Gorham, Maine, with her husband and three daughters. She enjoys sports, camping, photography, and reading. She has a degree in Animal Medical Technology from the University of Maine and is a graduate of Maine Medical Center's School of Surgical Technology. She has worked in the operating room at Mercy Hospital for over a decade.

Deans has written for both adults and children. Her book, *Decisions and Other Stories*, was the winner of the 1995 Maine Chapbook Award sponsored by Maine Writers & Publishers Alliance. Her children's books range from picture books to biography to young adult novels. She is the author of *Chick-a-dee-dee-dee: A Very Special Bird, His Proper Post: A Biography of Gen. Joshua Lawrence Chamberlain* (see page 197), and a young adult novel, *Brick Walls*.

When discussing writing, Deans advises students that they must write what they know. She adds, "Maine is where I live and what I know, and everyone of my books has a Maine connection." Deans claims that even before she knew how to write, she was *telling* stories. She believes that writing is a natural talent like drawing, singing, or acting; but "like any gift, it develops with practice." She does much of her writing when her children are in school and in the middle of the night when everyone else is sleeping.

ABOUT THE ILLUSTRATOR

Nantz Comyns is a native Mainer "born and bred, for better or worse." She currently lives in Scarborough, Maine, with her husband and two sons. She received a bachelor's degree in art from the University of Maine and a Master of Fine Arts degree from the University of Pennsylvania with an emphasis on sculpture. While in Pennsylvania, Comyns helped to design and create the nationally known "Please Touch Museum" for children in Philadelphia in 1982. This experience helped her to develop other creative educational experiences, such as her "Moose Smiles" program, which helps community groups to construct 10-14 foot moose sculptures out of trees, twigs, and reused materials. She also has created several Percent for Art Projects for Maine schools (in Hollis, Naples, and Greenbush).

Comyns enjoys illustrating as well as sculpting. She works in watercolors and gouache. The children's books that she has illustrated include *Chick-a-dee-dee-dee*, *A Very Special Bird*, and *Emily Bee and the Kingdom of Flowers*.

PRIZE IN THE SNOW

AUTHOR: Bill Easterling / ILLUSTRATOR: Mary Beth Owens
AGE LEVEL / LENGTH: 4-8 years / 32 pages
PUBLISHER / COPYRIGHT DATE: Little, Brown & Co. / 1994
FORMAT / ISBN: Hardcover / 0316224898 (recently out of print)
AWARDS: Lupine Award, 1994; Christopher Award, 1995; Please Touch Museum Book Award, 1995

Prize in the Snow tells the story of a boy and a rabbit. The boy walks into the wintry woods behind his house with a box, a carrot, and a stick with a string tied to it. The boy props up the box as a trap with the carrot underneath it. Then he hides at a distance, ready to tug on the rope when he sees an animal in his trap. The boy wants to be a "great hunter" like the older boys.

After a long wait, a rabbit hops up to the carrot. The boy tugs on the rope trapping the rabbit. But when the boy lifts the box to bring his prize home, he is surprised by what he sees. The rabbit is starving, its skeleton showing through its fur. The boy has a change of heart. He leaves the carrot for the starving rabbit and promises to return with more food the next day.

Prize in the Snow is a simple, yet beautiful book. Author Bill Easterling leaves young readers with a strong message about respect for nature, but the book is not at all "preachy." The watercolor drawings by Maine illustrator Mary Beth Owens nicely complement the text; she based the images upon the winter scenery found around her rural Maine home. *Prize in the Snow* is a rare "prize" of a book that young readers will return to time and again.

LEARNING ACTIVITIES

1. The rabbit in this story was starving in the middle of the winter. Read nonfiction books about a specific wild animal and learn how it survives in the winter. For example, if you select rabbits, try to learn what they eat in the winter, where they stay, how they protect themselves from their enemies. Or if you select deer, try to learn how they move through the woods in the winter, how they find food with snow on the ground, etc. Write a short report about what you learn.

2. Study a real rabbit. Visit a pet store or watch a friend's or classroom's pet rabbit. Notice how the rabbit moves, what sounds it makes, how it eats, etc. Then draw several "action" pictures of the rabbit doing something—eating, hopping, sniffing. Try to make your rabbit illustrations look realistic.

3. Write a follow-up story to *Prize in the Snow*. What happens the next day when the boy goes back with food for the rabbit? And the day after that? Will the rabbit's behavior change over time? How so? Will the boy's attitude change again? How so? What will the boy do if he discovers the older boys "hunting" again?

ABOUT THE AUTHOR

Bill Easterling works as a daily columnist for the *Huntsville Times* in Alabama. In fact, *Prize in the Snow* first appeared in a different version in one of his columns. The story is based upon an experience from Easterling's childhood. He is the father of two adult children, and he currently lives in Huntsville, Alabama.

ABOUT THE ILLUSTRATOR

See information about Mary Beth Owens on page 8.

THE STORY OF PAUL BUNYAN

> AUTHOR: Barbara Emberley / ILLUSTRATOR: Ed Emberley
> AGE LEVEL / LENGTH: 4-8 years / 32 pages
> PUBLISHER / COPYRIGHT DATE: Simon & Schuster / 1963; reissued 1994
> FORMAT / ISBN: Hardcover / 067188557X

The Story of Paul Bunyan has obvious Maine connections. First, and foremost, is the birth of legendary Paul Bunyan. However, the Emberleys' version has Paul Bunyan being born in Kennebunkport, rather than Bangor, which is more commonly designated as his birthplace.

From beginning to end, *The Story of Paul Bunyan* will cause readers to laugh aloud. Author Barbara Emberley does a masterful job of creating unusual and hilarious exaggerations in this tall tale. For example, when Paul Bunyan was born, she writes:

> I've been told that when the twelve storks brought baby Paul to his mother in Kennebunkport, Maine, he didn't weigh more than 104 or 105 pounds—and 46 pounds of that was his black, curly beard.

Barbara Emberley continues her exaggeration by telling how the residents of Kennebunkport placed baby Paul Bunyan in a huge cradle anchored offshore (so that he wouldn't keep destroying buildings onshore with his kicking). However, Paul Bunyan's rocking in the cradle "caused such high waves that one of the biggest towns in Maine at that time, Boston, was washed out to sea. It floated down to Massachusetts, where it still is to this day." The hyperbole continues with the giant ox Babe (actually called "Bebe" which is Franco-American for "Baby."), skating-length griddles, and a hinged-top bunkhouse. *The Story of Paul Bunyan* is a delight from its wonderful words to its witty woodcuts.

LEARNING ACTIVITIES

1. *The Story of Paul Bunyan* is a tall tale; that is, it uses exaggeration to tell a story. Reread the book and make a list of all the exaggerations that Barbara Emberley uses in the story. After making the list, discuss each exaggeration. What else could the author have used to exaggerate the story's details? Could Paul Bunyan's beard have been combed by a flock of clawing chickens or a hundred men with rakes rather than a pine tree? In each case, do you think the author chose the most effective example of exaggeration? Write a one or two page addition to *The Story of Paul Bunyan*. You might write about when he was a toddler learning to walk and talk. Or you might write about how he handled a hurricane that threatened his sawmill. Just make certain to include humorous exaggerations.

2. Ask an art teacher to help you make a woodcut. With an adult's guidance, carve out a design in a block of wood. Then roll ink on the woodblock and print the image onto paper. Afterwards, discuss woodcuts as art. How easy or hard do you think it was for Ed Emberley to create the illustrations in *The Story of Paul Bunyan?* Look at the book's illustrations again. How do you think Ed Emberley managed to create each detail?

3. Try to create a group tall tale. You might work with classmates or friends. First of all, think of a character for your tall tale. Will it be a person who's very teeny tiny? Or will it be a legend about the world's most creative artist? Or will it be a tall tale about Paul Bunyan's wife? After the group decides on the character, generate a list of four to eight details for your character, such as how the character eats, what the character wears, what the character does for work. Finally, combine these details to create a tall tale. You might tell your tall tale orally and tape-record it, or you might write down your tall tale and create illustrations for it.

ABOUT THE AUTHOR

Barbara Emberley was born in Chicago in 1932. She's married to children's book author and illustrator, Ed Emberley. They have two children. Emberley received a Bachelor of Fine Arts degree from the Massachusetts College of Art. She is the author of several children's books, including *One Wide River to Cross* (a 1967 Caldecott Honor Book and an adaptation of the Noah's ark story) and *Drummer Hoff* (the 1968 Caldecott Medal book and an adapted Mother Goose rhyme). Emberley has co-illustrated books with her husband, including *Crash, Rumble, and Roll,* and *The Moon Seems to Change.* Emberley lives with her husband in Massachusetts, where she enjoys her hobbies of herb gardening, collecting antiques, and sailing the Northeast coast.

ABOUT THE ILLUSTRATOR

Ed Emberley was born in Malden, Massachusetts, in 1931. Emberley graduated from the Massachusetts College of Art. After painting signs and creating cartoons, Emberley began his career as a children's book illustrator in the late 1950s. He is the illustrator of the 1968 Caldecott Medal book, *Drummer Hoff;* but he may be best known for his drawing book series, including *Ed Emberley's Drawing Book of Faces* and *Ed Emberley's Great Thumbprint Drawing Book.* Emberley's books are known for their humor and varied styles. He has experimented with different mediums, such as pen-and-ink, pencil, and woodcuts. He currently lives in Massachusetts, with his wife and frequent collaborator, Barbara Emberly.

CHRISTMAS ON AN ISLAND

AUTHOR / ILLUSTRATOR: Gail Gibbons
AGE LEVEL / LENGTH: 4-8 years / 32 pages
PUBLISHER / COPYRIGHT DATE: Morrow Junior Books / 1994
FORMAT / ISBN: Hardcover / 0688096786; Library binding / 0688096794

Christmas on an Island describes how the residents of a small island celebrate Christmas. The story is based on author/illustrator Gail Gibbons' seasonal home on Matinicus Island off the coast of Maine. The island Christmas includes many preparations, such as making gifts and wreaths, practicing the school play, cutting down and decorating Christmas trees, and baking goodies. When Christmas Eve arrives, the celebration begins at the island church. After a prayer of thanks, everyone enjoys a huge feast. Then hymns are sung and one of Santa's helpers passes out gifts. After their community celebration, everyone returns home with the lighthouse flashing in the distance. On Christmas Day, residents celebrate the holiday in smaller groups with their family and friends.

Christmas on an Island, with its bright, detailed illustrations and its joyful story, shows a universal yet unique holiday celebration. Gibbons captures the feel of island life and a close-knit community. For mainland readers, this book is the next-best-thing to actually celebrating Christmas on an island in the middle of the ocean.

LEARNING ACTIVITIES

1. Before reading this book, make a list of the ways you think celebrating Christmas on an island would be the same or different from celebrating Christmas elsewhere. Then after you read *Christmas on an Island*, recheck your list and see which of your guesses were correct. Did you learn any other ways that an island Christmas is the same or different from Christmas on the mainland? Add to your list of similarities and differences.

2. What do you think it would be like to celebrate another holiday on an island? What about New Years? Easter? Fourth of July? Halloween? Thanksgiving? Draw a picture showing what you imagine a selected holiday would look like on an island.

3. In *Christmas on an Island*, Gail Gibbons tells how one community, Matinicus Island, celebrates Christmas. How does your community celebrate Christmas? What special traditions or events does your town/city have? Write a short story telling about Christmas in your town.

ABOUT THE AUTHOR/ILLUSTRATOR

Gail Gibbons grew up in Illinois. She created her first book when she was only four; it was a four-page wordless picture book. Gibbons loved art and was often selected to do the artwork for school projects such as the scenery for plays. She received a degree in graphic arts from the University of Illinois. After college she did artwork for television stations. It was her work on a children's show that sparked her interest in writing and illustrating children's books.

Since 1975, Gibbons has devoted her time to writing and illustrating nonfiction children's books, with more than ninety books to her credit. Gibbons' books have always reflected her interests and experiences. A few of her recent titles include *Knights in Shining Armor*, *The Reasons for Seasons*, *The Great St. Lawrence Seaway*, *Cats*, *Deserts*, *The Moon Book*, and *Soaring with the Wind: The Bald Eagle*. She works in watercolors, black pen, and colored pencil. Gibbons explains that the research for each of her books takes much time and effort. She explains, "To me, putting a nonfiction book together is like watching the pieces of a puzzle finally fitting together. Bit by bit it takes its form."

Gibbons moved to the island of Matinicus, Maine, in 1986. Since then, many of her books have dealt with island life and topics. She currently spends four months each year living on Matinicus and the remainder of the year in Corinth, Vermont.

THE SEASONS OF ARNOLD'S APPLE TREE

AUTHOR / ILLUSTRATOR: Gail Gibbons
AGE LEVEL / LENGTH: 4-8 years / 32 pages
PUBLISHER / COPYRIGHT DATE: Harcourt Brace & Co./ 1984
FORMAT / ISBN: Hardcover / 0152712461; Paperback / 0152712453

Arnold has his own secret place, an apple tree. This book traces Arnold's special relationship with the apple tree through each of the four seasons. In spring, the boy climbs his tree, smells the apple blossoms, and watches bees gather nectar. In summer, he watches small green apples appear. In fall, he eats tasty ripe apples and watches the leaves change color and fall off. He also makes an apple pie and apple cider with his family. In winter, Arnold decorates his bare tree with popcorn and berries for the birds. Then it is spring, and the cycle begins once again.

Within this simple work of fiction, author/illustrator Gail Gibbons teaches numerous facts about an apple tree and how it changes through the seasons. Her detailed illustrations add to the story, showing honeybees collecting nectar from apple blossoms and a detailed diagram of how a cider press works.

LEARNING ACTIVITIES

1. At the back of *The Seasons of Arnold's Apple Tree*, illustrations show how the same branch of an apple tree looks during each of the four seasons. Select another part of the landscape (e.g., an oak tree, a waterfall, a mountain) and draw illustrations showing how it might look during each season.

2. Visit an apple orchard. See how the cider press works. Watch how apples are harvested. Learn about ways in which apples are used in different crafts and recipes. Write a story or draw a picture about your apple orchard visit.

3. Collect apple recipes and write them out on paper cut into the shape of apples. Combine the recipes into an apple booklet. Make two or three of the recipes and have an apple tasting party.

ABOUT THE AUTHOR/ILLUSTRATOR

See information about Gail Gibbons on page 39.

LOBSTER BOAT

AUTHOR: Brenda Guiberson / ILLUSTRATOR: Megan Lloyd
AGE LEVEL / LENGTH: 5-8 years / 32 pages
PUBLISHER / COPYRIGHT DATE: Henry Holt & Co. / 1993
FORMAT / ISBN: Hardcover / 0805017569 (recently out of print)

Lobster Boat tells the fictional story of a boy named Tommy who goes lobstering with his Uncle Russ. But the book also weaves many facts about lobsters and lobstering into the story. The two head out in a rowboat across the harbor to where their lobster boat, the "Nellie Jean," is docked. Tommy wonders if they will actually do any lobstering with all the fog around. Uncle Russ says they will go since the weather forecast predicts that the fog will burn off and a nearby storm will head south of them.

After loading up with fish bait, the "Nellie Jean" heads out of the harbor. A glow from a lighthouse helps them to find their way. They search for the yellow and red buoys which mark Uncle Russ' lobster traps. They pull traps up with a winch. Lobsters are measured to see which ones can be legally kept. A female with eggs is marked with a tail notch before she is thrown back so that future lobstermen will know not to keep her. Females must be saved so that they can reproduce to create more lobsters. Hovering seagulls are fed the old bait from traps before the traps are reset with fresh bait.

A radio call warns that the weather forecast has changed and a storm is now heading their way. Tommy and Uncle Russ move quickly back to shore, fighting the rain and waves. When they return safely to the harbor, they must tidy up the boat and sell their catch. Evening is a time for repairing traps, before they return to the sea the next day.

LEARNING ACTIVITIES

1. As you read *Lobster Boat*, write a list of lobster and lobstering facts that you learn from the story, such as: lobsters have a crusher claw and a ripper claw, a brass gauge is used to measure lobsters, a baiting iron is the tool used to load fish into a trap. Then double check your facts with a lobsterman or in nonfiction books about lobstering to make certain they are all correct.

2. Reread *Lobster Boat* and find all the onomatopoetic words; that is, words that sound like what they are referring to. Make a chart listing them and then add to the list more examples of onomatopoeia words that you hear or read during the next week. Make your list as long as possible.

3. In *Lobster Boat*, Tommy enjoys lobstering with his Uncle Russ. Write a story about an activity you enjoy doing with a relative. Make certain to include many details so that the story sounds realistic. Your story might even provide readers with information. Just as this

story helped its readers to learn about lobstering, so your story might help readers to learn more about fishing, gardening, hiking, or another subject.

ABOUT THE AUTHOR

Brenda Guiberson was born in Colorado and grew up in the state of Washington. In 1990 she began her career as a children's book author and has written several informational children's books, including *Lighthouses: Watchers at the Sea, Into the Sea,* and *Teddy Roosevelt's Elk.* Guiberson explains that each book requires many months of research and that she begins the actual writing only after she feels "very close" to the subject. After living on the Oregon coast and the Columbia River, Guiberson decided to write about lobsters in the book *Lobster Boat* "because they were new, unfamiliar, and fascinating and allowed her to take her water-side experiences to a new place."

Guiberson currently lives near Seattle, Washington, with her husband and son. Her hobbies include traveling, painting, and reading.

ABOUT THE ILLUSTRATOR

Megan Lloyd hails from Pennsylvania, but she fondly remembers her numerous vacations to Maine. In order to accurately illustrate *Lobster Boat,* Lloyd spent a day on a lobster boat with a lobsterman from South Brooksville, Maine. The lobsterman also brought along his dog, Shady Lady, (for whom the boat was named) and a young friend to pose as the boy in the book. She took many photographs in order to ensure the accuracy of her finished illustrations. For *Lobster Boat,* Lloyd used a combination of pen-and-ink and watercolors.

Lloyd has a Bachelor of Fine Arts degree in illustration from Parsons School of Design. She worked as an assistant to the art director at Harper & Row Publishers for a year, and then returned to Pennsylvania to pursue a full-time career in book illustration. The first book she illustrated was published in 1982. She currently has thirty books to her credit, including the widely popular *The Little Old Lady Who Was Not Afraid of Anything,* written by Linda Williams. Lloyd has collaborated with author Brenda Guiberson on four books. Their books represent each of the four corners of the United States: *Lobster Boat* from the northeast, *Spoonbill Swamp* from the southeast, *Cactus Hotel* from the southwest, and *Winter Wheat* from the northwest.

Lloyd currently lives on a small farm in south-central Pennsylvania. Her hobbies include spinning wool, gardening, hiking, boating, and antique-hunting (along with her husband who is an antiques dealer).

LOBSTER FOR LUNCH

AUTHOR: Bob Hartman / ILLUSTRATOR: Jo Ellen McAllister Stammen
AGE LEVEL / LENGTH: 5-8 years / 32 pages
PUBLISHER / COPYRIGHT DATE: Down East Books / 1992
FORMAT / ISBN: Hardcover / 0892723025

Lobster for Lunch is a humorous picture book which tells a wonderful parallel story. Larry is a boy who goes out to eat with his parents in a fancy restaurant. Little Lob is a boy lobster who lives with his parents in a tank at the same fancy restaurant. When Larry enters the restaurant, he is fascinated by the lobsters in the tank; and he presses his nose to the glass against his parents' warnings: "Don't stand so close! It's dirty!" Likewise, Little Lob is fascinated by the people; and he presses his antennae to the glass against his parents' warning: "Stop staring at those creatures!" Larry and Little Lob each are dragged off by a parent, but their paths will soon cross again.

Larry's mother decides to have a lobster for lunch as a special treat since it's her birthday. And Little Lob is finally told the "truth" about the tank he lives in—when a lobster is removed from the tank (as Uncle Crust once was) then it is that lobster's special "Eating Day;" that is, the lobster grows larger and larger outside the tank until it is big enough to eat one of the people.

Larry and Little Lob both come to the same terrible realization—the other one might be eaten. Larry tries to find a way to save Little Lob from being eaten by his mother, and Little Lob also tries to find a way to save Larry from being eaten by his father (the lobster selected by the waiter). In a marvelous, wordless, two-page spread, illustrator Jo Ellen McAllister Stammen shows Little Lob biting the waiter's thumb with his claw and Larry biting the waiter's ankle with his teeth. Their heroic efforts succeed, and there will be no lobsters or kids for lunch that day.

LEARNING ACTIVITIES

1. *Lobster for Lunch* is an upbeat book. The story is funny and so are the illustrations. Notice how illustrator Jo Ellen McAllister Stammen uses unusual perspectives to create humor—for example, when Larry's mother and father and the waiter look upward as Little Lob flies through the air as shown on the book's cover. Create your own drawing from an unusual perspective. Ask a friend to pose for you and then draw your friend from an unusual perspective (e.g., from above, from below, sideways, at an angle).

2. *Lobster for Lunch* is a parallel story; that is, two similar stories are happening at the same time. You'll notice Larry's and Little Lob's experiences are almost the same. Another parallel story is *Blueberries for Sal* by Robert McCloskey (see page 65); in that book, Little Sal and Little Bear's experiences are almost the same. Try to write your own

parallel story. You'll need to include two main characters in your story and make certain that their experiences in the story are almost the same. Share your parallel story with a friend.

3. In *Lobster for Lunch*, Larry's mother wants to eat a lobster as a special birthday treat even though lobsters are expensive. What do you like to eat for a special treat? What do others prefer? Survey family and friends to learn what meal is their favorite when cost is not a consideration. Draw graphs to show your survey results. Which foods were most popular over all? Most popular with grown-ups? Most popular with kids? Do your results show any trends?

ABOUT THE AUTHOR

Bob Hartman lives in Ben Avon, Pennsylvania, with his wife and two children. He works as a storyteller for The Pittsburgh Children's Museum and as a minister for an inner-city church. In fact, his college degrees are in theology, not writing; but he considers himself fortunate to have jobs which require creativity and which often inspire his written work. He is the author of more than ten children's books, including *The Bottom of the Boat*, *Aunt Mabel's Table*, and *The Lion Storyteller Bible*. For recreation, Hartman enjoys singing and playing in a Celtic band and working on cars.

ABOUT THE ILLUSTRATOR

Jo Ellen McAllister Stammen studied illustration at Parsons School of Design in New York City. She currently lives in Camden, Maine, with her husband and three children and works as a freelance artist. *Lobster for Lunch* was her first children's book. She is also the illustrator of several other picture books, including *Bears Out There* by Joanne Ryder; *A Snow Story* by Melvin J. Leavitt; *If you Were Born a Kitten* and *Sleep! Sleep!* by Marion Dane Bauer; and *Wild Fox: A True Story* (see page 63) which won the 1993 Lupine Award and was written by Cherie Mason. Her books are known for their soft, colored-pencil art which seems to create a dreamlike mood.

MOOSE ON THE LOOSE

AUTHORS: John & Ann Hassett / ILLUSTRATOR: John Hassett
AGE LEVEL / LENGTH: 5-8 years / 48 pages
PUBLISHER / COPYRIGHT DATE: Down East Books / 1987
FORMAT / ISBN: Paperback / 0892722452

Max is a very curious moose, especially when it comes to people. Who are these creatures who come to watch him? Where do they live? What do they eat? Max decides to follow some hikers and find out. *Moose on the Loose* traces Max's journey to, and through, the city of Bangor, Maine. He trots happily down a busy highway, wreaking havoc with traffic; sticks his head in a window and eats a plant; takes a dunk in a swimming pool; tries to get into a car at a gas station; and finally climbs to the top of a six-story building where he has to be rescued and brought back to the woods. At the end, Max is no longer a curious moose. After his adventure, he is content to act like a regular moose and eat some delicious pond weeds.

John and Ann Hassett's great sense of humor shines through this book. The Hassetts poke fun at the Maine pastime of moose-watching by reversing it with a moose who goes people-watching. The detailed, cartoonish illustrations add to the whimsy of the book.

LEARNING ACTIVITIES

1. Collect stories of moose and deer sightings. Most Mainers have seen their fair share of these animals. Cut out stories from newspapers and record interviews with people who have encountered these animals.

2. Create a story and/or cartoon personifying (i.e., bringing to life and giving human characteristics to) a different wild animal from Maine. You might try a puffin, porcupine, or lobster.

3. In *Moose on the Loose,* Max visits Bangor. How do you know? What clues do the story and pictures provide? Change the story and have Max visit your town. What changes will you have to make?

ABOUT THE AUTHOR/ILLUSTRATOR

As a child, John Hassett summered in South Bristol, Maine; and the Hassett family moved to Maine in 1987. *Moose on the Loose,* the Hassetts note, is "based on innumerable incidents of moose wandering into populated areas. No matter the frequency of such sightings, they always generate great excitement." Much of the story was written in a "dilapidated duck hunting shack on a tiny salt marsh island." The book was illustrated with ink, colored pencils, and acrylics.

Ann and John Hassett are also the author and illustrator of other picture books, including *Junior—A Little Loon Tale*, *We Got My Brother at the Zoo*, *Charles of the Wild*, and *Cat Up a Tree*. The Hassetts live in Waldoboro, Maine, with their two daughters. Their hobbies include gardening, shoveling snow, and other "out-of-doors stuff."

BIRDIE'S LIGHTHOUSE

AUTHOR: Deborah Hopkinson / ILLUSTRATOR: Kimberly Bulcken Root
AGE LEVEL / LENGTH: 4-8 years / 32 pages
PUBLISHER / COPYRIGHT DATE: Atheneum, a division of Simon & Schuster / 1997
FORMAT / ISBN: Hardcover / 0689810520

This book stands tall (6 x 12 inches) like the lighthouse it tells about. In this work of historical fiction, set in the year 1855, ten-year-old Bertha Holland ("but most folks call me Birdie") recounts a year of her life. In diary format, she tells how her family moved from a coastal Maine fishing village to Turtle Island, where she learned to become her father's assistant lighthouse keeper.

When her father becomes ill, Birdie must tend the lighthouse by herself during a fierce storm. Wet and exhausted, Birdie falls asleep in the lighthouse tower. She awakens to find it is too dark—"the lamps [are] almost out of oil." Birdie races to fill the lamps, and just in time, too, as the beacon leads a struggling boat away from dangerous rocks. The rescued boat is a fishing vessel on which her older brother works.

An author's note explains that *Birdie's Lighthouse* is based upon several real lighthouse heroines, including Maine's own Abbie Burgess, who assisted her father with the lighthouse on Matinicus Rock in the mid-1800s. Young readers of *Birdie's Lighthouse* will get a flavor of an earlier way of life, including the foods (fritters, salt pork, and cornmeal), the expressions ("smearin' in," "Mares' tails and mackerel sky, never twenty-four hours dry"), and the details of lighthouse keeping (filling the oil lamps, polishing the reflectors, trimming the wicks).

LEARNING ACTIVITIES

1. Make lists of similarities and differences. On one piece of paper write all the ways that your life is like Birdie's life. For example, did you both have pet cats or younger sisters? Did you both move to a new place? On a second piece of paper write all the ways that your life is different than Birdie's life—your hobbies, the foods you eat, the jobs of your parents, etc. Which list was longer—the ways your life was similar to Birdie's or different than Birdie's? Why do you think that list was longer?

2. *Birdie's Lighthouse* is written in a diary-format that is shaped like a lighthouse. Make your own specially-shaped diary that reflects an interest of yours. For example, you might cut papers into the shape of a fish if you enjoy fishing. Attach the papers together into a booklet. Then write about all your fishing adventures in your fish-shaped diary. Or you might make a diary in the shape of a wheel (to symbolize your bicycle) for writing your biking adventures. Or one in the shape of a shoe or boot to write about your hiking adventures, etc.

3. Explore Maine coastal maps. Is there really a Turtle Island off the coast of Maine? If so, where is it? Does it have a lighthouse on it? Look on the map at the places along the Maine coast where lighthouses are located. Why do you think lighthouses were located in those places?

ABOUT THE AUTHOR

Deborah Hopkinson grew up in Lowell, Massachusetts, but she vacationed every summer in Rangeley, Maine. Hopkinson states, "I believe that there are certain places where you somehow feel deeply at home. Maine is one of those special places for me." Hopkinson received a Bachelors degree in English from the University of Hawaii. She currently lives with her husband and two children, in Walla Walla, Washington, where she works as the Director of Development and Administrative Services at Whitman College.

Birdie's Lighthouse, a Junior Library Guild Selection, is Hopkinson's second picture book. She is also the author of *Sweet Clara and the Freedom Quilt* which won the 1994 International Reading Association Award and has been featured on public broadcasting's *Reading Rainbow*. Curriculum and classroom activities related to *Birdie's Lighthouse* can be found on Hopkinson's home web page: http://whitman.edu/hopkinda~.

ABOUT THE ILLUSTRATOR

Kimberly Bulcken Root created pen-and-ink and watercolor illustrations for *Birdie's Lighthouse*. She earned a Bachelor of Fine Arts degree from Parsons School in New York City. Root has illustrated many children's books, including *When the Whippoorwill Calls*, by Candace Ransom, which was a *New York Times* Best Illustrated Book in 1995; and *Papa's Bedtime Story*, by Lee Donovan, for which she received a silver medal from the Society of Illustrators.

Root currently lives in Lancaster County, Pennsylvania, with her husband and two young children. Her husband, Barry Root, also illustrates children's books.

BOUND BY THE SEA: A SUMMER DIARY

AUTHOR / PHOTOGRAPHER: Jean Howard
AGE LEVEL / LENGTH: 12 years–adult / 96 pages
PUBLISHER / COPYRIGHT DATE: The Tidal Press / 1986
FORMAT / ISBN: Hardcover / 0930954254; Paperback / 0930954262

Bound by the Sea: A Summer Diary is a fictional book written in journal format by fifteen-year-old Sandy Seymour during the summer of 1965. Sandy is staying on Outercliff Island, off the coast of Maine, with her parents. She comes to the island a loner except for her dachshund, Shag. Sandy plans to keep a diary during the summer as a school project so that she can impress her new high school English teacher and take an advanced course in creative writing in the fall. She also adds black-and-white photographs to the journal since her father gave her a camera and some photography books.

Sandy's journal is a wonderful glimpse into the mind of a teenage girl. She revels in the beauty around her—a lady slipper, the clouds, orchids, Indian paintbrushes, the waves, and more. Her photographs inspire her to create some poems about the images she has captured on film. In spite of her mother's hopes, Sandy is unable to make friends with any young people on the island. In fact, she seems more like their enemy when she gets into arguments with them over flowers and sailboats. And so, Sandy remains a loner, becoming more and more enthralled with her photography and the nuances of the island's beauty until she unexpectedly meets a new friend, Bob Stuart. Bob too enjoys photography and has his own darkroom. He's older than Sandy, and he becomes a mentor to her, sharing his expertise in picture-taking and developing. But it's a two-way friendship, as Sandy also helps Bob. Since he has difficulty moving due to the effects of childhood polio, Sandy moves for him, taking photos that he would not be able to take by himself. Their friendship is special, and Sandy begins to wish that it was more than a friendship.

Jean Howard has created a wonderful book. She speaks with the believable voice of a fifteen-year-old girl; and her striking photographs and thoughtful poetry complement the text of the journal. The book will serve as an artistic inspiration to teenage readers.

LEARNING ACTIVITIES

1. Discussion questions:

> —When referring to her writing. Sandy says "It's hard to get the words to equal the ideas." What does she mean by that sentence? Do you agree or disagree with her statement?
> —Do you believe Sandy had romantic feelings toward Bob? Why or why not?

—*Bound by the Sea* allows us to know the main character Sandy through her diary, her photographs, and her poetry. Using this information, in a paragraph or two, how would you describe Sandy?

—This book is set in 1965. Does the book feel like it was set more than thirty years ago? Why or why not? Find specific examples to support your opinion.

2. In this book, Sandy keeps a journal which documents her experiences as a budding photographer and poet. Select a new skill which you would like to learn (e.g., woodcarving, sculpting, knitting, drawing comics); and as you learn your new skill, keep a diary to record your experiences.

3. Select five photographs from *Bound by the Sea* and write a critique of them. What are the strengths of each photo? The weaknesses? Compare and contrast the photos with each other.

ABOUT THE AUTHOR/PHOTOGRAPHER

Jean Howard was born in Boston in 1921. She received a bachelor's degree from Sarah Lawrence College. For the past fifty years, Howard and her husband have lived much of the time in a house they built on Cranberry Isles, Maine. Howard is the author of three books for children and one for adults. She is also the co-owner of The Tidal Press.

The photographs for *Bound by the Sea* were taken by Howard during one summer on Cranberry. She claims that "the story grew from the photos and sometimes the photos from the story." For another of her children's books, *Half a Cage* (see page 116), Howard says that the story is based on her own family's experience of owning a spider monkey for a year. When remembering that experience, Howard says that "We loved her, she loved us, but it was a relationship doomed to fail. Humans should not have wild animals as pets!"

Currently, Howard and her husband divide their time—living six months in Maine and living six months in Boston. She enjoys winters in "the real city" and summers in "the real country" although she admits that it is a challenge to maintain two houses.

THE MEMORY QUILT

AUTHOR / ILLUSTRATOR: Elizabeth McKey Hulbert
AGE LEVEL / LENGTH: 6-10 years / 52 pages
PUBLISHER / COPYRIGHT DATE: Windswept House Publishers / 1989
FORMAT / ISBN: Paperback / 0932433421

Ethan comes to stay with his Grandma and Uncle Dicky at their island home off the coast of Maine. Ethan doesn't come to visit because he wants to; he comes to live because he has to—both of his parents have died. *The Memory Quilt* relates how Ethan and his grandmother adjust to his parents' death and to each other.

Ethan hates his new life. Grandma fixes him big breakfasts, but he's used to cereal and juice. Grandma gives him a scratchy blanket for his bed, when he's used to a puffy, warm quilt. Feeling sorry for himself, Ethan runs away. The Roode twins, neighbors on the island, tease him because he's a "norfan." Wanting to "show them," Ethan accepts their dare to row across the harbor, but the crossing is more than Ethan bargains for. After a scare, Ethan returns to shore and to his concerned family, Grandma and Uncle Dicky.

Author Elizabeth McKey Hulbert writes well about a difficult subject, grief. Her book, with simple but suggestive illustrations, can serve as a good beginning point for discussing ways to grieve.

LEARNING ACTIVITIES

1. *The Memory Quilt* includes many colloquial Maine words and phrases, such as "step lively," "servin' sorrow," "spittin' image," etc. Tape record (with their permission) some older native Mainers in conversation. From the tape, write down any words or phrases that seem particular to Maine. Research, then write down the meaning of these colloquial terms. Do the same for the Maine expressions in *The Memory Quilt*, and compile your own Maine dictionary.

2. Make a Maine quilt with cloth squares. Select images that represent Maine—animals, objects, or people. Use fabric crayons or markers. Then have an adult who sews help you assemble the squares into a quilt. If using cloth is too difficult, draw a quilt design onto a large piece of poster board.

3. Discussion questions:

> —In *The Memory Quilt*, compare how Ethan and his grandmother deal with the death of his parents.
> —Have you had any family members die? How did you deal with the death? What advice would you give to others in the same situation?

—Have you ever accepted a dare as Ethan did in this book? How did it turn out? Would you do it again?

4. At the end of *The Memory Quilt*, it appears that Ethan will adjust to his new family life. Write a brief follow-up to the book, a peek at Ethan's life with his grandmother one year later. Consider including a realistic conversation between the two, a look at their daily lives, an episode in which Ethan returns the gift of the quilt with one of his own, or whatever you feel would be an appropriate sequel.

ABOUT THE AUTHOR/ILLUSTRATOR

Elizabeth McKey Hulbert has summered in Maine for over forty years and has lived in the state year-round since 1981. She has been writing, drawing, and painting ever since she can remember. As a child, she always wanted to be an author and illustrator.

Hulbert wrote *The Memory Quilt* because she wanted to write about an island and use a situation that involved several generations. Her illustrations are black-and-white line drawings with a full watercolor cover. She also is the author and illustrator of four other children's books, including *Out and In, I Love to Ski*, and *Milkweed and Winkles: A Wild Child's Cookbook* (see page 294) which is based on her family's foraging experiences. In addition, she has written articles for *Down East* and *Yankee* magazines, as well as for newspapers in Maine, Delaware, and New York.

Hulbert currently lives in Manset, on Mount Desert Island, Maine, in a shorefront house facing Cranberry Isles. Her hobbies include hiking, cooking, traveling, and gardening.

LOBSTERMAN

AUTHOR / ILLUSTRATOR: Dahlov Ipcar
AGE LEVEL / LENGTH: 6-10 years / 36 pages
PUBLISHER / COPYRIGHT DATE· Down East Books / 1962
FORMAT / ISBN: Paperback / 0892720328

This informative book tells the story of Larry, a boy who lives in a fishing village on the Maine coast. Larry's father is a lobsterman, and together they build lobster traps, set them, and haul them. Larry even sets his own trap and catches three large lobsters on his first try. Eventually, Larry decides that he too will become a lobsterman when he grows up.

Author/illustrator Dahlov Ipcar details many aspects of lobstering and fishing harbors. She shows and tells about cormorants and gulls, sardine carriers and clam diggers, gaffs and lobster cars. Both text and illustrations are informative; young readers will know more about lobstering after reading this book.

LEARNING ACTIVITIES

1. Before reading *Lobsterman*, look at the book's inside covers (endpapers) and name as many of the pictured objects as possible. Then read the book and see how many more objects you can name afterwards. What new words did you learn?

2. *Lobsterman* was written in 1962. Research how lobstering has changed since then. For example, metal and plastic traps are now being used instead of wooden ones. What else has changed? Which parts of *Lobsterman* are still accurate or true? Read recent nonfiction books about lobstering and interview a lobsterman. Make a chart to show lobstering then and now.

3. Author/illustrator Dahlov Ipcar presents a fishing harbor in *Lobsterman*. Make your own trip to an active fishing harbor. Bring paper and write notes and make sketches of all that you see at the fishing harbor. Compare Ipcar's fishing harbor with the one you observe. How are they similar? How do they differ?

ABOUT THE AUTHOR/ILLUSTRATOR

Dahlov Ipcar has lived at Robinhood, on Georgetown Island, Maine, since 1937. She was born in Windsor, Vermont, was schooled in New York City, and has summered in Maine since she was five. Her parents, William and Marguerite Zorach, were artists. They owned the dairy farm where Ipcar and her family have lived for more than thirty years.

Ipcar is a self-taught artist. She illustrated her first book in 1945 — *The Little Fisherman* by Margaret Wise Brown. Since then, she has written and illustrated thirty books of her own including *The Calico Jungle, Bright Barnyard, The Marvelous Merry-go-round*, and *My Wonderful Christmas Tree* (see page 172). Unfortunately, most of Ipcar's books are now out of print, but many are still available at town and school libraries. Ipcar's artwork, including oils and watercolors, has been exhibited throughout Maine, including nine murals that are displayed at Maine schools and libraries.

Ipcar explains that she is first of all an artist. She thinks of the pictures first and then writes a story to go with them. "My writing is very visual," Ipcar explains, "I start with mental images." Ipcar's *Lobsterman* is based on her childhood memories of lobstering from a skiff with her brother. She describes herself and her work: "I am not a 'boater' but I love the water and Maine shores, and the colorful gear of fishermen. My illustrations are realistic, but simple and 'modern' in style. I like lots of color." Ipcar is also the author of a young adult novel, *A Dark Horn Blowing*.

Ipcar's hobbies include folk-song collecting and gardening. For more information about Dahlov Ipcar, read the biography of her, *Dahlov Ipcar, Artist* (see page 201) by Pat Davidson Reef.

A MOUSE'S TALE

AUTHOR / ILLUSTRATOR: Pamela Johnson
AGE LEVEL / LENGTH: 3-7 years / 32 pages
PUBLISHER / COPYRIGHT DATE: Harcourt Brace & Co. /
1991
FORMAT / ISBN: Hardcover / 0152560327

In *A Mouse's Tale*, an adventurous mouse longs to go to sea. But the mouse faces a dilemma. What kind of boat shall she use? A ship would be too big. A ferry boat would be too noisy. A tugboat would be too dirty. On and on, the little mouse considers each type of sea vessel, but each one seems to have a problem. Finally, the mouse invents her own boat using the odds and ends she discovers while beachcombing. At the end of the book, the mouse happily sets out to sea in a shell with a gull's feather as a sail. In Pamela Johnson's story and colored-pencil illustrations, a tiny mouse facing the gigantic sea seems like such a mismatch that the reader can't help but smile and root for the struggling mouse.

LEARNING ACTIVITIES

1. *A Mouse's Tale* mentions many different kinds of boats. Look in books about boats and try to find pictures of as many different kinds of boats as you can. Compare the pictures of boats. How are the boats alike? Different? Which boat looks like the kind you would like to take out to sea? Why?

2. The little mouse in this book goes beachcombing; that is, she explores the beach, finding different odds and ends. Go beachcombing yourself (or if you can't get to a beach, try meadow combing or woods combing). What did you discover on the beach? Try to make a creation with the objects you gather.

3. This book is called *A Mouse's Tale* and tells the story of a mouse finding a perfect boat. But if it was called "A Dog's Tale," then what would be a perfect boat for a dog? Or the perfect boat for an elephant in "An Elephant's Tale?" And so on with other animals. Or what if the mouse longed for a different adventure than going to sea? What if the mouse wanted to fly? What could she use? Or what could she use if she wanted to go skiing? Or bungee jumping? Or whatever other adventures you can imagine?

ABOUT THE AUTHOR/ILLUSTRATOR

Pamela Johnson grew up by the sea, on Cape Cod, Massachusetts, but she has lived on a rural farm in Sedgwick, Maine, since 1990. She has illustrated books written by Mary Stolz, and animal books for the Sierra Club. *A Mouse's Tale* is the first picture book that she has both written and illustrated. She illustrated it during her first winter in Maine. For *A Mouse's Tale*, Johnson used colored pencils on watercolor paper. Johnson says that she has no formal art training. She explains, "I have just always loved drawing (not necessarily illustrating!)."

Johnson's small farm includes a few sheep, cats, and a three-legged dog. She considers herself a market gardener and says that "the farm and gardens have taken over my life." She also makes dolls and spins the wool from her sheep to use for knitting.

COUSIN RUTH'S TOOTH

AUTHOR: Amy MacDonald / ILLUSTRATOR: Marjorie Priceman
AGE LEVEL / LENGTH: 4-8 years / 32 pages
PUBLISHER / COPYRIGHT DATE: Houghton Mifflin Co. / 1996
FORMAT / ISBN: Hardcover / 039571253X

Cousin Ruth's Tooth is a rollicking, rhymed story about Cousin Ruth who loses her tooth. Ruth's extended family searches "low and high" for the missing tooth. They turn the house topsy turvy as they check every place imaginable: "Check the hatbox. Check the cat box. Look inside the VCR." When they can't find the tooth, they try to whittle one from a stick, model one from clay, and even buy one at an L. L. Bean store. Still, no tooth. As a last resort, the family sends a fax to the Queen, who promptly faxes back her response, solving the mystery of the missing tooth. At the end, Cousin Ruth is all smiles (as will be all young readers of this humorous story).

Cousin Ruth's Tooth features the Fister family and is a follow-up to a 1990 book called *Rachel Fister's Blister*, by the same author and illustrator team. The rhyming text of *Cousin Ruth's Tooth* begs to be read aloud over and over, and the zany watercolor illustrations beg to be inspected time and again (perhaps even with a magnifying glass so as not to miss a speck of humor).

LEARNING ACTIVITIES

1. The Fister clan tries to buy Cousin Ruth a new tooth at an L. L. Bean store. Visit L. L. Bean in Freeport, Maine, or look into one of their catalogues. Do you think the Fisters will find a tooth at L. L. Bean? Maybe not, but they may find plenty of other things. Make a list of ten unusual items that can be found at L. L. Bean. Then do a little research on the company. Try to find out what year the store was started, how many visitors they get at the store each year, how many different items they offer for sale.

2. Study the rhyming pattern in *Cousin Ruth's Tooth*. Which lines rhyme? Is the pattern the same throughout the book? Try to create two additional pages to the book. Add different zany places where the Fister family might search for the missing tooth. When creating your pages, try to follow Amy MacDonald's rhyme pattern. Create crazy illustrations to go along with your words.

3. Even though the characters in this book might appear at first glance to be from an earlier time in history, they actually do some very contemporary things. Go back over the text and the illustrations and make a list of all the words and drawings that have current references (e.g., VCR, fax).

ABOUT THE AUTHOR

Amy MacDonald has lived in Maine since 1988, but she spent summers on Mt. Desert Island as a child. She and her husband (who is British) moved to Maine when he began his job as the director of the Maine Audubon Society.

MacDonald decided when she was in fifth grade that she wanted to become a writer, largely because a teacher encouraged her. She has written everything from news articles and feature stories to books and plays. Her children's books include *Rachel Fister's Blister*, the *Let's Explore* board books, *The Spider Who Created the World*, and *No More Nice* (which has a character based on a great-aunt MacDonald visited in Sorrento, Maine).

MacDonald came to write her first children's book *Little Beaver and the Echo* (see page 56) when she was staying at a pond with an echo. Her young son had never heard an echo. She decided to write a book that would tell him about echoes; she wrote it in 45 minutes! The pond where she lived for many summers had a beaver lodge at one end, and as a child she loved to canoe and watch the beavers. Thus the beaver was a natural choice for the main character.

Currently, MacDonald lives with her husband and three children in Falmouth, Maine. Her hobbies include canoeing, hiking, skiing, and swimming. She is also the president of a small theater company.

ABOUT THE ILLUSTRATOR

Marjorie Priceman grew up on Long Island. She now lives in New York City. She received a Bachelor of Fine Arts degree from the Rhode Island School of Design. She is the author and illustrator of *Friend or Frog* and *How to Make Apple Pie and See the World*. She also has illustrated books by other authors, including *A Mouse in My House* by Nancy Van Laan, *A. Nonny Mouse Writes Again* by Jack Prelutsky, and *Zin! Zin! Zin! A Violin* by Lloyd Moss.

LITTLE BEAVER AND THE ECHO

AUTHOR: Amy MacDonald / ILLUSTRATOR: Sarah Fox-Davies
AGE LEVEL / LENGTH: 3-7 years / 32 pages
PUBLISHER / COPYRIGHT DATE: G.P. Putnam's Sons / 1990
FORMAT / ISBN: Hardcover / 0399222030

Little Beaver and the Echo tells a simple and touching story of a little beaver's search for friendship. Little Beaver doesn't have any friends so he begins to cry. When he stops, he hears someone across the pond crying too. Little Beaver hollers across the pond, "I'm lonely. I need a friend." The voice answers back, "I'm lonely, I need a friend." Excited to find someone else in need of a friend, Little Beaver climbs into his boat and sets off across the pond in search of this friend.

Little Beaver never does find the voice, but he makes friends with a duck, otter, and turtle along the way. Finally, a wise old beaver explains to Little Beaver that the voice is the Echo, and that the Echo is always "on the other side of the pond no matter where you are." Little Beaver shouts, " I have lots of friends now," and sure enough from across the pond comes a voice repeating his happy words.

LEARNING ACTIVITIES

1. Create handmade puppets for each of the animals in the story. Then read the story aloud and use the puppets to act out the story. After acting the story, as it is read aloud, try acting the story again from memory. You may wish to have one person play the part of the narrator.

2. Visit a pond, and use paper and pencils, crayons, paints, etc. to record observations about the pond's animals, plants, and water using both words and pictures.

3. Research each of the animals in *Little Beaver and the Echo*. Then draw a simple chart with facts about each animal. For example, for a beaver the chart might show in words and/or pictures:

> —A beaver cuts down trees with its teeth.
> —A beaver lives in a lodge.
> —A beaver slaps its flat tail on the water to warn of danger.

Then play a guessing game about the chart with a friend. For example, one of you might say, "I'm thinking about the animal that lives in a shell. Which one is it?" Use the chart to help you find the answer (turtle). Continue with more turns. "I'm thinking of the animal that has a beak (duck)."

4. Discuss the concept of "echo." If possible, demonstrate a real echo in an empty room or outside. Then play an echo game. One person should stand on one side of the room and say a sentence. Then another person on the other side of the room plays the echo and says the sentence back exactly as it was said. Be sure to listen carefully and remember what was said (an echo does not change or add words).

ABOUT THE AUTHOR

See information about Amy MacDonald on page 55.

ABOUT THE ILLUSTRATOR

Sarah Fox-Davies is a graduate of the Hornsey School of Art in England. She is known for her natural history illustrations which have appeared in numerous publications and children's books. She currently lives in London.

INCH BY INCH:
THE GARDEN SONG

AUTHOR: David Mallett / ILLUSTRATOR: Ora Eitan
AGE LEVEL / LENGTH: all ages / 28 pages
PUBLISHER / COPYRIGHT DATE: HarperCollins / 1975-text/song lyrics; 1995-illustrations
FORMAT / ISBN: Hardcover / 0060243031; Paperback / 0064434818

This picture book captures the spirit of *The Garden Song*, a popular folk song written and performed by Maine musician, David Mallett. As the book's title suggests, most people refer to the song by its first line, "Inch by inch, row by row, gonna make this garden grow." The book depicts a little boy planting his garden along side his pet dog. The simple, childlike illustrations by Ora Eitan show the playfulness and hopefulness of the song. The young boy grows gigantic sunflowers and beets "with prayer and song." And as the song speaks about the feeling of freedom one finds in gardening, an accompanying illustration shows the boy and his dog sliding on a rainbow.

Inch by Inch: The Garden Song is a wonderful book to share between generations. It's hard to simply *read* it. Almost everyone who opens it will want to sing the words loudly over and over. And for those who don't know the tune, or wish for accompaniment, the music is included at the back of the book.

LEARNING ACTIVITIES

1. Create costumes and a set and perform this book/song as a play. How can you look like a gardener? What gardening tools will you need? What will you grow in your garden?

by David Mallett · pictures by Ora Eitan

When you perform your play, pass out a copy of the words and encourage the audience to sing along with you.

2. Select another song by a Maine performer (e.g., Rick Charette, Noel Paul Stookey, Malinda Liberty) and turn it into a picture book. Write down the song's words and add illustrations. Then share your song picture book with a friend.

3. Conduct a survey about the *Garden Song*. Sing or say the first line to this song. Then ask twenty-five people if they have heard of the song. For those who have heard of it, ask them what they think the title of it is. Write a summary of your survey results. How many people had heard of the song before? Did you notice a difference between age levels? How many people thought the song's title was *The Garden Song? Inch by Inch?* What other titles were suggested?

ABOUT THE AUTHOR

Born and raised in rural Maine, for thirty-five years Dave Mallett has worked as a singer, songwriter and performer, with ten albums of original songs to his credit. Mallett wrote *The Garden Song* in his family's garden plot in June 1975. He regularly tours throughout the United States, Canada, and Europe. He currently lives on the farm where he grew up in Sebec, Maine, with his wife and three children. Mallett's hobbies include hiking, fishing, and gardening

ABOUT THE ILLUSTRATOR

Ora Eitan is from Israel. She graduated from the Bezalel Academy of Art in Jerusalem. She teaches illustration at both the Bezalel Academy of Art and the Hebrew University in Jerusalem. She has illustrated many children's books and has received Israel's nomination for the Hans Christian Andersen Award.

BIZZY BONES AND THE LOST QUILT

AUTHOR: Jacqueline Briggs Martin / ILLUSTRATOR: Stella Ormai
AGE LEVEL / LENGTH: 3-7 years / 32 pages
PUBLISHER / COPYRIGHT DATE: Lothrop, Lee & Shepard / 1988
FORMAT / ISBN: Hardcover / 0688074073

Bizzy Bones is a mouse who lives near Paris Hill, Maine, with his Uncle Ezra. Their lives are filled with seeds and nuts and contentment until one day Bizzy loses his quilt. It's not just any quilt. It's *the* quilt that Bizzy lugs with him everywhere, the one that has stories about the squares, and the one that gives Bizzy good dreams at night. Even Uncle Ezra knows how special Bizzy's quilt is to him, claiming "Bizzy would be glad to ride a wheelbarrow to Aroostook County" if only he had his quilt with him.

Bizzy and Uncle Ezra look everywhere for the lost quilt. They enlist the help of the orchard mice who are "savers, swappers, and traders." Uncle Ezra even tries to make Bizzy a new quilt by nailing the patches together and filling in the spaces with birch bark. But Bizzy wishes for his old quilt back. Young readers will anxiously finish the story hoping that Bizzy's wish will come true.

Bizzy Bones and the Lost Quilt is a warm, universal story about the bond between a child and a prized possession. It is one of several books about this charming mouse; others in the series include *Bizzy Bones and Uncle Ezra* and *Bizzy Bones and Moosemouse*.

LEARNING ACTIVITIES

1. Draw a picture of your favorite blanket, toy, or other prized possession. Then tell a story to a friend about why your chosen possession is so special to you. What do you use it for? How long have you had it? Have you ever lost it?

2. Reread *Bizzy Bones and the Lost Quilt*. Afterwards turn to the map inside the covers of the book and locate with your finger all the places named in the story. For example, at the beginning of the story Bizzy and Uncle Ezra go from their home to the meadow. Trace the path they might have taken. Later, they visit the orchard mice. Find their home on the map. Can you find all the places named in the story on the map?

3. Interview someone who makes quilts. Look carefully at one of the quilts that this person has made. How was the quilt made? Where does the material come from? Is the quilt pattern planned? Are there stories behind any of the quilt squares? How long does it take to make a quilt?

ABOUT THE AUTHOR

Jacqueline Briggs Martin grew up on a dairy farm in Turner, Maine, that has been in her family for eight generations. During Martin's childhood, she found herself pausing to wonder what life must have been like for earlier generations that lived on the farm. She states, "I yearned to be able to travel back in time and see those earlier lives." Although Martin could not have her wish of actually traveling back in time, she could at least *imagine* earlier times and earlier lives. That's exactly what she did, and she set those imagined images down on paper to share with others.

Martin's first children's book, *Bizzy Bones and Uncle Ezra,* was published in 1984. It was based on her son's fear of the wind and was set next to a stone wall in a Maine pasture not far from Paris Hill.

Currently living in the small town of Mount Vernon, Iowa, Martin continues to write children's books. Her latest books include *Washing the Willow Tree Loon*; *Grandmother Bryant's Pocket* (see below); *The Green Truck Garden Giveaway*; *Higgins Bend Song and Dance* (see page 62); *Button, Bucket, Sky*; and *Snowflake Bentley*. When she's not writing, Martin enjoys camping, hiking, and gardening. She especially enjoys growing roses, tomatoes, hot peppers, and herbs. Martin returns to Maine every summer and at least once during the school year to visit family and friends.

ABOUT THE ILLUSTRATOR

Stella Ormai has no personal claims to Maine; but her husband, Richard Greene Flinn, is a descendant of the Greene family from Blue Hill, Maine. Ormai, a graduate of the Rhode Island School of Design, has been illustrating children's books for more than twenty years. She has more than twenty-five books to her credit, including *Soap Bubble Magic*, *Mole and Shrew*, *Sleeping Over*, and *Creatures*. Ormai, with her husband and two daughters, currently lives in Providence, Rhode Island, where she enjoys caring for numerous pets, working in her garden, and swimming.

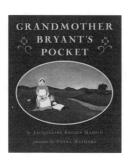

GRANDMOTHER BRYANT'S POCKET

AUTHOR: Jacqueline Briggs Martin / ILLUSTRATOR: Petra Mathers
AGE LEVEL / LENGTH: 5-8 years / 48 pages
PUBLISHER / COPYRIGHT DATE: Houghton Mifflin Co. / 1996
FORMAT / ISBN: Hardcover / 0395689848
AWARDS: Lupine Award, 1996

Grandmother Bryant's Pocket is set in Maine in 1787. It tells the story of eight-year-old Sarah whose dog Patches dies in a barn fire. Sarah has nightmares after the fire; and so she goes to stay with her grandparents in hopes that getting away from the ashes will help and that Grandmother Bryant's herbs will be able to cure her nightmares. Sarah enjoys her time at her grandparents. She helps her grandmother grow herbs in the garden, listens to her grandfather's stories, and befriends a stray one-eyed cat. But Sarah still has fears. She's afraid of the mean neighbor lady and her biting geese. After Grandmother Bryant allows Sarah to wear her special pocket, which carries soothing herbs and is embroidered with the words "Fear Not," Sarah begins to have sweet dreams. But in the end, Sarah must also confront the biting geese, as she has to overcome her other fears, in order to treat the mean neighbor after an accident.

Grandmother Bryant's Pocket is unique in several ways. Its small size (6 x 7 inches) and the way that it is divided into short chapters makes it an inviting book for beginning "independent" readers. Also, historical fiction tends to be more common in chapter books than in picture books. *Grandmother Bryant's Pocket* is a nice exception to this rule; it helps to make the 1700s in Maine accessible to young children through its story of one girl's fears. Readers learn about clothing during the 1700s (women wore a pocket tied around their waists since skirts had no built-in pockets); they'll get a feel for how farm life, chores, and bartering worked more than 200 years ago; and they'll learn about the importance of herbs to our ancestors (an appendix illustrates and describes herbs such as catnip, comfrey, and pennyroyal).

LEARNING ACTIVITIES

1. In *Grandmother Bryant's Pocket*, Sarah begins to have nightmares after her dog dies in a barn fire. Later, she is afraid of the mean neighbor and her biting geese. Discuss Sarah's fears. Did she have good reasons to be afraid? Why or why not? What do you think helped Sarah to overcome her nightmares and her fears in the story? Next, write a story or draw an illustration about a fear or nightmare you have had yourself. Then discuss your fear. Do you still have the fear or nightmare? If you stopped, why do you think you did so? If you still have the fear or nightmare, what do you think you could do to overcome it?

2. Select one herb and learn more about it. Read about your selected herb, talk with health food specialists, and, if possible, grow that herb with an adult's help. What does the herb look like? How does it grow? How is it used? Was your herb used for different purposes in the past than it is today? How many years has your selected herb been available? Give a short oral or written report about your herb after you finish your research.

3. *Grandmother Bryant's Pocket* is divided into very short chapters with simple titles, such as "Grandfather Bryant's Stories," "The One-Eyed Cat," and "The Neighbor." Select another picture book and try to divide it into short chapters. Then make up titles for the chapters.

4. Find an adult who knows how to sew and ask that adult to help you make a tie-on pocket like Grandmother Bryant's pocket. Help with the sewing as much as possible, then decorate the pocket, and finally wear it. What will you carry in your pocket? Why?

ABOUT THE AUTHOR

See information about Jacqueline Briggs Martin on page 59.

ABOUT THE ILLUSTRATOR

Illustrator Petra Mathers has no Maine connections other than the research she did for *Grandmother Bryant's Pocket*. Mathers grew up in postwar Germany and later emigrated to the U.S. with her husband and child. She has no formal art training, but she has been illustrating books for more than a decade She works in watercolor using a style similar to "American Folk Art with an eye on medieval times." In addition to *Grandmother Bryant's*

Pocket, Mathers lists some of the other "favorites" that she has worked on: *Sophie and Lou, Victor and Christabel, When It Snowed That Night,* and *Mrs. Merriwether's Musical Cat.* She writes children's books as well as illustrates them.

Mathers presently lives in Astoria, Oregon, with her husband in what she describes as "paradise." She explains: "Lewis and Clark camped where now our house stands. We look across seven miles of the mighty Columbia River before it goes around the bend to meet the sea. Sometimes an eagle watches me dry my hair in the mornings."

HIGGINS BEND SONG AND DANCE

AUTHOR: Jacqueline Briggs Martin / ILLUSTRATOR: Brad Sneed
AGE LEVEL / LENGTH: 4-8 years / 32 pages
PUBLISHER / COPYRIGHT DATE: Houghton Mifflin / 1997
FORMAT / ISBN: Hardcover / 0395675839

Simon Henry was a grumpy fisherman: "he didn't smile one day out of seven." He wouldn't even join in the Friday-Night-Potluck-Everybody-Come-and-Fling at Potato Kelly's Bait and Chowder Shop. He was too busy fishing. And there wasn't a fish Simon Henry couldn't catch—that is, until Oscar the catfish moved into the deep hole in the river by Higgins Bend. Oscar always managed to steal every kind of bait: cheese, chicken liver, live crickets, soap, cheeseballs, and cold french fries.

Simon Henry was determined to find a special bait to catch Oscar. He bet his friend Potato Kelly that he would sing with a bullfrog, dance with his fishpole, and eat his own socks if he didn't find a way to catch that "water burglar." Simon Henry tried one last special bait and Oscar bit! After a tremendous struggle, the townspeople weren't quite sure if Simon Henry caught the catfish or if the catfish caught Simon Henry. Nevertheless, Simon Henry joined the celebration at Potato Kelly's Bait and Chowder Shop with some singing, a waltz, and a bite of "sock" chowder.

Jacqueline Briggs Martin has created a fishing yarn that will keep readers chuckling long after the last page is read. Martin claims that the story is not specifically set in Maine, but that her "Maine roots poke through" in the characters who banter back-and-forth, like many people she knew growing up in Turner, Maine. She adds Maine touches of chowder, potatoes, and potluck suppers. Illustrator Brad Sneed amplifies the humor of the book with his visually detailed characters—such as big-eared, pointy-nosed Simon Henry, with his caved-in chest and saggy pants, which are held up by suspenders and a rope belt.

LEARNING ACTIVITIES

1. Turn *Higgins Bend Song and Dance* into a play. Decide on simple props and scenery.

A narrator should read the story aloud as others create the roles of different characters, performing the actions described in the book and repeating the conversations from the book. Be creative with your costumes. How can someone resemble Simon Henry? How can someone resemble Oscar? After rehearsing, perform the play for a small audience. You might want to serve chowder as a treat after the performance.

2. Learn about Maine catfish. Interview people who fish or a representative from your local Wildlife and Fisheries Department. What kind of catfish are found in Maine? Where are these catfish found? What do they eat? How large do they grow? Make a poster that shows the information you have learned.

3. Write your own creative humorous story—either about fishing or about a bet. You might want to base your story upon a real incident, but feel free to add some fictional details to exaggerate your story, making it into more of a yarn or tall tale, as Jacqueline Briggs Martin did in *Higgins Bend Song and Dance*.

ABOUT THE AUTHOR

See information about Jacqueline Briggs Martin on page 59.

ABOUT THE ILLUSTRATOR

Brad Sneed works as a freelance illustrator in Prairie Village, Kansas, where he lives with his wife. His hobbies include painting, sports, camping, and fishing. Sneed received a bachelor of fine arts degree from Kansas University. He has illustrated several picture books, including: *Grandpa's Song, Turkey in the Straw*, and *The Legend of the Cranberry*.

WILD FOX: A TRUE STORY

AUTHOR: Cherie Mason / ILLUSTRATOR: Jo Ellen McAllister Stammen
AGE LEVEL / LENGTH: 5 years–adult / 32 pages
PUBLISHER / COPYRIGHT DATE: Down East Books / 1993
FORMAT / ISBN: Hardcover / 089272319X
AWARDS: Lupine Award, 1993

This book tells the true story of a wild fox who visited the home of author Cherie Mason on Deer Isle, Maine. As if carrying on a conversation with the readers, Mason begins the book by asking, "Have you ever touched the nose of a wild red fox? I have." She then tells about finding a fox pup eating her strawberries one summer. The next winter the same fox returns to Mason's yard for bird suet. But this time the fox is injured; the fox's right paw has been nearly severed from a trap. Mason brings a chicken drumstick out for the fox. After that, the injured fox returns at regular intervals.

Maintaining her conversational style, Mason continues the story of the wild fox she names Vicky. Readers will feel as if they are simply chatting with the author as the story unfolds. After encountering Vicky, Mason's fascination with foxes led her to research them. She weaves factual information into her story so that readers learn without even realizing it. For example, foxes have been in existence for thirty million years—ten times longer than humans. Also, Native Americans believed that foxes had white-tipped tails because the end of their tails would sweep the snow, erasing their tracks. As the story ends, Mason realizes that Vicky will no longer be returning to her yard. The fox allows Mason a brief and rare moment of contact, refuses an offered blueberry muffin, and limps off without a glance backward.

Wild Fox: A True Story is a beautiful book, from its awe-filled story to its stunning illustrations to its elegant design. It's a celebration of nature for all ages, with only one noticeable flaw: there is no explicit warning for young readers to keep a safe distance from, and not to touch, wild animals. These days this warning is especially important in Maine and elsewhere, with the recent resurgence of rabies cases. But if adults who share this book with youngsters make certain to add this warning, then *Wild Fox: A True Story* can serve as a tale of respect for another species that will endure reading after reading.

LEARNING ACTIVITIES

1. Make a "fox fact list." Reread *Wild Fox: A True Story* and make a list of all the information about foxes (e.g., their coats become less bright in spring; foxes eat insects, frogs, rodents, and berries). Read nonfiction books about foxes and add to your fact list. Try to find fifty different fox facts.

2. Organize a debate. You and another person should take opposite sides on the following question: Should author Cherie Mason have touched the wild fox or not (see pages 26-27 in the book)? You should each plan a rationale for your answer and give evidence supporting your view. Invite others to watch your debate. Afterward, have a discussion as to who presented the best case in the debate, and why.

3. On the copyright page, Cherie Mason mentions the cruelty of the steel-jaw leghold trap. What are some other examples of how human actions or devices are dangerous to animals (e.g., litter, pollution, invading animals' habitats)? Learn more about one of these animal hazards and make a poster informing people about this hazard.

ABOUT THE AUTHOR

Cherie Mason has worked as an advertising executive, an actress, and environmental journalist. Mason moved to Maine several years ago from Chicago. In Maine she has been actively involved in environmental causes and organizations. She helped to obtain a federal grant for purchasing land around the Rachel Carson Wildlife Refuge in southern Maine, serves on the Deer Isle Conservation Commission, and is a trustee of Maine's Endangered & Nongame Wildlife Council.

Mason describes herself as an "evangelist for the environment and wild animals." She explains, "The reason I work so hard for animals and their habitats is that they are the innocents of the world. Because we have ruined so much, they are now in a position of needing us as protectors and advocates. Also of course, wild animals are so beautiful. Once you see them—not in cages, but on their own turf—they stay with you." Mason currently lives with her husband in Sunset, Maine, where she is at work on another children's book.

ABOUT THE ILLUSTRATOR

See information about Jo Ellen McAllister Stammen on page 44.

BLUEBERRIES FOR SAL

AUTHOR / ILLUSTRATOR: Robert McCloskey
AGE LEVEL / LENGTH: 3-8 years / 56 pages
PUBLISHER / COPYRIGHT DATE: Viking (hardcover); Puffin Books (paperback & cassette tape) / 1948
FORMAT / ISBN: Hardcover / 0670175919; Paperback / 014095032X; Cassette tape with Paperback / 0140951105

Little Sal goes blueberrying with her mother. Sal is more interested in eating blueberries than in picking and saving them for canning. Little Bear goes with his mother up Blueberry Hill, eating lots of blueberries to store up food for winter hibernation. Sal and Little Bear somehow get mixed up on Blueberry Hill and end up with the wrong mother— Sal with mother bear, Little Bear with Sal's mother. Each mother, human and bear, is shocked by the  mix-up and frantically searches for her own child. At the end, all is well; and the bears head down one side of Blueberry Hill, storing up on blueberries, and the people head down the other side of Blueberry Hill, storing up on blueberries.

Blueberries for Sal has remained a favorite of young readers for fifty years, and it will likely continue as a favorite for another fifty years. Robert McCloskey's story is simple yet brilliant; the playful, back-and-forth pattern between the humans' actions and the bears' actions will bring a smile to readers of all ages.

LEARNING ACTIVITIES

1. Go blueberrying. Pick or rake blueberries. Maine produces more blueberries than any other state; so it is a very important crop. Ask a blueberry cultivator questions about blueberries—how they are grown, when and how they are harvested, how they are packaged for sale out-of-state, etc.

2. Talk about storing food for the winter. Why do people store food? What kinds of foods can be stored? Following a recipe, help an adult to can, freeze, or pickle a food.

3. Study bears. What does a bear eat? What kinds of bears live in Maine? Where do they live? How do they survive in winter? Check bear books and encyclopedias for information. If possible, interview a game warden about bear sightings in the state.

4. Study the illustrations in *Blueberries for Sal*. They reflect life in the 1940s. Discuss the differences between the hair styles, cars, clothes, etc., then and now.

ABOUT THE AUTHOR/ILLUSTRATOR

Robert McCloskey was born and raised in Hamilton, Ohio. He showed an early interest in music, gadgets, and art. After going to Vesper George Art School in Boston and painting for awhile, McCloskey took a sample of his work (which included woodcuts of dragons) to a children's book editor in New York. The editor told him that he better go back to the drawing board and find an appropriate subject for his art. And so McCloskey did. His first book, *Lentil*, was published in 1940, and it reflected his Ohio roots.

After several more children's books and a stint in World War II, McCloskey moved to an island home in Maine with his wife. Once again he wrote from his experience. His Maine books include *Blueberries for Sal*; *One Morning in Maine*; *Time of Wonder*, and *Burt Dow, Deep Water Man*. McCloskey was the first artist to receive the prestigious Caldecott Medal twice, for *Make Way for Ducklings* (1941) and *Time of Wonder* (1958). The latter, McCloskey's first full color book, took him three years to complete.

In writing *Blueberries for Sal*, McCloskey imagined the bear, but the rest of the book was based on his real Maine world. He pictured his daughter, Sally, as Sal, and his wife, Peggy, as the mother. The kitchen in the book was McCloskey's, with the addition of his mother-in-law's (children's book author Ruth Sawyer) old stove transplanted from her home in Hancock, Maine.

McCloskey wrote and illustrated eight books and illustrated another ten books during his career. He stopped illustrating children's books in 1970, but his books have remained popular for generation after generation. McCloskey himself continues to hold a special place in the history of children's literature.

BURT DOW, DEEP-WATER MAN

AUTHOR / ILLUSTRATOR: Robert McCloskey
AGE LEVEL / LENGTH: 6-10 years / 64 pages
PUBLISHER / COPYRIGHT DATE: Viking Children's Books (hardcover); Puffin Books (paperback)/ 1963
FORMAT / ISBN: Hardcover / 0670197483; Paperback / 014050978X

This is the story of Burt Dow, a retired Maine fisherman who owns two old boats. In one, he grows geraniums and Indian peas. The other is the "Tidely-Idely," a leaky double-ender that Burt patches and paints and takes out fishing. He uses leftover paint from all the odds-and-ends painting jobs that he's done. He also has a giggling gull for a pet.

One day Burt Dow goes out fishing in the "Tidely-Idely." He catches a big one—a whale! The whale, being of the friendly variety, waits patiently while Burt snips the hook out of his tail. Burt even puts a peppermint-stripe bandage on the whale's tail where the "boo boo" is.

By the time Burt is finished caring for the whale, he notices that a big storm seems to be brewing. Burt knows the "Tidely-Idely" won't survive a big wind. "All hands aboard are headed for Davy Jones's locker," he declares. So Burt convinces the whale to swallow him, boat and all—temporarily—until the storm passes. And the whale does! After sitting in the whale's belly for a time, Burt is afraid that the whale misunderstood him and may have swallowed him permanently. Burt splatters everything he can find in the boat (left-over paint, sediment, bait, rusty fish hooks, and more) all over the insides of the whale's belly, trying to upset the whale's stomach so that he can get out. Burt succeeds—the whale burps, and out flies the fisherman, the boat, and the giggling gull. The adventure's not over yet. Burt finds himself in the middle of a lively school of whales, who won't let him pass to open water. Burt finds a fun and funny way to please the whales so that they will let him head for home.

Robert McCloskey shows a great sense of humor with this book. Not only does he tell a funny story, but his characters are lively, his made-up words (slish-cashlosh, clackety-bangety) are fun to say, and his bright color combinations enliven the pages.

LEARNING ACTIVITIES

1. Tape record the story of *Burt Dow, Deep-Water Man*. As it's read, add sound effects to the story (e.g., laughing for the seagull, banging for the engine). Listen to the story played back with the sound effects.

2. Inside the whale, Burt Dow expresses his "personality in paint." Use a large piece of paper to paint an image of your own personality. What colors will you use? What designs?

3. Write a follow-up story to *Burt Dow, Deep-Water Man*. What other ocean adventures might Burt Dow have? What if he met a shark? What if he had to rescue his giggling gull? How would he rescue himself if the "Tidely-Idley" actually sank? Write a story about one of these adventures or one of your own choosing.

ABOUT THE AUTHOR/ILLUSTRATOR

See information about Robert McCloskey on page 66.

ONE MORNING IN MAINE

AUTHOR / ILLUSTRATOR: Robert McCloskey
AGE LEVEL / LENGTH: 4-8 years / 64 pages
PUBLISHER / COPYRIGHT DATE: Viking Children's Books (hardcover); Puffin Books (paperback)/ 1952
FORMAT / ISBN: Hardcover / 0670526274; Paperback / 0140501746

Sal, the little girl in *One Morning in Maine*, wakes up to a day full of excitement. She looks forward to a boat trip with her father to Bucks Harbor, and she discovers that she has her first loose tooth. Sal's mom congratulates her now that she's a "big girl." Sal learns that she can save her tooth when it comes out, put it under her pillow, and make a wish.

Sal is so busy showing off her loose tooth—to a fish hawk, a loon, a seal, and her Dad—that when it comes out, she accidentally loses it. Unable to find it, she is disappointed that she won't get a chance to make her wish. But Sal finds a tooth substitute, a seagull feather, and makes her wish, hoping for the best. Sal boats to Bucks Harbor with her family. She proudly shows everyone that her tooth is missing. And before leaving, much to her excitement, her wish comes true.

Robert McCloskey's large-format illustrations transport the reader back in time with 1950s styles of clothing, furniture, and vehicles. But McCloskey's story remains timeless with its warm humor and universal situation of a child losing a first tooth.

LEARNING ACTIVITIES

1. Keep a tooth diary. Record the time, date, and place that you lose each tooth, as well as how it comes out and what you wish for. Ask friends to keep a tooth diary also, and then compare your diaries.

2. Start a tooth collection. Ask a veterinarian for samples of animal teeth. Compare them with children's teeth. How are they alike? Different? Do young animals lose their teeth the same as children do?

3. Have a round-robin wish in your classroom. In *One Morning in Maine*, Sal wished for a chocolate ice cream cone. What would the children in your room wish for? Each student must think of something that starts with the same letter as the first letter in their names. And so, Tim might wish for a tuna sandwich, Beth might wish for a Barbie doll, Frita might wish for a frog, and so on. To make the round-robin challenging, everyone must not only say their wish aloud, but also repeat all the wishes of the students who have spoken before them.

ABOUT THE AUTHOR/ILLUSTRATOR

See information about Robert McCloskey on page 66.

TIME OF WONDER

AUTHOR / ILLUSTRATOR: Robert McCloskey
AGE LEVEL / LENGTH: 6-10 years / 64 pages
PUBLISHER / COPYRIGHT DATE: Viking Children's
Books (hardcover); Puffin Books (paperback);
Audio Bookshelf (audio book) / 1957
FORMAT / ISBN: Hardcover / 0670715123; Paperback / 0140502017; Audio Book / 1883332176
AWARDS: Caldecott Medal, 1958

Set in Penobscot Bay on the coast of Maine, *Time of Wonder* presents the glories of island summer life. Fog and fiddleheads, high tides and low tides, hummingbirds and hurricanes are all a part of this Maine setting.

Unlike Robert McCloskey's other picture books, *Time of Wonder* is not so much a story as a slice of life. McCloskey captures with poetic words and large-format illustrations the different moods of island life. McCloskey speaks of "salty young silhouettes on the old scars made by glaciers." And he describes a late night row in the ocean with the words "the stars are gazing down, their reflections growing up." Best of all, McCloskey captures the fury of an island hurricane with his streaked illustrations and talk of gulls flying backward and salt spray blowing in under the doorsill. As the family packs to leave the island at the end of the book, the reader too feels the sadness of summer's ending.

LEARNING ACTIVITIES

1. Reread *Time of Wonder* along with a Maine map. Notice the names of all the places mentioned by McCloskey in the book. Try to locate these places on the map. Can you tell where *Time of Wonder* must have taken place? How do you know? What hints does the story give you?

2. McCloskey provides a dramatic picture of a hurricane off the Maine coast. Collect true hurricane stories. Interview Maine people who remember any of these hurricanes:

> 1938-The Great Hurricane
> 1954-Hurricane Carol
> 1954-Hurricane Edna
> 1955-Hurricane Diane
> 1960-Hurricane Donna
> 1985-Hurricane Gloria
> 1991-Hurricane Bob

Tape-record their recollections. Then paint pictures to accompany their words. Combine the paintings and words into a taped picture book.

3. Robert McCloskey finishes the book with people leaving the island at summer's end. What favorite place have you had to leave? Write a poem, create a song, or paint a picture that expresses your feelings of farewell.

4. There are many things to pause and wonder about as one reads McCloskey's story. For example, the narrator asks, "Where do hummingbirds go in a hurricane?" Create your own wonder list with questions, such as: why do bats hang upside down? or, how do hibernating animals know when to wake up? Try to find answers to the questions on your list.

ABOUT THE AUTHOR/ILLUSTRATOR

See information about Robert McCloskey on page 66.

GRANDFATHER'S CHRISTMAS CAMP

AUTHOR: Marc McCutcheon / ILLUSTRATOR: Kate Kiesler
AGE LEVEL / LENGTH: 4-8 years / 32 pages
PUBLISHER / COPYRIGHT DATE: Clarion Books (a Houghton Mifflin Co. imprint) / 1995
FORMAT / ISBN: Hardcover / 0395696267; Paperback / 0395866294

Lizzie and her grandfather will not be spending Christmas Eve at home. Mr. Biggins, their three-legged dog, has disappeared; and they must hike up the mountain to look for him. Lizzie bundles up and follows her grandfather, "a mountain man." They holler for Mr. Biggins, but he doesn't come. Grandfather thinks that he is too busy chasing deer.

The trail is steep, and Lizzie is cold, but she refuses to tell her grandfather. Finally, they stop and make a fire. Grandfather cooks venison and cheese sandwiches, which he hopes will attract Mr. Biggins. Lizzie and her grandfather watch the stars, then build an igloo for the night. Lizzie dreams Christmas dreams, then awakens to a snout in her face — Mr. Biggins is back. Lizzie crawls out of the igloo to find a special Christmas treat from her grandfather.

Marc McCutcheon and Kate Kiesler have created an evocative book, filled with fine metaphoric language. For example: "The snow swirls a carousel of sugar and doilies;" and "A three-legged brown missile with a jangling collar." Kiesler's oil paintings are exquisite; the reader can almost touch the snow, feel Grandfather's gruffness, and smell Mr. Biggins' breath. *Grandfather's Christmas Camp* is a welcome story for Christmas time or anytime.

LEARNING ACTIVITIES

1. Author Marc McCutcheon uses unusual vocabulary words in this book. The words blend into the story and can be understood from the way they are used in the story. Reread *Grandfather's Christmas Camp* and try to guess the meaning of vocabulary words that are unfamiliar to you. For example, what is an "alpenhorn" on page 7, a "switchback" on page 12, "venison" on page 19, "bivouac" on page 22, and "swaybacked" on page 30? Look these words up in the dictionary to see if your guesses were correct.

2. *Grandfather's Christmas Camp* tells a story, but there's more to this story than you actually find in its 32 pages. What do you think is the story "behind" the story and "after" the story? How did Mr. Biggins become three-legged? Why did Mr. Biggins really go up the mountain? Why does Lizzie live with her grandfather? How did the grandfather become such a mountain man? What was the rest of Christmas day like for Lizzie?

3. Learn more about the stars mentioned on page 21 of *Grandfather's Christmas Camp*. Check nonfiction books about stars and constellations. Is Betelgeuse really red? Is Rigell blue? Where are they located in the sky? How far away are they? Watch a winter night-time sky. Can you find Orion? What other constellations and stars do you see?

ABOUT THE AUTHOR

Marc McCutcheon grew up in Maine. He now lives in South Portland, Maine, with his wife and two children. *Grandfather's Christmas Camp* began as a bedtime story for his daughter, Kara.

McCutcheon comes from a family of writers; he is the great-nephew of Lucy Maud Montgomery, the author of *Anne of Green Gables. Grandfather's Christmas Camp* is McCutcheon's first children's book, although he has written several reference books for adults, as well as screenplays. He is the author of *The Writer's Guide to Everyday Life in the 1800s* and *The Writer's Guide to Everyday Life from Prohibition Through World War II.*

ABOUT THE ILLUSTRATOR

Kate Kiesler grew up in Stowe, Vermont. She states that she grew up painting and drawing, which eventually led her to study at the Rhode Island School of Design. She has been illustrating professionally for three years. She has illustrated two books with Maine connections: *Grandfather's Christmas Camp* and *Into the Deep Forest with Henry David Thoreau* (see page 220). She is also the illustrator of *Temple Cat* and *Bright Christmas*, both by Andrew Clements, *The Great Frog Race* by Kristine George, *Out of Darkness: The Story of Louis Braille* by Russell Freedman, and *Twilight Comes Twice* by Ralph J. Fletcher. She uses oil paints to create her illustrations. Kiesler currently lives in Taos, New Mexico, where she pursues her hobbies of reading, rock climbing, gardening, and photography.

GRANDFATHER'S TROLLEY

AUTHOR / PHOTO-ILLUSTRATOR: Bruce McMillan
AGE LEVEL / LENGTH: 3-7 years / 28 pages
PUBLISHER / COPYRIGHT DATE: Candlewick Press / 1995
FORMAT / ISBN: Hardcover / 1564026337

Grandfather's Trolley transports young readers back in time to the early 1900s, when trolleys were a common means of transportation. In this story, a little girl meets her grandfather's trolley at the Arundel station. He has saved her a favorite seat way in back. She holds on tight as the trolley speeds along swaying from side to side and with the breeze blowing in her face. The woods are a blur as the trolley gains speed. At the other end of the line, the girl helps her grandfather to change the controls from one end of the car to the other, and she acts as his assistant conductor on the trip back. At the end, the girl skips up a dirt road toward home as her grandfather watches. One gets the feeling that she'll be back soon for another ride on this special trolley with her special grandfather.

Bruce McMillan's striking photographs capture both the feel of a trolley ride and the special bond between a grandfather and granddaughter. McMillan dedicated this book to his grandfather, who was actually a trolley car driver in Boston from 1883 to 1927. The trolley car featured in the book was fully restored in 1975. It is now a working trolley at the Seashore Trolley Museum in Kennebunkport, Maine. In addition, McMillan used a unique method for coloring the photographs in *Grandfather's Trolley*. He shot the photos in black and white, and then toned the prints brown, and finally hand-tinted them with oil colors. This photography method was the one actually used in the early 1900s, before color film was available.

LEARNING ACTIVITIES

1. Learn more about trolleys. Find pictures of them in nonfiction books. If possible, visit the Seashore Trolley Museum in Kennebunkport, Maine, and ride the trolley in the story. Talk with history buffs from your town. Where was the nearest trolley? What route did it follow? What years did it run? Draw a picture or write a paragraph describing what you learned about trolleys.

2. Bruce McMillan used an old-fashioned method for coloring the photographs in *Grandfather's Trolley.* Look at some old-fashioned photos. What makes these older photos look different from the photos taken today? Do you like older or newer photographs better? Why?

3. The little girl in this story has a special relationship with her grandfather. Write and draw a story that shows you doing a special activity with one of your grandparents. Maybe you can show the two of you cooking together, or a time you visited your grandparent at work, or a time you slept over at your grandparent's house. After creating your story, share it with your grandparent.

ABOUT THE AUTHOR/PHOTO-ILLUSTRATOR

See information about Bruce McMillan on page 5.

ONE SUN: A BOOK OF TERSE VERSE

AUTHOR / PHOTO-ILLUSTRATOR: Bruce McMillan
AGE LEVEL / LENGTH: 2-7 years / 32 pages
PUBLISHER / COPYRIGHT DATE: Holiday House / 1990
FORMAT / ISBN: Paperback / 0823409511

One Sun: A Book of Terse Verse was photographed on the beaches of York County in Maine. Bright, vivid pictures of the seashore accompany "terse verse." Terse verse consists of a two-word rhyme. The two words must each be one syllable in length. For example, one terse verse in McMillan's book is "sand hand," which is illustrated with a photo of a child's hand covered with sand. Another terse verse, "wet pet," is paired with a photo of a white dog coming out of the ocean. The back cover of the book even features its own terse verse with McMillan's signature happy ending; it shows a child wrapped in a blue towel looking off at the blue ocean and blue sky with the words "blue view." McMillan has also written and photo-illustrated a companion book of terse verse called *Play Day.*

LEARNING ACTIVITIES

1. Create your own book of terse verse with drawings or photographs. Select a theme for a book. Bruce McMillan used the seashore. You might try a winter, food, toy, or animal theme for your book.

2. Have a terse verse scavenger hunt. Make a list of terse verse items to search for. For example, your list might have "phone tone" (for a phone with its dial tone) or "bare chair" (for an empty chair) or other two-word combinations. Write the terse verses on separate pieces of paper and challenge others to locate all your terse verse objects by placing the papers on the objects.

3. Visit a York County beach (or another beach). Before going, make a list (a written list or a picture list) of things you expect to find at the beach. While at the beach look for all the items on your list. Cross off each one as you find it. Were you able to find everything on your list?

ABOUT THE AUTHOR/PHOTO-ILLUSTRATOR

See information about Bruce McMillan on page 5.

THE REMARKABLE RIDERLESS RUNAWAY TRICYCLE

AUTHOR / PHOTO-ILLUSTRATOR: Bruce McMillan
AGE LEVEL / LENGTH: 4-8 years / 48 pages
PUBLISHER / COPYRIGHT DATE: Apple Island Books (originally published by Houghton Mifflin) / 1978, 1985
FORMAT / ISBN: Paperback / 0934313008

The Remarkable Riderless Runaway Tricycle tells the story of Jason's tricycle. His parents throw it out because they think it is "too rickety and worn out." But the tricycle somehow escapes from the Kennebunkport dump and takes off—past Mr. Moulton's cow, over the trolley tracks, onto the pier, into a lobsterboat, and on and on. As if "it had no other choice," it finally returns to Jason.

The Remarkable Riderless Runaway Tricycle is set in Kennebunkport, Maine. The book shows President Bush's summer home on page 25. Yet the book's true appeal lies in its portrayal of everyday people and commonplace locations in Kennebunkport. Bruce McMillan often brings along the tricycle from this book when he gives talks, and he claims *The Remarkable Riderless Runaway Tricycle* is his autobiography. But McMillan says that he is not the little boy in the story, but rather the *tricycle*—that is, a "creature" with a vision and great perseverance.

LEARNING ACTIVITIES

1. A number of vocabulary words are shown in context through photographs in *The Remarkable Riderless Runaway Tricycle*. Select several vocabulary words and discuss them. For example, what is a winch? How do you know? What is a boardwalk? Why is it called that?

2. On a Maine map, find Kennebunkport. Former President George Bush has a vacation home there. Write to the Kennebunkport Chamber of Commerce to get more information about the town.

3. Visit a local dump/sanitary landfill. What happens there? How can garbage be reduced and recycled? If possible, interview a worker at the landfill, take a few photos, and write a book about your landfill.

4. Make up your own story following the pattern of *The Remarkable Riderless Runaway Tricycle*. Pretend, for example, that a toy car has been thrown in the trash can. Brainstorm ideas for how it escapes, the places it goes, and where it ends up. Turn these ideas into a book.

ABOUT THE AUTHOR / PHOTO-ILLUSTRATOR

See information about Bruce McMillan on page 5.

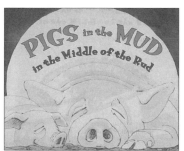

PIGS IN THE MUD
IN THE MIDDLE OF THE RUD

AUTHOR: Lynn Plourde / ILLUSTRATOR: John Schoenherr
AGE LEVEL / LENGTH: 3-7 years / 32 pages
PUBLISHER / COPYRIGHT DATE: The Blue Sky Press/ Scholastic / 1997
FORMAT / ISBN: Hardcover / 0590568639

Pigs in the Mud in the Middle of the Rud finds Grandma and family heading out for a drive. But their Model-T Ford can't drive in the rud (Maine word for road) because some pigs are in the way. So someone's got to shoo the pigs. But who? Brother tries, but the pigs won't budge. Next, there are hens in the rud. Sister tries to shoo them, but the hens won't scatter. And on and on. Mama can't get the sheep to shuffle; Papa can't get the bulls to charge. Finally, the whole family and all the animals are blocking the rud. The only one left to do the shooing is Grandma. Can she do it? The feisty grandmother in this story gives it her all to clear the rud. Young readers will have fun watching Grandma take charge.

Pigs in the Mud in the Middle of the Rud works best as a read-aloud. The story includes a predictable pattern and a repetitive chant which invites children to join in "reading":

> Oh no. Won't do.
> Gotta shoo. But who?

John Schoenherr's watercolors are full of fun details (e.g., smiling pigs, Papa's jacket hanging from a bull's horn, Grandma's mega-bonnet) which complement the playful, rhyming text.

LEARNING ACTIVITIES

1. Add another animal in the "rud" to this book: ducks or goats or horses or whatever. Write words to go with your new animal following the pattern of the book. Try to come up with rhyming words for the situation when your animal gets shooed from the "rud." Draw illustrations to go along with your words.

2. Perform *Pigs in the Mud in the Middle of the Rud* as a play. Assign parts, create simple costumes and props, and practice it. One person should be the narrator. When performing the play, invite the audience to join in during the chant. They can say the words and perform the following gestures:

WORDS	GESTURES
"Oh no."	(put hands up to cheeks with wide-eyed, shocked look)
"Won't do."	(shake head no)
"Gotta shoo."	(brush hands away from body, as if shooing something away)
"But who?"	(raise hands to side and shrug shoulders, as if questioning)

3. "Rud" is a Maine word for road. Make a list of other Maine words or expressions and their meanings. You might interview some Mainers to learn about any regional words they use.

ABOUT THE AUTHOR

Pigs in the Mud in the Middle of the Rud is Lynn Plourde's first picture book. She was inspired to write the story when she looked out of her window one day and saw a bunch of pigs running down the middle of the road. She is also the author of three up-coming picture books: *Thank you and Goodbye, Wild Child,* and *Grandpappy Snippy Snappies.*

Plourde grew up in Skowhegan, Maine, and attended the University of Maine in Orono, receiving bachelor's and master's degrees in speech-language pathology. She has worked as a speech-language therapist for fifteen years in Maine public schools, and has written

ten instructional books since 1985 including the best-selling *Classroom Listening and Speaking* series (published by Communication Skill Builders of San Antonio, Texas). Co-author of *A Celebration of Maine Children's Books*, Plourde currently lives on a dirt "rud" in Winthrop, Maine, with her husband and three children.

ABOUT THE ILLUSTRATOR

John Schoenherr has illustrated more than forty children's books, including *Owl Moon* by Jane Yolen, for which he received the Caldecott Medal in 1988. He is the author and illustrator of two picture books: *Bear* and *Rebel*. He has also illustrated such classic stories as *Julie of the Wolves, Rascal,* and *Gentle Ben*. Schoenherr is also a wildlife and landscape artist. He frequently travels to Alaska and Montana to find scenes for his paintings. Schoenherr currently lives in an 1865 New Jersey farmhouse with his wife. *Pigs in the Mud in the Middle of the Rud* is Schoenherr's first humorous picture book. He did the research for his watercolor illustrations by taking photographs of his neighbor's sheep, chicken, bulls, and Model-T Ford, but he made the pigs up. He also checked with his official "humor consultants"—his granddaughters—for their final approval of the book.

A PENNY FOR A HUNDRED

AUTHOR: Ethel Pochocki / ILLUSTRATOR: Mary Beth Owens
AGE LEVEL / LENGTH: 6-12 years / 32 pages
PUBLISHER / COPYRIGHT DATE: Down East Books / 1996
FORMAT / ISBN: Hardcover / 0892723920

Nine-year-old Clare can hardly contain her excitement. For the first time, she is old enough to help harvest the potatoes on her family's farm in Aroostook County. But the harvest will be different this year. It's 1944, and German prisoners of war (POWs) have been brought in to help with the crop. Clare is curious about the "enemy," but as she befriends an English-speaking POW named Peter, she realizes that he is not very different from her older brother Patrick who has gone overseas to fight for this country.

When winter comes, the POWs stay in the area to help with logging. As Christmas approaches, Peter and the other POWs are lonely for their families and their own Christmas traditions. Clare comes up with a plan to create a special Christmas surprise for Peter. He, in turn, surprises Clare with a special homemade present. Clare's and Peter's Christmas celebration in 1944 is unlike any they have ever had before, yet one they will each cherish for the rest of their lives.

Author Ethel Pochocki and illustrator Mary Beth Owens have combined their talents to create a book with an important message. Their book also helps to fill a void in Maine children's literature with this story set in Aroostook County during a potato harvest.

Readers will also find a special bonus at the end of the book: a copy of the recipes for the Christmas surprise that Clare made for Peter.

LEARNING ACTIVITIES

1. Learn more about potato harvesting in Maine. Read nonfiction books and visit a potato farm, if possible, during its harvest, or interview a potato farmer. When are potatoes planted? Harvested? How do farmers today get rid of potato bugs? Do schools in Aroostook County still close during the fall for the harvest? What kind of potatoes are grown in Maine? How large is Maine's potato crop? What weather conditions help and hurt the crop? Write a report about the information you learn.

2. Prepare a Christmas dish with adult supervision. Either make Clare's stollen or a traditional Christmas food from your family's heritage. Follow the directions carefully. When you are finished, share your creation with friends or family, and tell the story or tradition behind the recipe.

3. Interview someone who remained in Maine during World War II (WWII). Find out what life was like for that person during the war. Were any POWs brought to their area to work? Did people raise victory gardens? Which goods were in short supply? How did people in Maine help with the war effort? Write an essay describing what you learned.

ABOUT THE AUTHOR

Ethel Pochocki was born and raised in Bayonne, New Jersey. When she was sixteen, she read *The Little Locksmith* by Katherine Butler Hathaway. "From that moment," Pochocki explains, "I yearned to live in Maine; even more, I knew it would happen." More than thirty years later, Pochocki finally made it to Maine and lived in Brooksville, across the bay from Castine—where Hathaway wrote *The Little Locksmith*.

Pochocki first began writing as a young mother, with five children under the age of ten. "I needed something to keep my sanity and my mind out of the diapers," she explains, "Writing was a wonderful cottage industry while raising my family, which had grown to eight children." She has since had close to thirty books published, as well as numerous stories in children's magazines. Her books include *The Attic Mice*, *The Mushroom Man*, *Wildflower Tea*, and *The Gypsies' Tale*.

Pochocki explains the story behind her creation of *A Penny for a Hundred*. Years ago she had read an article by a Maine columnist who described the unpleasant task of picking off potato bugs, for which her father paid her "a penny for a hundred." Pochocki mentally tucked that idea away, and a few years later she read a story in *Echoes (A Journal of Northern Maine)* about WWII German prisoners of war who helped with the potato harvest. Pochocki then visited the Caribou/New Sweden area and interviewed older residents about their memories of WWII in the County. She also worked in the potato fields herself "under that glorious expanse of Aroostook sky." Pochocki explains that it took her four years to finish the story from the initial idea to the final draft.

Pochocki now lives in Brooks, Maine, with seven cats. She describes her current life as follows: "In winter, I write and read and enjoy the solitary delight of burrowing and holing up. In summer, I write and garden and turn extrovert to be hostess for summer visitors. It is the best of all lives, a lovely balance."

ABOUT THE ILLUSTRATOR

See information about Mary Beth Owens on page 8.

THE TOWN THAT GOT OUT OF TOWN

AUTHOR / ILLUSTRATOR: Robert Priest
AGE LEVEL / LENGTH: 6-10 years / 48 pages
PUBLISHER / COPYRIGHT DATE: David R. Godine, Publisher / 1989
FORMAT / ISBN: Hardcover / 0879237864

In *The Town That Got Out of Town*, the city of Boston decides to go on its own Labor Day vacation. After all the people have left town, the buildings pull themselves out of the ground and head for Portland, Maine. Boston's buildings and Portland's buildings share town stories and memories. Boston's buildings then return home, just in time for the returning people.

The Town That Got Out of Town is an unusual book. It features large-format black-and-white scraperboard illustrations. The people and the animals in the book appear surreal. Author Robert Priest pokes fun at human vacations by replicating their experiences with the buildings' vacation; the buildings have traffic jams on bridges and exchange souvenirs. Another interesting aspect of the book is its architectural accuracy. If they look carefully, young readers will find Portland's Museum of Art, the Longfellow House, and Custom House.

LEARNING ACTIVITIES

1. Create your own version of *The Town That Got Out of Town*. Draw pictures of recognizable buildings from your town heading off for a vacation. Where will they visit? How will they get there? What will they do on their vacation?

2. Research the cities of Portland and Boston: their history, population, landmarks, etc. How are the cities similar? How are they different? Which would you rather live in and why?

3. Challenge some of your friends or classmates to learn the names for landmarks in different Maine towns and cities. Then play a memory game about the landmarks. For example, the first player might say, "Portland went to Augusta to visit Fort Western." The next player repeats that sentence and adds a new one "Portland went to Augusta to visit Fort Western, and Augusta went to Skowhegan to visit the world's largest wooden Indian sculpture." Continue with more landmarks as long as players can remember the towns and landmarks correctly.

ABOUT THE AUTHOR/ILLUSTRATOR

Robert Priest has been an artist for the past fifteen years. He claims that he simply added words to his drawings to become a writer. Priest lives in Boston, but has a summer home in Limington, Maine. He frequently visits the city of Portland because of its accessibility and architecture. Using Boston and Portland as the subjects for *The Town That Got Out of Town* was, in his words, "a natural choice."

SNOW

AUTHOR: Steve Sanfield / ILLUSTRATOR: Jeanette Winter
AGE LEVEL / LENGTH: 4-8 years / 32 pages
PUBLISHER / COPYRIGHT DATE: Philomel Books (The Putnam & Grosset Group) / 1995
FORMAT / ISBN: Hardcover / 0399227512 (recently out of print)

Snow celebrates the wonder of a snowfall. A child awakens to see the world covered with snow. The child bundles up and heads out to savor the snow experience from snow-covered tree limbs to drifted snow sculptures to "busy" animal tracks. Everything looks new and different in this snowy world.

Steve Sanfield's text is deceptively simple, yet poetic. This book is an unusual "snow" book in that it has little of the color white. Illustrator Jeanette Winter provides readers with a colorful snow experience including aqua, raspberry, and lavender acrylics. Each illustration is framed by a wide, patterned border giving readers the feeling that they are peeking into a magical world.

LEARNING ACTIVITIES

1. Look at the animal tracks in *Snow*, and try to identify each track. Use a nature guide to help you. What makes each track distinct so that you can identify it? Try drawing your own animal tracks.

2. *Snow* tells about many different experiences in the snow. Select another topic such as "trees" or "water" or "rocks" and write a short story or poem about that topic. Try to include as many different ideas and images as you can for your selected topic.

3. Study the borders of Jeanette Winter's illustrations. Do the borders repeat an image found in the illustrations? Do they use colors found in the illustrations? Which border do you like the best? Why is it your favorite? Try creating your own bordered illustration about a subject that interests you.

ABOUT THE AUTHOR

Steve Sanfield grew up in Massachusetts. As a young boy, he traveled to Maine with his father, who sold supplies to mills. Many years later, his first book of poems, *Water Before & Water After*, was published by Blackberry Books of Brunswick. Sanfield has been writing since he was eight years old. He claims to spend very little time at the typewriter, yet he finds himself "writing in his head" all the time. Some of his children's books are *The Great Turtle Drive*, *Bit by Bit*, and *The Girl Who Wanted a Song*. He has also traveled the country as a professional storyteller. Sanfield currently lives in the mountains of California, where his nearest neighbor is a half mile away.

ABOUT THE ILLUSTRATOR

Jeanette Winter grew up in Chicago. She says, "I can't remember a time when I didn't love to draw." As a child, she treasured her deluxe 64-color box of crayons; and if paper was not available, then she drew on the cardboard that came with laundered shirts. In high school, Winter began taking art lessons at the Art Institute of Chicago. Winter went to college in Iowa, and later moved to Texas to raise her family. Several years ago, Winter moved to Frankfort, Maine, with her husband; and she claims that "rural Maine has now begun making its way into my books" (notice the Frankfort bridge in *Snow*).

Winter's other children's books include *Follow the Drinking Gourd*, *Diego*, *Cowboy Charlie*, *The Christmas Tree Ship*, and *Josefina*. She is also the illustrator of *The Day of the Dead* (about a Mexican Holiday) by Tony Johnston, and *The Tortilla Cat* (about a magical cat) by Nancy Willard. She uses acrylic paints for her illustrations. When she creates a book, Winter enjoys doing the research. She surrounds herself with books on her chosen topic. She uses photographs for references—many of which she has taken herself. While working, Winter enjoys playing music and watching the crows in the field outside her studio window. Winter currently divides her time between Texas, New York City, and Frankfort, Maine.

JOURNEY CAKE, HO!

AUTHOR: Ruth Sawyer / ILLUSTRATOR: Robert McCloskey
AGE LEVEL / LENGTH: 4-8 years / 48 pages
PUBLISHER / COPYRIGHT DATE: Puffin Books / 1953
FORMAT / ISBN: Paperback / 0140502750
AWARDS: Caldecott Honor Book, 1954

Johnny is a "bound-out" boy. He lives with an old woman, Merry, and an old man, Grumble. They do their chores and live happily until trouble after trouble strikes them. With only enough food left for two, Johnny must leave. He is sent on his way with a Journey Cake. But as he walks down the logging road, the Journey Cake rolls off his pack and comes to life, challenging everyone to catch him and eat him. Johnny chases the Journey Cake, as do a cow, a duck, two sheep, and more, as the Journey Cake leads them on a journey "home."

This playful tale tells how the Johnny Cake was named. Sawyer's simple, repetitive text helps to build the pace of the story as the Journey Cake gains speed: "Away and away rolled the Journey Cake . . . faster and faster, faster and faster!" Robert McCloskey's illustrations are hilarious, from the character's mismatched clothes to the zany animal parade behind the Journey Cake.

LEARNING ACTIVITIES

1. *Journey Cake, Ho!* tells the story of how the Johnny Cake came to be named. Select another food—such as Apple Brown Betty, Blueberry Buckle, Whoopie Pies, Dynamites, or another regional food—and make up a story about how it got its name.

2. Try a rolling experiment. Set up two ramps, one for an object to roll down, one for an object to roll up, with a space between the two ramps. Gather objects that can roll, such as balls (golf, baseball, etc.), a Frisbee, a tin can, a spool. Roll each object down one ramp and up the other. Before doing so, guess which object will roll the farthest and the fastest. Then roll the objects to see if your predictions are correct.

3. Put on *Journey Cake, Ho!* as a skit. Make and plan the costumes. As the story is read,

each character should say and do their part. Put on the skit for others. You might even serve Johnny Cakes for refreshments.

ABOUT THE AUTHOR

Born in 1880 in Boston, Ruth Sawyer was raised in New York. She spent most summers in Maine. Sawyer studied folklore and storytelling at Columbia University. She started a storytelling program for children at the New York Public Library. Her daughter, Margaret, married Robert McCloskey.

Sawyer was a prolific writer of children's books, including such titles as *The Long Christmas*, *The Enchanted Schoolhouse*, and *The Year of the Christmas Dragon*. She had a passion for writing folktales and Christmas stories. She also wrote a handbook for storytellers called *The Way of the Storyteller*. Sawyer won the Newbery Medal in 1937 for her book, *Roller Skates*, which she described as autobiographical. She was pleased when her son-in-law wanted to illustrate *Journey Cake, Ho!*. The book went on to be selected as a Caldecott Honor Book in 1954. Sawyer was the recipient of the 1965 Laura Ingalls Wilder Medal for her enduring contribution to children's literature. Sawyer died in 1970 in Hancock, Maine.

ABOUT THE ILLUSTRATOR

See information about Robert McCloskey on page 66.

FOGBOUND

AUTHOR / ILLUSTRATOR: Steven Shepard
AGE LEVEL / LENGTH: 8-12 years / 29 pages
PUBLISHER / COPYRIGHT DATE: Landmark Editions / 1993
FORMAT / ISBN: Library Binding / 0933849435
AWARDS: Landmark Editions' 1992 Written & Illustrated by . . .
Awards Contest for Students

Fogbound is a realistic Maine adventure story, with finely detailed illustrations. It's a quality book, but what makes it truly remarkable is that it was written and illustrated by a thirteen-year-old. With *Fogbound*, Steven Shepard won first place in the 10-13 age category for Landmark Editions' 1992 Written & Illustrated by . . . Awards Contest for Students.

This story is told from the perspective of twelve-year-old Jason. Jason "borrows" his father's new knife, without permission, to show it off to his friends. He forgets the knife on an island, so he feels that he must retrieve it with his skiff before his father returns from a business trip and discovers it is missing. But Jason runs into many obstacles: first, he must bring along his six-year-old sister whom he is babysitting for the day, then he must escape from a gruff lobsterman who chases after him, and finally he must find his way home amidst thick fog and strong currents. Jason succeeds in the end, returning home with a lesson that's more valuable than the prized knife.

LEARNING ACTIVITIES

1. *Fogbound*, by Steven Shepard, won a student writing contest, and his prize was having his book published. Challenge yourself and your friends or classmates to each write and illustrate a picture book. Then "publish" your books and display them and read them aloud at a "Student Book Night."

2. Enter a student writing contest or try to get something you wrote published in a magazine. For lists of contests and magazines which publish children's work, check the library for the latest edition of *Market Guide for Young Writers: Where and How to Sell What You Write,* by Kathy Henderson (published by Writer's Digest Books), and the latest edition of *Children's Writer's & Illustrator's Market,* from Writer's Digest Books, which includes a chapter called "Young Writer's and Illustrator's Markets."

3. When creating *Fogbound,* Steven Shepard had to make many revisions in both his written story and his illustrations. Select a piece of writing or an illustration that you have completed within the past year; then work to revise and improve your writing or illustration. Make several revisions, getting feedback from others, until your work is the best you can possibly make it. Afterward, write about your revision process. How did you know what to change? Which revisions were the easiest to make? Which were the most difficult? Why? What did you learn during the revision process that can help you the next time you write or draw?

ABOUT THE AUTHOR/ILLUSTRATOR

Steven Shepard wrote and illustrated *Fogbound* when he was thirteen years of age. That book won the 1992 national Landmark Editions' Written & Illustrated by . . . Awards Contest for Students in the 10-13 age category.

Shepard lives in Great Falls, Virginia, with his parents and younger brother; but he based his prize-winning story on his summer experiences in Maine. Ever since Shepard was three-years-old, he has spent summers in a cottage near Boothbay Harbor, Maine. The house in *Fogbound* is based on his grandparents' white farmhouse, and the skiff "Hushpuppy" from the story is just like Shepard's own family skiff.

Shepard has had other writing successes. He was the editor of his intermediate school's literary magazine and yearbook. He also has had poetry and short stories published in *Stone Soup* and *Creative Kids* magazines.

MUWIN AND THE MAGIC HARE

AUTHOR: traditional Passamaquoddy tale, retold by Susan Hand Shetterly /
ILLUSTRATOR: Robert Shetterly
AGE LEVEL / LENGTH: 6-10 years / 32 pages
PUBLISHER / COPYRIGHT DATE: Atheneum / 1993
FORMAT / ISBN: Hardcover / 0689316992

Muwin and the Magic Hare is a retelling of a Passamaquoddy "trickster" tale. Muwin, the bear, tries to catch Mahtoqehs, the Great Magic Hare of the Woods, for one last feast before returning to his den for the winter. But the hare keeps eluding Muwin by turning into Passamaquoddy people who wear strange, hare-like feathers and shoes. Each of the Passamaquoddies welcomes the bear, shares a meal of hare, and finally tells the bear a story. After the good company, the fine food, and the interesting stories, Muwin falls asleep, only to awaken each morning with no sign of the Passamaquoddies. It's as if each experience were only a dream. Finally, Muwin is too tired to chase after the hare any longer. He only wants to return to his den for a long winter of sleep. And that's exactly what he does after being led there by a Passamaquoddy boy—or was it a hare?

The Shetterlys have created a wonderful tale. They have helped to fill a void since few Native American legends that include Maine tribes have been published in a format which is appropriate for children. A subtle wit fills the book. Young readers will especially enjoy Robert Shetterly's cock-eyed hare's ears and feathers which pop up throughout the story.

LEARNING ACTIVITIES

1. Turn *Muwin and the Magic Hare* into a skit. Prepare simple costumes and props, divide up roles, and practice the story as a play. Have one person be the narrator. Decide how you will show the hare transforming into Passamaquoddy people. Will the transformation happen behind a barrier? Or with a simple passing of the rabbit's ears? How else could the transformation take place? After rehearsing, perform your play for others.

2. Ask a librarian to help you find another trickster tale. Read the new tale and make a list comparing all the ways the two trickster tales (the new tale and *Muwin and the Magic Hare*) are similar and different.

3. Learn more about the Passamaquoddy Indians of Maine. Read nonfiction books and write to or interview a Passamaquoddy from the Pleasant Point State Indian Reservation in Perry, Maine, or from another location. What traditions did the Passamaquoddies practice in the past and which ones do they continue today? What are some special words or vocabulary used by Passamaquoddies? What role do animals have in the Passamaquoddy culture? Can you find other Passamaquoddy tales that have been written down?

ABOUT THE AUTHOR

Susan Hand Shetterly moved to Maine in 1970, after growing up in New York and Connecticut. Shetterly's father was a writer and read poetry to her when she was a child. She wrote poetry, and an occasional piece was published in journals for young writers. Shetterly traces her interest in writing to time spent alone when her father moved her family to Mallorca, an island off the coast of Spain. "I suppose a person who is a writer has to learn how to be on the outside—even for a short time—and to look in, to observe," Shetterly says. "My time in Spain gave me that."

Shetterly, who lives in Surry, Maine, is the author of several other children's books, including *The Tinker of Salt Cove, The Dwarf-Wizard of Uxmal,* and *Raven's Light.* She also is a nature essayist, with articles appearing in *The Maine Times.* Shetterly's hobbies include gardening and rehabilitating wild birds.

ABOUT THE ILLUSTRATOR

Robert Shetterly grew up in Cincinnati, Ohio. He studied literature and art at Harvard. He currently works as a printmaker and painter, as well as an illustrator. He is the illustrator of *The Dwarf-Wizard of Uxmal* and *Raven's Light,* both with Susan Hand Shetterly. His illustrations have also appeared in the National Audubon Society's children's newspaper, *Audubon Adventures.* Shetterly lives in Brooksville, Maine.

LOST MOOSE

> AUTHOR: Jan Slepian / ILLUSTRATOR: Ted Lewin
> AGE LEVEL / LENGTH: 4-8 years / 36 pages
> PUBLISHER / COPYRIGHT DATE: Philomel Books (Putnam & Grosset Group) / 1995
> FORMAT / ISBN: Hardcover / 0399227490

In *Lost Moose,* a moose and her calf become separated while crossing a lake during a storm. The calf wanders onto an island. A little boy named James discovers the moose calf, only he thinks it must be one of Santa's reindeer. James quietly follows the young moose hoping to see Santa when he comes to retrieve his "reindeer." But when the calf wanders out of the woods near a dining hall, James waves his arms and shouts for him to go back into the woods. Suddenly, there is a noise. James wonders if it is Santa coming. It's not—it's the mother moose! Just then James's mother arrives too. Both mothers stand protectively in front of their children and stare at each other. Finally, they each back down and head off in separate directions.

Lost Moose is a beautiful book. Author Jan Slepian tells a simple, almost poetic tale. Her word choices ring true: "the moose and the boy slipped through the woods together as if joined by a cord" and "disappointment made his nose stuffy." Ted Lewin's vibrant water-colors perfectly complement the text. In particular, the confrontation between the bristling mother moose and James's flaming red-headed mother says more than words could ever say about maternal instinct.

LEARNING ACTIVITIES

1. Compare this book with *Blueberries for Sal,* by Robert McCloskey. They both tell the stories of a lost animal and a lost child. Make a chart listing all the ways these two books are alike and the ways they are different.

2. A baby moose is called a calf. Make a list of as many other Maine animals as you can. Then use reference books to learn what each animal's baby is called. Are any of the baby terms the same? Which ones?

3. Using Ted Lewin's illustrations in *Lost Moose* as a guide, try drawing your own pictures of a moose. Study a moose's head, body, legs, etc. Try to reproduce each part to create a realistic-looking moose.

ABOUT THE AUTHOR

Jan Slepian grew up in New York City. She attended Brooklyn College and the University of Washington in Seattle, where she received degrees in psychology and speech pathology. She began her writing career with speech therapy articles and materials, including *The Listen-Hear Books.* After taking a children's literature course, Slepian decided to try her hand at writing fiction for young people. She wrote a chapter book called *The Alfred Summer* which was based on her experiences of growing up with a handicapped brother.

Slepian is the author of numerous chapter books including *Pinocchio's Sister, Back to Before, Risk N' Roses,* and *Lester's Turn.* Her picture book *Lost Moose* is based upon a "real" lost moose which Slepian saw on Sandy Island in Lake Winnipesaukee in New Hampshire.

ABOUT THE ILLUSTRATOR

Although the author of *Lost Moose,* Jan Slepian, admits that the story was based on an incident in New Hampshire, the book's illustrator, Ted Lewin, says that he actually photographed all the landscape images for the book in Maine. His Maine photos then served as the models for the book's watercolor illustrations.

Lewin grew up in Buffalo, New York, with unusual pets such as a lion, iguana, and chimpanzee. Lewin studied at the Pratt Institute of Art. He raised money for college by working as a wrestler, which he chronicles in his autobiographical book, *I Was a Teenage Professional Wrestler*. A freelance illustrator since 1956, he is the illustrator of more than seventy books. Many of his books reflect his deep concern for the environment; and he has traveled to wilderness areas around the world in order to gather material for his books. His illustrations are included in the books *Matthew Wheelock's Wall, I Wonder if I'll See a Whale, Market!, Paperboy*, and the Caldecott Honor Book *Peppe the LampLighter*.

Lewin currently lives in New York City, with his wife, Betsy, who is also a children's book author/illustrator. Lewin's hobbies include scuba diving, bird watching, and observing wildlife.

PUMPKIN PUMPKIN

AUTHOR / ILLUSTRATOR: Jeanne Titherington
AGE LEVEL / LENGTH: 2-6 years / 24 pages
PUBLISHER / COPYRIGHT DATE: Greenwillow (hardcover); Mulberry (paperback) / 1986
FORMAT / ISBN: Hardcover / 0688056954; Paperback / 0688099300; Library Binding / 0688056962

Jeanne Titherington shows and tells the simple story of how a pumpkin seed is planted and grows to become a pumpkin and then is carved into a Jack-o'-lantern (from which the seeds are saved for planting the next year). Titherington's soft, detailed, colored-pencil illustrations and simple text invite the youngest reader to learn a science lesson about pumpkins. The main character of the book is a curious, fun-loving little boy who will make young readers giggle.

LEARNING ACTIVITIES

1. Explore a pumpkin—inside, outside, even the stem. Carve it with an adult's help. Feel the slimy, slippery insides. Make a chart to show what you discover about the pumpkin. Include information on your chart about how the pumpkin looks, how it feels, how it tastes, etc.

2. Do some pumpkin cooking (e.g., pumpkin seeds, pumpkin pie, pumpkin muffins) with adult supervision. Follow the directions carefully. While your pumpkin food is cooking, retell each step in the recipe. Try to remember all the steps in the correct order.

3. Play a variation of the game "Button, Button, Who Has the Button?" using a pumpkin seed. Take turns placing a pumpkin seed secretly into someone else's hands. Others playing must guess who has the pumpkin seed. Continue with more turns, hiding the pumpkin seed, and guessing who has it.

ABOUT THE AUTHOR/ILLUSTRATOR

Jeanne Titherington grew up in Falmouth, Maine. She attended both the Portland School of Art and the University of Maine. She has spent much of her adult life in Maine, living in Portland then Rockland. Currently, Titherington lives in Houston, Texas, with her husband and two young children. She continues to summer in Bremen, Maine. Her hobbies include working out, reading, and needlepoint.

Titherington claims to have entered the world of children's books "through the back door." In art school, she experimented with box constructions and collages. But after graduation, she didn't have enough space for her "junk constructions," so she devoted herself to drawing. A friend suggested that Titherington try her hand at book illustration. And so she made an "unorganized" trip to publishing companies in New York and Boston, and received her first book contract. Since illustrating Jack Prelutsky's *It's Snowing, It's Snowing*, Titherington has gone on to both write and illustrate her own books, including *Baby's Boat, A Child's Prayer, Sophy and Auntie Pearl*, and *Bonkers Fellini*. Her illustrations are done with colored pencils.

Pumpkin Pumpkin was inspired by many years of growing pumpkins herself. "I grew them for no practical reason whatsoever, just because I love big pumpkins. I also love the changing of the seasons, and I thought I could present a sense of that wonderful change by showing a pumpkin from seed to Jack-o'-Lantern, to seed again."

Titherington created her book *Where Are You Going, Emma?* (see the following page) to celebrate the fall season and to capture a common childhood experience. Titherington explains, "Fall is my favorite time of the year, the smells of fallen leaves and ripe apples sending chills up my spine. It's a beautiful time, but also a melancholy one, and I suppose I wanted a touch of sadness in *Emma*. The story itself is made up, but I was trying to express memories that are very true and real, memories of times when I was a child and got lost. It was always only a short step from feeling safe and secure to suddenly feeling lost or abandoned or afraid. I wanted to catch that 'short step,' primarily in a visual way."

WHERE ARE YOU GOING, EMMA?

AUTHOR / ILLUSTRATOR: Jeanne Titherington
AGE LEVEL / LENGTH: 3-6 years / 24 pages
PUBLISHER / COPYRIGHT DATE: Greenwillow (hardcover) / 1988
FORMAT / ISBN: Hardcover / 0688070817; Library Binding / 0688070825

Emma and her Grandpa go to the orchard. Grandpa stops to pick apples, but Emma wanders—over the orchard wall, across the brook, past the bushes, and through the meadow. Then Emma stops and, in a breathtaking double-page spread, Titherington shows the reader that the little girl has wandered too far. But all's well, and Emma is happily reunited with her Grandpa and the apples.

LEARNING ACTIVITIES

1. Visit an apple orchard. If possible, help to pick apples. Watch how cider is made. Ask an adult to take photographs of your apple orchard visit. When the photos are developed, use them to create a picture book about your own orchard visit.

2. Have a discussion about getting lost. Have you ever gotten lost? Have your friends? Where were you? How did you get "found?" What can you learn from your own experiences and Emma's experiences?

3. How will Emma's grandmother use the apples when they are brought home? What would you use the apples for? Help an adult to make a recipe that uses apples. Afterward, while your apple creation is cooking, draw a picture showing all the steps in your recipe. When your apple dish is ready, eat and enjoy!

ABOUT THE AUTHOR/ILLUSTRATOR

See information about Jeanne Titherington on page 89.

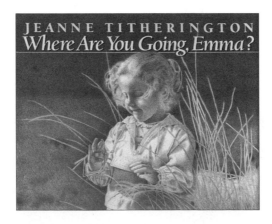

MORE MAINE PICTURE BOOKS

Below is a list of quality Maine picture books thay have recently gone out of print. You are likely to find many of them at your local library. They are listed alphabetically by author.

NEAR THE SEA
written & illustrated by Jim Arnosky, 8 years–adult, 1990, Lothrop, Lee & Shepard, 32 pages. This book presents eleven paintings of a Maine island–including a tidal pool, a boatyard, and a salt marsh–and the story behind the creation of each illustration.

NEW KID ON SPURWINK AVE.
written by Michael Crowley, illustrated by Abby Carter, 4-8 years, 1992, Little Brown & Co., 32 pages. This book, set in Cape Elizabeth, tells of a new boy who moves to the neighborhood and how he finally fits into the Spurwink Gang.

SHACK AND BACK
written by Michael Crowley, illustrated by Abby Carter, 4-8 years, 1993, Little Brown & Co., 32 pages. In this follow-up to *New Kid on Spurwink Ave.*, the boys and girls of the Spurwink Gang get into a disagreement and almost lose a bet to the Broad Cove Bullies.

SOMETHING MAGIC
written by Maggie Davis, illustrated by Mary O'Keefe Young, 4-8 years, 1991, Simon & Schuster, 32 pages. A mother reminisces with her daughter about the summers she spent with her grandmother on the Maine coast, raking blueberries, digging clams, and more.

SURROUNDED BY THE SEA: LIFE ON A NEW ENGLAND FISHING ISLAND
written & illustrated by Gail Gibbons, 4-8 years, 1991, Little Brown & Co., 32 pages. Life on a Maine fishing island (Matinicus) is described through the four seasons.

HUBKNUCKLES
written by Emily Herman, illustrated by Deborah Kogan Ray, 4-8 years, 1985, Crown Publishers, 32 pages. This Halloween story presents a ghost named Hubknuckles who revisits a family every year.

MOLLY'S SEASONS
written & illustrated by Ellen Kandoian, 3-8 years, 1992, Cobblehill Books, 32 pages. Young readers will learn what the four seasons are like for a girl named Molly who lives in Maine and how the seasons in Maine differ from those in other parts of the world.

FOURTH OF JULY BEAR
written by Kathryn Lasky, illustrated by Helen Coganberry, 4-8 years, 1991, Morrow Junior Books, 40 pages. A girl named Rebecca reluctantly spends the summer on a Maine island where she finds friendship and a starring role in the island's Fourth of July parade.

MY ISLAND GRANDMA
written by Kathryn Lasky, illustrated by Amy Schwartz, 4-8 years, 1993 (originally published-1979), Morrow Junior Books, 32 pages. This story tells of special summertime activities shared between a granddaughter and her grandmother on a Maine island.

ISLAND RESCUE
written & illustrated by Charles E. Martin, 4-8 years, 1985, Greenwillow Books, 32 pages. A girl breaks a leg and must be rescued and brought to the mainland in this story which is part of the author's series set on Monhegan Island including *Island Winter, Sam Saves the Day, Summer Business,* and *For Rent.*

THE FINEST HORSE IN TOWN
written by Jacqueline Briggs Martin, illustrated by Susan Gaber, 4-8 years, 1992, HarperCollins, 32 pages. This story focuses on the author's two great-aunts who owned a hardware store and "the finest horse in town" in a Maine village during the early 1900s.

THE LIGHTHOUSE KEEPER'S DAUGHTER
written by Arielle North Olson, illustrated by Elaine Wentworth, 6-10 years, 1987, Little Brown & Co., 32 pages. This picture book is based upon Abbie Burgess' ordeal at the Matinicus Rock Lighthouse during a severe storm in the 1850s.

QUIET
written & illustrated by Peter Parnall, 4-8 years, 1989, Morrow Junior Books, 32 pages. In this poetic story a boy rests quietly in a field where he sees a raven, a chickadee, a mouse, and more.

WOODPILE
written & illustrated by Peter Parnall, 4-8 years, 1990, Macmillan Publishing Co., 32 pages. This book is a close-up look at the animals and insects that live in a woodpile.

GOOD MORNING, RIVER!
written by Lisa Westberg Peters, illustrated by Deborah Kogan Ray, 4-8 years, 1990, Arcade Publishing, 32 pages. A little girl Katherine and an old man Carl share the seasonal joys of the St. Croix River on the Maine-Canadian border.

ROSEBUD AND RED FLANNEL
written by Ethel Pochocki, illustrated by Mary Beth Owens, 5-10 years, 1989-text, 1991-illustrations, Henry Holt & Co., 32 pages. In this romantic story, an elegant nightgown and a pair of long johns are hung out to dry on a clothesline one day when a snowstorm blows in, and then Red Flannel, the long johns, must struggle to protect his true love, Rosebud.

THE ISLAND MERRY-GO-ROUND

written by Ruth Sargent, illustrated by Pam DeVito, 4-8 years, 1988, Windswept House, 40 pages. Ruth Sargent has written a story within a story of how a merry-go-round came from Norway to a Maine island and continued to give pleasure even after it had broken down.

SPRUCE THE MOOSE CUTS LOOSE

written & illustrated by Sarah Stapler, 3-7 years, 1992, G.P. Putnam's Sons, 32 pages. This animal fantasy features a moose named Spruce whose ever-growing antlers interfere with his daily life.

MAROONED

written by Ken Thomas, illustrated by Middy Chilman Thomas, 5-9 years, 1990, St. Martin's Press, 32 pages. Two brothers go clamming on Long Island, off the coast of Maine, in the 1920s and become stranded.

CHAPTER BOOKS

FUDGE-A-MANIA

AUTHOR: Judy Blume
AGE LEVEL / LENGTH: 8-12 years / 148 pages
PUBLISHER / COPYRIGHT DATE: Dutton (hardcover); Dell (paperback) / 1990
FORMAT / ISBN: Hardcover / 0525446729; Paperback / 0440404908

Almost-seventh-grader Peter Hatcher is about to have the worst summer of his life. His five-year-old brother, Fudge, is planning to marry his arch enemy, Sheila Tubman. To add insult to injury, his mother and father have decided to vacation in Southwest Harbor, Maine, in the house next door to the Tubmans. Some vacation! He will be stuck in an isolated corner of the world with Fudge and Sheila, "Queen of the Cooties," for three weeks.

But the summer is not as bad as Peter anticipates—it's worse! The Hatchers' house is not next door to the Tubmans; it's in the same building. His little brother Fudge brings along his pet mynah bird which escapes. Peter's father takes them on a near-fatal sail. Peter tries to impress a famous baseball player, but ends up being the Error King of the game. Finally, Peter's grandmother has a surprise which could leave Peter related to Sheila Tubman for the rest of his life.

LEARNING ACTIVITIES

1. Author Judy Blume includes several businesses and community members which are actually in Southwest Harbor, Maine. Write a short story in which you use some of the businesses or community members from your own hometown in your story.

2. Judy Blume captures the humor of a family vacation. Interview family members about the most unusual or funniest vacation they ever experienced. Write up these experiences and make a vacation booklet telling about your family's vacations. Share your finished booklet with your family.

3. In her book *Fudge-a-Mania*, Judy Blume creates a sport's legend, Big Apfel, a former Boston Red Sox player. What famous sports figures actually come from Maine? Select one and research that sports figure. You might interview (by mail, phone, or in person) your selected sports figure—if that person is available and willing to be interviewed. Turn the information you gather into a brief biography about the player.

ABOUT THE AUTHOR

Judy Blume was born and raised in New Jersey. She attended Boston University and New York University, receiving a teaching degree. Blume started writing when her own two children were young and she needed an outlet for her creativity. She took a course on how to write for children (the same course, twice) and slowly defined her own special style of writing—strong on humor, full of true-to-life, youth-oriented material. Blume claims that she writes the kinds of books she would have liked to have read as a child. Her first book, *The One in the Middle is the Green Kangaroo*, was published in 1969. Since then, she has written more than twenty books for kids and adults, including the famous "Fudge" books, which are based on her son's experiences.

Blume did not set out to write *Fudge-a-Mania*. When she spent the summer of 1989 at a rented house on Southwest Harbor, Maine, she was planning to write a different book, but her mind kept returning to the characters of Fudge, Sheila, and Peter. *Fudge-a-Mania* (originally titled "Fudge-a-Maine-ia") was born. She based some of the story on her own experiences in Southwest Harbor, including visits to Bicycle Bob's, Oz Books, and the ice cream parlor. Blume rode a bicycle to town every day and remembers the summer as "cold and foggy." By the time she left Southwest Harbor, she had written three chapters and had a notebook full of vignettes (going blueberrying, sailing, etc.) to include in her book. It took her a year, and three rewrites (her usual number), to finish writing *Fudge-a-Mania*.

Blume currently lives in New York City, with her husband, George, who also writes. He's the one who led Blume to Maine—one of his favorite places to sail.

CHESHIRE MOON

AUTHOR: Nancy Butts
AGE LEVEL / LENGTH: 8-14 years / 112 pages
PUBLISHER / COPYRIGHT DATE: Front Street Books, Inc. / 1996
FORMAT / ISBN: Hardcover / 1886910081

Twelve-year-old Miranda is spending the summer with her aunt on Summerhaven, an island in Penobscot Bay off the coast of Maine. Miranda has spent many summers on the island, but this summer will be different from all the rest. It will be her first summer on Summerhaven without her best friend Timothy; he was lost at sea last year. Miranda is deaf, and Timothy knew sign language well, making communication between the two of them easy. Now Miranda must try to survive in the "hearing" world where no one seems to understand her.

As she tries to deal with her grief over Timothy's death, Miranda is forced into an unfriendly relationship with a boy named Boone. When Miranda learns that Boone is having the same strange dream about a mysterious island that she is also having, she asks him to help her find the island of their dreams. She believes the island will lead her to answers about Timothy and her own identity, but Boone believes the island may lead Miranda to her death.

Author Nancy Butts claims that her fictional island of Summerhaven in *Cheshire Moon* is actually based on Islesboro. In this, her first novel, Butts creates an intriguing story with well-developed characters. She realistically portrays the special conflicts and self-doubts faced by a deaf child; yet at the same time, she gives readers the feeling that Miranda's struggles to learn who she is are like those of any other preteen—hearing or deaf.

LEARNING ACTIVITIES

1. Discussion questions:

> —In *Cheshire Moon*, Miranda came close to throwing her hearing aids into the sea. Do you believe she should have thrown them into the sea? Why or why not?
> —How does the relationship between Miranda and Boone change over time? Why do you think it changes?
> —How could Miranda and Boone have had the same dream? Do you believe that was possible? What did their dream mean?
> —Do you think it was more difficult for Miranda to deal with Timothy's death or for Boone to deal with his father walking out? Support your answer.
> —Project into the future. What will Miranda's life on Summerhaven be like one year later from the time the novel ends?

2. Learn more about being hearing-impaired. Read nonfiction books and "shadow" a hearing-impaired student in your school system (with permission, of course). What's the difference between the terms "hearing-impaired" and "deaf?" In what different ways do hearing-impaired people communicate? What challenges does the student you shadow face on a daily basis? How does that student meet those challenges? Write a story or poem or create a drawing depicting what you have learned.

3. The Cheshire moon is one phase of the moon. Learn more about phases of the moon—when they occur, how they were named. Research any sayings or legends related to them. Write a report or give a speech about what you learn.

ABOUT THE AUTHOR

Nancy Butts lives in Barnesville, Georgia; but she has vacationed in Maine several times including a stay on Islesboro, the location on which she based her fictional island of Summerhaven in *Cheshire Moon*. Butts' voice quickens as she recalls her stay on Islesboro. She had been working on the book for awhile, but something was missing. When Butts arrived on Islesboro, she realized that Islesboro had to be the setting for her story. Butts then spent her vacation walking around with a notebook and taking notes about "the water, the smells, the sounds" of the island. Butts claims that the book then came together quickly; and when she was finished, the setting "almost seemed like a character" to her.

When she was eleven-years-old, Butts had her first poem published—in her principal's dissertation! She has been writing ever since. She worked first in the medical field and then as a journalist. She also became fascinated with sign language, took numerous courses in signing, and then began volunteering with hearing-impaired children in her local school system. After joining a children's writers' group in Atlanta, Butts began working full-time on *Cheshire Moon*. It took her three years to complete the book. Her second children's book is *The Door in the Lake*, a science fiction story about a boy who disappears from a family camping trip and reappears two years later not a day older.

Butts makes her home with her husband, her eleven-year-old son, and three dogs in a 110-year-old Victorian house with no ghosts (but she wishes there were!). Butts enjoys herb gardening, quilting, and walking by the ocean.

THE ENCHANTED: AN INCREDIBLE TALE

AUTHOR: Elizabeth Coatsworth / ILLUSTRATOR: Stephen Petroff
AGE LEVEL / LENGTH: 12 years–adult / 160 pages
PUBLISHER / COPYRIGHT DATE: Blackberry Books / 1951-original text; 1992-reprint
FORMAT / ISBN: Paperback / 0942396650

A young man named David Ross buys a deserted farm in the northern Maine woods near the Dead River. The area is known as the Enchanted (see Upper and Lower Enchanted Townships on a Maine map); and legend claims that it is a place of magic where deer change to bear and music comes out of the air. David is warned by an elderly neighbor to stay away from an odd family, known as the Perdrys, or he might find himself "in the middle of one of them legends."

However, David grows lonely in this desolated region, and he befriends the large Perdry clan. One night, to his own surprise, David finds himself proposing to Molly, one of the Perdry daughters. Once they are married, David learns that Molly has some unusual traits—she panics when she is alone, she avoids eating meat, and she mysteriously disappears with her large family without a goodbye or a trace. When Molly returns, David finally understands the mystery of the Perdrys and the magic of the Enchanted.

The Enchanted is an unusual and mysterious novel. Author Elizabeth Coatsworth creates a strong sense of place; the Enchanted seems more like a character than a setting. Coatsworth skillfully and subtly weaves hints about the Perdrys' true identity throughout the novel.

LEARNING ACTIVITIES

1. Discussion questions:

> —Why do you think David Ross decided to buy the deserted farm in the first place?
> —What hints can you find throughout the novel that suggest the true identity of the Perdrys?
> —Do you believe David really loved Molly? Why or why not? And do you believe Molly really loved David? Why or why not?
> —Would you like to visit a place like the Enchanted? Why or why not?

2. Elizabeth Coatsworth created a magical, mysterious place in the Enchanted. Write a short story that is a mystery and is set in your own town. You will need to decide what your mystery will be and how you will slowly give hints to its solution throughout your story. It might be helpful to create a backwards outline that shows first of all how your story will end (solves the mystery) and then backtracks logically to the opening scene where your story will set up the mystery. Share your final story with some peers.

3. Learn more about Elizabeth Coatsworth. She wrote more than one hundred books, many of them for children. Most of her books are now out of print, though many are still available through libraries. In previous decades, she received both critical praise and recognition for her writings, including the 1930 Newbery Medal for *The Cat Who Went to Heaven*. Coatsworth was married to naturalist and author Henry Beston, and she lived for more than forty years on a farm in Nobleboro, Maine. Research Coatsworth in author biography sources, such as *Something About the Author*, by Gale Research (available in many library reference sections) and *Children's Books and Their Creators*, edited by Anita Silvey. Also read one or more of Coatsworth's other novels. Then write a paper about Coatsworth, describing her life and her writing style.

ABOUT THE AUTHOR

Elizabeth Coatsworth was born in Buffalo, New York, in 1893. Her first publication came in 1923 with a book of adult poetry called *Fox Footprints*. But she was best known for her children's books, including the 1930 Newbery Medal-winning novel, *The Cat Who Went to Heaven*, which was based on a Japanese legend; and a popular classic from 1934 called *Away Goes Sally*, which tells of a girl's wintertime move from Massachusetts to Maine.

Coatsworth lived at Chimney Farm in Nobleboro, Maine, with her husband, Henry Beston. Their daughter, Kate Barnes, is also a well-known Maine writer and poet. Coatsworth attended Vassar College and Columbia University. She died in 1986 at the age of ninety-three and was buried in the graveyard on Chimney Farm.

EMERGENCY RESCUE! NIGHTMARE AT NORTON'S MILLS

AUTHOR: James & Lois Cowan
AGE LEVEL / LENGTH: 8-12 years / 115 pages
PUBLISHER / COPYRIGHT DATE: Scholastic Inc. / 1993
FORMAT / ISBN: Paperback / 0590460196 (recently out of print)

Emergency Rescue! Nightmare at Norton's Mills is a unique chapter book. Written by two EMTs (Emergency Medical Technicians) and set in Maine, the book is divided into five episodic chapters. Each chapter tells the story of a different emergency situation featuring Matt Rich and Davey Mountain, junior members of the Camden, Maine, Rescue Squad. Each episode is an action-packed fictional story which incorporates much factual information.

The emergency situations featured in *Emergency Rescue! Nightmare at Norton's Mills* include saving a person from drowning, keeping two people safe who are in an accident with live wires touching their car, dealing with hypothermia when someone falls through the ice, stopping the bleeding from a severe cut, and helping to rescue someone lost in the Maine woods. Each chapter concludes with a description of the skills required for the emergency situation and a completed emergency report. In addition, the book includes a decoder guide explaining the meaning of emergency code numbers (e.g., Ten-32 is a person with a weapon, Ten-55 is a vehicle accident, Ten-71 is a bomb threat) and a comprehensive glossary of emergency vocabulary (e.g., containment area, heat reduction, shunt, string line). This book is one of a series of books by the Cowans and published by Scholastic. Another book in the series, entitled *Emergency Rescue! Trouble at Moosehead Lake*, includes five new emergency situations, such as dealing with poisonous gas and an allergic reaction to a bee sting.

LEARNING ACTIVITIES

1. Using the decoder guide in the front of *Emergency Rescue! Nightmare at Norton's Mills*, listen to a scanner. Does the guide help you to understand information on the scanner? What other codes do you hear on the scanner that are not included in the book's guide? For example, what does PI refer to in a Ten-55? Which codes were used most frequently as you listened to the scanner?

2. Select one of the chapters in *Emergency Rescue! Nightmare at Norton's Mills* and write a quiz testing knowledge of the emergency information included in that chapter. Then share your quiz with a friend. Have your friend complete the quiz before reading the chapter (a pre-test) and then again after reading the chapter (a post-test). How did your friend do on your quiz? Did your friend increase his or her knowledge of emergency information after reading the chapter?

3. Write an additional chapter for *Emergency Rescue! Nightmare at Norton's Mills*. Select a different emergency situation, research what should be done in such a situation, and then write a chapter, including the book's main characters, Matt Rich and Davey Mountain. Afterward, share your chapter with a local EMT and ask for input as to whether your chapter contains the correct emergency information.

ABOUT THE AUTHORS

James and Lois Cowan are a husband-and-wife writing team who have lived in Maine since the mid 1980s—first in Camden for eight years, and in Islesboro for the last several years. The Cowans are practicing paramedics in Islesboro, Rangeley, Windsor, and for a state-wide Wilderness Rescue Team. The Cowans have written more than thirty books, including fiction and nonfiction for adults and children. Their stories are based upon their experiences as emergency medical providers, and their settings feature Maine locations where they have lived, worked, or visited.

The Cowans live on Islesboro with a St. Bernard rescue dog and a pea-pod boat which they double row. They have eight children and two grandchildren "scattered throughout the country."

CALICO BUSH

AUTHOR: Rachel Field / ILLUSTRATOR: Allen Lewis
AGE LEVEL / LENGTH: 12 years–adult / 224 pages
PUBLISHER / COPYRIGHT DATE: Simon & Schuster (hardcover); Dell (paperback) / 1931; reissued 1966, 1987
FORMAT / ISBN: Hardcover / 0027346102; Paperback / 0440403685
AWARDS: Newbery Honor Book, 1932

Calico Bush is the story of Marguerite Ledoux's life during the year 1743. Marguerite is French, but her family (her grandmother and her uncle) has recently died, so she becomes a "bound-out girl." A bound-out girl is someone who is taken in by a family and is given shelter and food until the age of eighteen in exchange for help with chores and domestic work.

The Sargent family takes Marguerite as a bound-out girl in spite of her background (the French were viewed negatively by the colonists during this time, due to the French alliance with the Indians against the English). Marguerite, or Maggie as she is known to the family, accompanies the Sargents on the ship "Isabella B.," sailing from Massachusetts to Maine. The Sargents want to get away from an overpopulated Massachusetts and stake their claim on land near Mt. Desert Island.

The book is divided into four sections corresponding to the seasons. The hardships of a Maine winter, run-ins with Indians, dealing with death, and many other trials are vividly portrayed. Happier moments, such as a house-raising, corn-shelling bee, and singing and dancing, provide a balanced view of life in the 1700s on the coast of Maine.

LEARNING ACTIVITIES

1. Visit or read about Mt. Desert Island. Try to imagine it from Maggie's point of view in the 1700s. How must it have looked to her? How has it changed over the years?

2. Keep a seasonal diary as Maggie did. For each of the seasons, note changes in your surroundings. What looks different? What are people doing differently for work and recreation? How do each of the seasons make you feel?

3. Write some of the French words found in *Calico Bush*. Translate them, using a French-English dictionary. Practice pronouncing them correctly. Add to your French list any other French words that you know.

4. Discussion questions:

> —There are marked differences in conveniences between the Maine of the 1700s and the one we live in now. For example, Maggie has only one dress to wear, even though she is outgrowing it. What would have inconvenienced you most living in Maine back in the 1700s?
> —Maine has a strong French heritage. Does your family have any French roots? How so?
> —Discuss foreshadowing in *Calico Bush* (e.g., the death of the baby and the use of the Maypole). How did author Rachel Field "signal" to readers about future events in her novel?
> —Reread sections of *Calico Bush* where Indians appear. Do you feel that Field's depiction of the Indians was a fair one? Why or why not?

ABOUT THE AUTHOR

Rachel Field was born in New York City in 1894 and grew up in western Massachusetts. She attended Radcliffe College. Her first job was as a writer at a company that produced silent pictures. She then started to write and illustrate her own books, including children's plays, adult novels, and poetry. Her first children's book was published in 1926.

As an adult, Field summered on Sutton's Island, off Mt. Desert. She said that she loved islands and included them as settings in many of her writings.

Field had not planned to write a book such as her Caldecott-winning *Hitty: Her First Hundred Years* (see book-entry below). She and illustrator Dorothy Lathrop discovered a doll in an antique shop in New York. They bought the doll and found a yellowed tag attached to her with the word "Hitty." They began to imagine what the doll's "story" would be. That story, *Hitty: Her First Hundred Years*, resulted in Field being the first woman to be awarded the Newbery Medal. Field died in 1942; but a compilation of some of her best work was published in 1957 in a book called *Poems*. In addition, several of her poems have surfaced as picture book texts in recent years, including *General Store* (see page 170).

HITTY: HER FIRST HUNDRED YEARS

AUTHOR: Rachel Field / ILLUSTRATOR: Dorothy P. Lathrop
AGE LEVEL / LENGTH: 10 years–adult / 220 pages
PUBLISHER / COPYRIGHT DATE: Simon & Schuster (hardcover); Dell (paperback) / 1929
FORMAT / ISBN: Hardcover / 0027348407; Paperback / 0440403375
AWARDS: Newbery Medal, 1930

Hitty: Her First Hundred Years tells the story of a hand-carved, mountain-ash doll. The story is written from the doll's perspective, as a memoir of her first 100 years. The doll's life is a series of constant adventures, starting in Maine with her first owner, Phoebe Preble. Hitty becomes stranded in a crow's nest, gets left under a church pew, and then travels to sea on a whaling ship with the Preble family. She circles the world and has many owners before she finally returns to Maine almost 100 years later.

Although *Hitty: Her First Hundred Years* might initially seem a bit outdated to today's young readers, a reminder of when the book was published (1929) is likely to whet their appetites for a trip back in time. *Hitty* truly was a unique book in its day since it was told from the doll's point of view.

LEARNING ACTIVITIES

1. After reading *Hitty*, create an outline for what might have happened to her during her second hundred years. Include more modern adventures, such as a ride in an airplane or a trip in a space shuttle.

2. Hitty is supposed to be a lucky doll because she's made out of a kind of tree called mountain ash. Do a survey to determine what objects people today consider to be lucky. Write a summary of your survey results and note any trends.

3. Find the oldest object in your household and research its history. Who owned it first in the family? Where did it come from? Are there any special stories about the object? Where is it kept? Has the object had any mishaps? After gathering this information, write a short story from the object's point of view.

4. Visit an antique toy exhibit, such as those found at the Maine State Museum in Augusta or the Webb Museum in Island Falls. How are these toys different from modern toys? What materials are they made from? Imagine the "story" behind one of these toys. Who might have first owned it? What was a typical day like for the toy?

ABOUT THE AUTHOR

See information about Rachel Field on page 104.

WESTERN WIND

AUTHOR: Paula Fox
AGE LEVEL / LENGTH: 8-14 years / 202 pages
PUBLISHER / COPYRIGHT DATE: Orchard Books (hardcover); Dell (paperback) / 1993
FORMAT / ISBN: Hardcover / 0531068021; Paperback / 0440409918; Library binding / 0531086526

In *Western Wind*, twelve-year-old Elizabeth Benedict is sent away for a month to stay with her grandmother on Pring Island, off the coast of Maine. Elizabeth is not happy. She's certain that her parents want to get rid of her so that they can dote over her new baby brother. On top of that, Gran's little cottage has no electricity and no bathroom, the Maine ocean water is too cold for swimming, and there's only one other family living on the island—a very strange family.

While Elizabeth's grandmother spends her days painting, Elizabeth is free to explore the island. As she does so, she discovers that she enjoys her new-found peace and solitude. She also forms a new friendship with the boy next door, Aaron. Aaron is usually "hyper" and out of control with his family, but he calms down when he is with Elizabeth. She enjoys the way he speaks his mind. Elizabeth also grows close to her grandmother, learning more about her in one month than she'd known during the previous twelve years.

As Elizabeth's month on Pring Island draws to a close, she faces several crises. Aaron becomes lost on the island, and Elizabeth is the one who finds him in a dense fog. Gran suddenly becomes very ill and must be transported to the mainland hospital by a Coast Guard boat. Elizabeth discovers the real reason she was sent to Pring Island and learns much more about herself in the process.

LEARNING ACTIVITIES

1. Aaron Herkimer and the rest of his family are odd characters. How does author Paula Fox create such characters? What traits does she give them? How does she make them talk? Even though the Herkimers are unusual characters, are they still believable? Do you like any of them? Why or why not? Write a description of someone you know who is unique (e.g., who has unusual habits, who talks in a special way). Work to make your description believable.

2. Elizabeth must live without many modern comforts on Pring Island. She takes sponge baths, she uses an outhouse, and she reads by kerosene lanterns. Learn more about living without modern conveniences. Interview elderly relatives or neighbors and learn what daily life was like for them as children. What did they use for transportation? How were meals prepared? What supplies and devices were used for cleaning houses? What did they do for pastimes or hobbies? As you listen to their experiences, think about whether you would have enjoyed living in the world they describe. Why or why not?

3. Discussion questions:

> —Why do you think Paula Fox gave her book the title, *Western Wind?* What does the title mean? Does it refer to any other work of literature?
> —During Elizabeth's visit, her grandmother frequently reminisces about her earlier life Why do you think she does this reminiscing?
> —Do you believe there is anything wrong with Aaron Herkimer? Do you think Aaron's family is responsible for his strange behavior? Support your answer.
> —How do Elizabeth's feelings change during her month on Pring Island—her feelings toward her grandmother, toward the Herkimer family, toward her baby brother, toward her parents, toward herself?
> —How do you think Elizabeth will spend her next summer? Why?

ABOUT THE AUTHOR

Paula Fox has been writing for over thirty-five years, with more than twenty-two titles for children to her credit. Her notable children's books include *The Slave Dancer* (1973), which won the Newbery Medal, and *One-Eyed Cat* (1984), a Newbery Honor Book. Her more recent novel, *Monkey Island* (1991), is a touching story of homelessness. In 1978, Fox won the prestigious Hans Christian Andersen Medal in honor of her total body of work.

Fox was born in New York City in 1923. She moved frequently as a child and attended schools in Cuba, Canada, and the United States. A steady force throughout Fox's childhood was books; she often visited public libraries and was a voracious reader. As an adult, she worked as a teacher, journalist, and television writer. Fox currently lives in Brooklyn, New York. She has three grown children and seven grandchildren. She claims to have no time for hobbies other than, in her words, "playing the piano (badly!) and writing."

Paula Fox fell in love with the state of Maine when she first visited it fifty years ago. Since then, she has spent several summers near Blue Hill, on Deer Isle, and near Bath. She decided to set *Western Wind* in Maine because of her affection for the state. Furthermore, rural Maine island life seemed well-suited to her storyline and in particular to the character of the grandmother in the book.

ASH: A NOVEL

AUTHOR: Lisa Rowe Fraustino
AGE LEVEL / LENGTH: 14 years–adult / 176 pages
PUBLISHER / COPYRIGHT DATE: Orchard Books / 1995
FORMAT / ISBN: Hardcover / 0531068897; Library Binding / 0531087395

Ash Libby is changing. The once-revered older brother, son, and community idol is obsessed with substance use, partying, and playing music with his friends to the point of scaring and embarrassing his family, neighbors, and the community of Calvin Cove in Downeast Maine.

ASH: A Novel, written in a journal format by Ash's younger brother, Wes, chronicles Ash's relationship with Wes and the rest of the family as Ash falls deeper into the grip of substance abuse and mental illness. Wes's journal tells how Ash was the reason that Wes's best friend did not speak to him for a year, how sharing a bedroom with Ash made Wes feel scared, and how Ash's frequent disappearances and erratic behavior brought an end to Libby family traditions and life as they had known it. Despite the realistic portrayal of the negative impact of mental illness, the book manages to celebrate family strength and love in the face of hardship.

Author Lisa Rowe Fraustino has written a gripping and powerful story which deals effectively with a difficult subject. She makes her serious topic more readable and believable by creating a very strong narrator's voice. The novel sounds like a real journal written by a real fourteen-year-old boy from rural Maine. Fraustino adds simple line drawings to look like sketches drawn by Wes, and she has the teen write with grammatical errors and Maine slang (e.g., cunning, gawmy, staved in). In addition, the book has large doses of teen humor. Ash and Wes Libby's teenage sister, Deena, creates many "ASH" word plays throughout the book when teasing her oldest brother, such as, "You should be ASHamed of yourself," and "Ash is acting like a real ASHwipe." Fraustino also has humor woven into the story: when referring to his strict father, Wes writes "There's a fine line between his sense of humor and his belt." When speaking of his place in the family, Wes writes,

"Dad's the drill sergeant, but Mama's the major. And Grammy's the 4-star General. Me, I'm on KP." The book's lighter aspect helps make the story's anguish bearable.

LEARNING ACTIVITIES

1. Wes Libby claims to have written his journal so that someday he could share it with his brother, Ash; but in reality, Wes probably wrote the journal as a form of therapy and healing for himself. Have you ever kept a journal as a way of understanding and dealing with difficulties in your life? If at any time keeping a journal seems appropriate and useful, try it.

2. Ash Libby's mental illness is diagnosed as schizophrenia. Some other types of mental illness are depression, hysteria, neurosis, phobia, and psychosis. Select one type of mental illness and research it. What are its causes, its symptoms, and its treatments? In addition to checking reference books, try to find a personal account of the illness in a magazine or biography. Write an informational pamphlet about what you learn, one that educates the public.

3. When Wes's journal concludes, there is no magical fairy tale ending with everyone living happily ever after. Continue Wes's journal five or ten years into the future. How would his life have changed? What would he be writing about? On your first draft, try to get your ideas of the storyline down; but on subsequent revisions, work hard to make the journal sound as though Wes actually wrote it. Study his drawings, his "voice," his grammar and his humor in *ASH: A Novel,* and try to replicate Wes's characteristics with your own journal entries.

ABOUT THE AUTHOR

Lisa Rowe Fraustino was born in Dover-Foxcroft, Maine, and spent most of her childhood in Piscataquis County. She graduated from Piscataquis Community High School in Guilford, and then went on to major in English at the University of Maine in Orono. Fraustino claims to have been writing "ever since she could hold a crayon," but she has been writing professionally since she graduated from college. Her freelance writing career has included book and restaurant reviews, articles for national magazines, and educational texts for a correspondence school. In the 1980s, she had her first writing for children published in children's magazines, including her story "Back to the River," which won the *Highlights* Fiction Contest in 1992.

Fraustino's first children's novel, *Grass and Sky* (see next page), was published in 1994. She claims to have worked on it "on and off and on" for almost ten years before it was published. Her writing was slowed while she raised her three children and while she worked on her Ph.D. in English/Creative Writing. In fact, her second book *ASH: A Novel* served as her doctoral dissertation. *ASH* was selected as a Best Book for Young Adults by the American Library Association. Fraustino claims that *ASH* is her truest Maine book to date since it is written in a Maine accent. She says, "the narrator, Wes Libby, is very much like many of the boys she knew at Piscataquis Community High School—not very good at English, but a wicked good storyteller with a lot to say." *ASH* is set in Calvin Cove, a fictional town near Machias; and Fraustino is currently at work on a "Calvin Cove Cycle" of books. Fraustino's newest book is a collection of short stories, which she edited. She has also authored one of the stories in *Dirty Laundry: Stories about Family Secrets* (Viking Children's Books, scheduled to be published in June 1998).

Fraustino currently lives in Kingston, Pennsylvania, with her husband and three children. She continues to summer in Maine, on the Bowerbank Shore of Sebec Lake. Fraustino teaches fifth-grade English during the school year and summer courses at Hollins College in Virginia in their Graduate Program in Children's Literature. Fraustino claims that her favorite hobbies are reading and writing, but she also enjoys working out at a gym, playing tennis, baking, surfing the Internet, and "goofing off with her family."

GRASS AND SKY

AUTHOR: Lisa Rowe Fraustino
AGE LEVEL / LENGTH: 8-12 years / 160 pages
PUBLISHER / COPYRIGHT DATE: Orchard Books / 1994
FORMAT / ISBN: Hardcover / 0531068234; Library Binding / 0531086739 (recently out of print)

Eleven-year-old Timmi Lafler is not very happy about her Fourth of July plans. She wants to be back in Pennsylvania as the star baseball pitcher in the Independence Tourney. Instead, she's going to be stuck at a camp in Maine with her little sister and a grandfather she doesn't even know.

After Timmi's parents travel to a high school reunion in Dexter over the holiday weekend, Timmi is left to watch after her little sister who is afflicted with asthma (their grandfather doesn't even have the sense not to smoke his pipe around her), to put together jigsaw puzzles that don't have all the pieces, to pitch in an "out-in-the-sticks" baseball game in Patten, and to listen to her grandfather complain about a group of rowdy drunks who disturb the peace and cause chaos at the lake.

At times, Timmi begins to feel close to her grandfather as he reminisces about the past, tells terrific tall tales, and shows signs of genuine affection toward his granddaughters. But Timmi resists her feelings. There's a mystery behind her grandfather's absence all those years; and she decides if he didn't care about her in the past, then she won't care about him in the present. However, after several crises—a fire and her sister's severe asthma attack—Timmi learns that she can depend on her grandfather after all. She also learns the reason for her grandfather's mysterious absence in the past.

Author Lisa Rowe Fraustino has crafted an interesting novel with believable characters. She tackles the difficult topic of alcoholism and families in a realistic, non-moralistic manner.

LEARNING ACTIVITIES

1. Timmi Lafler is named after her grandmother, Timothea. Trace the names in your family for several generations. Were you named after a particular relative? Why? Was anyone else in your family named after a relative? Draw a chart showing your family tree and connect the names of relatives who have the "same" name (Remember to check family connections for middle names also, not just first names. Look for variations of names—such as, a girl, Roberta, being named after a grandfather, Robert.).

2. Timmi's grandfather enjoyed putting jigsaw puzzles together; and Timmi also enjoyed their challenge. Try putting together a difficult jigsaw puzzle. If you can do a 200-piece puzzle easily, then try a 500-piece one; or if you are used to 500-piece puzzles, then try a 1,000-piece puzzle. Before beginning, write down your strategy for making the puzzle. In what order will you do the puzzle? What sorting strategies will you use? Afterwards, check to see if you actually followed your puzzle strategy. Why or why not? How would you adjust your strategy for another puzzle?

3. Select a relative whom you don't know very well. It might be a great-aunt or a second cousin or a grandparent who lives far away. Then try to learn more about that relative. Get together for several conversations if you live close to each other. Or exchange letters and audio or video tapes if you live far apart. As you get to know this relative better, think about what you've learned. Did your relative turn out to be the kind of person you thought he or she would be? What surprised you most about your relative? Which things about your relative were consistent with your preconceived image? Did you learn anything new about your family from this relative?

4. *Grass and Sky* deals with two illnesses—asthma and alcoholism. Select one of these two illnesses or an illness that has directly affected your own family. Research your selected illness. Read nonfiction books, write for informational pamphlets from organizations which deal with the illness, and interview people who have lived with or have been affected by the illness. Write a report summarizing what you have learned.

ABOUT THE AUTHOR

See information about Lisa Rowe Fraustino on page 109.

THE FIRE BUG CONNECTION:
AN ECOLOGICAL MYSTERY

AUTHOR: Jean Craighead George
AGE LEVEL / LENGTH: 8-12 years / 160 pages
PUBLISHER / COPYRIGHT DATE: HarperCollins / 1993
FORMAT / ISBN: Hardcover / 0060214902; Library Binding /
0060214910; Large Type Hardcover / 0614095557

Maggie Mercer has an unusual twelfth birthday. As her day begins at the Biological Research Center in the Maine woods, a raven flies at Maggie. Maggie is concerned because she remembers her grandmother warning that when a raven flies at you, there will be a murder. And her grandmother's saying seems to be coming true, as the fire bugs she receives as a birthday present from a European graduate student begin to die mysteriously. But what is killing them? Is it acid rain, global warming, the raven's curse?

Maggie, who is a young naturalist and the daughter of two science professors from the University of Maine in Orono, tries to solve the mystery of the dying fire bugs. She gets help from Mitch Waterford, another professor's ten-year-old son who has a reputation for being a computer wizard as well as a prankster. Maggie and Mitch set up experiments, gather information on the Internet, and research the paper-making process at the Rumford Paper Mill. As they try to solve the mystery, they also explore and learn more about ravens, bats, spiders, and wasps. In the end, Maggie not only discovers what has been killing her fire bugs, but she helps to further the scientific research of insecticides.

Author Jean Craighead George has created an unusual Maine mystery with *The Fire Bug Connection*. Her characters are well-rounded, and young readers will become caught up in solving the fire bug mystery without realizing how much scientific information they are learning. This book is a must read for young naturalists and future scientists.

LEARNING ACTIVITIES

1. As you read *The Fire Bug Connection*, keep a log of all the information you learn about the fire bugs, chapter by chapter. Then at the end of each chapter, make a guess as to what is stopping the development of the fire bugs and killing them. Does your guess change as you learn more information? Why or why not? When did you learn what was actually killing the fire bugs? How did you know?

2. Learn more about one of the animals in *The Fire Bug Connection*—ravens, bats, spiders, wasps, or another wild animal of your choice. Read and gather research from non-fiction books, interview biologists or animal experts, and if possible observe your selected animal in its natural setting. Then write a picture book including the information you have learned.

3. In *The Fire Bug Connection*, Maggie and Mitch needed to learn more about the paper-making process, so they visited the Rumford Paper Mill. Learn how paper is made today. If possible, visit a Maine paper mill. What steps are involved? What materials are used? Does paper-making have an effect on the environment? If so, how? Is the effect harmful? Create a brochure on paper-making, summarizing what you have learned.

ABOUT THE AUTHOR

Jean Craighead George is the author of more than sixty children's books, including the 1973 Newbery Medal-winner, *Julie of the Wolves*, and the 1960 Newbery Honor book, *My Side of the Mountain*. Her books celebrate nature and are set in varied locations throughout the world. Two of her current books are sequels to *Julie of the Wolves*: *Julie* (1994) and *Julie's Wolf Pack* (1997).

George was born in Washington, D.C., and raised in a family of naturalists. She claims that she has been writing since third grade and professionally since graduating from Pennsylvania State University, where she received dual degrees in English and in science. In the 1940s, George worked as a member of the White House Press Corps and a reporter for *The Washington Post*. George currently lives in Chappaqua, New York, where she enjoys hiking, canoeing, making sourdough pancakes, and reading to her grandchildren. George is the mother of three grown children; and she describes how she raised her children and 173 pets in her 1996 autobiography, *The Tarantula in My Purse*.

Jean Craighead George explains that "her deep love for Maine" began when she worked as a counselor at a camp on Lake Sebago at the age of eighteen. Since then, George has returned frequently to Maine to canoe and hike. She has spent summers in Cape Elizabeth and Hancock. Her ecological mystery book, *The Fire Bug Connection*, is based upon her experiences visiting Dr. Bernard Heinrich's camp and "Raven Haven" in western Maine, near the White Mountain National Forest.

LOOK FOR ME BY MOONLIGHT

AUTHOR: Mary Downing Hahn
AGE LEVEL / LENGTH: 12 years–adult / 198 pages
PUBLISHER / COPYRIGHT DATE: Clarion Books (hardcover); Avon (paperback) / 1995;
FORMAT / ISBN: Hardcover / 039569843X; Paperback / 038072703X

Sixteen-year-old Cynda comes to Maine to stay with her father, whom she has not seen in two years, and her pregnant stepmother and little stepbrother, neither of whom she has met before. She's unhappy about being stuck at their isolated Downeast inn in the middle of the winter. She feels abandoned by her mother and stepfather, who decided to move to Italy. She feels like an outsider in her father's family. Also, rumor has it that their inn is haunted by the ghost of a teenage girl who was murdered sixty years ago. Cynda feels a glimmer of hope when she meets a nice neighborhood boy named Will.

Cynda's life is changed forever one night during a blizzard, when a mysterious stranger named Vincent Mothanos arrives at the inn. Cynda is immediately drawn to this handsome, mesmerizing, older man. Vincent, during his extended stay at the inn, works his magic on Cynda, making her feel like he is the only one who understands her feelings. He weaves Cynda tighter and tighter into a web of deceit and danger, which not only threatens her life, but the life of her little stepbrother as well.

Author Mary Downing Hahn has created a mysterious and fast-paced novel. She makes readers care about her characters in *Look for Me by Moonlight* and then keeps readers on the edge of their seats as they wonder if Cynda can ever escape from the eternity of horror which awaits her.

LEARNING ACTIVITIES

1. Research vampires. Historically, when were vampires first written about? Geographically, where were vampires reported to have been sighted? What common characteristics have been reported for vampires? Can they appear in daylight? What protects a person from a vampire? What can kill a vampire? Write a report about your findings.

2. Write your own horror story set in Maine. Include ghosts and vampires if you wish, or write a more realistic horror story if you'd rather. Map out your story first. How will you build tension and suspense? How will you make your characters believable? How can you make readers care about your main character? Share your first draft with a peer and ask for suggestions on how to improve your story. Then try revising your horror story one or more times to polish it.

3. Cynda feels as if she doesn't belong in her new stepfamily. Her feelings are not unusual. If you are part of a stepfamily, write a reflective piece about your own sense of belonging. Do you feel that you belong? Have you always felt that way? Have you resented any members of your stepfamily? Why? Based on your experiences, what advice would you give to other teens in stepfamilies? If you are not a part of a stepfamily, interview a teen who is and (with permission) write about that person's experiences.

ABOUT THE AUTHOR

Mary Downing Hahn worked as a children's librarian before she turned to writing full-time. She is known for writing a broad range of books from realistic fiction to fantasy to ghost stories. Her first book, *The Sara Summer*, was published in 1979. Her other books include *The Doll in the Garden; Time for Andrew: A Ghost Story;* and *The Gentleman Outlaw and Me, Eli,* as well as the Scott O'Dell Award-winner for historical fiction,

Stepping on the Cracks. Hahn claims that getting the idea for a story is the easy part of writing; the difficult part for her comes when she has to sit down at her computer to do the actual writing.

Hahn was born in Washington, D.C., in 1937. She currently lives in Columbia, Maryland, with her husband. Hahn is the mother of two grown daughters.

THE LIBERTY POLE

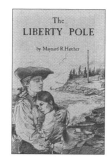

AUTHOR: Maynard R. Hatcher
AGE LEVEL / LENGTH: 12 years–adult / 200 pages
PUBLISHER / COPYRIGHT DATE: Windswept House Publishers / 1987
FORMAT / ISBN: Paperback / 0932433324

The Liberty Pole, an historical novel set in 1775 in Machias, Maine, records the naval battle between the British ship *Margaretta* and the American ship *Unity.* This was the first naval battle of the Revolutionary War. The book also tells the story of nineteen-year-old Luke Cole, who inadvertently becomes the hero of the battle after being captured and impressed into the British navy. The book focuses on Luke's struggle to become an adult—what career he will choose, whom he will marry, and how he will fulfill his responsibility to his community and country.

The Liberty Pole is a realistic portrayal of the daily life of people in Machias, Maine, in 1775. It describes work at a sawmill, as well as the lumbering and shipbuilding industries. A case of racial discrimination is also presented, as shown through Luke's romance with a woman who is a French Abenaki Indian.

LEARNING ACTIVITIES

1. If possible, plan a visit to Machias to view Fort O'Brien, the Burnham Tavern, and the Gates House, Machiasport's historical society. You might also write to the Chamber of Commerce in Machias for information about the town and its history.

2. Interview someone who currently works at a sawmill, or as a lumberer or shipbuilder. Compare that person's modern-day experiences with those described in *The Liberty Pole.*

3. Using a dictionary, research some of the early American vocabulary words found in *The Liberty Pole.* Rewrite a page of the book in a modern idiom.

4. In *The Liberty Pole,* Luke has a difficult time finding his way on poorly marked roads. Many roads back in the 1700s were little more than paths. Discuss what it would have been like to find one's way through the wilderness. To get a sense of such an adventure,

take a hike (tell others where you are going, and be careful not to become lost) and imagine what it would be like to travel without trail markers.

5. Rachel DuBois' last name means "of wood." Scan a Maine telephone book to find other French names. Use a French-English dictionary to learn the English translation of these names.

ABOUT THE AUTHOR

Maynard Hatcher was from Virginia, where he died in 1997. He had always been a history buff. After he retired in 1977, Hatcher vacationed in many places and studied local history as he traveled. In 1982, Hatcher visited the Porter Memorial Library in Machias, Maine. He warmly remembered "a sumptuous local history room" where he came across George W. Drisko's *History of Maine*. What he read fascinated him, and he subsequently made oral notes on a tape recorder.

Hoping to fulfill his lifelong dream of becoming a writer, Hatcher enrolled in a writing course. He had his Machias information first published as a magazine article, "The Lexington of the Sea," in *New England Senior Citizen* in 1984. The Machias material continued to "call" to Maynard Hatcher, and he decided it warranted more than an article—it should be a book of historical fiction. *The Liberty Pole* continued to take shape for several years, until its publication in 1987.

HALF A CAGE

AUTHOR / ILLUSTRATOR: Jean Howard
AGE LEVEL / LENGTH: 12 years–adult / 319 pages
PUBLISHER / COPYRIGHT DATE: The Tidal Press / 1978
FORMAT / ISBN: Hardcover / 0930954076

Half a Cage opens with a prologue set in 1932 in which a young girl wishes desperately for a pet monkey as a birthday present. She is crushed when she discovers that her present is actually a *toy* monkey. But life has a way of coming full circle. As the novel opens in 1965, that young girl is now grown and married, with a family of her own. It just so happens that her daughter, Ann Carpenter, desperately wants a pet monkey for her twelfth birthday. Ann's mother cannot disappoint her daughter as she herself had been disappointed years earlier. Ann gets a pet monkey, and the family gets chaos.

The rest of the book chronicles the family's experiences during "the year of the monkey." Ann discovers soon after getting the monkey that it is very sick. She struggles to nurture her new pet, Diana, back to health and to teach it some semblance of order and routine within their household. But Diana is a wild, not a tame, animal; and worse yet, she has a stubborn streak. Ann hopes that during the family's summer vacation to her grand-mother's in Maine that she will have the time and her grandmother's help to tame Diana. The summer by the lake is filled with moments of wonder as Diana entertains the family with her skilled acrobatics; with moments of humor as Diana kisses strangers and wears underwear for a hat; and with moments of despair as Diana screeches, bites, and ransacks the camp when she is left alone or doesn't get her way. Ann's grandmother is supportive, but wise. When Diana ruins a new friendship that Ann has made with a boy across the lake, Ann's grandmother suggests that it may be time for Ann to consider other alternatives for Diana. Ann struggles with her decision—she loves Diana more that she thought it was possible to love a pet, but she's also frustrated to tears and overwhelmed by the thought of caring for Diana once school begins in the fall. As she reaches her final decision about Diana, Ann emerges as a character who is older and wiser, one who has learned much about life and herself during "the year of the monkey."

Half a Cage is a well-written novel. Author Jean Howard writes with a passion and a poignancy that could only be possible if she had lived the experience herself. And she did. Howard, her husband, and their two children actually owned a pet monkey for a year.

LEARNING ACTIVITIES

1. As you read *Half a Cage*, take notes on any special features or characteristics of spider monkeys (e.g., information about their fur, tails, temperament.). Then after you finish the book, research spider monkeys, learning as much as possible about them. View one at a zoo, if possible, and study its tendencies. Read nonfiction books about spider monkeys. How does the information you learn compare with the portrayal of Diana in *Half a Cage?* Write a report about your spider monkey information.

2. "The Lake," where Ann's Gram lives in Maine, is a much-loved summer retreat. What place serves as a retreat for you and your family? Write a description of your retreat.

3. Ann Carpenter helps her grandmother at a church fair. That church fair bustled with activity—sales of home-baked goods, white elephant tables, craft sales, a baked bean lunch, three-legged races, and more. Discover the story behind a church or school fair in your community. What preparations are needed? How many people help? What activities are included in the fair? How many years has the fair been in existence? Write an article about the church or school fair you select and offer it for publication in the church's or school's newsletter/bulletin.

4. Interview someone who has owned an unusual pet. Prepare your questions ahead of time. Try to learn how that person decided to own an unusual pet, what research they had to do about the pet, whether the pet met their expectations, unusual incidents involving the pet, and more. Tape record or videotape your interview. For a video, try to tape the actual pet or photos of the pet.

ABOUT THE AUTHOR

See information about Jean Howard on page 49.

THE MOSQUITO TEST

AUTHOR: Richard Kent
AGE LEVEL / LENGTH: 12 years–adult / 153 pages
PUBLISHER / COPYRIGHT DATE: Windswept House Publishers / 1994
FORMAT / ISBN: Paperback / 1883650038

Sophomore Scott Cinador has cancer. A small lump on Scott's chest turns his world as he knows it upside down: no more contact sports, his friends treat him differently, and coping with chemotherapy uses all his energy. With his mother's encouragement, Scott tries the game of tennis and makes a new friend, Eric, who has cystic fibrosis. Tennis becomes the focal point that Scott and Eric need to help them deal with their illnesses.

Richard Kent creates a powerfully candid novel written in the first person. *The Mosquito Test* rings true from its life-like characters to its realistic dialogue. It's a novel that is difficult to put down and one that will be remembered by teens long after the last page is read.

LEARNING ACTIVITIES

1. Research cystic fibrosis or a specific type of cancer. Read articles and books. If possible, interview someone who has the disease. With permission, write a report about your research, including the facts and the "emotions."

2. Help at a local fundraiser. Find a local fundraiser in a local newspaper or through a local service organization. Contact the people organizing the fundraiser and offer your help. For example, you might offer to sell tickets for a fundraising event or work at a booth at such an event. Write a summary of this fundraising experience.

3. Using *The Mosquito Test* as a guide, write a first-person story about someone with a disease. You will need to interview someone with the disease in order to get a "real picture" of what it is like to live with that disease. Work to make your short story's character seem real, not idealized like a saint.

ABOUT THE AUTHOR

Richard Kent's grandparents summered in Maine in the 1920s. They purchased land in Weld on Lake Webb. Kent's parents eventually moved to Maine in the late 1940s; the author himself was born in the state in the 1950s.

After a three-year stint as a speaker for an Indianapolis-based educational foundation, Kent decided, with the urging of the award-winning poet Jared Carter, to move back to Maine and write. He made $5.00 from writing during his first three months in Maine. He now has been writing professionally for twenty years.

Kent is also an English teacher at Mountain Valley High School in Rumford, Maine. He directs The Writing Center at the school and also has coached numerous sports. Kent has received several teaching awards, including the Maine's Teacher of the Year for 1993 and a 1994 National Educator Award from the Milken Family Foundation.

Kent is the author of two young adult novels, both published by Windswept House Publishers. His first, called *Play On!* (see below), is a sports novel. Kent is donating his royalties from his most recent book, *The Mosquito Test*, to the Jimmy Fund of the Dana Farber Cancer Institute and to the Cystic Fibrosis Foundation.

PLAY ON!

AUTHOR: Richard Kent
AGE LEVEL / LENGTH: 10-15 years / 124 pages
PUBLISHER / COPYRIGHT DATE: Windswept House Publishers / 1985
FORMAT / ISBN: Paperback / 0932433049

Skeez Gilpatrick, a fourteen-year-old boy, lives in the fictional western Maine town of Bedford. After Skeez's parents die in a car accident, he must live at a Boys' Home, and he hopes that someday he will be adopted. The one bright spot in Skeez's life is soccer—he lives for the sport.

Bedford has never had a soccer team before, but Skeez manages to pull together a most unusual team called the "Stinkers." The Stinkers have an elderly female English teacher for a sponsor, an athletic girl for a star player, and the old "town bum" for a coach. The team makes up in spirit what the players lack in ability; their lively cheer begins, "We rot, we rot. / We smell a lot."

Play On! is a fictionalized account of the formation of the author's first soccer team in Rumford, Maine. Kent dedicates his book to "the real stinkers, the kids I've coached."

LEARNING ACTIVITIES

1. Select a sport and research its history and tradition in your town. When was the sport first played locally? Interview older townspeople and read historical newspaper accounts. Write an article for your school or town newspaper about your findings.

2. What is adoption like in the state today? Do children stay in residential facilities or are they placed in foster homes until they can be adopted? How long does an adoption take? Is there a difference in the process of adopting a baby or an older child?

3. Discuss how Skeez deals with his parents' deaths in *Play On!* Is his reaction realistic or not? Why? Discuss how you and others have dealt with deaths of friends or family members. Invite a grief counselor, hospice worker, or funeral director to your school to speak about death and ways to deal with it.

4. Discussion questions:

> —Kish, the coach, is misunderstood in *Play On!* He's thought of as the town bum, when in fact he's someone very different. How did Kish get labeled as the town bum? What are some of the consequences of stereotyping people? Have you ever been stereotyped, or stereotyped others?
> —Bedford High has some strong cliques—football, druggies, etc. Does your high school have cliques? What kind are they? What purpose do they serve? In what ways are they harmful?

ABOUT THE AUTHOR

See information about Richard Kent on page 118.

THE LAST VOYAGE OF THE MISTY DAY

AUTHOR: Jackie French Koller
AGE LEVEL / LENGTH: 10-14 years / 154 pages
PUBLISHER / COPYRIGHT DATE: Atheneum (imprint of Simon & Schuster) / 1992
FORMAT / ISBN: Hardcover / 068931731X

Fourteen-year-old Denny Townsend thinks of her new home on Phinney's Island as "a godforsaken lump of an island clinging by a string to the coast of Maine." Her life is in turmoil. She's suddenly had to move from New York City to an isolated Maine island, after her father dies unexpectedly. Money's tight. Her mother still cries every night. And Denny hates her new school, Moose Hollow Regional Secondary School.

But Denny develops an unusual and mysterious friendship with an old man who lives on a boat on the next island (which can only be reached by foot at low tide). He calls himself Mr. Jones, but he seems to have connections to Rufus Day, a legendary ghost who sailed the seas for twenty years in a boat called the "Misty Day." In fact, Mr. Jones is restoring that same boat, the "Misty Day," readying it for a summer voyage. Denny grows closer to Mr. Jones as they work side by side on his boat, but she still wonders about many unanswered questions. Why does he claim to be Mr. Jones when family photos show that's not his real name? Why is he hiding Captain Rufus Day's ship's log? And why won't he go see a doctor for his ailing leg? In the end, Denny must risk her own life to save Mr. Jones. She willingly does so and finally learns the answers to all her questions.

The Last Voyage of the Misty Day is well-written. The characters have depth and the story is tight and focused. Author Jackie French Koller makes the unusual friendship between Denny and Mr. Jones believable. The story's touch of mystery will keep young readers turning page after page to learn the secrets of Mr. Jones, Rufus Day, and the "Misty Day."

LEARNING ACTIVITIES

1. As you read *The Last Voyage of the Misty Day*, stop reading at the end of Chapter 22 (page 122) and write your guess as to what will happen in the rest of the book. What is the answer to the mystery surrounding Mr. Jones, Rufus Day, and the "Misty Day?" Do you think Mr. Jones is who he says he is? Why or why not? What's the story behind the ship's log? Why hasn't Mr. Jones seen a doctor about his leg? After writing down your guesses, read the rest of the book to see if your guesses were correct.

2. In *The Last Voyage of the Misty Day*, Denny and her mother must overcome their grief after the unexpected death of Denny's father. Mr. Jones also had to deal with the death of his wife. Who is the closest person to you that has died? How did you deal with that person's death? Write a reflective piece about your experiences dealing with loss. Based upon your experiences, the experiences of people you know, and of the characters in *The Last Voyage of the Misty Day*, what advice would you give to someone who had to deal with the death of a close relative or friend?

3. Denny's impression of Maine people changes as the story progresses and she gets to know them better. Write about a time when your impressions of someone changed. What were your impressions of the person initially? What happened to change your impressions? What were your impressions of the person afterward? Discuss this issue with some peers. Did they have experiences similar to yours? What, if any, lessons have you learned about judging others?

ABOUT THE AUTHOR

Author Jackie French Koller based her novel *The Last Voyage of the Misty Day* upon her father. Koller's father was in the navy and has always loved the sea and boats. Koller also describes her father as a tinkerer and a bit "crusty" on the surface with "a heart of gold beneath"—just like the elderly Mr. Jones in *The Last Voyage of the Misty Day*. The author decided to set this novel in Maine because it needed a remote, shoreline setting. Koller has vacationed on the Maine coast and has friends who live in the state.

Koller wrote her first novel in sixth grade. She continues telling stories to this day with fourteen-plus books for children and young adults published. Her books include the picture book *Mole & Shrew*, the chapter books *The Dragonling* and *The Falcon*, and a novel called *A Place to Call Home* about a family of homeless children.

Koller currently lives on ten acres on a mountain top in western Massachusetts with her husband, three nearly grown children, and two Labrador retrievers. Her hobbies include painting, gardening, walking, and making gingerbread houses. In addition to writing books for children and young adults, Koller enjoys reading them. Her husband teases her and asks if she will ever read a "grown up" book again. She answers, "Maybe, someday, but I hate to lower my standards."

FIRE IN THE WIND

AUTHOR: Betty Levin
AGE LEVEL / LENGTH: 10 years–adult / 138 pages
PUBLISHER / COPYRIGHT DATE: Greenwillow Books / 1995
FORMAT / ISBN: Hardcover / 0688142990; Paperback / 0688154956

The Yeadons are an extended family living in a farmhouse in Prescott Falls, Maine. Meg has become "the defender" of her younger brother, Paul, and her older cousin, Orin. She protects them from the bullies at school and in the community. Orin has always been simple-minded, unlike his intelligent older brother Champ, who was killed in World War II.

When a raging forest fire strikes Prescott Falls, a new family hero emerges. Orin saves his cousins Meg and Paul when they are caught in the middle of the fire. Meg is grateful that Orin saved their lives, but at the same time she worries that Orin may have been responsible for setting the fire in the first place. Meg is torn. She must decide whether to keep the fire incident a secret, further defending her cousin and keeping her promise to her late cousin, Champ, that she would always watch out for Orin, or to make the incident public, possibly placing Orin in trouble with his family and the law.

Fire in the Wind, an historical novel set in Maine during the forest fires of October 1947, explores the dynamics of the extended family and community as they learn to recognize everyone's value and place in the world. Levin's writing is powerful, especially during the fire scenes, and she provides her readers with a unique hero.

LEARNING ACTIVITIES

1. Further research Maine's devastating forest fires of October 1947. Check contemporary newspapers and town histories. Even though *Fire in the Wind* is fictional, it is based

on actual fires at that time. Where did the fires occur? How much damage did they do? How were the fires fought? Write a report about what you learn.

2. Rewrite a chapter from *Fire in the Wind* from a different character's perspective. How would the first chapter (when Meg defends her younger brother Paul on the playground at school) be written from Paul's point of view? Or how would the actual fire scene be written from Orin's point of view? Or how would Chapter 7 (when Orin returns from fighting fires) be written from Uncle Frank's perspective? Or select another chapter to rewrite.

3. Write your own disaster story. It may be fiction or based on a real event, such as a storm, fire, or accident. Work to make the disaster seem realistic and action-packed. You may wish to reread Chapters 19 and 20 in *Fire in the Wind* to notice how author Betty Levin made the fire scene seem true to life.

4. Research your family history. Does your family have any "heroes?" Interview family members and gather information. Then write an account of an act of heroism by your family's "hero." Share it with your family.

ABOUT THE AUTHOR

Betty Levin was born in New York City in 1927. She grew up in Bridgewater, Connecticut, in New York City, and in Washington, D.C. Levin fondly remembers summers spent on the family farm where she was surrounded by animals. Levin claims that she has been writing all her life, but that she did not have anything published until she started writing stories and books for her own children. Her first book was published in 1973; she has had close to twenty books published to date. Levin also has worked as a critic and teacher of children's literature. She currently lives in Lincoln, Massachusetts, where she works as a sheep farmer—selling wool and breed stock. She also trains Border Collies.

Many of Levin's novels have Maine connections and are based upon her experiences in the state. She summered in Castine for more that twenty years and then in Brooksville for sixteen years. She also has sailed in Maine frequently and has helped to gather sheep on Maine islands many times. For ten years, she did sheep dog demonstrations at the Common Ground Fair in southern Maine. A trilogy, that Levin wrote in the 1970, included the books *The Sword of Culann*, *A Griffin's Nest*, and *The Forespoken* (all out of print) and told the story of a girl from a Maine island who traveled back in time. In addition, a 1984 mystery/fantasy novel by Levin called *A Binding Spell* (out of print) told the story of a girl who moves to Maine and sees a ghost horse. Levin's more recent Maine books include *The Trouble with Gramary* (see page 151), *Brother Moose* (see page 151), *Gift Horse*, and *Island Bound* (see page 124).

ISLAND BOUND

AUTHOR: Betty Levin
AGE LEVEL / LENGTH: 10-16 years / 218 pages
PUBLISHER / COPYRIGHT DATE: Greenwillow Books (a div. of William Morrow) / 1997
FORMAT / ISBN: Hardcover / 0688152171

Because he accepted a dare, Chris Fossett is spending one week alone on deserted Fowlers Island off the coast of Maine. He must meet the challenge by sleeping outside, finding his own food, and refraining from contact with anyone else (the sheep who graze there and the island's ghost don't count!). But the island is not deserted after all. On its other side, Joellen Roth is determined to stay in the island's old lighthouse in order to escape from her father and his new girlfriend who are in a yacht moored offshore and who make daily visits to the island to do puffin research. Chris and Joellen discover each other and become reluctant partners as they try to free a sheep and its lamb from a large hole. They discover a mysterious object in the hole which leads them on an adventure as they attempt to solve the mystery of the island's ghost.

Author Betty Levin has crafted an intricate novel. She skillfully weaves interesting facts and information into the story. Readers will learn about survival skills, the puffin transplant project, sheep-raising on an island, and the story of Irish immigrants during the potato famine of the mid-1800s.

LEARNING ACTIVITIES

1. As you read *Island Bound,* make a list of Survival Do's and Don'ts. If someone was trying to survive in the wilderness for a week, what should they do and what should they not do? You may want to check nonfiction survival guides to gather more information for your lists.

2. In *Island Bound,* Chris Fossett learned the story behind some of his ancestors. Learn more about one of your ancestors, and then write a story loosely based upon that ancestor. For example, you might write a story about your grandmother who had a pet pig as a little girl. Or you might write a story about your great-grandfather who worked on the river log drives. Your story doesn't need to be strictly factual. Add fictional information as needed to help make your story more interesting and complete.

3. This book tells information about Irish immigrants during the potato famine of the mid-1800s. Select a different immigrant group and research their story. To gather information, use books, records at your local historical society, and interviews with immigrants or descendants of immigrants. Then prepare an oral report describing your selected immigrant's group experiences—where they came from, why they left, the conditions of their immigration journey, why they settled where they did, and so forth.

ABOUT THE AUTHOR

See information about Betty Levin on page 123.

FIND A STRANGER, SAY GOODBYE

AUTHOR: Lois Lowry
AGE LEVEL / LENGTH: 12-16 years / 192 pages
PUBLISHER / COPYRIGHT DATE: Houghton Mifflin (hardcover); Dell (paperback) / 1978
FORMAT / ISBN: Hardcover / 0395264596; Paperback / 0440205417

The primary setting of *Find a Stranger, Say Goodbye* is rural Maine. The story starts with eighteen-year-old Natalie Armstrong ready to graduate from Bradford High School. She is very attractive, does well academically, has an understanding and caring boyfriend, and has recently been accepted to one of the top medical schools in the country. What else could she ask for? She wants to find out the identity of her biological mother and meet her. Natalie's adoptive parents are understanding and loving, but the teenager has an inner need to find out her true identity and the reasons she was put up for adoption.

With a great amount of support from her adoptive parents, Natalie spends her eighteenth summer researching her past. Eventually, she uncovers her parents' identity and the reasons for her adoption. She also establishes a close relationship with her real grandfather, whom she has never known.

LEARNING ACTIVITIES

1. In *Find a Stranger, Say Goodbye*, Natalie researches her genealogy. Study your own family's past. Where did your family come from? Do you have any well-known ancestors? Interview your oldest living relative. Tape-record the interview and transcribe it.

2. Discuss the concept of "small town Maine." What are small towns in Maine like? How do they differ from Maine's larger towns or cities? Are there differences between small towns in northern Maine and those in other parts of the state?

3. The main character, Natalie, plans to attend a prominent medical school. Is this a typical dream or plan for a high school senior in Maine? Survey 25-50 high school seniors to learn what their postgraduate plans are. Make a chart or graph summarizing the results. Look for trends according to gender, socioeconomic status, parent's careers, etc.

ABOUT THE AUTHOR

As a child, Lois Lowry lived in Hawaii, Pennsylvania, and Japan. As an adult, from 1963 to 1979, she lived in three Maine locations—Portland, Falmouth, and Kennebunkport. During that time, she also graduated from the University of Southern Maine. Lowry studied writing in college and graduate school and then worked as a freelance journalist for magazines and newspapers, including the *Maine Times* and *Down East*. Since then she has become a full time writer of fiction for young people, with more than twenty books to her credit, including the well-known series about Anastasia Krupnik, and a recent chapter book entitled *Dog Keeper*.

Lowry's books have achieved both wide-spread popularity and critical acclaim. Her 1989 book *Number the Stars* and her 1994 novel *The Giver* were both Newbery Award winners. Two of Lowry's novels are set in Maine: *Find a Stranger, Say Goodbye* and *A Summer to Die* (see below). Both were written while Lowry lived in Maine. Lowry says that *Find a Stranger, Say Goodbye* is entirely fiction, although many of the locations are real. In 1981, it was made into a TV movie, under the title, *I Don't Know Who I Am*.

Lowry currently divides her time between her home in Cambridge, Massachusetts, and an 1815 farmhouse in rural New Hampshire. Some of Lowry's fiction has reflected upon death and loss. Lowry has had to deal with close personal losses several times—the death of her sister when she was a child (the inspiration for her first novel, *A Summer to Die*) and the 1995 accidental death of one of her adult children. These days, Lowry enjoys spending time with her other three adult children and her two grandchildren.

A SUMMER TO DIE

AUTHOR: Lois Lowry
AGE LEVEL / LENGTH: 12-16 years / 160 pages
PUBLISHER / COPYRIGHT DATE: Houghton Mifflin (hardcover); Bantam (paperback) / 1977
FORMAT / ISBN: Hardcover / 0395253381; Paperback / 0440219175

A Summer to Die is a book about the everyday life of two very different sisters. Meg wears glasses, loves photography, is insecure and a bit of a misfit. Her older sister, Molly, is blond, pretty, very popular, and sure of what she wants from life. When the family moves to a rural section of Maine so that their father can finish writing a book, Meg and Molly have to share a bedroom. They both hate it.

Meg retreats into her own world, taking photos and developing them in her own lab; she also makes friends with the eccentric old man down the road and the hippy couple next door. Molly becomes ill over the summer and has to go into the hospital. Meg feels guilty and somehow responsible for Molly's illness; at the same time, she is angry and jealous of all the attention Molly is getting. Meg's world is thrown into chaos when she realizes that her sister is going to die.

A *Summer to Die* was author Lois Lowry's first published book. She wrote the book in memory of her sister, Helen, who died when she was young. Lowry's own experience with the death of a sister helps to make A *Summer to Die* a poignant and believable novel.

LEARNING ACTIVITIES

1. Meg is a photography fanatic. Learn as much as you can about photography. Read books on the subject, interview a photographer, observe the developing process, and try your own hand at taking photos. Write a "how to" photography booklet for kids.

2. Sibling rivalry is the norm in most families. If you have a brother or sister, keep a journal of your own experiences. Write down your feelings and observations. How well do you get along with your siblings? Discuss your findings with a friend who has kept a similar journal. How are your experiences similar/different?

3. Death is a difficult subject. Collect poems, other writing, and/or pictures about death. Make a collage with your collection. Try to focus your collection on one aspect of death (e.g., death of pets, the funeral, grieving).

ABOUT THE AUTHOR

See information about Lois Lowry on page 125.

SKYLARK

AUTHOR: Patricia MacLachlan
AGE LEVEL / LENGTH: 7 years–adult / 96 pages
PUBLISHER / COPYRIGHT DATE: HarperCollins / 1994
FORMAT / ISBN: Hardcover / 0060233281; Paperback / 0064406229; Library Binding / 0060233338; Large Type Hardcover / 0614206200

Skylark is the sequel to the Newbery Award-winning book, *Sarah, Plain and Tall*. As this nineteenth-century story continues, Sarah, who is the mail-order bride to Jacob and the stepmother to his children Caleb and Anna, must face the dilemma of a drought on the prairie. Sarah is from Maine, where she could see the endless ocean and the land was green. But now she must face dust and fires.

As the drought worsens, Sarah leaves for Maine with Caleb and Anna. Jacob will remain behind to rebuild their burned-down barn and to wait for rain. The children enjoy Maine—the cool weather, swimming in the ocean, being spoiled by Sarah's aunts. But mostly they miss their Papa and worry that they will never be reunited as a family. The closing chapters of *Skylark* bring rain, hope, and a celebration for Sarah and her family.

Patricia MacLachlan is a masterful writer. She has created a simple yet profound novel. *Skylark* is told from the point of view of the daughter, Anna, including entries from her journal. The writing is poetic, and the story is deeply moving.

LEARNING ACTIVITIES

1. Why do you think Maine is special to Sarah? Do you think her new home on the prairie will ever be as special to her? Why or why not? Why is Maine special to you? Do you think you will ever find another state as special to you as your home state?

2. Write letters to a friend or relative who used to live in Maine, but now lives out of state. As you correspond, share differences in your day-to-day lives.

3. Write a follow-up chapter to *Skylark*. Make your chapter take place one year after *Skylark* ends. What will happen in your chapter? How will the family's lives be different?

ABOUT THE AUTHOR

Patricia MacLachlan was born in Cheyenne, Wyoming, and grew up in Minnesota. She was an only child and a voracious reader. After public school, she attended the University of Connecticut and then taught English.

As a board member of a family service agency, MacLachlan wrote articles on adoption and foster mothers. Since then, she has written both picture books and chapter books which reflect her strong concern for family relationships. Her 1985 Newbery-Medal-winning novel, *Sarah, Plain and Tall*, the story of a mail-order bride, was based on a true family incident. Both *Sarah, Plain and Tall* and *Skylark* have been made into TV movies. MacLachlan's other books include *Journey; Arthur, for the Very First Time; The Fact and Fictions of Minna Pratt*; and *Cassie Binegar*. MacLachlan currently lives in western Massachusetts.

TURN THE CUP AROUND

AUTHOR: Barbara Mariconda
AGE LEVEL / LENGTH: 10-14 years/148 pages
PUBLISHER / COPYRIGHT DATE: Delacorte Press / 1997
FORMAT / ISBN: Hardcover / 0385322925

Twelve-year-old Evie Johannson lives in Cozy Cove on the Maine coast with her two younger brothers and her grandmother. The children have lived with their grandmother for the past six years, since their mother died and their father went to a hospital too sick to see anyone. During the summer, Evie helps her grandmother with the guests at their bed-and-breakfast inn. This summer is different than past ones. They will have the same guests for the whole summer at their inn. Also, it is a summer filled with mystery. A white cat with one green eye and one blue eye suddenly appears. And Evie discovers paintings in a deep crevice between rocks along the coast. The mystery paintings are fresh and are washed away with each high tide; then a new, different painting appears. Evie's grandmother reads her fortune in her coffee grounds and warns her of a change in her life and of the dangers of getting tangled in a web. Evie also has a reoccurring nightmare that has haunted her for years—a nightmare that seems more real each time she dreams it.

In *Turn the Cup Around* author Barbara Mariconda has created a satisfying, fast-paced mystery and a memorable character. Young readers will find themselves rooting for Evie as she discovers the answers to the physical mysteries of the cat and the paintings, and to the emotional mysteries of her dreams and family secrets.

LEARNING ACTIVITIES

1. Write an epilogue to *Turn the Cup Around*. What will Evie's life be like a year after the story ends? Include information about her brothers, the cat, her father, her grandmother, and her new friend, Michael Elliott.

2. Evie takes art lessons in this novel. Julia, her art teacher, teaches her about using negative space when drawing. Have an art teacher show you how to draw using negative space. Then create a drawing of an object that is representative of you and your life (e.g. something you collect, a favorite keepsake) and draw it using negative space. How did your drawing turn out? Was it easy or hard to draw? Why? Did your drawing accurately represent your chosen object? Why or why not?

3. The white cat in *Turn the Cup Around* is reported to be deaf since he has eyes that are different colors. Do you think that is a true fact or a myth? Research cats to learn the answer and other interesting facts or myths about cats. You might inquire as to where cats originated, when cats were first tamed, who believed cats were sacred, who believed they were evil, and so forth. Write a report about cats.

ABOUT THE AUTHOR

Barbara Mariconda lives in Stratford, Connecticut, with her husband, two teenagers, and a pet poodle. She works as a writer, teacher, and musician. She enjoys traveling, especially to the Maine coast. She is the author of two early reader books about a city witch and a country witch, *Witch Way to the Country* and *Witch Way to the Beach*.

CROSSING THE STARLIGHT BRIDGE

AUTHOR: Alice Mead
AGE LEVEL / LENGTH: 8-12 years / 122 pages
PUBLISHER / COPYRIGHT DATE: Simon & Schuster / 1994
FORMAT / ISBN: Hardcover / 002765950X; Paperback / 068980105X

Nine-year-old Rayanne Sunipass finds her life suddenly thrown into turmoil. Her father unexpectedly leaves the family. Then when Rayanne's mother can no longer afford to support the two of them at their home on Two Rivers Island in Maine, they must leave for a nearby town and move in with Rayanne's grandmother. Rayanne doesn't want to leave behind her Penobscot heritage on the reservation, the river she loves, her best friend, and her pet rabbit.

This novel chronicles Rayanne's struggle to start a new life. With time, patience, and the help of her grandmother and her crayons, Rayanne begins to enjoy her new life. She draws upon her heritage, as revealed through her grandmother's stories, and her artistic talent, to create her own special niche.

Crossing the Starlight Bridge is a well-written, quickly-paced story. Rayanne's struggle to deal with her family crisis and her search for her identity are realistically portrayed. Young readers will end the book with a sense of hope about adjusting to change and learning to find essential answers from within oneself.

LEARNING ACTIVITIES

1. Look at the designs drawn at the end of each chapter in *Crossing the Starlight Bridge*. Author Alice Mead notes that these designs are important symbols to the Wabanaki people, including the Penobscot. How are the designs similar? Different? What patterns repeat in the designs? Can you guess the meaning of any of the designs? Research non-fiction books, including *The Wabanakis of Maine and the Maritimes: A Resource Book About the Penobscot, Passamaquoddy, Maliseet, Micmac, and Abenaki Indians* (see page 272), and try to learn more about Wabanaki drawings and designs. Copy or create designs following the same pattern.

2. Select one of the Native American stories told by Rayanne's grandmother in *Crossing the Starlight Bridge* (see pages 47-51 or pages 90-94). Turn the story you select into a picture book. Add illustrations to accompany the words. Then share this picture book with a younger relative or student at your school.

3. Discussion questions:

— How did Rayanne deal with her father leaving the family? Which coping strategies worked for her? Which strategies did not work? How had her attitude toward her father changed by the end of the book?

—What do you think Rayanne missed most about her home on Two Rivers Island? Have you ever moved? What did you miss most about the home you left behind?

—Besides Rayanne, who is your favorite character in *Crossing the Starlight Bridge?* Why?

—In what ways did Rayanne's grandmother help Rayanne to stay in touch with her Penobscot heritage? In what ways does your family help you to stay in touch with your heritage?

ABOUT THE AUTHOR

Alice Mead was born in New York, but she has lived in Maine for over twenty years. Mead has a bachelor's degree in English from Bryn Mawr College in Pennsylvania, a master's degree in elementary education from the University of Southern California, and a bachelor's degree in art education from the University of Southern Maine. She has worked as an art teacher and flute instructor in Maine schools, and has founded and directed preschools in Portland.

Mead has also founded her own press, called Loose Cannon Press, which has a goal of "publishing silent and unheard voices." Mead's books include *Crossing the Starlight Bridge, Walking the Edge* (see below), *Journey to Kosova, Junebug, Adem's Cross,* and *Giants of the Dawnland.*

Mead currently lives in Cumberland, Maine, with her husband, two teenage sons, and a student from the former Yugoslavia. Another important member of her "family" is an "aging, but strong-willed beagle lab named Tony." Mead enjoys gardening, photography, and painting landscapes.

WALKING THE EDGE

AUTHOR: Alice Mead
AGE LEVEL / LENGTH: 10-14 years / 190 pages
PUBLISHER / COPYRIGHT DATE: Albert Whitman & Co. / 1995
FORMAT / ISBN: Hardcover / 0807586498

Thirteen-year-old Scott Easton lives in the small coastal village of Prescott Harbor, in Down East Maine. Scott's life is in turmoil. His parents are divorced, but his abusive, alcoholic father keeps returning and stirring up trouble. Worse still, there are rumors around town that Scott's father is involved in something illegal. Scott's mother works at a factory shucking clams, but there's never enough money. Scott and his brother have only cereal and peanut butter sandwiches to eat most days. Also, Scott and his best friend, his only friend, have grown apart. Scott feels frustrated; even more, he feels an intense anger that he has never known before, an anger that scares him.

As Scott struggles to deal with his problems, he finds comfort and security from two sources—from his close relationship with his grandfather and from his involvement in a new 4-H project at school (a project to raise clams for restocking the bay). The more Scott's world seems to fall apart, then the more he "throws himself" at his grandfather and into the clam project. But even his two sources of security begin to fail him. As Scott works long weekend hours clamming and lobstering side by side with his grandfather, he notices signs that his grandfather is not well. And it appears that the clam project—which Scott has worked many hours to develop, and which has taught him so much—will end abruptly due to complaints from the community. Scott won't even have a chance to plant the clams he's worked so hard to raise.

But as life seems to become more unfair, Scott looks within himself for answers. Scott knows that he cannot give up the project he loves without a fight. And in the end, Scott wins that fight through his own resourcefulness.

Alice Mead has created a unique and convincing Maine novel. She visits the not-so-glamorous-but-still-very-real Maine issues of poverty, abuse, the struggle to make a living in Down East Maine, and the tendency of small towns to be set in their ways.

LEARNING ACTIVITIES

1. Beals Island, in Washington County, Maine, is the town that was used as the basis for Prescott Harbor. Write to or plan a visit to the Clam Hatchery on Beals Island. Learn all you can about how a clam hatchery works. How do they raise juvenile clams? How do they "plant" the clams they raise? Where is the best place to stock clams? How many clams that are raised actually survive? Write a report about what you learn.

2. Scott Easton was so poor that he often was hungry. Plan a project to raise money and/or food donations for your local food cupboard. You might hold a variety show with the price of admission being a food item. Or you might start a group penny collection for a month with the money raised going toward food for the food cupboard. Or develop other possible fund-raising ideas. Work hard and do what you can—every little bit helps.

3. Invite a local law enforcement official to speak at your school about illegal drug activity in your area. How do drugs get into your area (by boat, train, plane)? Is drug activity decreasing or increasing in your area? How do law enforcement officials "catch" drug dealers? What are the penalties and sentences for drug conviction in the state? After the talk, create an informational pamphlet using your research.

4. Reread some sections of *Walking the Edge* that depict Scott when he is angry. How does author Alice Mead let us know he is angry? What are his words? His actions? Write a description of a time that you became angry.

ABOUT THE AUTHOR

See information about Alice Mead on page 131.

SONGS IN THE SILENCE

AUTHOR: Catherine Frey Murphy
AGE LEVEL / LENGTH: 8-14 years / 188 pages
PUBLISHER / COPYRIGHT DATE: Macmillan Publishing Co.; available from Catherine Frey Murphy / 1994
FORMAT / ISBN: Hardcover / 0027677303

Eleven-year-old Hallie blames herself for her younger brother Josh's injury. If she had acted quicker when the barbecue grill overturned and caught Josh's pants on fire, his injuries would not have been as serious. But instead she froze. And now Josh is in the hospital, and Hallie can't even visit him because of a rule that no one under twelve is allowed.

One morning after the accident, Hallie's guilt and depression leads her out into the ocean in her neighbor's skiff. She wants to be completely alone and have a chance to cry. But instead, she becomes lost in a thick fog and finds herself caught between waves and rocks. The skiff overturns and Hallie is thrown into the freezing ocean waters. She flounders under the dark ocean waters and nearly drowns when, out of nowhere, a soothing voice coaches her to safety. Hallie is mystified. Whose voice could that have been? When the voice speaks to her again, she realizes it is the voice of a pilot whale, Melae. A whale had saved her life! Hallie's and Melae's relationship develops as Melae helps Hallie to understand and cope with her brother's injuries. When Melae seeks Hallie's help for an injured whale named Globo, Hallie reaches deep inside herself and finds strength and courage that she never knew she had.

Catherine Frey Murphy has written a fascinating and insightful book with well-developed characters. Garnet Island is modeled after Peaks Island in Casco Bay.

LEARNING ACTIVITIES

1. Write a position paper. A position paper is where you take a stand on an issue. Your paper may either be called "Why I Believe in Animal-Human Communication" or "Why

I Do Not Believe in Animal-Human Communication." Be sure to support your rationale. Why do you believe the way you do?

2. Research pilot whales. What do they eat? Where do they live throughout the year? How big are they? What sounds do they make? What is their life expectancy? Write a report about the information you find, and create a cover with a drawing of a pilot whale.

3. In *Songs in the Silence,* Hallie blames herself for her brother's injury. Do you think she was really to blame? Why or why not? Think of something you have blamed yourself for. Write about that experience—the details, your feelings, what others said. Do you still think you were to blame for the situation? Why or why not?

ABOUT THE AUTHOR

Catherine Frey Murphy spent her early childhood in the Southern Tier of New York state. She says that she has been writing ever since she learned to read. She wrote her first book in second grade. She has a bachelor's degree in art and elementary education, and she has had her illustrations as well as her writing published. She is also the author of *Alice Dodd and the Spirit of Truth.* Murphy lived in Maine from 1980 to 1986 and graduated from the University of Maine Law School.

Her college roommate was Anne Sibley O'Brien, another Maine children's author and illustrator (see page 265). The two were also neighbors on Peaks Island. Murphy first got the idea for *Songs in the Silence* while commuting on the daily ferry between Peaks and Portland. For several weeks, a pod of deep-sea pilot whales stayed in Portland Harbor. Murphy vividly recalls that experience:

> I could see the whales from the windows of my island home, and each day, the captain would steer close enough to the whales so that we ferry passengers could lean over the rail and gaze into their joyful, mystifying faces. I wondered so intensely what had brought those whales into the harbor, what they thought about, what they cared about, that in time, the story of a Maine island girl who discovers that she can communicate with a pilot whale began to take shape in my mind.

Murphy currently lives with her husband and three children on a dairy farm in upstate New York, with 140 Jersey cows, chickens, goats, and "far too many barn cats." Even though Murphy no longer lives in Maine, she claims that it will "always be a spiritual home" for her. Her oldest child was born in Portland, she returns to the state to visit friends as often as possible, and she believes that she will write more Maine stories in the future.

DANCING ON THE TABLE

AUTHOR: Liza Ketchum Murrow / ILLUSTRATOR: Ronald Himler
AGE LEVEL / LENGTH: 8-12 years / 120 pages
PUBLISHER / COPYRIGHT DATE: Minstrel Pocket (Simon & Schuster) / 1990
FORMAT / ISBN: Paperback / 0671738291

Jenny has always had a special relationship with her grandmother, Nana. They share special mischief days together exploring the coast of their Maine island. But things are about to change: Nana announces her plans to get married. Jenny doesn't like the idea of her grandmother getting married, she doesn't like her grandmother's fiance, but most of all she doesn't like the fact that Nana will move away to New York after the wedding.

Jenny is the flower girl in the wedding, and she does everything in her power to wreck the celebration. She even gets some help from a hurricane that strikes the island. In the end, after a nearly tragic accident, Jenny rediscovers her love for her grandmother.

LEARNING ACTIVITIES

1. As with the wedding in *Dancing on the Table*, special events in Maine are often affected by the weather. Recollect a time when the weather influenced an event in which you were involved. Write a short story or picture book about that time.

2. Nana's wedding is a lively family affair. What wedding customs and traditions are there in your family? Look at family photos; and interview parents, grandparents, and other relatives about family weddings. What food was served? What did the bride and groom wear? What music was played? Compare your family's celebrations with those of others.

3. Discussion questions:

   —Do you think Jenny is justified in trying to jinx her grandmother's wedding? Why or why not?
   —Jenny believes a rabbit's foot will bring her luck and fulfill her wishes. Do you think it does? What, if any, superstitions do you believe in?
   —Jenny had to be brave to leave the car during the hurricane. Would you have been brave in the same situation? Describe a time when you acted bravely.

ABOUT THE AUTHOR

Liza Ketchum Murrow, who currently goes by the name of Liza Ketchum (young fans should look for new books by this author under her Ketchum name), started writing when she was seven-years-old. She created tiny stapled books with crayons and construction paper. She even recalls writing some of her stories under the covers with a flashlight when she was supposed to be asleep. In eighth grade, Ketchum made a career decision to become a writer. She studied writing in college, but then became a teacher and only had time to write magazine articles. Finally in 1984, Ketchum began to write full-time; her first novel, *West Against the Wind*, was published in 1987. Since then, she has had more than ten books published, including *Allergic to My Family*, *Twelve Days in August*, *The Gold Rush*, and *Blue Coyote*. Ketchum claims that she does more *re*writing than writing and that it takes her six to nine months to complete a novel. She also teaches fiction writing at a Boston college and makes school visits as an author.

Ketchum tells the story behind her two novels set in Maine. She has close friends on Orr's Island and in Kezar Falls. Visits with these friends helped to shape both novels. For *Dancing on the Table*, Ketchum had been caring for her friend's house on Orr's Island when it struck her that a Maine island would be the perfect setting for this novel which was based upon a real event in the author's life. Ketchum's own grandmother had remarried when she was a little girl and had left for the honeymoon during a violent storm. Ketchum realized that a hurricane on a Maine island would be much "scarier and more dramatic"—perfect for *Dancing on the Table*. The idea for her other Maine novel, *The Ghost of Lost Island* (see below), came about when she helped a friend care for his sheep on Richmond Island. Ketchum's friend told a spooky story by lantern light about a young woman who drowned trying to cross the breakwater during the incoming tide. These sheep experiences and the "ghost" made their way into Ketchum's *The Ghost of Lost Island*.

Ketchum currently lives in Acton, Massachusetts, with her husband. She has two grown sons. Her hobbies include playing the piano, swimming, hiking, biking, canoeing, camping, and visiting art galleries.

THE GHOST OF LOST ISLAND

AUTHOR: Liza Ketchum Murrow
AGE LEVEL / LENGTH: 8-12 years / 165 pages
PUBLISHER / COPYRIGHT DATE: Holiday House (hardcover); Simon & Schuster (paperback) / 1991
FORMAT / ISBN: Hardcover / 0823408744; Paperback / 0671753681

For many years Gabe O'Day's grandfather has raised sheep on deserted and haunted "Lost Island" off the coast of Maine. This winter Gabe will accompany his grandfather to the island to help him shear the sheep. Gabe cannot be happier; he will finally be able to prove to everyone that he is mature and responsible.

While rounding up the sheep on the island, Gabe and his sister, Ginny, come face to face with the real living ghost of Lost Island, Delia Simpson. Delia had been a milkmaid and was rumored to have drowned many years before. As Gabe and his sister learn more about Delia, a special bond of friendship grows between them, a bond so strong that the children risk their lives helping the "ghost" woman to escape from the island before their grandfather or anyone else finds out about her.

Liza Ketchum Murrow has written a fast-paced mystery. Young readers will eagerly read to learn the secret of the island's "ghost." At the same time they will learn about raising and shearing sheep; and they will get caught up in the believable sibling rivalry between Gabe and Ginny.

LEARNING ACTIVITIES

1. Learn about sheep-shearing. Visit a sheep farm or an agricultural fair while sheep are being sheared. Watch all the steps and compare them to those described in *The Ghost of Lost Island*. Write and illustrate a simple "How to Shear a Sheep" booklet.

2. Delia is homeless, the fate of a number of Mainers today. Contact and visit a local homeless shelter or soup kitchen. Consider doing some volunteer work, such as helping to prepare or serve meals. Keep a journal of your experiences.

3. Study the glossary at the back of *The Ghost of Lost Island*, which includes dog commands and special terms related to sheep-shearing. Many professions and hobbies have a special vocabulary. Select a hobby or interest (e.g., snowmobiling, canning vegetables, building models, bird-watching) and create a glossary for that topic.

4. Simplify the story of *The Ghost of Lost Island*. Rewrite it, add illustrations, and turn it into a picture book. Then share it with younger children.

5. Discussion questions:

> —In *The Ghost of Lost Island*, Gabe has to overcome his fear of darkness. Discuss fears. What purpose do they serve? Have you ever overcome a fear? How?
> —Gabe and Ginny compete with each other for privileges and adult attention. Is there any sibling rivalry in your family? Describe and try to understand the experience of sibling rivalry
> —Does your community have any ghost stories? What are they? Are the stories based on fact or legend? How did they get started?

ABOUT THE AUTHOR

See information about Liza Ketchum Murrow on page 135.

BECKY'S ISLAND

AUTHOR: Elisabeth Ogilvie
AGE LEVEL / LENGTH: 12-16 years / 187 pages
PUBLISHER / COPYRIGHT DATE: Amereon House / 1961
FORMAT / ISBN: Hardcover / 0884113264

Becky's Island tells the story of Vicky Conrad. The story is set in the early 1900s. Vicky and her extended family (aunts, uncles, cousins) come from Massachusetts to the Maine coast for a summer vacation at the family cottage. Vicky is depressed. She's not young enough to play with the little children, and her teen cousins seem to be outgrowing her, caring only for affairs of the heart. She misses the days when they were younger, foolish, and carefree.

Vicky mostly keeps to herself. During one of her lone ventures in a dory, she discovers two abandoned and scared children on a deserted island. Vicky returns the children to their home on Becky's Island, a place rumored to be inhabited by convicts and crazy people. Vicky believes that her good deed is a one-time occurrence, but she gets overwhelmed by the poverty and neediness of the people on Becky's Island, and spends the rest of the summer secretly helping them. Among other things, she teaches the children how to read and write. Finally, against great odds, Vicky gets a school built on the island.

Becky's Island is based on Maine history. In the early 1900s there was an island called Malaga, near Harpswell, known for its odd population—with intermarriages, people who had abandoned ships, and people of different races. The people of Malaga were reported to be very poor. No help was offered to these people until a couple from Massachusetts who summered in Maine began to visit the island to teach the children Sunday school. Sunday school turned into the teaching of reading and writing. Eventually, the out-of-staters petitioned the state to help the people of Malaga. Author Elisabeth Ogilvie found this history intriguing and thought it would be fun to have a teenager save the island. Thus *Becky's Island* was born.

LEARNING ACTIVITIES

1. Discussion questions:

    —Who's your favorite character in *Becky's Island*, and why?
    —How does Vicky change during the course of the story?

—Do you know anyone like Vicky, Georgie, Luke, King Harry, or Fraustino?

—What are some of the differences between life in Maine in the early 1900s and now? How do vacations, clothing, poverty, and relationships (family, peer, romantic) differ between then and now?

2. Learn about poverty in your community. Contact local officials to learn about what assistance and services are available for poor people. With adult supervision, plan and carry out a "poverty" project. Possible activities could include working in the local soup kitchen, having a fundraiser for the Red Cross, or providing childcare for low-income parents so that they can go back to school.

3. Interview retired teachers and learn what schools were like in the early 1900s. Then reenact a school day from that time. You may wish to plan such a day for younger children at an elementary school.

ABOUT THE AUTHOR

In 1917, Elisabeth Ogilvie was born in Boston. She grew up in Massachusetts, but her Maine connections began before she was born when her mother, as a young child, visited Criehaven Island off the coast of Maine. As an adult, Ogilivie's mother continued to bring her children to Crichaven.

Ogilvie reports that she always liked to create stories and that when she was a young child her mother claimed that Ogilvie walked around telling herself stories. Ogilvie found a writing role-model in her mother who wrote poems, plays, and sketches "on the spur of the moment" for special family and school occasions.

At the age of fifteen, Ogilvie decided to become a writer. She describes it as a courageous decision since it was the middle of the Great Depression. She sold her first story when she was nineteen; and her first novel, *High Tide at Noon*, was published in 1944, the year she moved to Maine. Since then she has written more than forty books for adults and young people. The publishing company Amereon House continues to make some of Ogilvie's books available. They produce very small press runs of books and will go to press once they receive enough orders (at times as little as 30 or 50 books). Contact Amereon House (see page 312) for a complete listing of Ogilvie's books and their availability.

Ogilvie continues to write every day. She claims, "I'm a morning writer, and I feel deprived if anything keeps me away from a few hours of work." The author says that she had no formal education after high school, but that her high school gave her a good start to writing because they expected "everyone to write *something*, correct in spelling and grammar." Since then, Ogilvie claims that she's educated herself—"a process which is still going on."

Ogilvie continues to split her time between summer island life and her winter home in Cushing, Maine. She describes herself as a "professional" aunt. She has supported a dozen children through the Foster Parents' Plan. Her hobbies include walking, rowing, island-living, listening to music, and writing for fun in between book contracts.

ISLAND IN THE BAY

AUTHOR: Dorothy Simpson
AGE LEVEL / LENGTH: 12 years–adult / 192 pages
PUBLISHER / COPYRIGHT DATE: Blackberry Books / 1956 (original); 1993 (reprint)
FORMAT / ISBN: Paperback / 0942396626

Sixteen-year-old Linn Robertson has something to prove. He must prove that he has a right to stay on Lee's Island. Linn lives with his Grampa Swenson on this lobstering island 25 miles off the coast of Maine. But his grandfather kicks him out of the house after a disagreement, and Linn must try to fend for himself. Linn's luck keeps getting worse. Someone is sabotaging his lobster traps so that he cannot earn any money, and then he is falsely accused of stealing rope. The residents spread the word that there is no room on their island for a thief.

But when it seems that Linn is defeated and must leave, he reaches inside himself and discovers new-found strength and courage. Linn knows that he must continue living and lobstering on Lee's Island—it's the only happiness he has ever known. With the help and support of a neighborhood girl and a few other friends, Linn devises a plan to catch the person sabotaging him. His plan succeeds, and Linn proves to himself, his grandfather, and the community that he is a mature and valuable resident of Lee's Island.

Dorothy Simpson has created a marvelous coming-of-age Maine novel. Even though *Island in the Bay* was originally published forty years ago, its theme of learning to depend upon oneself still rings true for today's readers. Simpson's characters are fully realized, her description of island life is richly detailed, and her plot is well-paced and engaging.

LEARNING ACTIVITIES

1. Discussion questions:

—Do you think Linn's grandfather was too hard on him? Why or why not?
—What do you think was the most important lesson that Linn Robertson learned in the story? Support your answer.
—Do you believe that the islanders should give bait to those who need it? What about food? Shelter?

—Linn went into debt to get a new boat so that he could trap more lobsters and earn more money. But Linn's grandfather believed that any kind of debt was an evil mistake; he thought that one should buy something *only* when one had saved enough for it. Who do you believe is right, and why? Why do you feel some people feel differently than you do? —Project into the future for Linn. One year later, after the time this novel is finished, what do you believe Linn's relationship with his grandfather will be like? What about his relationship with Randy Mears? With Polly Armstrong?

2. Write a character analysis of one of the characters from *Island in the Bay*. Explain what motivated your selected character. Describe how your character changed during the course of the novel. Support your observations with specific quotes and details from the novel.

3. Linn Robertson and Randy Mears had a disagreement that grew and grew. Think of a disagreement that you have had with someone. Write about that disagreement from two points of view—from your point of view and from the viewpoint of the person you disagreed with. How difficult was it for you to consider the other person's point of view?

ABOUT THE AUTHOR

Dorothy Simpson grew up on Criehaven Island off the coast of Maine. As the oldest of eleven children, Simpson would entertain her younger brothers and sisters with stories that they could all act out. Her stories often featured lobstering since all of her male relatives were lobstermen. In fact, her book, *Island in the Bay*, is based upon the relationship between one of Simpson's brothers and their Norwegian grandfather. Four of Simpson's other books—*The Honest Dollar*, *A Lesson for Jamie*, *A Matter of Pride*, and *New Horizon*—tell the continuing story of one Maine island girl; Simpson says they are "partly biographical."

Simpson enjoys island life in the summer and spends winters on the mainland in Cushing, Maine. Her hobbies include reading and listening to music. Simpson continues to write but says, "Times having changed, my last few manuscripts have met with some enthusiasm; but those 'enthusiastic' people are always outnumbered! Making trap-heads (for lobster traps) pays a lot better than unpublished manuscripts."

THE SIGN OF THE BEAVER

AUTHOR: Elizabeth George Speare
AGE LEVEL / LENGTH: 8-14 years / 144 pages
PUBLISHER / COPYRIGHT DATE: Houghton Mifflin (hardcover); Dell (paperback) / 1983
FORMAT / ISBN: Hardcover / 0395338905; Paperback / 0440227305; Vinyl Bound Braille Edition / 1569565635
AWARDS: Newbery Honor Book, 1984

Twelve-year-old Matt is left alone in the Maine wilderness in the late 1700s, while his father returns to Massachusetts to bring the rest of the family back to their new home. Matt feels he can handle himself and the responsibility of watching over the new family home and their crops. One day, while trying to gather honey from a tree, Matt is attacked by swarms of bees. Luckily he is rescued by an Indian chief and his grandson, Attean.

To show his appreciation, Matt agrees to teach Attean the "white man's worlds and ways." As they grow to know each other, Matt and Attean become close friends and teach each other the ways of their own culture. They become so close that when Matt's family fails to return on schedule, he must decide whether to join Attean's family or continue to live alone.

The Sign of the Beaver is a well-written, fast-paced adventure story which brings history to life for young readers. It's a perfect read-aloud for younger readers or a terrific discussion novel for older readers.

LEARNING ACTIVITIES

1. Plan a visit to an Indian reservation in Maine, such as the Passamaquoddy reservation in Princeton or the Penobscot reservation in Old Town. Observe and discuss Native American customs, school, daily living, and work. What traditions are still continuing? Which have changed? Why?

2. Research trapping. How are different animals trapped? What equipment is used? What are the laws for trapping? How has trapping changed over the years? Interview someone who is familiar with trapping.

3. Read all or part of Daniel Defoe's *Robinson Crusoe,* which was published in 1719. Why do you think this book was so interesting to Matt and Attean? What makes *Robinson Crusoe* a book that has remained popular for almost 300 years?

4. Research the beaver. Where and how does it live? What does it eat? What does it do in the winter? Are there different kinds of beavers? How large do they grow? Create a display or a simple informational pamphlet about what you learn.

ABOUT THE AUTHOR

Elizabeth George Speare was born in 1908. She was raised in Melrose, Massachusetts. She attended Smith College and Boston University and worked as a high school English teacher. Speare spent her whole life in New England and began to write as her children grew older. She wrote articles for *Woman's Day* and *Better Homes and Gardens* magazines. Her first novel, *Calico Captive*, based upon an historical diary, was published in 1957. Speare's strong interest in history continued to influence her writing, including her two Newbery Medal-winning books, *The Witch of Blackbird Pond* and *The Bronze Bow*. More than twenty years later, Speare's historical novel, *The Sign of the Beaver*, was selected as a Newbery Honor book. In 1989, Speare won the Laura Ingalls Wilder Award in recognition of her complete body of work. Speare died in November 1994.

HUGH PINE

AUTHOR: Janwillem van de Wetering / ILLUSTRATOR: Lynn Munsinger
AGE LEVEL / LENGTH: 8-12 years / 96 pages
PUBLISHER / COPYRIGHT DATE: Morrow / 1980
FORMAT / ISBN: Paperback / 0688117996 (recently out of print); Large Type Paperback / 0614095883

Hugh Pine is an almost-human porcupine with strong Maine characteristics, such as an abundance of common sense, a strong desire to be left alone, and slow-moving, slow-talking mannerisms. He lives in Sorry (Surry), near Rotworth (Ellsworth). Hugh solves his porcupine problem of being an easy target for cars on the road by donning a floppy red hat and overcoat and teaching himself to walk upright. People driving-by think he's an old man, so they slow down and pass him carefully. Unfortunately, the other porcupines in the woods are not able to learn Hugh Pine's "human tricks," so they ask him to help them think of a way to protect themselves from getting "smashed" on the roads.

Hugh Pine seeks the help of a real human, Mr. McTosh, who is a short, fat, scruffy man who happens to look a lot like a porcupine. After a well-intentioned, but unsuccessful attempt by Mr. McTosh to save the porcupines, Hugh Pine comes up with his own simple but clever solution. In the end, all is well and the porcupines are saved.

LEARNING ACTIVITIES

1. While reading *Hugh Pine*, jot down porcupine facts mentioned in the text, such as that they eat mushrooms, sleep in trees, cannot run, and have orange teeth. Using nonfiction books about porcupines, try to verify as many of these facts as possible.

2. Select another Maine animal and make a list of its greatest dangers or problems. Then think of creative ways to solve them.

3. On pages 10 and 11 of *Hugh Pine*, the reader learns how Hugh Pine gets his name. Write down the names of family and friends' pets, and explain how they were named.

4. Hugh Pine looks a lot like a person; Mr. McTosh looks a lot like a porcupine. Cut pictures of people and animals out of magazines. Paste them onto a paper and then add details to make the humans look like animals and vice versa.

ABOUT THE AUTHOR

Janwillem van de Wetering was born in Holland in 1931, the youngest of six children. He was living in Rotterdam when the German military bombed and captured the city during World War II. He went to business college and became a world traveler living in South Africa, London, and Japan. In his first children's book, *Little Owl,* he attempted to help children understand Buddhism. Van de Wetering now lives in Surry, Maine, and is the author of a series of detective novels for adults, as well as three Hugh Pine children's books: *Hugh Pine, Hugh Pine and the Good Place,* and *Hugh Pine and Something Else.* (These Hugh Pine books are currently out of print.)

TREE BY LEAF

AUTHOR: Cynthia Voigt
AGE LEVEL / LENGTH: 12 years–adult / 192 pages
PUBLISHER / COPYRIGHT DATE: Atheneum (hardcover); Fawcett (paper) / 1988
FORMAT / ISBN: Hardcover / 0689314035; Paperback / 0449703347

Set in 1920 on a peninsula along the Maine coast near Ellsworth, *Tree by Leaf* recounts a week in the life of twelve-year-old Clothilde Speer. Clothilde's life suddenly becomes very confused and complicated when her father, who has been away fighting in World War I, returns with injuries that have disfigured his face, making him look like a "monster." He refuses to be seen and shuts himself away in an old boathouse on the peninsula. Clothilde's older brother, Nate, deserts the family, running away to live with his grandfather. The family's servant girl, Lou, who is one of Clothilde's few friends, faces her own tragedy and must leave the state. And perhaps most upsetting of all, the family is considering selling Speer Point in order to have enough money to live.

Clothilde is overwhelmed. Speer Point was left to her personally when her great-aunt died. It is the one place where she finds comfort and solace. Speer Point is a part of her, and she doesn't want to give it up; but her opinion doesn't count—she's "only a child."

In order to cope with these struggles, Clothilde turns to nature. She spends hours observing the rocks, trees, clams, and seaweed. She talks to nature, and one day it seems that nature talks back to her. She expresses her wishes to it; and in return she is allowed to see nature in a new, wonder-filled way. When her wishes begin to come true, but in unexpected and unpleasant ways, Clothilde wonders if nature's voice has deceived her.

Cynthia Voigt's *Tree by Leaf* might seem like a difficult story for some young readers because of its psychological nature and mystical happenings, but the book is worth the work. Young readers who stick with the novel will enjoy sharing the rewards of Clothilde's struggle and survival.

LEARNING ACTIVITIES

1. In *Tree by Leaf*, Clothilde retreats to her peninsula, Speer Point, when life's demands become too great. Speer Point is her get-away haven. Where do you go to get away? What does your haven look, sound, feel, and smell like? Try to capture the essence of this favorite place in a creative way, through poetry, music, a drawing, or a dance.

2. Discussion questions:

> —In *Tree by Leaf*, Clothilde asks the "Voice" to grant her wishes. If you could retreat to the magical world of fairy tales and be granted three wishes, what would your wishes be, and why?
> —In *Tree by Leaf*, Clothilde blames herself when things start to go wrong. Do you think she's really to blame? Why or why not? Have you ever blamed yourself for something? If so, what and why? Were you really to blame?
> —As you read *Tree by Leaf*, what do you learn about the roles of women and children back in 1920? How have these roles changed?

3. Clothilde's father is disfigured during World War I. His reaction to his handicap is strong and negative. How are physically handicapped people treated today? How do they perceive themselves? Arrange to interview several physically-challenged people. With their permission, arrange to audiotape or videotape the interviews. Ask them to explain their handicap and others' reactions to them. Invite them to share their suggestions on how people can improve their relationships with physically-challenged people.

4. In the epilogue of *Tree by Leaf*, Clothilde is an elderly lady looking back on her childhood. As she reminisces about her early life, some of its mystery is lost. Most of the unknowns and curiosities of her childhood suddenly make sense—they fit into the giant jigsaw puzzle of her life. Write your own epilogue. Pretend you're an old person looking back at your childhood. In your mind, make your childhood make sense as a piece of the giant jigsaw puzzle of your life.

ABOUT THE AUTHOR

Cynthia Voigt was born in Boston, Massachusetts, and grew up in Connecticut. She decided in ninth grade that she wanted to become a writer. After attending boarding school and college, she worked at an advertising agency and also worked toward her teaching accreditation. While teaching fifth graders in Annapolis, Maryland, Voigt discovered children's literature and began to write. Since then, Voigt has written more than twenty novels for young people, including the popular and critically-acclaimed series of books about the Tillerman family (*Homecoming*; *Dicey's Song*, which won the Newbery Medal; *A Solitary Blue*, a Newbery Honor Book; *The Runner*; and *Seventeen Against the Dealer*). While Voigt's earlier books are set in Maryland, since moving to coastal Maine, Voigt has written several novels set in her new "home" state, including *Tree by Leaf* and *The Vandemark Mummy* (see below). Voigt also says that much of the natural setting for her fantasy novel *On Fortune's Wheel* is based upon Maine. Two of Voigt's most recent books are *Bad Girls* and its sequel, *Bad, Badder, Baddest*.

Voigt currently lives in Deer Isle, Maine, with her husband and two pets, Bongo and Tazzy. When not writing, she enjoys playing tennis, going for walks, and reading.

THE VANDEMARK MUMMY

AUTHOR: Cynthia Voigt
AGE LEVEL / LENGTH: 10-14 years / 208 pages
PUBLISHER / COPYRIGHT DATE: Atheneum (div. of Simon & Schuster)(hardcover); Fawcett (paper) / 1991
FORMAT / ISBN: Hardcover / 0689314760; Paperback / 0449704173

Sam Hall is a new instructor at Vandemark College in Portland, Maine. His job includes being the curator of an Egyptian collection recently donated to the college. The collection, complete with mummy, seems to bring a curse to Hall and his two children, twelve-year-old Phineas and fifteen-year-old Althea. First the mummy is stolen, then it is mysteriously returned, and finally Althea disappears. Phineas plays sleuth in an attempt to locate his sister.

The Vandemark Mummy also deals with complicated family relationships. The mother of Phineas and Althea is in Portland, Oregon, working at a new job. Even though it was a family decision to live apart, the children still feel abandoned and worry that their parents might get a divorce. Throughout the mystery of the mummy, Phineas and Althea grow closer to each other and realize that family is what is most important—even if their family structure is a bit unusual.

LEARNING ACTIVITIES

1. Universities and colleges often are the benefactors of special gifts or collections. Visit the nearest college to you and view one of their special collections. Learn as much as possible about it. How was it acquired? What restrictions are there on the collection and its use?

2. Some of the characters in *The Vandemark Mummy* try to play down Althea's disappearance—after all, they say, this is Maine, not Boston or New York City. Learn what actual crimes occur in your community. Interview your local police chief or sheriff and learn which crimes occur most often, which ones are on the rise, which are decreasing, etc. Combine this information into a crime profile for your community, complete with graphs and helpful "crime prevention" tips for citizens.

3. *The Vandemark Mummy* is fiction, but Maine has its own share of real-life mysteries. Interview a reporter, police officer, or historian to learn about a real Maine mystery. Research the mystery in newspaper archives. If possible, interview someone who has knowledge of the event. Write a summary of the mystery, providing your own solutions based on what is known.

ABOUT THE AUTHOR

See information about Cynthia Voigt on page 146.

CHARLOTTE'S WEB

AUTHOR: E. B. White / ILLUSTRATOR: Garth Williams
AGE LEVEL / LENGTH: 8-12 years / 188 pages
PUBLISHER / COPYRIGHT DATE: HarperCollins / 1952
FORMAT / ISBN: Hardcover / 0318529319; Paperback / 0061070106; Large Type Hardcover / 0060263857
AWARDS: Newbery Honor Book, 1953

In *Charlotte's Web*, E.B. White personifies the animals on his North Brooklin, Maine, saltwater farm. The novel traces the life of Wilbur, the pig. A runt at birth, Wilber is saved from an early death by Fern, a farm girl who believes all life should be given a chance.

After Wilbur's initial brush with death, he lives happily for a time in the barn getting fatter and fatter. Wilbur makes friends with the other animals in the barn; but his special, best friend is Charlotte, a spider. Once the animals realize Wilbur is being fattened for slaughter, Charlotte comes up with a plan to save her best friend. She weaves webbed messages about Wilbur. Wilbur becomes a celebrity in the neighborhood and beyond as he is shown at the county fair (modeled after the Blue Hill Fair in Maine). A weak Charlotte weaves one last heroic message at the fair to save her friend.

E.B. White's *Charlotte's Web* has been described as one of literature's greatest books (for children and adults). White creates memorable characters, such as wise, maternal Charlotte the spider and greedy, scrounging Templeton the rat. Readers cannot help but cheer and cry during this amazing novel of friendship and death.

LEARNING ACTIVITIES

1. If one were to judge from his children's books alone, E.B. White seems to have enjoyed animals more than people. Reread sections of *Charlotte's Web*, or White's other two children's books, *Stuart Little* and *The Trumpet of the Swan*. How does White express his love and respect for nature and animals in his books? What words does he use?

2. If possible, visit the area of Maine where E.B. White lived, Brooklin. Go to the Brooklin Public Library. How does the library pay tribute to E.B. White? Visit the local schools, town hall, stores, etc. What signs can you find that E.B. White was an important part of the town?

3. Select one animal from *Charlotte's Web* (e.g., pig, sheep, rat, goose, spider). Research that animal, using nonfiction books and firsthand observations, if possible. Then write a factual report about your chosen animal.

ABOUT THE AUTHOR

E.B. White—that is, Elwyn Brooks White—was born on July 11, 1899, in Mount Vernon, New York, and died on October 1, 1985, in North Brooklin, Maine. White grew up in New York, the youngest of six children. His Maine connections began as a child when his family summered on the Belgrade Lakes. He attended Cornell University and was the editor of the college newspaper. After working as a newspaper journalist for a time, White found his niche as a columnist for the *New Yorker* magazine. He also wrote books of essays and poetry. His writing was known for its clear, witty, and personal style.

Children know E.B. White for his three children's books: *Stuart Little* (1945), *Charlotte's Web* (1952), and *The Trumpet of the Swan* (1970). White moved to a farm in North Brooklin, Maine, in 1938; the next year he began writing *Stuart Little*. All three of his children's books were written on his Maine farm. *Charlotte's Web* grew out of White's experiences with raising pigs and a "magical" time when he saw a spider spin a web. It took White three years to write and revise *Charlotte's Web*, which was selected as a Newbery Honor book in 1953. White received the Presidential Medal of Freedom in 1963 and a Pulitzer Prize special citation in 1978, both in honor of the quality and far-reaching impact of White's total body of writing.

REBECCA OF SUNNYBROOK FARM

AUTHOR: Kate Douglas Wiggin
AGE LEVEL / LENGTH: 12 years–adult / 292 pages
PUBLISHER / COPYRIGHT DATE: William Morrow & Co. (hardcover); Signet
Classics/Penguin (paperback); also published by many other publishers / 1903
FORMAT / ISBN: Hardcover / 0688134815; Paperback / 0140367594

Rebecca of Sunnybrook Farm, by Kate Douglas Wiggin, is a classic. First published in 1903, it tells the story of Rebecca Randall, who grew up (on a Maine farm called Sunnybrook) with her mother and her six brothers and sisters. But when Rebecca's mother finds it more and more difficult to support her large, fatherless family, she sends Rebecca to live with two elderly, frugal aunts and to get a proper education in Riverboro, Maine.

Rebecca is a lively, free-spirited, and outspoken child who turns her aunts' house topsy-turvy. Rebecca gets wet paint on one of her dresses, clogs the well to the house after tossing her parasol into it, and invites an "unwelcomed" missionary family to stay at her aunts' home. But amidst all the chaos she creates, Rebecca also brings joy to others. She raises money to buy a special lamp for the town's poorest family; she acts like an adopted daughter to an elderly couple in town; and she wins the hearts of her teachers, who see her as the best student they have ever had. Rebecca even gains favor with her Aunt Miranda by the end of the novel, as shown by the generous gift Aunt Miranda leaves Rebecca in her will.

In some ways, *Rebecca of Sunnybrook Farm* is difficult to read. Like other Romantic novels from the late nineteenth and early twentieth centuries, it has many descriptive passages and flowery language. But the extra time and effort that it might take young readers is well worth it. (Young readers who would like to read the story in a more updated and easier version might try a 1994 series of three books entitled *Rebecca of Sunnybrook Farm* by Eric Wiggin and Kate Douglas Wiggin and published by Bethel Publishing Co./1819 South Main Street/Elkhart, Indiana 46516.) In particular, young readers who enjoy the *Anne of Green Gables* series by L.M. Montgomery will find in Rebecca Randall another great heroine of juvenile literature.

LEARNING ACTIVITIES

1. Research author Kate Douglas Wiggin. What were her Maine roots? What authors influenced her writing? What else did she write? Was Wiggin considered a successful author during her lifetime? What impact did Wiggin have upon education in this country? How was Wiggin's life similar to Rebecca Randall's life? Give an "author talk" about the information you learn.

2. Select one scene from the original *Rebecca of Sunnybrook Farm* and rewrite it using a more modern style. Update the dialogue, simplify the descriptions, and use a less formal style of writing.

3. Play a drama game about *Rebecca of Sunnybrook Farm* with someone else who has read it. Take turns playing the part of a character from the book or acting a scene from the book. Try to guess the character or scene the other person is depicting.

ABOUT THE AUTHOR

Kate Douglas Wiggin was born in Philadelphia in 1856, but she grew up in Hollis, Maine. As a child, Wiggin had a passion for reading. In particular, she enjoyed the books of Charles Dickens; in fact the family's pets and farm animals were all named after characters from Dickens' books. Wiggin actually met Dickens by chance once on a train and proceeded to give him a review of his novels.

Wiggin moved to Santa Barbara, California, with her family. She had her first piece of writing published in *St. Nicholas* magazine. Wiggin's interest turned to education as an adult, and she founded the first free kindergarten in the West. To support her education projects, Wiggin wrote and sold children's stories. Her first published book in 1887 was *The Birds' Christmas Carol*, which is still in print. Wiggin wrote more than twenty books for young readers; but her best known work, *Rebecca of Sunnybrook Farm* (1903), has withstood the test of time and has been favorably compared to such classics as *Little Women* and *Anne of Green Gables*. *Rebecca of Sunnybrook Farm* was made into a play and a movie. Wiggin died in 1923 in England.

MORE MAINE CHAPTER BOOKS

Below is a list of quality Maine chapter books that have recently gone out of print. You are likely to find many of them at your local library. They are listed alphabetically by author.

ASK ME TOMORROW
written by Betty Bates, 12-16 years, 1987, Holiday House, 135 pages. A fifteen-year-old boy fights his family's traditions and their plans for him to take over the family apple orchard in southwest Maine.

THE MYSTERY OF HILLARD'S CASTLE
written by Kathy Lynn Emerson, 10-15 years, 1985, Down East Books, 160 pages. This mystery features a fourteen-year-old girl who is forced to move with her mother, an aspiring author, to a castle in western Maine that is full of strange noises and a genealogical surprise.

ALMOST HOME
written by M.C. Helldorfer, 10-14 years, 1987, Bradbury Press, 211 pages. A girl leaves New York City to spend the summer with her grandfather on a Maine island where she befriends an island misfit and becomes obsessed with solving a mystery of an old locket, a lost ship, and a pirate.

BROTHER MOOSE
written by Betty Levin, 10-16 years, 1990, Greenwillow, 213 pages. This historical novel, set in the late 1800s, presents two foster girls who are led to their foster home in Maine by an elderly Indian and his grandson.

THE TROUBLE WITH GRAMARY
written by Betty Levin, 12-16 years, 1988, Greenwillow, 208 pages. A girl is caught in the middle of a dispute in Ledgeport, Maine, between her outcast, sculptor grandmother and the townspeople who are set in their ways.

SUMMER GIRL
written by Deborah Moulton, 10-14 years, 1992, Dial Books for Young Readers, 133 pages. A thirteen-year-old girl must leave behind her mother who is dying of cancer and spend the summer in Maine with her estranged father.

SEAL CHILD
written by Sylvia Peck, 8-12 years, 1991, Bantam Skylark, 192 pages. This is a story of friendship on Ambrose Island, off the coast of Maine, between two girls, one of whom acts strangely—appearing out of nowhere, playing in the cold for hours, and acting as though she's never tasted candy before.

THE TINKER OF SALT COVE

written by Susan Hand Shetterly, 10-16 years, 1990, Tilbury House, 57 pages. This fictional story of a tinker in Salt Cove, Maine, is based upon a real-life tinker who actually wandered Hancock and Washington counties in the late 1800s.

HARPOON ISLAND

written by Pieter Van Raven, 10-14 years, 1989, Charles Scribner's Sons, 158 pages. A schoolmaster attempts to start a new life on a Maine island, but his withdrawn son is rejected by the islanders as an "idiot." The schoolmaster's German heritage is then questioned as World War I breaks out.

ANTHOLOGIES, SHORT STORIES, AND COLLECTIONS

THE WIND EAGLE AND OTHER ABENAKI STORIES

AUTHOR: Joseph Bruchac / ILLUSTRATOR: Kahionhes
AGE LEVEL / LENGTH: 10-14 years / 40 pages
PUBLISHER / COPYRIGHT DATE: Bowman Books, The Greenfield Review Press / 1985
.FORMAT / ISBN: Paperback / 091267864X

The Wind Eagle and Other Abenaki Stories is a short collection of six Abenaki stories. The stories are well told, and the nine black-and-white drawings add to the mood of the book. The book's foreword explains that the Abenaki, who have lived in the Northeast for 11,000 years, called themselves "The People of the Dawn" because they lived on the land where the sun rose first everyday. The Abenaki people were known to be gentle with their children. Rather than spanking them for misbehaving, they simply told them stories which contained lessons. This book shares some of those stories.

All the stories are about Gluskabi, the one who called the Abenaki his grandchildren. The first story, "The Coming of Gluskabi," tells how he was created and then learned that it would be his role to make the world a good place for his grandchildren, the humans. "Gluskabi and the Game Animals" tells how Gluskabi tricked all the game animals into hiding in his game bag; but wise Grandmother Woodchuck teaches Gluskabi an important lesson about sharing the game and finding the right balance between man and wild animals. In the title story, "Gluskabi and the Wind Eagle," Gluskabi finds and then hides the wind so that he can hunt ducks more easily. But he learns that a world without wind is worse than one with wind; and so he removes the wind from its hiding place and negotiates a deal so that the wind will blow some of the time, but not all of the time. The last three stories in the book have Gluskabi searching for tobacco, water, and summer to share with his people.

LEARNING ACTIVITIES

1. In the foreword to *Wind Eagle and Other Abenaki Stories*, storyteller Joseph Bruchac explains that when he retells Abenaki stories, he tries to continue the tradition of involving the audience in storytelling. For example, if the story includes a song, then he teaches the song to the audience so that they may sing along during the story. Select one of the stories from this book and plan several ways to involve an audience as you read or retell the story. Then read or retell the story as you planned to an actual audience.

2. In several of the stories in *The Wind Eagle and Other Abenaki Stories*, readers learn how some animals got their special characteristics (e.g., why the woodchuck's belly is bare, why the owl winks). Create your own story telling how an animal got its special characteristics (e.g., why giraffes' necks are so long, why skunks have stripes, why loons have a difficult time when taking off to fly).

3. Select one of the stories in *The Wind Eagle and Other Abenaki Stories* that you think would make a good picture book. Then simplify and rewrite the story. Add illustrations to create an Abenaki picture book. Share your book with a young child.

ABOUT THE AUTHOR

See information about Joseph Bruchac on page 27.

A WHITE HERON

AUTHOR: Sarah Orne Jewett / ILLUSTRATOR: Wendy Anderson Halperin
AGE LEVEL / LENGTH: 10 years–adult / 64 pages
PUBLISHER / COPYRIGHT DATE: Candlewick Books; many other editions available / original-1886; reprint-1997
FORMAT / ISBN: Hardcover / 0763602051

Sarah Orne Jewett's classic short story, *A White Heron,* is set in the late 1800s. It tells the story of Sylvia, a nine-year-old girl who has gone to live on a Maine farm with her grandmother. Previously Sylvia lived in a dirty city. Her move to the country brings a new spirit and life to the once-shy girl. One evening a young man happens by. Looking to add another trophy to his collection of "stuffed" birds, he wants to find the elusive white heron. Sylvia must struggle with conflicting emotions: her fondness for the young man, her desire for the money he offers as a reward for finding the bird, and her love for the beautiful heron.

A White Heron is widely regarded as one of Sarah Orne Jewett's best short stories. Although its language may be difficult to understand for some modern-day readers, its message of respect for nature is as timeless today as when it was written more than one hundred years ago. This Candlewick Treasures edition will appeal to young readers because of its small format and Halperin's simple watercolor illustrations.

LEARNING ACTIVITIES

1. Study the life of Sarah Orne Jewett. Read some of her work and, if possible, visit her house in South Berwick, Maine. Plan and present a speech about why this author's literary work is as appealing today as it was one hundred years ago.

2. Research the "white heron" (probably a snowy or common egret). Where does it live? What does it eat? Is it endangered? How big is it? How does it care for its young? Write a report about what you learn.

3. At the time Sarah Orne Jewett was writing, language was more formal; written sen-

tences tended to be longer. Rewrite a section of *A White Heron* in a more modern prose style. Compare your rewritten section with the original story. Which do you like better? Why?

ABOUT THE AUTHOR

Sarah Orne Jewett was born on September 3, 1849, in South Berwick, Maine. As a child Jewett had arthritis, and it was recommended that she spend as much time outdoors as possible. She started to accompany her father, a country doctor and a graduate of Bowdoin College, on his visits to patients. During these visits Jewett started to collect observations of the people and places she saw.

Her writing was noted for its strong New England sense of values, dialect, and characterizations. Her books included *Deephaven* (1877), sketches about rural Maine; and *The Country of the Pointed Firs* (1896), with its stories about people from an isolated Maine seaport. Jewett was a respected author during her lifetime, and she enjoyed friendships with other noted authors such as Henry James and Willa Cather. Jewett wrote more than 150 stories and had ten books published. She was also the first woman to receive an honorary doctorate degree from Bowdoin College in Brunswick.

A White Heron was written in 1886 and was dedicated to Jewett's sister Mary. In 1901, on her fifty-second birthday, Jewett fell from a carriage and suffered head and spinal injuries which left her partially paralyzed. She lived another eight years but was not able to continue her writing. Jewett died in 1909.

MAINE SPEAKS: AN ANTHOLOGY OF MAINE LITERATURE

EDITOR: The Maine Literature Project
AGE LEVEL / LENGTH: 12 years–adult / 466 pages
PUBLISHER / COPYRIGHT DATE: Maine Writers and Publishers Alliance / 1989
FORMAT / ISBN: Hardcover / 0961859210; Paperback / 0961859229

Maine Speaks: An Anthology of Maine Literature is a representative collection of the rich and varied literature of Maine. This anthology combines Abenaki legends with modern short stories by the likes of Sanford Phippen and Carolyn Chute; the poetry of E.A. Robinson and Edna St. Vincent Millay with that of contemporaries, such as Lee Sharkey and Baron Wormser; original accounts of Maine as an infant state, along with stories by Ruth Moore and Elisabeth Ogilvie, which describe twentieth-century Maine. The collection is divided into five major themes: Identity, Origins, Work, Nature, and Communities. Brief author biographies are included at the end of the book.

Maine Speaks is perhaps best used as a resource for middle schools, high schools, and colleges. Young readers can pick and choose from the 100+ selections and 77 authors who are represented. It's a book which represents the richness of Maine literature from the early 1600s through the 1980s. Having sold more than 10,000 copies, the book is in its fourth printing and continues to "speak" to Maine readers.

LEARNING ACTIVITIES

1. Select two authors from *Maine Speaks,* one early and one modern. Research their lives and writings to find out as much as you can about them. For modern authors, try to get first-hand information via a personal interview or questionnaire. Compare and contrast the lives and writings of your selected authors.

2. Create a visual representation for one of the selections in *Maine Speaks.* Use sculpture, painting, collage, or another medium, to capture the essence of the written piece. If a classroom tries this activity, display the artwork and try to guess which *Maine Speaks* selection is represented by each piece.

3. Select a few pieces from *Maine Speaks* and bring them to life using a reader's theater format, with participants giving choral and individual oral readings. Try to choose pieces that reflect a common theme, such as rural life in Maine, Maine's Native American heritage, or Maine's wildlife. Practice and perform these selections.

ABOUT THE EDITORS

Maine Speaks was the result of a collaboration between the Maine Writers and Publishers Alliance and the Maine Council for English Language Arts. An editorial board, under the direction of Jeff Fischer, selected the pieces to include in *Maine Speaks,* with input from Maine teachers and librarians, during a summer institute called the Maine Literature Project. The book was three years in the making.

THE QUOTABLE MOOSE:
A CONTEMPORARY MAINE READER

EDITOR: Wesley McNair
AGE LEVEL / LENGTH: 14 years–adult / 269 pages
PUBLISHER / COPYRIGHT DATE: University Press of New England / 1994
FORMAT / ISBN: Paperback / 0874516730

The Quotable Moose: A Contemporary Maine Reader is a treasury of some of the best contemporary poetry and short stories written by Maine's modern-age authors. Editor Wesley McNair brilliantly weaves poetry and short stories together amidst new themes of Maine life: Arrivals, Traveler's Advisories, Neighbors and Kin, and State of Mind. The book features the writings of forty authors from 1977 to 1994. Brief biographies of the contributing authors are included in the back of the book.

Susan Hand Shetterly's "Mallards," a short story of an elderly woman's tragic death while stopping to view a pair of ducks; Baron Wormser's "Somerset County," a poem discussing the realities of living in rural Maine; Cathie Pelletier's "Civil Defense," a short story of one woman's struggle to cope with and understand her aging mother-in-law; and William Carpenter's "Man Climbing Katahdin," a poem vividly describing a man's experience of conquering Maine's highest peak, are a just few of the anthologized works that may become classics for young and adult readers.

LEARNING ACTIVITIES

1. Study the poems in *The Quotable Moose*, and then try writing a poem about one of your own Maine experiences. Share your poem with some peers and make revisions based on their feedback. In which section of *The Quotable Moose* would your poem best fit?

2. Select one poem or story from *The Quotable Moose*. Write what you believe is "the story behind" your selected piece; that is, how do you think the author came to compose that piece, and which experiences led to its writing.

3. Work with some peers or classmates to develop a short anthology of your own community's writings. Invite students through senior citizens to contribute poems and stories about your community. Edit, organize, and make copies of this anthology to share with town residents (you might sell it to raise money for your local library). Arrange for a publishing party/celebration when your anthology is completed.

ABOUT THE EDITOR

Wesley McNair has lived in Maine since 1987, when he became a professor at the University of Maine at Farmington. Currently, he is the director of the Bachelor of Fine Arts program in Creative Writing at the University. He is the father of four children, and he lives in Mercer, Maine, with his wife.

McNair says that he has been writing poetry for twenty five years. His published volumes of verse include *The Faces of Americans in 1853* and *The Town of No*, as well as three volumes inspired by Maine subjects: *Twelve Journeys in Maine, My Brother Running*, and *Love Handles*. McNair has also written a prose book about poetry, called *Mapping the Heart*. McNair has been the recipient of numerous awards and fellowships, including a Guggenheim Fellowship, a Fulbright Lectureship, and the Theodore Roethke Prize.

THE BEST MAINE STORIES

EDITORS: Sanford Phippen, Charles Waugh & Martin Greenberg
AGE LEVEL / LENGTH: 14 years–adult / 320 pages
PUBLISHER / COPYRIGHT DATE: Downeast Books / 1986
FORMAT / ISBN: Paperback / 0892723513

The Best Maine Stories is a fine collection of short stories about Maine and her people. The stories are arranged thematically by the four seasons. The earliest story is Henry James's "A Bunch of Letters" written in 1879. The most recent is Rebecca Cummings's "Berrying," written in 1985. Dates of composition and brief biographical notes on authors are included.

From Arthur Train's "The Viking's Daughter" (about the issue of a rich son of a wealthy businessman wanting to marry the daughter of a lobsterman) to Sarah Orne Jewett's "A White Heron" (about a young girl's struggle to decide whether to share her most prized secret) to Sanford Phippen's "Step-Over Toe-Hold" (a humorous account of growing up in Hancock County), *The Best Maine Stories* is a downhome collection of Maine stories—some well-known and others now rediscovered.

LEARNING ACTIVITIES

1. Select two stories from *The Best Maine Stories* and read them carefully. Then write a comparison of the two stories. How are they alike and different in terms of their plots, characterizations, themes, and writing styles? After you finish your comparison, decide which of the two stories you liked best. Why?

2. Search your library and read recent issues of Maine journals and magazines. Select a story to add to *The Best Maine Stories*. Which season will your "new" story best fit into? In what order will you place it within the book? Write a paper defending your selected story (e.g., why you chose it, why it "belongs" in this collection).

3. The cover illustration by Sarah Knock for *The Best Maine Stories* shows a hodgepodge of houses and buildings in a rural setting. Do you think the illustration is a good match for the book? Why or why not? Study the covers of other anthologies and collections. How do you think the covers were selected for each book? Next, design and illustrate your own cover for an anthology or collection of stories. Explain the rationale behind your cover illustration and design.

ABOUT THE EDITORS

Sanford Phippen was raised in Hancock, Maine. He graduated from Sumner Memorial

High School in East Sullivan, Maine, as well as the University of Maine and Syracuse University. He currently teaches at Orono High School. Phippen is the author of several books, including *The Police Know Everything, Cheap Gossip*, and *Kitchen Boy*, all of which feature Phippen's strong Down East voice and humor. Phippen states that it took two years of reading and research before the editors compiled the final list of stories to include in *The Best Maine Stories*.

For information about Charles Waugh see page 162.

Martin Greenberg is a professor of political science at the University of Wisconsin at Green Bay. He has worked as the editor and co-editor of more than 700 anthologies.

STORIES FROM THE OLD SQUIRE'S FARM

AUTHOR: C. A. Stephens / EDITORS: Charles G. Waugh & Eric-Jon Waugh
AGE LEVEL / LENGTH: 14 years–adult / 416 pages
PUBLISHER / COPYRIGHT DATE: Rutledge Hill Press / 1995
FORMAT / ISBN: Hardcover / 1558533346

Stories from the Old Squire's Farm is a collection of thirty-six quasi-autobiographical stories by C.A. Stephens, a Maine writer of the late 1800s and early 1900s. The collection traces the adventures of six young cousins, orphaned by the Civil War, as they come to live with their grandparents, the Old Squire, and his wife, in rural Maine.

Humorous tales of the young children include their escape from the wrath of a nest full of angry hornets while "taking care" of the neighbor's angry bull in "A Fight with Hornets," as well as the creation of a very messy and smelly chemistry experiment in "Making Mug-Bread." In "Three Days at the County Fair," the children take their "wares" to the county fair in an attempt to make their fortunes; and they try to create the biggest and fastest sled in the county in "The Old Rantum-Scooter."

The selections in *Stories from the Old Squire's Farm* make this book one to be savored and enjoyed over time. It also is a wonderful book to read aloud. For interested Stephens' fans, his stories continue with *Sailing on the Ice*, a second volume of Stephens' stories published by Rutledge Hill Press and edited by Charles Waugh and Larry Glatz, of the Friends of C.A. Stephens organization.

LEARNING ACTIVITIES

1. *Stories from the Old Squire's Farm* is an enjoyable book to read aloud for "children" of all ages. Select one chapter from the book and turn it into a skit or an oral reading. Add props and costumes if you wish. Then perform your chapter twice—once for a class of

young children and once for a group of senior citizens at a nursing home. Which audience was the most receptive? Why?

2. Interview your own grandparents and older relatives to collect several stories from your own family's past. Write these stories down (or encourage your relatives to do so) and compile them into your own collection of family stories. Make copies of this collection as a special present for family members.

3. One of the editors for *Stories from the Old Squire's Farm*, Charles Waugh, claims that when reading Stephens' numerous stories he actually combined two or three of the original stories to create one story or chapter in this book. Try the same thing. Read several short stories on the same topic or by the same author and then try to combine these stories into one story. Be careful not to make your new story seem choppy. Share your final story with a peer. Could the peer tell your story was a combination of several other stories? Why or why not?

ABOUT THE AUTHOR

Charles Asbury Stephens was born in Norway, Maine, on October 21, 1844. He attended local schools, including Kents Hill Academy and Bowdoin College. Stephens wrote more than 2,500 stories and 31 books. Most of his stories were published in *The Youth's Companion*, a popular children's magazine of the time. Stephens wrote under 60 different pen names. He also obtained a medical degree from Boston University, and his studies on human aging led him to be described as a "pioneer of American gerontology." Stephens married twice; his second wife was Minne Scalar of West Paris, Maine, who was an internationally known opera singer. Stephens died in his hometown of Norway in 1931. Historical archives of Stephens' work can be found at Bowdoin College, Brown University, and the Norway Historical Society. Fans of Stephens can write for information about the author to: Friends of C.A. Stephens, 151 Main St., Norway, ME 04268.

ABOUT THE EDITORS

Charles and Eric-Jon Waugh are a father-and-son team. Charles Waugh has edited more than 180 anthologies and collections during the past eighteen years. He works as a professor of psychology and communication at the University of Maine at Augusta. He lives in Winthrop, Maine, with his wife who is also an author. Eric-Jon Waugh is a former student at Kents Hill School, C.A. Stephens' alma mater. At Kents Hill, the younger Waugh wrote for the school's newspaper and literary magazine, and managed the cross country team. He is also an amateur actor.

MORE MAINE ANTHOLOGIES, SHORT STORIES, AND COLLECTIONS

Below is a list of quality Maine anthologies, short stories, and collections that have recently gone out of print. You are likely to find them at your local library.

THE FASTEST HOUND DOG IN THE STATE OF MAINE
written by John Gould, 12 years–adult, 1953, North Country Press, 98 pages. This short story is actually a long Maine joke about a man who buys the fastest hound dog in the state of Maine and then must get the dog home to Wytopitlock.

A WHITE HERON
written by Sarah Orne Jewett, illustrated by Douglas Alvord, 10 years–adult, text-1886, illustrations-1990, Tilbury House Publishers, 28 pages. This classic short story about Sylvia, a bird collector, and the white heron is beautifully illustrated by Douglas Alvord's black-and-white drawings which help make the story more accessible to younger readers.

POETRY

I SWAM WITH A SEAL

AUTHOR / ILLUSTRATOR: Charlotte Agell
AGE LEVEL / LENGTH: 3-7 years / 32 pages
PUBLISHER / COPYRIGHT DATE: Harcourt Brace & Co. /
1995
FORMAT / ISBN: Hardcover / 015200176X

I happened on a heron
fishing in the stream.
She stalked by me,
quiet as a dream.

In *I Swam with a Seal*, a girl and a boy copy the actions of different Maine animals in a series of rhyming poems. In each case, the animals playfully ask about a difference between the child and themselves. For example, the seal wants to know where the girl's flippers are. The gull wants to know where the boy's beak is.

Author/illustrator Charlotte Agell encourages young readers to consider an early science concept of differences between species. Her childlike, brightly-colored watercolors add to the playfulness of the book. Young readers can easily imagine slithering like a snake by the old stonewall and meandering like a moose in the bog.

LEARNING ACTIVITIES

1. Focusing on other Maine animals, continue the book *I Swam With a Seal*. How would you act like (but still be different from) a chickadee, or a lobster, or a deer? Try to write a poem and draw pictures about the new animals. Follow the same pattern that Charlotte Agell uses in her book.

2. After reading *I Swam With a Seal*, write a list of even more ways that children and the animals differ from each other. For example, for a beaver, not only is the boy missing a strong tail, but he also doesn't have big teeth for chewing wood, doesn't build dams, and isn't covered with fur. How many differences can you think of for each animal?

3. The only adult appearing in *I Swam with a Seal* is the girl's and boy's grandfather, who tucks them into bed at night. Think of a time when you have either slept overnight at your grandparent's house or a grandparent has tucked you into bed at your house. How is it different being tucked into bed by a grandparent rather than a parent? Does your grandparent have different bedtime routines? Draw a picture of your experience and then speak about the picture.

ABOUT THE AUTHOR/ILLUSTRATION

See information about Charlotte Agell on page 16.

TO THE ISLAND

AUTHOR / ILLUSTRATOR: Charlotte Agell
AGE LEVEL / LENGTH: 2-6 years / 32 pages
PUBLISHER / COPYRIGHT DATE: DK Ink / 1998
FORMAT / ISBN: Hardcover / 078942505X

Author-illustrator Charlotte Agell describes her picture book *To the Island* as a "celebration of a Maine summer day for very young children." The story begins with a rabbit waking up to a day of great expectations: "Dark / Light! / Shadows creep / Hello morning— Farewell sleep / Today is the day! / Today is the day we go to the island." Rabbit meets three friends (dragon, cat, and chicken) and they set sail for an island. After journeying through a gale, they go ashore on the island and enjoy a picnic and swim. All too soon, it's time to return home. On the way back, there is no wind; so they all must row. Darkness falls, and they return to a harbor filled with twinkling lights. The story comes full circle with rabbit going to bed to dream about his special day on the island. Agell's simple yet bright watercolor illustrations, and her brief yet rhythmic text, help to capture the joy of a summer day in Maine for very young children.

LEARNING ACTIVITIES

1. Act out the book *To the Island* as a play. Friends will need to play the rabbit, the dragon, the cat, and the chicken. You may use simple props if you want, such as a towel spread out on the floor for rabbit's bed or wooden rulers for oars. As the story is read aloud and the pictures in the book are shown, everyone should act out their parts. Invite an audience to your play, if you wish.

2. Have your own island picnic, but you don't have to go to a *real* island. Instead, select an area in your yard at home or at school to be your pretend island. Mark off the area where your island will be; for example, outline the area by laying down jump-ropes. When your island area is marked, pack a picnic to take to your pretend island. Grab the picnic and travel to your island.

3. Make a *paper* bag mask (*not* a plastic bag—you should never put plastic on your head or near your face) to look like one of the characters from *To the Island*—the rabbit, dragon, cat, or chicken. Draw and color the mask for your selected character. Then have an adult help you to cut eye and mouth holes in your mask. Try your mask on and look in the mirror.

ABOUT THE AUTHOR / ILLUSTRATOR

See information about Charlotte Agell on page 16.

BIG RED BARN

AUTHOR: Margaret Wise Brown / ILLUSTRATOR: Felecia Bond
AGE LEVEL / LENGTH: 2-6 years / 32 pages
PUBLISHER / COPYRIGHT DATE: HarperCollins / text-1956; illustrations-1989
FORMAT / ISBN: Hardcover / 0694006246; Big book / 0060207507

Big Red Barn is a warm and soothing bedtime book—for animals! All the animals on a farm are shown first in daytime. They squeal and play and stomp and bray. The bright red of the barn and the bright green of the field enliven the pages. But as nighttime comes, the animals return to a darkened barn and to sleep.

The simple rhyming text and the large-format illustrations make this book a perfect choice for the youngest "readers." They will find comfort in the familiar animals and their sounds. They will enjoy the playfulness of the animals romping in the pasture. Finally, they will be lulled by the slow-paced text and increasingly darkened illustrations.

LEARNING ACTIVITIES

1. Using *Big Red Barn*, play a simple "Where's the Animal?" game. Can you find the page with the rooster, the page with the scarecrow, etc.? Tell your friends which animals to find by using questions such as, "Where's the cat?" or "Where's the horse?"

2. Add animal sounds to *Big Red Barn*. Read the book and add appropriate sound effects, such as "neigh" for the horse, "moo" for the cow.

3. Draw a group mural about *Big Red Barn*. On a large piece of paper encourage friends to draw a farm, barn, scarecrow, etc. Draw many different animals and parts of the farm.

ABOUT THE AUTHOR

See information about Margaret Wise Brown on page 23.

ABOUT THE ILLUSTRATOR

Felecia Bond was born in Japan. At the age of five, she decided that she would be an artist. She studied painting at the University of Texas in Austin. While living in Canada in her early twenties, she pulled together a portfolio of her drawings to be considered for children's books. Her first book was a "Let's Read and Find Out" science book for T.Y. Crowell Publishers. Since then, she has both written and illustrated numerous books, including *Wake Up, Vladimir, The Halloween Performance,* and *If You Give a Mouse a Cookie,* written by Laura Numeroff.

GENERAL STORE

AUTHOR: Rachel Field / ILLUSTRATOR: Nancy Winslow Parker

AGE LEVEL / LENGTH: 5-8 years / 24 pages

PUBLISHER / COPYRIGHT DATE: Greenwillow (div. of William Morrow & Co.) / text-1926; illustrations-1988

FORMAT / ISBN: Hardcover / 0688073530

Rachel Field's poem shows a young girl imagining and pretending that one day she will own a general store. The young girl plans to sell "bolts of calico," "jars of peppermint," "kegs of sugar," and "sarsaparilla." This large-format book shows busy pictures with drawers, cases, baskets, and barrels full of goods. Field's poem captures the spirit of a child's love of make-believe. Nancy Winslow Parker's illustrations give young readers the feel of browsing in a 1920s general store.

LEARNING ACTIVITIES

1. Study Nancy Winslow Parker's illustrations in *General Store*. How can you tell the store is from the 1920s? What items are for sale? How are the items displayed and packaged? What jobs does the girl do as she works at the store? Compare the store in this book with a store you would visit today.

2. The poem *General Store* is full of "old-fashioned" words (e.g., bolts, calico, crockery, sarsparilla). In the context of the poem and by looking at the illustrations on each page, guess the meaning of each of these words. Then check a dictionary to see how accurate your definitions are.

3. Draw a picture which shows what you would like to do when you grow up. Ask a friend to do the same thing. Afterwards, share your pictures with each other and talk about your hopes and dreams.

ABOUT THE AUTHOR

See information about Rachel Field on page 104.

ABOUT THE ILLUSTRATOR

Nancy Winslow Parker worked in the public relations field for twenty years. During this time, she also worked as a writer. After eighty-eight rejections slips on a variety of manuscripts, Parker made a career change, with the 1974 publication of her first children's book, *The Man with the Take-Apart Head*. Her other books include *Paul Revere's Ride* (by Henry Wadsworth Longfellow), *At Grammy's House* (by Eve Rice), *No Bath Tonight* (by Jane Yolen), and her own books: *Love From Aunt Betty*, *The Christmas Camel*, and *Locks,*

Crocks, and Skecters: The Story of the Panama Canal. Her illustrations are done with watercolors, color pencil, and black pen. She currently lives in New York City.

Parker is proud of her Maine connections. Her father was born in the state and she has traced relatives back to the 1600s. She has dedicated several of her books to her Maine-based grandfather and great uncles who served in the Civil War. In fact, one of Parker's hobbies is wood sculpting for which she uses her grandfather's carpentry tools.

SUMMER LEGS

AUTHOR: Anita Hakkinen / ILLUSTRATOR: Abby Carter
AGE LEVEL / LENGTH: 3-8 years / 32 pages
PUBLISHER / COPYRIGHT DATE: Henry Holt & Co. / 1995
FORMAT / ISBN: Hardcover / 0805022627 (recently out of print)

Actually *Summer Legs* doesn't best fit into poetry books or picture books—it can best be called a *musical* book. The rhyming, tongue-twister stanzas feel like song-lyrics as they are read aloud. The rhythm is strong, and it's hard to read *Summer Legs* without clapping or tapping along with the beat of the words.

Summer Legs is a celebration of summer legs, their activities and summer "scars." Activities include climbing, swimming, jump-roping, and swinging; summer "scars" include mosquito bites, mustard drips, tree-climbing scrapes, and paint splats. Each page has four lines describing a different summer activity. For example, the page at the seashore reads:

> Sandy are my summer legs
> Seashell-sprinkled summer legs
> Beachybummy ho-humdrummy
> At-the-ocean legs

Author Anita Hakkinen and illustrator Abby Carter have created a vibrant, bouncy book. Hakkinen's background as a music teacher has helped her to create a playful text filled with wonderful made-up words. Carter's fun watercolors perfectly complement the text with unusual perspectives and visual jokes.

LEARNING ACTIVITIES

1. Add one more page to *Summer Legs*. Write about a summer activity that is not already in the book, such as bike-riding, roller-blading, or hammock-laying. Write a poem about your selected activity that follows the pattern used by Anita Hakkinen. It may take you several tries to get the words to work the way you want them to. Then draw an illustration to go along with your words.

2. Write a short story from your own legs' perspective. Have your legs tell the story of what they did during a day. Your story doesn't need to be set in the summertime; it can take place anytime. Just make certain you write it as if your legs were actually telling the story.

3. As a class or a family, work together to write your own story about another body part. For example, you might write about "Winter Nose" or "Thanksgiving Tummy." Make a list of as many examples as you can think of for how that body part looks, feels, and acts during your chosen situation.

ABOUT THE AUTHOR

Anita Hakkinen grew up in Minnesota. She has worked as a music teacher, and she currently teaches fifth grade in Alaska.

ABOUT THE ILLUSTRATOR

In 1967, when still a child, Abby Carter began summering in Friendship, Maine. She moved to the state in 1970. Carter says that she can't remember when she didn't have a pencil in her hand. She has always loved to draw. She majored in art at Wesleyan University in Connecticut and has been working as an illustrator since 1983. She has done illustrations for both chapter books and picture books, including *Never Ride Your Elephant to School, New Kid on Spurwink Ave.* (see page 91), *Shack and Back* (see page 91), *I Thought I'd Take My Rat to School,* and *The Invisible Day.* Her illustrations are done in watercolor and color pencil. Many of Carter's illustrations–deriving from her "childhood adventures in Friendship"–show the ocean and Maine coast. Carter currently lives with her husband and two young children in Cape Elizabeth.

MY WONDERFUL CHRISTMAS TREE

AUTHOR / ILLUSTRATOR: Dahlov Ipcar
AGE LEVEL / LENGTH: 5-8 years / 32 pages
PUBLISHER / COPYRIGHT DATE: Gannet Books; available from Maine Writers & Publishers Alliance / 1986
FORMAT / ISBN: Paperback / 0930096851

My Wonderful Christmas Tree is a poem describing what the author sees as she looks out the window of her Maine farm on Christmas night. Ipcar sees a tree with "one shining star." From there, her imagination takes over as she sees "two velvety black bears," "three bobcats with spotted coats," "four round black pincushion porcupines," and so on. Ipcar's verse is filled with vivid imagery. For example, she describes bluejays as "spreading their tails like Chinese fans," and chipmunks by saying "running up and down their backs, black and white stripes like railroad tracks." Eleven different kinds of wild Maine animals fill her "wonderful Christmas tree."

LEARNING ACTIVITIES

1. Test your memory. After reading *My Wonderful Christmas Tree*, try to remember, in order, all of the animals presented in the book. How many can you remember? If you forget some, reread the book and try once more to remember all the animals in order. How many can you remember this time?

2. Make stick puppets and use them to present *My Wonderful Christmas Tree*. Try to match Dahlov Ipcar's bright, bold animals when creating your puppets. Use the puppets to retell the story of *My Wonderful Christmas Tree* to an audience of nursery school children. You will need to make the outline of a large tree for the story, or perhaps you can use a real Christmas tree and place the puppets on it.

3. Make a list of other Maine animals (e.g., moose, deer, fox, eagle) not included in *My Wonderful Christmas Tree*. Follow Ipcar's format for an eight line rhyming verse for each animal, and compose your own poem describing the new animals as they join the Christmas tree.

ABOUT THE AUTHOR/ILLUSTRATOR

See information about Dahlov Ipcar on page 52.

THE CHILDREN'S HOUR

AUTHOR: Henry Wadsworth Longfellow / ILLUSTRATOR: Glenna Lang
AGE LEVEL / LENGTH: 4-10 years / 32 pages
PUBLISHER / COPYRIGHT DATE: David R. Godine, Publisher / 1993; poem written in 1859
FORMAT / ISBN: Hardcover / 0879239719

This picture book gives young readers a glimpse into the life of the famous American poet, Henry Wadsworth Longfellow. *The Children's Hour* presents a special time that Longfellow spent with his three daughters. The three girls sneak down the stairs and into their father's study, his "castle." They seize and capture him in the middle of his writing: "They almost devour me with kisses, Their arms about me entwine." Longfellow compares his daughters' attack to one upon a tower in Germany. The poet "captures" his daughters at the end in the "tower" of his heart and with the lines of this immortal poem.

The Children's Hour is a large-format book with warm illustrations which bring the poem to life. It's a book that helps make this classic Longfellow poem easily accessible for another generation of readers.

LEARNING ACTIVITIES

1. Work together with your family or your classmates to select another poem, or section of a poem, by Henry Wadsworth Longfellow (e.g., "Paul Revere's Ride," "The Village Blacksmith," "The Song of Hiawatha") and draw pictures to represent that poem. Be certain to discuss your selected poem first so that everyone understands its meaning. Divide the poem into sections, with each person drawing illustrations for a different part. Then combine the drawings in order to make a book of the poem.

2. Henry Wadsworth Longfellow was born in 1807. He grew up in Portland, Maine (then part of Massachusetts) and attended Bowdoin College, in Brunswick, Maine, at the age of fifteen. Longfellow then became a professor at Bowdoin at age of eighteen. Learn as much as you can about poet Henry Wadsworth Longfellow's life and his Maine connections. Check the encyclopedia and biographies about the author. If possible, visit the Henry Wadsworth Longfellow House in Portland, or the Hawthorne-Longfellow Library at Bowdoin College in Brunswick. Tape record a list of all the information you learn about the poet. Make your tape available in the biography section of your classroom or school library.

3. *The Children's Hour* tells about a special family time in Longfellow's household. Write a poem or story about one of your own family's special times, customs, or rituals.

ABOUT THE AUTHOR

Henry Wadsworth Longfellow was a famous U.S. poet during the 1800s. His poetry was both popular at the time he wrote it and is still widely read today, more than 100 years later.

Longfellow was born in Portland, Maine (then part of Massachusetts), on February 27, 1807. He enjoyed growing up in a seaport, and the ocean was a frequent topic in his poetry. Longfellow's first poem was published by a Portland newspaper when he was just thirteen-years-old. He began college at Bowdoin College in Brunswick, Maine, at age fifteen. He studied foreign languages in college. After graduating at age eighteen, he became Bowdoin's first professor of modern languages. Along with his interest in foreign languages, Longfellow enjoyed traveling throughout Europe.

Longfellow's first book of poetry, *Voices of the Night*, was published in 1839. Longfellow became a professor at Harvard College in Cambridge, Massachusetts. He lived in a yellow mansion in Cambridge, called the Craigie House, which is today known as the Longfellow National Historical Site. Longfellow and his wife Frances Appleton raised their six children at this home, including his three daughters Alice, Allegra, and Edith who are immortalized in *The Children's Hour.*

Longfellow wrote such famous poems as "Paul Revere's Ride," "Evangeline," "The Song of Hiawatha," and the "The Courtship of Miles Standish." He received many honorary degrees and awards during his life. In 1882, Longfellow died at the Craigie House.

ABOUT THE ILLUSTRATOR

Glenna Lang majored in Fine Arts at the University of Chicago and received a Master of Fine Arts in printmaking from the School of the Museum of Fine Arts in Boston. She has done freelance illustration work for numerous magazines and newspapers. She has also illustrated several picture books, including *When the Frost is on the Punkin,* by Robert Louis Stevenson, and *The Runaway,* by Robert Frost. Her illustrations are painted in gouache.

For *The Children's Hour,* Lang studied the life of Henry Wadsworth Longfellow and visited The Longfellow National Historic Site on Brattle Street in Cambridge, Massachusetts. Lang used her daughter as one of the models for the book. She currently lives in Cambridge, Massachusetts.

DREAMING

AUTHOR / ILLUSTRATOR: Bobette McCarthy
AGE LEVEL / LENGTH: 3-7 years / 28 pages
PUBLISHER / COPYRIGHT DATE: Candlewick Press / 1994
FORMAT / ISBN: Hardcover / 156402184X

In this short book, author/illustrator Bobette McCarthy tells a lyrical tale of a dog going to bed in his house by the ocean. McCarthy's illustrations show the dog's bed being transformed into a rowboat, his blue blanket becoming a sailor's coat, and his dog dish becoming his sailor's hat. Then, at high tide, the dog rows far out to sea amidst playful dolphins, a bright full moon, and bone-shaped clouds. As morning comes, the dog rows back home and wakes up in his own dog bed—it was all a dream!

Dreaming is a deceptively simple book at first glance. But as one revisits the book, one notices many details that do not seem obvious at the beginning—the transformation of the dog's belongings into seafaring equipment, the ever-changing shapes of clouds, and the game that dolphins play with the dog's sailor hat. The mood of the book is soft and soothing with its sea green watercolors and poetic phrases "Through mizzle and moon-mist," making it a perfect bedtime book.

LEARNING ACTIVITIES

1. *Dreaming* tells a poem of a dog's late night row out to sea. But there's much more than the dog's actions going on. Look through the book several times and tell, in your own words, the other "stories" in the book. For example, one time you might tell a story about the changing clouds. Another time you might tell a story about the dolphin's actions.

2. Draw a picture of what you most like to dream about. Since it's a picture of a dream, it's okay to have make-believe things in the picture. When you finish, talk with a friend about your picture.

3. On a cloudy day, find a partner and lay on the grass so that you can both see the clouds. Stare at the clouds to see if they remind you of anything. Does one look like a smokestack, or a donut, or an elephant? You and your partner should point out the cloud shapes you discover and talk about them. Do the shapes stay the same or change? Do you and your partner each see the same cloud a different way? If you try to look for a specific objects in the clouds, such as a banana or a heart, are you able to find a cloud that looks like that object?

ABOUT THE AUTHOR/ILLUSTRATOR

Bobette McCarthy grew up on the craggy Harpswell islands. As a child she often went fishing with her father. McCarthy believes that she was lucky to grow up by the ocean because it was ever-changing. McCarthy is also the author and illustrator of *Buffalo Girls*. She currently lives in Auburn, Maine.

CATS IN THE DARK

AUTHOR: Kate Rowinski / ILLUSTRATOR: Bonnie Bishop
AGE LEVEL / LENGTH: 3-7 years / 32 pages
PUBLISHER / COPYRIGHT DATE: Down East Books / 1998
FORMAT / ISBN: Hardcover / 0892724277

Two children wake with a start in their lighthouse home. They hear "a crash, a bang, and a rumble" and worry that cats are turning their house "into jumble." In this rhyming picture book, things are not as they seem. The children race around the lighthouse, trying to catch a glimpse of what sounds like "a hundred, a thousand, a million or so" cats. But all they find in the end is their one mischievous little kitten creating chaos in the beam of the lighthouse.

Author Kate Rowinski and illustrator Bonnie Bishop have created a fun book with *Cats in the Dark*. The rhyming text with its repetitive words "a hundred, a thousand, a million or so" invites young readers to join in with the story. The yellow and black-and-white illustrations playfully alternate between light and dark to reflect the flashes of the lighthouse beacon. Wide borders on each page feature a multitude of cats, while each illustration for the story hints at a single mysterious cat shown in the shadows or as a pair of eyes peeking out of the dark.

LEARNING ACTIVITIES

1. Play a hide and seek game with friends or classmates. Cut out two round circles from yellow construction paper, and add a black mark in the middle of each circle to make them look like cat eyes. Place a small piece of masking tape on the back of each eye; wrap the masking tape in a backwards circle with the sticky side out so that it will stick to the paper on one side and other objects on the other side. Then take turns having one person leave the room while another person sticks the cat eyes somewhere in the room. Don't hide the cat eyes under or inside things so that they are not visible. Rather, stick them someplace where they can be seen; for example, you might stick them to the bottom of a door, or on the leg of a chair, or the top of a windowsill. After the cat eyes have been placed, the person who left the room must come back and find the cat eyes. Continue taking turns hiding the cat eyes around the room in different places for someone to find.

2. Play a flashlight game. Make a room as dark as possible (with lights off and shades down). One person will hold the flashlight and flash it around the room. Everyone else must stay still. As the flashlight is flashed around the room, the people staying still must try to make movements such as waving their hands or shaking their heads *without* being "caught" by the flashlight beam. If the flashlight shines on someone when they are moving, they are "caught" and must take the flashlight and flash it around the room, trying to catch someone else moving. Each time someone is caught moving in the beam of the flashlight, that person shines the flashlight to continue the game. The object of the game is to move without getting caught by the flashlight.

3. Pretend to be a cat. Take turns with friends or classmates doing a cat action, such as pretending to lap milk, pretending to play with a ball of yarn, pretending to clean yourself with your paws, and so on. Try to guess each other's cat actions.

ABOUT THE AUTHOR

Kate Rowinski has worked as a professional writer for the past twenty years. Her copywriting work includes developing advertising and catalogue material for the Freeport, Maine, mail-order business, L. L. Bean. In fact, Rowinski developed the idea for L. L. Bean's mascot, L. L. Bear. She also has written three children's books based upon that character: *L. L. Bear*, *Ellie Bear & the Fly-Away Fly*, and *Trailfinder Bear*. In addition, Rowinski has written articles for the children's magazine, *Ranger Rick*.

Cats in the Dark is based upon an experience in Rowinski's own family. Her daughter Brooke brought home the family's first cat. Night after night the family would be awakened by loud noises. Could it be just one cat making all that noise? Yes, indeed. And so Rowinski wrote the story of *Cats in the Dark* several years ago as a Christmas present for Brooke. The mother of four children, Rowinski currently lives in Yarmouth, Maine. Her hobbies include gardening and caring for pets.

ABOUT THE ILLUSTRATOR

Bonnie Bishop grew up in Connecticut. She has a bachelor's degree in art from Skidmore College and a master of fine arts degree in illustration from Syracuse University. She lived in New York City for ten years and worked as an art editor and art director at Scholastic. After seeing the publishing side of children's books, Bishop decided to try her hand at creating her own. She authored two books about a parrot, *No One Noticed Ralph* and *Ralph Rides Away*, which were illustrated by Jack Kent. She also illustrated the children's book, *Miracle at Egg Rock*, written by Doris Gove.

Bishop moved to central Maine in the late 1970s. She has worked as the director of publications at Colby College, in Waterville, and currently runs her own studio.

Bishop was the book-designer for *Cats in the Dark*, as well as the illustrator. She has stated, "I believe this is a book about fear and how our imaginations run away with us." She explained that the central illustration on each page represents reality while the borders show the imagination of the child. Bishop decided to feature a Maine coon cat as the mischievous kitten in the lighthouse. She also explained that she has always considered herself a dog-lover, but while doing this book she gained a new appreciation for cats. Bishop believes that "the natural world and animals in particular have a lot to teach us."

A HOUSE BY THE SEA

AUTHOR: Joanne Ryder / ILLUSTRATOR: Melissa Sweet
AGE LEVEL / LENGTH: 3-7 years / 32 pages
PUBLISHER / COPYRIGHT DATE: Morrow Junior Books / 1994
FORMAT / ISBN: Hardcover / 0688126758

In this rhyming story, a little boy imagines what it would be like to live in a house by the sea. He imagines sharing fish-eyed pie with some seals, rocking to sleep on the back of a whale, having an octopus keep house for him, and much more. This whimsical tale, along with Melissa Sweet's playful watercolors, invites young readers to play a game of "what if" in their own minds.

LEARNING ACTIVITIES

1. Find another poem about the sea. Read it several times. Then draw one or more illustrations to accompany the poem. Make a poster with the written poem and your illustrations.

2. Turn *A House by the Sea* into a play. Collect pails, shovels, sunhats, and other beach paraphernalia. Decide how you can look like a seal, or a whale, or an octopus. You don't need fancy costumes or props. Keep them simple. For example, for the octopus several friends might stand with their backs to each other and their arms sticking out, or for the whale one person might wear black and white clothes. Then act out the book as it is read aloud, pretending to do all the silly activities that are described.

3. Work with a partner to think of one more verse, or part, to this poem. For example, what if you added a lobster to the story? Or a shark? Or a clam? What silly things would happen?

ABOUT THE AUTHOR

Joanne Ryder grew up on Long Island, New York. At an early age, Ryder was encouraged to write by her family and teachers. She went on to study journalism at Marquette University and learned the importance of research. Ryder worked for several years as an editor of children's books in New York. Then she turned to full-time writing. She now has more than forty books to her credit, including *One Small Fish, My Father's Hands, When the Woods Hum, Winter Whale,* and *White Bear, Ice Bear.* Ryder strives "to paint pictures with words" in her books. Many of her books reflect her love of nature, especially the sea. Ryder has enjoyed several vacations to Maine. She currently lives in Pacific Grove, California, with her husband, Lawrence Yep, who is also an author.

ABOUT THE ILLUSTRATOR

Melissa Sweet has summered in Waldoboro, Maine, for the past fifteen years; and she has lived in Portland year-round since 1993. Sweet has worked as a freelance illustrator for sixteen years. Her illustrations can be found on stationery, in major magazines, and in many books. She also has illustrated hundreds of greeting cards for Renaissance Greeting Cards in Springvale, Maine, as well as more than thirty children's books. Her books include *Sing Me a Window,* by Elizabeth Lee O'Donnell; James Howe's *Pinky and Rex* series; and *Will You Take Care of Me,* by Margaret Park Bridges. She has also adapted and illustrated an American folksong, *Fiddle-i-Fee: A Farmyard Song for the Very Young.*

Sweet's illustrations are primarily done in watercolor with pen-and-ink and color pencil. Sweet continues to attend school at the Maine College of Art., where she is studying collage and French. She also is an avid gardener.

MORE MAINE POETRY BOOKS

Below is a list of quality Maine poetry books that have recently gone out of print. You are likely to find them at your local library. They are listed alphabetically by author.

GENERAL STORE
written by Rachel Field, illustrated by Giles Laroche, 5-8 years, text-1926, illustrations-1988, Little Brown & Co., 24 pages. Rachel Field's rhyming tour of an old general store is creatively depicted with objects and collage art.

BRICKYARD SUMMER
written by Paul Janeczko, 12 years–adult, 1989, Orchard Books, 53 pages. This book of poems is based on the author's experiences of growing up in a mill town (Lewiston) by the Androscoggin River

THE BALLAD OF THE HARP-WEAVER
written by Edna St. Vincent Millay, illustrated by Beth Peck, 8 years–adult, text-1922, illustrations-1991, Philomel Books, 32 pages. This poem, Millay's tribute to her mother who raised her in Camden, tells of a poor boy and mother who only own a harp.

BIOGRAPHIES, AUTOBIOGRAPHIES, AND JOURNALS
(This section is arranged alphabetically by the name of the
the person/animal that is featured in the book)

THE STORY OF ANDRE

AUTHOR: Lew Dietz / ILLUSTRATOR: Stell Shevis
AGE LEVEL / LENGTH: 8-14 years / 88 pages
PUBLISHER / COPYRIGHT DATE: Down East Books
(paperback); Audio Bookshelf (audio book) / 1979
FORMAT / ISBN: Paperback / 0892720522; Audio
Book / 1883333060

The Story of Andre is the fascinating account of Harry Goodridge's pet harbor seal, as told from the perspective of Harry's daughter, Toni. The story takes the reader through twenty years of Andre's life from being an abandoned seal pup in Penobscot Bay, to adoption and domestication by the Goodridge family, to learning to coexist with the human world. Many of Andre's playful antics and skillful tricks are described: playing hide-and-seek in seaweed, kissing strangers in their boats, and retrieving a lost button from the ocean.

Andre captured world attention, with stories appearing in newspapers and on TV, when he was released from the New England Aquarium in Boston at the end of winter and instinctively swam home to the Goodridge family. As his fame grew, Andre captivated the hearts of the people of Rockport, Maine, and visitors from around the world applauded his command performances in the harbor. The closing chapter describes the unveiling of the Andre Statue in Rockport Harbor.

LEARNING ACTIVITIES

1. Learn more about Andre. If possible, visit Rockport and view the bronze statue of Andre by Jane Wasey. Interview residents who remember Andre. Research newspaper archives from the time when Andre died, the summer of 1986. Write a follow-up chapter to *The Story of Andre*, including some of the new information you discover.

2. Visit an aquarium and view some harbor seals, or try to see some seals on the coast. Take photographs of the seals and describe them in words—their looks, their movements, and the sounds they make. Arrange the photos and words to make a harbor seal collage.

3. Interview people who fish, and learn their perspective on harbor seals. Do seals interfere with their fishing? Does the seal population need to be managed or controlled? If so, in what ways? Write a paper describing what you learned about the fishing/seal debate

ABOUT THE AUTHOR

Lew Dietz was born in Pittsburgh, Pennsylvania in 1906, was raised in New Jersey, and educated in New York City. But for most of his adult life, Dietz called Maine home. He worked as an editor for such publications as the *Camden Herald, Maine Coast Fisher-*

man, and *Outdoor Maine.* He also helped to established *Down East* magazine. His first book, *Jeff White: Young Woodsman,* was published in 1951. This book was the first of a series of adventure books for children set in northern Maine. He went on to write many books for adults and children, most of them reflecting his love of the outdoors. In addition to the children's book, *The Story of Andre,* Dietz co-authored (with Andre's master, Harry Goodridge) a book about Andre for adults, titled *A Seal Called Andre.* Dietz lived in Rockport, Maine, for many years and died in April 1997, at the age of ninety.

ALL FOR MAINE: THE STORY OF GOVERNOR PERCIVAL P. BAXTER

AUTHOR: Liz Soares / PHOTOGRAPHER: photographs from a variety of sources
AGE LEVEL / LENGTH: 10 years–adult / 102 pages
PUBLISHER / COPYRIGHT DATE: Windswept House Publishers / 1995
FORMAT / ISBN: Paperback / 1883650178

All for Maine: The Story of Governor Percival P. Baxter presents the life of an engaging Maine politician and philanthropist. Born in Portland in 1876, Percival P. Baxter grew up in a wealthy family. He tended to live frugally, however, and frequently contributed money and land to the causes he believed in. His greatest cause, passion, and legacy was purchasing and donating the land around Mount Katahdin to the state of Maine for the purpose of creating what was to become Baxter State Park.

Author Liz Soares gives readers insights into Baxter's unusual life. As a young man, this future governor of Maine spent a night in jail. A police officer had accused him of leading a demonstration of Bowdoin College's Young Republicans against the Presidential candidate, William Jennings Bryant. Baxter was elected several times to the political offices of state representative and state senator, but he also lost many elections. Baxter's support waned after he became a vocal opponent of selling electricity out of state and of the land monopolies being created by rich owners, such as Great Northern Paper Company. Baxter became Maine's forty-sixth governor after Governor Parkhurst died in office. As the president of the Maine Senate, Baxter was next in line for the governor's office.

As governor, Baxter refused the allowance for maintaining the governor's mansion, the Blaine house. He showed a strong interest in education and visited over 200 schools during his first year in office. He was also the first governor to appoint females to state offices. Baxter walked from the Blaine House to the Capitol each day and was greeted by his first name by passing citizens. Baxter was a bachelor, with a "family" of Irish setters. In fact, when one of his most beloved dogs, Garry, died while he was governor, he ordered flags to be flown at half staff. He also sent a homeless dog to the Maine State Prison to keep the prisoners company. Baxter continued to work hard after leaving office—acquiring and donating land to the state, developing rules that would maintain the wilderness around Katahdin, and helping to start the Governor Baxter School for the Deaf at his family's summer retreat on Mackworth Island. At age ninety, Baxter still worked three hours a day in his office and went for a daily walk and drive. He died in 1969 at the age of ninety-two. As he requested, his ashes were scattered atop Mount Katahdin.

All for Maine: The Story of Governor Percival P. Baxter also includes a timeline of Baxter's life, a listing of places to visit, a bibliography, a dozen photographs, maps, and drawings related to Baxter's life. The book would have benefited from a table of contents and an index, but overall it succeeds as the extraordinary personality of Percival P. Baxter shines through its pages.

LEARNING ACTIVITIES

1. Visit one or more of the "Baxter" places described on pages 94-95 of *All for Maine*. During your visit, watch for signs that show you why this place was special to Governor Baxter. Take photos, if possible. After your visit, create a "guide" to the place you visited.

2. Invite some friends or classmates to join you in a debate. Create two teams. One team should speak in support of Governor Baxter's decision to order flags flown at half staff after the death of his Irish setter Garry; the other team should speak against his decision. Each team should carefully plan their reasoning and arguments.

3. Write a "Dear Governor Baxter" letter to update him on the condition of Baxter State Park today. How many visitors does it receive each year? Have any changes been made to his list of park rules? Has any land been added to the park? You will need to contact officials of Baxter State Park in order to gather information for your letter.

ABOUT THE AUTHOR

Liz Soares has lived in Maine since 1986, first in Lewiston and then in the Augusta area. She grew up in Somerset, Massachusetts, and graduated from Providence College in Rhode Island. Soares claims that she has been writing since she was ten-years-old, but didn't get paid for it until she was twenty-three. As a child, she published a family newspaper. Then she worked on her junior high, high school, and college newspapers. As an adult, she has worked as a newspaper reporter, editorial writer, and columnist. Since 1987, she has written a column for the *Kennebec Journal*. Soares also works as a middle school librarian.

All for Maine is Soares' first book. It took her a year and a half to research and write. Soares claims to write her first draft very quickly; then she goes back and does the painstaking task of rewriting. Soares says that "journalism is a good place to learn to write—you learn to write fast and on a deadline—and to write *every*day."

Soares is married to a reporter and lives in Augusta. Her hobbies include writing, reading, traveling, and gardening. She also is interested in politics and history, and loves to "surf" the Internet.

SIMPLY THE BEST: THE CINDY BLODGETT STORY

AUTHOR: Ron Brown / PHOTOGRAPHER: photographs from a variety of sources
AGE LEVEL / LENGTH: 10 years–adult / 262 pages
PUBLISHER / COPYRIGHT DATE: Furbush-Roberts (printer); available from
Magazines Incorporated, Bangor, Maine / 1994
FORMAT / ISBN: Hardcover / 096344591

These days, basketball fans and Cindy Blodgett fans are synonymous in the state of Maine. One can't love the sport of basketball without appreciating Cindy Blodgett. Fans will enjoy an inside look at Blodgett's basketball career, as told in *Simply the Best: The Cindy Blodgett Story*. Author Ron Brown, a sportswriter, details Blodgett's experiences playing basketball from the first grade up through high school. As a child, Blodgett played basketball for hours in the driveway of her Clinton, Maine, home. In fact, she played so much that she would wear out two or three balls each year.

Blodgett's story includes her impressive high school highlights: four state championships with the Lawrence Bulldogs, becoming the all-time highest scorer in Maine high school basketball history with 2,596 points, and numerous other basketball records and awards. Blodgett's story presents her as an extremely positive role model. She states, "I don't think I'm any better than anyone else. I just think I work harder." *Simply the Best* includes more than 75 black-and-white photos; numerous play charts; and a transcript of a televised broadcast of the big, come-back, regular season game between Lawrence and Cony during Blodgett's senior year.

This book whets the appetite of fans, leaving them hoping for follow-up books that will feature her college career, Olympic career, pro career, coaching career. (Hey, if Cindy can dream, so can her fans!) Profits from the sale of *Simply the Best* go to several charities and nonprofit organizations, including the Kidney Foundation of Maine and the University of Maine Foundation.

LEARNING ACTIVITIES

1. Write a follow-up chapter to *Simply the Best: The Cindy Blodgett Story*. Summarize Blodgett's basketball experiences since the book was completed. You may refer to newspaper and magazine articles for information.

2. Select a sports "hero" from your own high school. Interview that student, watch the stu-

dent in action, and then write a short biographical story. You might try to get your story published in your school or community newspaper.

3. Learn how girls' basketball has changed over the years. Interview players and coaches from today and from 10, 20, or 30 years ago. Have the rules changed over time? In what ways? What changes have occurred with ball size, with uniforms, with post-season play, with fan loyalty? Make a comparison chart showing girls' basketball, then and now.

ABOUT THE AUTHOR

Ron Brown was born in Camden in 1950. He has lived and worked in the state most of his adult life. Brown has been writing professionally for twenty-one years. He is the author of five basketball books, including *Back to Basics* and *Basketball 2000*. He has worked as a journalist, including writing the "Time Out" column for the *Bangor Daily News*, and as a boys basketball coach at the Bangor Christian School. He currently lives in Bangor, Maine, with his wife and two sons.

A VERY YOUNG MUSICIAN

AUTHOR / PHOTOGRAPHER: Jill Krementz
AGE LEVEL / LENGTH: 8-12 years / 48 pages
PUBLISHER / COPYRIGHT DATE: Simon & Schuster / 1991
FORMAT / ISBN: Paperback / 0671792512 (recently out of print)

Nationally-known photo-journalist Jill Krementz visits Portland, Maine, to show and tell the story of ten-year-old Josh Broder. Josh plays the trumpet. *A Very Young Musician* follows the boy's experiences at home, school, practice, and music camp. Color photographs clearly depict Josh's musical life. The reader learns how this one youngster dedicates his life to a future career in music. The message is strong: work hard everyday at something you love and one day you'll excel in your chosen field. Josh's love for music fills the book.

LEARNING ACTIVITIES

1. Select a child from your community to profile, someone you know or who has been recommended by others. He or she should have a special hobby or interest. Then follow Krementz's model in *A Very Young Musician* to show the daily life of this person.

2. Interview members of a school band or orchestra from your community. How many members are there? When did members first start playing? How often do they practice? What awards have they received? Combine this information into an article for your school newspaper.

3. In *A Very Young Musician,* Josh attends a music camp in Michigan. Maine has many of its own music camps. If possible, visit a music camp in the state and learn about its history, traditions, and philosophy. Write up your findings in a brochure advertising the camp.

4. Take a survey. Ask people: "Who is your favorite musical performer?" Look for trends in terms of types of music (e.g., country, rock, rap) and the age level of those surveyed.

ABOUT THE AUTHOR

Jill Krementz grew up in Morristown, New Jersey. She attended Drew University and Columbia University. She was hired as the first woman photographer for the *New York Herald-Tribune.* Her photographs have appeared in *The New York Times, Life, Time, Newsweek,* and many other publications.

Her first photograph book, *The Faces of South Vietnam,* was published in 1968. Since then, she has written and photo-illustrated more than two dozen books for young readers. *A Very Young Musician* is one of a series of "Very Young" books by Krementz. The series started in 1976 with *A Very Young Dancer,* and has included portraits of a gymnast, skater, and skier. She also has written and photographed books in a "How It Feels" series, including *How It Feels When a Parent Dies, How It Feels to Be Adopted,* and *How It Feels When Parents Divorce.*

Krementz currently lives in New York City.

MARGARET WISE BROWN:
AUTHOR OF GOODNIGHT MOON

AUTHOR: Carol Greene / PHOTOGRAPHER: photographs from a variety of sources
AGE LEVEL / LENGTH: 4-7 years / 48 pages
PUBLISHER / COPYRIGHT DATE: Childrens Press / 1993
FORMAT / ISBN: Paperback / 0516442546; Library Binding / 0516042548

Margaret Wise Brown: Author of Goodnight Moon is part of the "Rookie Biography" series for young children. With numerous photos and five short chapters, the book shows and tells about the life of the famous children's book author, Margaret Wise Brown. The book describes Brown's love for playing make-believe when she was a child, how she came to write many of her famous books, and how much she enjoyed her Maine island home which had "no electricity, no phone, and no bathroom, but nature was all around." The final chapter tells of Brown's unexpected death at the age of forty-two. Young readers also learn that Brown wrote more than 100 children's books, books that continue to bring enjoyment to children more than 50 years after the author's death.

Margaret Wise Brown: Author of Goodnight Moon is an easy book which beginning readers can read independently. Photographs of Brown's books are included, as well as a listing of important dates from her life, and a simple index. It is likely that the first books many children experience are by Margaret Wise Brown. Now they may enjoy a beginning biography of this revered author.

LEARNING ACTIVITIES

1. Reread your favorite Margaret Wise Brown book; then write or tell why it is your favorite. What part of the book did you like best? Why do you think kids today still enjoy this book?

2. Margaret Wise Brown loved animals. She had as many as twenty pet rabbits at a time when she was a child. When she grew up, she wrote a book about rabbits, called *The Runaway Bunny*. Write and draw a story about one of your own pets. Share your story with a friend or family member.

3. Go on a Margaret Wise Brown book search. She wrote more than 100 children's books. Many of her books are still available today. As you visit the school library, the public library, and bookstores, look for books written by Margaret Wise Brown. Keep a list of all the books you find by her. How many different books can you find?

ABOUT THE AUTHOR

Carol Greene has worked as an editor and writing teacher. She has written more than 100 books, including those in the Childrens Press Rookie Biographies Series. She currently lives in Webster Groves, Missouri.

ABBIE BURGESS: LIGHTHOUSE HEROINE

AUTHOR: Ruth Sexton Sargent & Dorothy Holder Jones
AGE LEVEL / LENGTH: 10-14 years / 190 pages
PUBLISHER / COPYRIGHT DATE: Ruth Sargent, available from Lighthouse Depot / 1969
FORMAT / ISBN: Paperback / 0892720182

This biography tells the story of Abbie Burgess, who helped her father tend the lighthouse on Matinicus Rock, off the coast of Maine, during the mid-1800s. Abbie arrived on Matinicus Rock in 1853 with her family. Even though she was only fourteen-years-old, she had many family and work responsibilities, since her mother was sickly and her only brother soon left the family for a job as a fisherman.

Abbie learned to light and tend the lamps in the twin towers by herself. When her father needed to sail to Rockland for supplies or to sell the lobsters he had caught, Abbie was in charge. During several severe winter storms, including the Great Storm of 1856, Abbie kept the lights burning even as ice coated the lighthouse windows, as waves swept away some buildings, and as the food supply dwindled to just eggs and cornmeal. Abbie's hero-ism became well-known, and she received special presents and awards from sailors and the townspeople of Rockland. When Abbie's father's appointment as lighthouse keeper was finished, Abbie dreaded the thought of leaving her beloved lighthouse. She stayed on to teach the new keeper's family how to run the lighthouse. Abbie's lighthouse destiny continued, as she fell in love with and married one of the keeper's sons.

Young readers will enjoy the heroic story of Abbie Burgess. They will also be transported back in time to see what life was like in the mid-1800s. The food, clothing, schooling, pastimes, and chores were very different from those of today. Authors Ruth Sargent and Dorothy Jones make this earlier time come to life for young readers.

LEARNING ACTIVITIES

1. Abbie Burgess's experiences during the Great Storm of 1856 have been featured in numerous anthologies and several picture books. Select a different part from *Abbie Burgess: Lighthouse Heroine* and turn it into a picture book. Reread your selected section several times; then rewrite that section as a story, with simpler text and add illustrations if you wish. Share your picture book with a younger child.

2. Using *Abbie Burgess: Lighthouse Heroine* as a guide, create a chart with a list of food, clothing, school subjects, pastimes, chores, etc. from the mid-1800s. Then create a simi-lar list for the present time. Compare and contrast the two lists. How is life today similar and different than it was in the 1850s? Do you think you would have enjoyed living in the mid-1800s? Why or why not?

3. The weather was of vital importance to Abbie Burgess's life. See the weather poems and sayings on page 61 of the book. Discuss them. Have you heard them before? What does each one mean? Do you believe any of them are true? Then try to collect other weather poems or sayings. Put them into a booklet. Create some of your own original weather poems and sayings, and add them to the booklet.

ABOUT THE AUTHORS

Ruth Sargent was a Midwesterner who moved, more than forty years ago, to Peaks Island, off the Maine coast near Portland. She worked for three Portland newspapers over the course of a decade, providing coverage of the Casco Bay Islands' news. She also wrote articles for magazines and the Associated Press.

Sargent has been writing for the past thirty years and claims that "writing takes precedence over housework and social life." Her advice to aspiring writers is to "write about what one knows, but additional research is like a treasure hunt." Sargent credits her family with helping her to write. Her son who fell in love with the sea at age four serves as her "nautical adviser," and her daughter who enjoys cooking keeps Sargent fed when she is immersed nine hours a day in writing a book.

Sargent has authored several books, including *Island Merry-Go-Round* (see page 93), *The Tunnel Beneath the Sea*, *The Littlest Lighthouse*, and *The Casco Bay Islands* (a photo essay book for the "Images of America" series by Arcadia Publishing). She also has self-published several of her own books, including *Always Nine Years Old: Sarah Orne Jewett's Childhood* (see page 203), *Five Girls Aboard the Mayflower's Voyage to Freedom*, and *How to Do a Who-Done-It*.

The co-author of this biography of Abbie Burgess was Dorothy Holder Jones, who was born in Houston, Texas, and lived in Atlanta, Georgia, and then Falls Church, Virginia. While raising her two children, she worked as a freelance writer. She had several hundred articles and stories published in magazines, as well as five novels for teenagers. Jones died several years ago.

KEEP THE LIGHTS BURNING, ABBIE

AUTHOR: Peter and Connie Roop / ILLUSTRATOR: Peter E. Hanson
AGE LEVEL / LENGTH: 6-9 years / 40 pages
PUBLISHER / COPYRIGHT DATE: Carolrhoda Books (book); Live Oak Media (audio tape) / 1985
FORMAT / ISBN: Paperback / 0876144547; Library binding / 0876142757; Hardcover with audio tape / 0874991358; Paperback with audio tape / 087499134X

Keep the Lights Burning, Abbie tells the true story of Abbie Burgess, a lighthouse keeper's daughter in the mid-1800s. When her father takes a boat to town to get food, supplies, and medicine for his sick wife, Abbie is left not only to watch over her family, but also to tend the lights at Matinicus Rock lighthouse. A fierce storm moves in for several weeks. Abbie keeps the lights burning in the lighthouse night after night. She grows weary and hungry—there are only eggs from the chickens left to eat. Finally, the sky is light, the storm passes, and Abbie's father returns.

This book is a special treat because it is an easy-reader; there are not many biographies that are easy-readers. The Roops succeed in telling a compelling story with short sentences and simple words. The watercolors of illustrator Peter Hanson help to clarify the story and set the scene of life at a lighthouse almost 150 years ago.

LEARNING ACTIVITIES

1. Research lighthouses. How do they work? How is their signal selected? How many lighthouses are there in Maine? Are there any manned lighthouses left in the state? Visit a lighthouse if possible. Write to or interview a lighthouse keeper (the Coast Guard might be helpful). Write a report using the information you have learned.

2. Find an old diary to read. Check with older family members or your local library or historical society. How was life different during the time when the diary was written than it is today? Can you easily understand the diary? Why or why not?

3. Create a tape recording of *Keep the Lights Burning, Abbie*, complete with sound effects. How can you create the sounds of the chickens, the storm, etc.? Share the tape and the book with a group of younger children.

ABOUT THE AUTHORS

Peter and Connie Roop are a husband-and-wife writing team. Peter has been coming to Maine since he was a child to visit his grandparents in York, where they had an antique store. Since 1969, the Roops have owned a house in Stonington, Maine, where they come every summer to "read, relax, camp, and eat lobster!"

While researching and writing a travel article about Maine islands, the Roops came across the story of Abbie Burgess. To research their story on Abbie Burgess, they flew over Matinicus Rock in an airplane, read actual letters written by Burgess, visited Maine in January to get a feel for the state's winter weather, and gathered information from the Shore Village Lighthouse Museum in Rockland. *Keep the Lights Burning, Abbie* was a featured book on the *Reading Rainbow* television show, and it has been adopted by five reading series.

The Roops are fulltime teachers as well as authors. Peter teaches grades 1 and 2, and Connie teaches high school science. They have been writing since 1980, and have had twenty children's books and five teaching guides published. Their books include *Buttons for General Washington, Ahyoka and the Talking Leaves,* and *Seasons of the Cranes.*

During the winter, the Roops live in Appleton, Wisconsin, with their two children. Their hobbies include camping, canoeing, island hopping, and playing games.

RACHEL CARSON

AUTHOR: Leslie A. Wheeler / PHOTOGRAPHER: photographs from a variety of sources

AGE LEVEL / LENGTH: 10-14 years / 138 pages

PUBLISHER / COPYRIGHT DATE: Silver Burdett Press (div. of Simon & Schuster) / 1991

FORMAT / ISBN: Paperback / 0382241746; Library binding / 0382241673

Rachel Carson, by Leslie A. Wheeler, is part of the "Pioneers in Change" series, published by Silver Burdett Press. The series consists of biographies of scientists, inventors, and social innovators who did pioneering work which changed the way the world lives and thinks. Rachel Carson was a perfect choice for this series. Her work as a biologist and a writer had a marked impact on the way people see and interact with nature.

This biography traces the life of Rachel Carson from her birth in 1907 in Springdale, Pennsylvania, to her death in 1964, at the age of fifty-six. It extends beyond her death with a look at the posthumous awards she received and the continued impact her books, such as *The Sea Around Us* and *Silent Spring,* had into the 1970s and 1980s. Carson's early love of writing is documented; she had her first story published in *St. Nicholas* magazine when she was just eleven-years-old. Her love of the sea and "call" to be a marine biologist are also shown through samples of her writing and detailed descriptions of her college years and her early scientific work. And Maine is not forgotten. Carson's love of the Maine seashore and her cherished visits to her summer cottage in West Southport, Maine, are described fully by author Leslie Wheeler.

The message that shines through this biography is that Rachel Carson was a woman on a mission. She seemed born to be a writer and a scientist, and she followed her chosen careers with a passion. Carson was never married, but she raised two nieces and a grand-nephew, and cared for her elderly mother for many years. Even when Carson was very ill with cancer and heart disease, she still made time to work most days. She felt a sense of duty to share her love of the sea and her concerns about pesticides with the world.

Leslie A. Wheeler has created a fine, readable biography that adults as well as children will enjoy. Wheeler manages to make difficult scientific terms understandable to young readers. The black-and-white photographs add further interest to the book. The book includes a helpful list of important dates, a complete bibliography, and a detailed index.

LEARNING ACTIVITIES

1. Borrow one of Rachel Carson's books from the library: *Under the Sea Wind, The Edge of the Sea, The Sea Around Us, Silent Spring,* or *The Sense of Wonder.* Read a section of the book. What do you think of Carson's writing? Does she make scientific information

easy to understand? How so? Can you sense Carson's love of nature when you read her words? In what ways? Write an essay on what you have learned.

2. Author Leslie A. Wheeler makes it clear in this biography that Rachel Carson had a "calling" to become both a writer and a scientist. Even as a child, Carson loved writing and nature. Interview an adult you know who loves his/her career. Ask questions about the adult's childhood hobbies and interests. Can you find any "hints" from the adult's childhood that would have indicated his/her chosen career as an adult? Next, look at your own life. What "hints" do you have as to what your future career might be?

3. Rachel Carson received the Presidential Medal of Freedom, the nation's highest civilian award, posthumously (after her death) in 1980. Research what other Mainers have received the Presidential Medal of Freedom. Make a chart showing what you learn—which Mainers received the Presidential Medal of Freedom, when, and for what reason.

ABOUT THE AUTHOR

Leslie A. Wheeler is also the author of *Jane Addams*, another biography in the Silver Burdett Press "Pioneers in Change" series. Wheeler is originally from California. She now lives in Massachusetts. Her hobbies include hiking, cross-country skiing, and watching wildlife near her Berkshire Hills home.

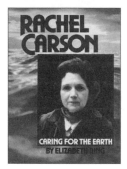

RACHEL CARSON: CARING FOR THE EARTH

AUTHOR: Elizabeth Ring/ PHOTOGRAPHER: photographs from a variety of sources
AGE LEVEL / LENGTH: 6-10 years / 48 pages
PUBLISHER / COPYRIGHT DATE: The Millbrook Press / 1992
FORMAT / ISBN: Hardcover / 1562940562; Paperback / 1562947982

Rachel Carson: Caring for the Earth is an early biography about Rachel Carson, famous biologist and writer. Author Elizabeth Ring writes simply but clearly and with many details about Carson's childhood, her job as a scientist, the books she wrote, and Carson's special affection for Maine. In particular, the book explains that Carson raised her grandnephew Roger (after his mother died) and spent hours exploring the seashore and woodland with him near her West Southport, Maine, cottage. Years later, Carson wrote a book called *A Sense of Wonder* about the experiences she shared with Roger.

This biography opens and closes by asking young readers to question and wonder as Rachel Carson must have done. At the beginning of the book, readers are asked how they would feel if they lived in a pretty little town where trees, flowers, and animals suddenly died. This hypothetical situation is the same one posed by Rachel Carson at the beginning of her most famous book, *Silent Spring*. Then the end of the book asks young readers to guess which areas of the environment Rachel Carson would be most involved in if she were still alive today. By posing questions and speaking directly to young readers, Elizabeth Ring helps to make this biography an "active" one that encourages children to think, wonder, and question about human life and its effect on the environment.

LEARNING ACTIVITIES

1. Read the first three paragraphs on page 5 of *Rachel Carson: Caring for the Earth*. Then write a story or draw illustrations to show how you would feel if the beautiful living things in your town suddenly began to die.

2. Find a copy of Rachel Carson's *A Sense of Wonder* at the library. Read parts of this book and study the photographs in it. What things in nature did Carson and her grandnephew Roger "wonder" about? Have you wondered about those same things? What other things in nature make you wonder and ask questions?

3. Pretend to be Rachel Carson. Write or tell a speech warning others about an environmental concern or danger in the world today.

ABOUT THE AUTHOR

Elizabeth Ring says that her "Maine" connection began when her family used to go camping in Acadia. Then her family summered in Trenton for ten years in an old farmhouse on 30 acres overlooking Union Bay. Ring says that she still returns to camp in Maine, often at Lamoine State Park, but that her family no longer owns the old farmhouse.

Ring's interest in Rachel Carson began when she read Carson's books and explored the Maine shores that Carson had written about. She first wrote about Carson in a magazine article for *Ranger Rick*. In addition to *Rachel Carson: Caring for the Earth*, Ring has written *Henry David Thoreau: In Step with Nature*, a biography which refers to Thoreau's journey into the Maine woods. Ring has authored several photo-essay picture books photographed by Dwight Kuhn of Dexter, Maine, including *Night Flier*, *What Rot! Nature's Mighty Recycler*, and *Lucky Mouse* (see page 281). She is also the author of the recent picture book, *Loon at Northwood Lake*.

Ring grew up in Rowayton, Connecticut. She attended school in Massachusetts and graduated from Middlebury College in Vermont. She also studied fiction writing at New York University. Ring has two daughters and four grandchildren. She lives with her husband in Woodbury, Connecticut. Her hobbies include music, reading, painting, hiking, and camping.

RACHEL CARSON: PIONEER OF ECOLOGY

AUTHOR: Kathleen V. Kudlinski / ILLUSTRATOR: Ted Lewin
AGE LEVEL / LENGTH: 8-14 years / 64 pages
PUBLISHER / COPYRIGHT DATE: Puffin Books (div. of Penguin Books USA) / 1988
FORMAT / ISBN: Paperback / 0140322426

Rachel Carson: Pioneer of Ecology is part of the "Women of Our Time" series, which features twentieth-century women who have had a positive impact upon the world. This biography is well-written, making a complex person easily accessible to young readers.

Author Kathleen V. Kudlinski begins her story with Rachel Carson as a small girl who has a conch shell pressed to her ear. Even as a child who had never seen the sea, Carson still felt drawn to the ocean. Carson's early love of nature is stressed. Readers learn how she talked her older brother out of hunting and how insects found inside the Carson household were simply captured and released outside. Carson's early interest in writing is also highlighted in a chapter called "Big Plans."

When Carson goes to college, she finds that she loves both writing and science, and feels she must make a choice between the two. Readers learn how Carson turned to an Alfred Tennyson poem for inspiration; Tennyson's poem, which told her that her "own path led to the sea," was prophetic. Carson turned to the sea as a scientist and as a writer, but also as a human being who considered herself part of nature. Carson felt most at home in a house she had built beside the sea in West Southport, Maine.

LEARNING ACTIVITIES

1. Rachel Carson had a difficult time deciding between a career in writing or science—she loved both. At the time she lived, no one believed it was possible to combine the two careers. Interview several adults to learn how they decided upon their career choices. Have they ever changed careers? Do they believe they will change careers in the future? After these interviews, and after reading *Rachel Carson: Pioneer of Ecology*, write a paper describing what you have learned about choosing a career.

2. Rachel Carson felt drawn to the sea even before she ever saw it, and that was the topic about which she wrote most of her books. What part of nature or the environment interests you the most? Learn more about your area of interest by reading nonfiction books and observing that part of nature. Afterwards, write a report about what you have learned.

3. Rachel Carson is one of many famous Mainers. Hold a "Famous Mainers" fair or exhibit in your classroom or at your school. Classmates may work alone or with partners to study a famous Mainer and then prepare a report and exhibit about that person. Select a time for the public to visit your exhibit.

ABOUT THE AUTHOR

Kathleen V. Kudlinski was inspired by Rachel Carson when she was a teenager. After reading Carson's books, Kudlinski decided to become a scientist herself. After teaching for many years, Kudlinski became a writer. While researching *Rachel Carson: Pioneer of Ecology*, Kudlinski spoke with Carson's friends, listened to her taped speeches, read the draft versions of Carson's works, and visited Carson's home in West Southport, Maine.

HIS PROPER POST: A BIOGRAPHY OF GEN. JOSHUA LAWRENCE CHAMBERLAIN

AUTHOR: Sis Deans / PHOTOGRAPHER: photos from a variety of sources
AGE LEVEL / LENGTH: 10 years–adult / 170 pages
PUBLISHER / COPYRIGHT DATE: Belle Grove Publishing Company / 1996
FORMAT / ISBN: Hardcover / 188392605X; Paperback / 1883926076

His Proper Post: A Biography of Gen. Joshua Lawrence Chamberlain follows the life of Joshua Chamberlain from his birth, in 1828, in Brewer, Maine, until his death in 1914. Although a man of few words, Chamberlain was a man of many accomplishments–at least early in his life. Chamberlain had a severe stutter and avoided certain words and social situations; so many mistakenly thought him to be shy. But as Chamberlain's accomplishments grew—a Civil War military hero, a four-term governor of Maine, President of Bowdoin College—Chamberlain became known as an "elegant speaker."

This biography presents Joshua Chamberlain as a rich, fully-developed character thanks to the thorough research and numerous details included by author Sis Deans. Young readers will learn about Chamberlain's knack for learning foreign languages, the fact that he was a self-taught musician, his dedication to his horse, Charlemagne (shot three times while carrying his master in battles), Chamberlain's ability to think quickly when he mistakenly crossed to the enemy's side, and much more. The hardships and realities of the Civil War, and the heroism of Chamberlain and his Twentieth Maine Infantry, are all detailed.

In *His Proper Post*, Sis Deans begins each chapter with a quote by or about Chamberlain. She then briefly relates her own personal experiences and thoughts on writing each particular chapter. For example, in the chapter entitled "The 20th Maine Infantry," Deans actually visited Gettysburg and Little Round Top and described her impressions of the battlefields. The back of *His Proper Post* includes extensive footnote information, descriptive summaries of generals from the Civil War, a glossary, bibliography, and index; the only noticeable omission is a timeline of Chamberlain's life. Young and old readers alike will be captivated by this fascinating story of one of Maine's most versatile, heroic, and compassionate men.

LEARNING ACTIVITIES

1. Create a Joshua L. Chamberlain display. Gather information, photos, maps, and charts from *His Proper Post* and other biographical resources. You might create a clay model of an important incident from Chamberlain's life, a family tree showing Chamberlain's life—whatever comes to mind. Work to make your display interesting, and make it interactive, if possible. When you are finished, invite others to view your display.

2. Select several incidents from Chamberlain's life that you believe young children could most readily understand and identify with. Then write a short story or create a picture book about your selected incidents. Share your story/book with a classroom of younger students.

3. The author of *His Proper Post*, Sis Deans, claims that everyone who writes fiction should also experience writing a biography since doing so teaches a writer so much about telling a story, developing a character, and writing in a disciplined way. Take Deans' s advice and write a brief biography of another Mainer. You might write about someone famous, someone from your family, whomever you'd like. Just make certain to research thoroughly, and to create an interesting and true story. After writing a brief biography, reflect upon what you learned from the experience.

ABOUT THE AUTHOR

See information about Sis Deans on page 34.

LOST ON A MOUNTAIN IN MAINE

AUTHOR: Donn Fendler, as told to Joseph B. Egan / PHOTOGRAPHER: photos from a variety of sources
AGE LEVEL / LENGTH: 8 years–adult / 125 pages
PUBLISHER / COPYRIGHT DATE: Cricketfield Press (hardcover);
William Morrow (paperback); Audio Bookshelf (audio book) / 1939
FORMAT / ISBN: Hardcover / 0897251008; Paperback / 068811573X;
Audio book / 1883332044

Lost on a Mountain in Maine tells the true story of twelve-year-old Donn Fendler. While hiking down from the top of Mount Katahdin in July 1939, Fendler became cold and impatient and ran ahead of a friend to meet his father and brothers further down the trail. Instead, he became hopelessly lost. For nine days the boy fought to survive in the Maine wilderness with hunger, wild animals, mosquitoes, the weather, and rough, unmarked terrain working against him.

His journey to an inhabited cabin on the east branch of the Penobscot River was nothing short of a miracle. Photographs from a variety of sources, including newspaper reports of Donn's rescue, add a further touch of realism to the ordeal. *Lost on a Mountain in Maine* is a classic survival tale that thousands and thousands of school children from across the country have enjoyed for close to sixty years. The book reads like fiction; but the fact that it is a true story makes it all the more incredible and inspirational to young readers.

LEARNING ACTIVITIES

1. Study a map of the hiking trails in Baxter State Park. Can you see how it was possible for Donn Fendler to get lost? Write to a ranger at the park. How many people are lost on Katahdin each year? In what ways are trails marked and hikers kept safe? Who is responsible for searching for lost hikers?

2. Talk with rangers, guides, and scout leaders about wilderness safety. Read safety manuals. Then write and design a wilderness safety guide for children.

3. *Lost on a Mountain in Maine* captures the day-to-day trials of Donn Fendler's wilderness trek. Find out what the reaction of the outside world was to his ordeal by reading newspaper stories about Fendler's experiences, starting from July 17, 1939.

4. Donn Fendler did not write his own story, but rather he shared his recollections with Joseph B. Egan. Egan then wrote *Lost on a Mountain in Maine* from Fendler's perspective, using the boy's own words as much as possible. Find someone who has had an adventure (even a small one). Interview that person to learn details about the person's adventure. Then write a description of that person's adventure, trying to make it sound realistic and believable. Did you find it more difficult to write someone else's story than writing a story about yourself? Why or why not?

ABOUT THE AUTHOR

Since his brush with death in Baxter State Park more than fifty years ago, Donn Fendler has received hundreds of letters, mostly from Maine school children, which he says he always answers. He still visits many Maine schools every year.

Fendler currently lives in Clarksville, Tennessee, but summers in Newport, Maine. He attended Maine Central Institute, in Pittsfield, and the University of Maine. Fendler is retired from the U.S. Army.

Fendler says that this book was not dedicated to anybody, but if he was to dedicate the book today, it would be to the Boy Scouts of America. Fendler's love for and appreciation of scouting is shown by his active involvement in scouting, attaining the rank of Life Scout.

A WEEKEND WITH WINSLOW HOMER

AUTHOR: Ann Keay Beneduce / PHOTOGRAPHER: photographs from a variety of sources, including numerous photographs of Winslow Homer paintings
AGE LEVEL / LENGTH: 8 years–adult / 64 pages
PUBLISHER / COPYRIGHT DATE: Rizzoli International Publications / 1993
FORMAT / ISBN: Hardcover / 0847816222; Paperback / 0847819191

A *Weekend with Winslow Homer* is a unique art book written as though it were told by Winslow Homer himself. Legendary American artist Winslow Homer (1836-1910) welcomes young visitors to his art studio at Prouts Neck, Maine, and shares the story of how he came to be an artist. Homer was born in Boston and grew up in rural Cambridge. Even as a child, he was always drawing and enjoying the out-of-doors.

Homer began his career by doing sketches for publications such as *Harper's Weekly*, including drawings of the inauguration of President Lincoln. His early works were published as wood engravings. He later worked with oils, and finally with watercolors. Homer visited Paris and England for inspiration. Over time, Homer's work evolved from playful, carefree scenes of people in nature to darker, more serious paintings which pitted man against nature, and finally paintings which showed the awesome power of nature. Many of his later works were inspired in Maine.

A *Weekend with Winslow Homer* includes approximately forty photographs—a few photos of the artist and numerous reproductions of his paintings. The end of the book includes a listing by state of places to see Homer's original works, a three-page listing of important dates from Homer's life, and a description of each of his works included in the book. This book succeeds wonderfully in making a great American artist from the past come alive for today's youth.

LEARNING ACTIVITIES

1. Select your favorite Winslow Homer work from A *Weekend with Winslow Homer* and write a critique of it. Why is it your favorite work? What medium does Homer use? Where is your eye first drawn to in the work? What is the theme of the work? Share your critique with a friend and see if your friend agrees with your comments.

2. Select a local artist. Interview that artist and watch him or her at work. View several samples of the artist's work. Then write a booklet about the artist called "A Weekend with (artist's name)." Write the booklet as if the artist was actually telling the story.

3. Using the guide in the back of A Weekend with Winslow Homer, plan a visit to a museum that has one or more pieces of Homer's work. As you view Homer's real work, notice how it makes you feel. How is a real painting different from a photographic reproduction? Why do you think Winslow Homer was known as the greatest American artist of his time? Write a journal entry about your museum visit.

ABOUT THE AUTHOR

Author information on Ann Keay Beneduce was unavailable.

DAHLOV IPCAR, ARTIST

AUTHOR: Pat Davidson Reef / PHOTOGRAPHER: photographs from a variety of sources
AGE LEVEL / LENGTH: 8-12 years / 48 pages
PUBLISHER / COPYRIGHT DATE: Kennebec River Press; available from Dickinson Family Publications / 1987
FORMAT / ISBN: Paperback / 0933858205

This biography traces, with text and photographs, the life and work of Georgetown Island resident Dahlov Ipcar—painter, sculptor, and children's book illustrator. At an early age Ipcar painted a frieze on her bedroom wall and made sketches depicting life around her. As she matured, so did her work, which includes oil paintings of farm scenes, paintings incorporating intricate tapestry designs, cloth sculptures, needlepoint tapestries, and large murals. Dahlov Ipcar, Artist also includes a section with children's questions about the artist's work and Ipcar's responses.

Dahlov Ipcar, Artist gives young readers a chance to visit a "museum" of sorts while seeing numerous samples of Ipcar's work. Author Pat Davidson Reef clearly details Ipcar's creative childhood and artistic heritage so that young readers can learn how Dahlov Ipcar developed her true vocation as an artist.

LEARNING ACTIVITIES

1. Locate several children's books by Dahlov Ipcar at the library, such as Lobsterman (see page 51), My Wonderful Christmas Tree (see page 172), Bug City, and A Flood of Creatures. Study the illustrations in these books. If possible, also view some samples of her artwork, listed on page 46 of Dahlov Ipcar, Artist. Then write about her artwork. How are her works similar or different from each other? What subjects does she choose to paint or sculpt? What materials does she use most often? What styles and patterns are repeated throughout her work?

2. Part of Ipcar's success as an artist is her versatility—her ability to produce art in many different forms. Decide on a picture/image that you would like to create. Then use two different means to produce your image. For example, if you want to show a sunset, you might use photography and painting; if you want to produce a work of art based on a flower, you might use collage and sculpture. Compare your two methods.

3. Dahlov Ipcar's career as an artist makes perfect sense considering she had a famous sculptor for a father and an artist for a mother (William and Marguerite Zorach). Trace three or four generations of careers in your family. What jobs did your great-grandparents have, what were their children's jobs, etc.? Does a family tree of occupations exist for your family? Did your relatives continue in careers that their parents had followed? What about other people's families? Do you think someone like Dahlov Ipcar became a famous artist because she inherited artistic ability or because she was exposed to art experiences throughout her childhood?

ABOUT THE AUTHOR

Pat Davidson Reef was born in Portland, Maine, in 1939. She is a graduate of Wayneflete School, Emerson College, and the University of Southern Maine. She has worked as a high school English and humanities teacher as well as a college instructor of children's literature courses.

Reef has been writing for twenty years. For eight years she worked as the regional editor of *Art New England*, an arts journal. She also writes arts articles for *The Morning Sentinel* and *Kennebec Journal*. She currently writes and edits for the *Central Square Times*, a small southern Maine newspaper that focuses on arts, health, and human interest stories. She also edits *Kids Ink*, a newspaper for Maine students by Maine students. Reef's interest in the arts led her to write two children's books on artists: *Dahlov Ipcar, Artist* and *Bernard Langlais, Sculptor* (see page 204). She is working on two books, one about Henry Wadsworth Longfellow and the other about Maine artist, William Thon.

Reef lives in Falmouth, Maine, where she enjoys encouraging the "artist" inside each of her five grandchildren. She also enjoys doing needlepoint, taking nature photographs, and reading children's books.

ALWAYS NINE YEARS OLD:
SARAH ORNE JEWETT'S CHILDHOOD

AUTHOR: Ruth Sargent
AGE LEVEL / LENGTH: 8-12 years / 51 pages
PUBLISHER / COPYRIGHT DATE: Ruth Sargent; available from Maine
Writers and Publishers Alliance / 1985
FORMAT / ISBN: Paperback / no ISBN

Always Nine Years Old: Sarah Orne Jewett's Childhood gives readers a rare glimpse into the childhood of a famous writer. The book describes Jewett's early childhood and relates her special relationships with her grandfather (a sea captain) and her father (a country doctor). Jewett's heritage, her health problems, and her passion for her hometown of South Berwick are all explored in the book. The book also shows that Jewett was well on the way to becoming a writer, even as a child.

The story revolves around Jewett's magical ninth birthday. On her ninth birthday, Jewett went on a surprise picnic with her family. She received many wonderful gifts—a gold pen, a box of writing paper, a glass boat inkwell; she learned that she had won a story contest; and best of all, she was allowed to sleep over at her grandfather's house in her own special room. The magic of young Jewett's birthday continued as she listened down the stairway to the adults' conversations below. She even heard her grandfather's friends, a famous poet and a magazine editor, praise her writing and speak of her promising future as a writer. The next morning, Jewett woke to one more birthday surprise, her own mahogany desk. As Sargent explains in the epilogue, the same desk can still be seen today at the Jewett House in South Berwick.

Always Nine Years Old: Sarah Orne Jewett's Childhood was written by Sargent for a Sarah Orne Jewett Conference held at Westbrook College in 1985. The story is well-worth reading in spite of some surface flaws (e.g., plain format, typographical errors, the use of direct quotes from a century and a half ago with no reference to the source of the quotes). The story will attract readers to Jewett's writing and will serve as a true inspiration to Maine's aspiring young writers.

LEARNING ACTIVITIES

1. Look through *Always Nine Years Old: Sarah Orne Jewett's Childhood* again and find as many references as you can to young Jewett's passion for writing. Make a list of these references. Is it obvious from the list that Sarah Orne Jewett was going to become a writer one day? Now make a list of your own "passions." What is it that you love to do? What are your hobbies? How do you spend your free time? Does your list hint at what you might do as an adult? If you were to make a prediction on your future career, what would you predict?

2. Plan a visit to the Jewett House in South Berwick. Before going, make a list of all the objects mentioned in *Always Nine years Old: Sarah Orne Jewett's Childhood* that you hope to see (e.g., the mahogany desk, the glass boat inkwell, the "miniature" of Jewett). Bring your list on your visit. Did you find the objects on your list? How did they differ from your expectations? How were they similar? Write a description of your visit.

3. Research another famous Mainer (read biographies, check newspaper or magazine articles, interview the famous Mainer if possible, etc.). Target your research toward the famous Mainer's childhood. Gather information about one specific experience from that Mainer's childhood, and write a short story about that experience.

ABOUT THE AUTHOR

See information about Ruth Sargent in page 190.

BERNARD LANGLAIS, SCULPTOR

AUTHOR: Pat Davidson Reef / PHOTOGRAPHER: photographs from a variety of sources

AGE LEVEL / LENGTH: 8-12 years / 48 pages

PUBLISHER / COPYRIGHT DATE: Kennebec River Press; available from Dickinson Family Publications / 1985

FORMAT / ISBN: Paperback / 093385806X

This biography of Bernard Langlais (1921-1977) provides facts about this well-known Maine sculptor's life, as well as black-and-white photographs of him and his work. The text gives the reader a feel for Langlais's life—his artistic roots, his passion for sculpting large animals, his creation of the world's largest wooden Indian. An appendix in the book includes listings of Langlais's awards, locations of private and public collections of his work, a glossary of art terms, plus a brief description/credit for each black and white photograph in the book.

Author Pat Davidson Reef has created a wonderful biography. The story gives young readers a glimpse into the mind of a creative artist, while the photographs help to bring Langlais and his sculptures to life.

LEARNING ACTIVITIES

1. Bernard Langlais's most famous sculpture is the wooden Indian located in Skowhegan. The Indian stands 65 feet high. Measure and mark off a 65 foot section outside. Can you imagine what it would be like to sculpt something so large? Write a list of all the special considerations you'd have when creating such a large sculpture.

2. Pat Davidson Reef tells the story of one Maine artist. The state of Maine has attracted many painters and sculptors. Talk with an artist from your area. Through interview questions and viewing artistic work, write a brief biography of the artist.

3. Learn more about Bernard Langlais. Try to view samples of his work. Read newspaper clippings about Langlais's work, such as the published articles dating from 1969, when he finished work on the Skowhegan Indian. Combine this new information into an addendum, or follow-up section, to Pat Davidson Reef's biography.

ABOUT THE AUTHOR

See information about Pat Davidson Reef on page 202.

EDNA ST. VINCENT MILLAY: POET

AUTHOR: Carolyn Daffron / PHOTOGRAPHER: photographs from a variety of sources
AGE LEVEL / LENGTH: 12 years–adult / 112 pages
PUBLISHER / COPYRIGHT DATE: Chelsea House Publishers / 1989
FORMAT / ISBN: Hardcover / 15554666680; Paperback / 0791004449

Edna St. Vincent Millay: Poet is part of the "American Women of Achievement" series, published by Chelsea House. Edna St. Vincent Millay was a world famous poet from Camden, Maine. This book succeeds at presenting her poetic genius and zest for life.

Millay was born in Rockland in 1892. Her parents were divorced when she was young, and her mother raised Millay and her two young sisters in Camden, while working as a visiting nurse. Millay's mother tended to her daughters' cultural needs as much as their physical needs. If the family had a choice between spending their limited resources on heat or books, they typically chose books. Millay wrote her first poem when she was five; by the age of nine, she had read most of Shakespeare's plays and poems, as well as works of traditional Latin literature.

Millay loved her family and the Camden countryside, but at the same time she felt like a prisoner in her small town, with no chance to escape. She expressed her feelings in a poem entitled "Renascence," and ironically that poem helped her gain her freedom when it was published in a poetry contest anthology to wide critical acclaim. Edna St. Vincent Millay became a legendary American poet during her lifetime, achieving both popular and critical success. She received the 1923 Pulitzer Prize for poetry. Millay was frequently ill and considered fragile, yet she still produced prolific quantities of poetry. At the age of 58, she died from a heart attack while climbing a staircase; some believe she was on the way to her upstairs study to write a final poem—inspired until the end.

LEARNING ACTIVITIES

1. Read Millay's poem "Renascence." Then visit Camden, Maine, where Edna St. Vincent Millay found much of her inspiration. Climb Mount Battie and enjoy the view. Then reread "Renascence." Do you believe the view from the top of Mount Battie inspired this poem? Why or why not? Did your understanding and appreciation of the poem change after you saw the view from atop Mount Battie? Write a summary of what the poem means to you.

2. Plan a celebration of Edna St. Vincent Millay's life and work. For example, you might read her poems and select several to read before an audience. You could also share a summary or write a play about this fascinating author's life. You might also have a visual display showing pictures of the author and a timeline of her life. Whatever your formulation—find a way to share Millay's talent with a new generation.

3. Turn Edna St. Vincent Millay's story into a picture book for young readers. Simplify her biography, select sections from her poetry that would be easily understood by children, and add drawings or copies of photographs to elaborate on her work and her life. Share your finished book with a group of children.

ABOUT THE AUTHOR

Carolyn Daffron works as a lawyer and a writer. She graduated from the University of Chicago and Harvard Law School. She currently lives in Philadelphia, with her husband and son. Daffron is the author of two other biographies in the "American Women of Achievement" series: *Gloria Steinem* and *Margaret Bourke-White*.

GEORGE MITCHELL: IN SEARCH OF PEACE

AUTHOR: Alberta Gould / PHOTOGRAPHER: photographs from a variety of sources
AGE LEVEL / LENGTH: 12 years–adult / 136 pages
PUBLISHER / COPYRIGHT DATE: Heritage Publishing / 1996
FORMAT / ISBN: Hardcover / 0929537041

In this biography, young readers can learn about one of Maine's most respected and famed politicians—George Mitchell. Mitchell grew up in Waterville, Maine, in a small Lebanese-American neighborhood, known as Head of Falls, on the Kennebec River. He grew up poor in finances, but strong in values. Mitchell's parents taught their five children that to succeed in life they must be willing to work hard. George Mitchell worked hard in school and was a good student; he also had numerous jobs while growing up: delivering newspapers, washing cars at an auto dealership, mowing lawns, shoveling snow, and doing janitorial work. Mitchell attended Bowdoin College and graduated with a degree in history and plans to become a history teacher. After serving in the Army in West Berlin, Mitchell decided to attend law school at Georgetown University.

Mitchell's political career began when he was hired to work on Edmund Muskie's campaign for the U.S. Senate. Later, he became chairman of Maine's Democratic Party. After losing in his first bid for office to James Longley for the governorship, Mitchell practiced law and then was appointed to a federal judgeship. When Ed Muskie became U.S. Secretary of State, Mitchell was appointed to fill Muskie's Senate seat, even though he had never before served in any elected public office. Mitchell thrived in the Senate, writing the Clean Water Act, and was eventually elected Senate Majority Leader in 1988. Mitchell was respected by both parties in his leadership of the Senate. After fourteen years in Washington, Mitchell surprised everyone by announcing that he would not seek reelection. The book ends with Mitchell facing a new challenge as an advisor on economic development and peace initiatives in Ireland.

George Mitchell: In Search of Peace includes numerous photos from Mitchell's childhood and career. The full text of Mitchell's statement to Lt. Col. Oliver North at the Iran-Contra hearings, and his speech upon receiving the Bowdoin Prize in 1995, are included at the end of the book. A bibliography and index are also included.

LEARNING ACTIVITIES

1. George Mitchell's mother was a Lebanese immigrant. In what ways do you think the fact that his mother was an immigrant influenced Mitchell's life and career? Interview another Mainer who is an immigrant or whose parents were immigrants. Learn that person's story. What struggles—linguistic, financial, cultural—did that person face? Write a summary of your interview.

2. Research the position of Senate Majority Leader. How long has that position been part of the Senate? What famous people have served in that position? What responsibilities go with the job? Write a report about what you learn.

3. George Mitchell loves to play cribbage. Learn the game if you do not already know how to play it. If you do, then practice and brush up on your skills. Afterwards, hold a cribbage tournament.

ABOUT THE AUTHOR

Alberta Gould is a Skowhegan native with a lifelong interest in Maine history and personalities. Gould has always written for herself, including journals and poetry, but she had never tried writing a book for others until deciding to undertake a biography of Margaret Chase Smith. *First Lady of the Senate: A Life of Margaret Chase Smith* (see page 208) grew out of her teaching experience. As a reading tutor, Gould was working with a group of fourth graders on a famous-person project. These students wanted to learn more about Margaret Chase Smith, but there was no material appropriate for young readers. Gould decided she'd fill this gap by writing a junior biography of Skowhegan's famous senator. Gould did much of her research at the Margaret Chase Smith Library, where she interviewed Senator Smith.

Since then, Gould, seeing another gap in junior biographies, has written *George Mitchell: In Search of Peace*. When writing biographies, Gould says that she reads and researches a great deal before she ever begins to write. Then once she starts writing, she watches for "holes in the information" and returns to do more research and interviews in order to fill in these holes.

Gould is the mother of two married daughters and "Nanny" to a grandson. She currently lives in central Maine with her husband. Her hobbies include traveling, reading, and gardening.

FIRST LADY OF THE SENATE: A LIFE OF MARGARET CHASE SMITH

AUTHOR: Alberta Gould / PHOTOGRAPHER: photographs from a variety of sources
AGE LEVEL / LENGTH: 10-15 years / 87 pages
PUBLISHER / COPYRIGHT DATE: Windswept House Publishers / 1995
FORMAT / ISBN: Paperback / 1883650275

First Lady of the Senate: A Life of Margaret Chase Smith traces the life of Margaret Chase Smith from her birth in Skowhegan, Maine, in 1897, through her 90s, when she still actively participated in school visitations to her Margaret Chase Smith Library. The back cover includes an update describing the circumstances of Margaret Chase Smith's death in 1995.

Margaret Chase Smith's childhood experiences are related, including hanging May baskets, fishing at a summer camp on North Pond in Smithfield, and having "big" birthday parties with up to eighty children. Her education, early job, and marriage to Clyde Smith are also detailed. The majority of the book focuses on Smith's political career, which began when she assumed her late husband's post in the House of Representatives in 1941. She later became a senator, serving from 1949 to 1973. As the first woman from a major political party to run for the Presidency of the United States (in 1964), Smith was considered a political pioneer. Her famous "Declaration of Conscience" speech in 1950, which challenged Senator Joseph McCarthy's rampant accusations of Communism in the United States, put Smith in the national as well as the local spotlight. A final chapter describes Smith's return to Skowhegan and the creation of the Margaret Chase Smith Library.

First Lady of the Senate: A Life of Margaret Chase Smith includes the full text of Smith's "Declaration of Conscience" speech, an introduction by Maine Senator George Mitchell, and forty black-and-white photographs showing Smith with five U.S. Presidents and several world leaders. Although this book could have benefited from a table of contents, chapter titles, and stronger editing, it still goes far in fulfilling its purpose of introducing young readers to one of Maine's greatest politicians.

LEARNING ACTIVITIES

1. If possible, visit the Margaret Chase Smith Library in Skowhegan or call (207-474-7133) for information. Plan your visit. Using *First Lady of the Senate* as a guide, make a checklist of exhibits you want to observe (e.g., elephant collection, doctoral degrees). After your visit, write a descriptive summary of it.

2. Make three parallel time lines. On the first, list important dates in the life of Margaret Chase Smith (e.g., when she was born, graduated from high school, was elected to Congress, received the Congressional Medal of Freedom). On the second time line, write the dates of major world events (e.g., World War I, the Great Depression, World War II). On the third time line, mark important dates in your own family's history (e.g., immigration of an ancestor, grandparent's birthdates, dates that an ancestor served in a war, parents' wedding date). Interview family members to gather information about important dates in your family. Study these three time lines. How are they related? Do some events overlap to all three time lines?

3. Research and write a biography of another famous Mainer (e.g., Billy Swift, Joan Benoit Samuelson, Stephen King, Olympia Snowe). Gather information from nonfiction books, newspapers, and magazines. If the Mainer is living, write to that person for information, or even request an interview. Consider what to include in a biography (childhood, school years, career, etc.).

ABOUT THE AUTHOR

See information about Alberta Gould on page 207.

HIGHLIGHTS OF MARGARET CHASE SMITH'S LIFE

AUTHOR / ILLUSTRATORS: Woolwich Central School, Mrs. Driver's 1993-94 fourth grade class
AGE LEVEL / LENGTH: 8-12 years / 48 pages
PUBLISHER / COPYRIGHT DATE: Biddle Publishing Co. / 1994
FORMAT / ISBN: Paperback / 1879418169

Highlights of Margaret Chase Smith's Life is a book written by kids for kids. This delightful book features informational essays by a class of Woolwich, Maine, fourth graders about different aspects of Margaret Chase Smith's life. The book includes sections called "Family and Childhood," "Wedding," "Political Career and Community Service," and "Did You Know?" Individuals or small groups of students wrote about specific topics and/or drew illustrations of roses for the book. They gathered their information by reading articles and books about Margaret Chase Smith (their bibliography is included), by researching information at the Margaret Chase Smith Library in Skowhegan, and by actually interviewing Margaret Chase Smith.

The facts and trivia that the student-authors include in the book are often fun and reflect a child's perspective. For example, readers will learn that Margaret Chase Smith collected Russian dolls and elephants (the symbol of the Republican Party). Her first job was at a five-and-dime store where she earned thirty-five cents a day. On her wedding day, Margaret Chase Smith wore a royal blue lace dress from Paris along with "pink flowers, white gloves, crystal clear beads, and blue heels with straps." Margaret Chase Smith had a pet Chihuahua that liked ice cream. And on and on—the book contains many interesting tidbits.

In addition, *Highlights of Margaret Chase Smith's Life* includes black-and-white photos from the Margaret Chase Smith library. The back of the book contains students' comments about what they learned from the project and a log describing all the steps involved in creating the book. The book is a child's eye-view and celebration of Margaret Chase Smith's life, but it is also a celebration of a hands-on learning project.

LEARNING ACTIVITIES

1. The fourth graders from Woolwich Central School worked very hard on their first book, *Highlights of Margaret Chase Smith's Life*. They had to rewrite their pieces many times. Select one section from the story and read it carefully. Then write a critique of it. What did the student do well? Were any parts unclear or confusing? What suggestion would you make to the author on how to improve the writing?

2. Create your own group book. Invite friends or classmates to join you in writing a book about another Maine topic or person. Follow a similar process to the one used by the

Woolwich students, described on pages 41-46 of the book. Be sure to agree on a Maine topic, find a way to divide up that topic, and allow plenty of time for researching, writing, and rewriting about your topic. Also have a celebration after you complete your book. Your book doesn't have to be published by an official publishing company—you can "publish" it yourselves and share copies with friends and family.

3. Study the rose illustrations in *Highlights of Margaret Chase Smith's Life*. Try to draw a rose yourself. Use a real rose as a model. Ask your art teacher for suggestions, and try to create roses out of different materials. Can you sculpt one from clay? Can you make one from tissue paper? How else could you create roses?

ABOUT THE AUTHORS/ILLUSTRATORS

The student authors/illustrators of *Highlights of Margaret Chase Smith's Life* all attended Mrs. Janice Driver's fourth grade classroom during the 1993-94 school year. When the students began a research project on Margaret Chase Smith, they couldn't find all the information they wanted, so they decided to "write their own book." The students were familiar with the writing process before starting this book and had "published" numerous stories for friends and family. As sixth graders, the same group of students have worked to produce a newscast for their local cable TV channel.

JOURNEY TO THE SOVIET UNION

AUTHOR: Samantha Smith / PHOTOGRAPHER: photographs from a variety of sources
AGE LEVEL / LENGTH: 8-14 years / 122 pages
PUBLISHER / COPYRIGHT DATE: Little, Brown, & Co. / 1985
FORMAT / ISBN: Hardcover / 0316801755; Paperback / 0316801763

In *Journey to the Soviet Union*, ten-year-old Samantha Smith joins the ranks of other Maine people who have "led the way" as inventors, writers, politicians—she became a world-famous young diplomat. The book reprints Smith's letter to Soviet leader Yuri Andropov, in which she asks, "Are you going to vote to have a war or not?" His response and Smith's subsequent journey for peace to the Soviet Union are recounted in detail. Smith and her parents are shown visiting the Red Square, the Pioneer Camp on the Black Sea, a state farm, the Kirov Ballet, Moscow's Puppet Theater, and much, much more. One hundred photos make the book feel like a scrapbook of a family's trip.

The story is told from Samantha Smith's perspective. The reader gets a view of the Soviet Union through a ten-year-old's eyes. The text is wonderfully honest and innocent. For example, Samantha tells about getting hugged by Madame Krouglova, head of the Friendship Societies: "When she hugs you it's like your ribs are going to crack." She also tells how their guide Natasha showed her a way to cut chicken Kiev "so the butter wouldn't squirt you in the eye." And as Samantha reflects on her journey, she writes: "the people of the world would seem more like people in my own neighborhood. I think they are more like me than I ever realized. I guess that's the most important change inside me." Young readers of *Journey to the Soviet Union* will also view the world differently after reading this book.

LEARNING ACTIVITIES

1. This book shares a triumphant time in Samantha Smith's life, but there's more to her story. She went on to become an ambassador for peace, speaking at conferences around the world. She also began a career as an actress, only to die soon after in a tragic plane crash. Learn more about Samantha Smith's short life. Plan a visit to the Samantha Smith Memorial statue located in front of the Maine State Museum in Augusta, research newspaper archives about her life, and then write your own Samantha Smith story.

2. Learn more about the former Soviet Union. This area of the world has changed dramatically in recent years. Read nonfiction books to learn as much as possible about it. If possible, interview someone who has visited there. What were the visitor's experiences like? How is living there different from living here?

3. Samantha Smith is one young Mainer who made a difference in the world. Other Maine children are also making a difference by working at a homeless shelter, pushing for recycling efforts in their town, or starting their own business. Create a magazine called "Kids Who Make a Difference." Interview boys and girls from your community, and have classmates do the same. Then turn the articles into a magazine. Make copies and sell them to raise money for your own special cause.

ABOUT THE AUTHOR

Samantha Smith was born in Houlton, Maine, in 1972. Later she lived and attended schools in Manchester, Maine. She gained fame when she wrote a letter to former Soviet leader Yuri Andropov asking him why his country wanted to conquer the United States. Andropov answered Smith's letter, assuring her of his desire for peace and inviting her to take a two-week tour of his country. The national and international press followed Smith's adventures in the Soviet Union.

With her new-found fame, Smith made numerous television appearances. She interviewed the 1984 Democratic Presidential candidates for the Disney channel, and had a role in the television series *Lime Street* with Robert Wagner. Smith died in a plane crash in 1985, at the age of thirteen. Her father was also killed in the crash. After Smith's death, she was honored with a Soviet commemorative stamp.

SAMANTHA SMITH: A JOURNEY FOR PEACE

AUTHOR: Anne Galicich / PHOTOGRAPHER: photographs from a variety of sources
AGE LEVEL / LENGTH: 8-12 years / 72 pages
PUBLISHER / COPYRIGHT DATE: Dillon Press (Silver Burdett Press of Simon & Schuster) / 1987
FORMAT / ISBN: Library binding / 0875183670

Samantha Smith: A Journey for Peace traces the life of Samantha Smith from her birth in Houlton, Maine, in 1972, through her Soviet Union adventures, to her death in a 1985 plane crash. Samantha Smith started her diplomatic career at the age of five with a letter of admiration to Queen Elizabeth. When Samantha Smith was ten, she wrote to another world leader. This letter was to Yuri Andropov, the leader of the Soviet Union, expressing her concern about a nuclear war. She received a personal reply from Andropov and an invitation to visit the Soviet Union. Her trip to the Soviet Union received world-wide attention.

Upon her return to Manchester, Maine, Smith continued to stay in the spotlight with her ongoing efforts for peace and her beginning career as an actress. The book also includes some of the tributes paid to Smith after her death, and relates her mother's continued efforts for world peace through the Samantha Smith Foundation.

LEARNING ACTIVITIES

1. Write a biography about yourself to date. Follow author Anne Galicich's writing style. Include a table of contents, chapter titles, photographs, and an index. Plan your story ahead of time. Which information is the most important? Which information should you leave out? Which information can be grouped together? Write a first draft of your autobiography and then get feedback from others on how to improve it. After making revisions, share your autobiography with family members and save it: you might want to reread it and possibly update it each year on your birthday.

2. Samantha Smith's mother founded and continues to work for the Samantha Smith Foundation. Learn more about the Foundation by writing for information:

> Samantha Smith Foundation
> 9 Union Street
> Hallowell, ME 04347

3. Samantha Smith got to know children from other parts of the world during her visits to the Soviet Union and Japan. You may not be able to visit a foreign country, but you

can still get to know a child from another country by corresponding with one as a pen-pal. To find a penpal, write to one of the following organizations:

Peace Links
747 Eighth Street SE
Washington, DC 20003

International Pen Friends
P.O. Box 290065
Brooklyn, NY 11229

Children Around the World Resource Center
P.O. Box 40657
Bellevue, WA 98004

World Pen Pals
1694 Como Ave.
St. Paul, MN 55108

ABOUT THE AUTHOR

Anne Galicich has traveled frequently in Maine. She graduated from Stanford University and currently lives in New York City, working as a freelance writer. Galicich learned about Samantha Smith while teaching an English class at Horace Mann School in New York City. Galicich felt that Smith's story would be an inspiration to both children and adults.

SAMANTHA SMITH: YOUNG AMBASSADOR

AUTHOR: Patricia Stone Martin / ILLUSTRATOR: Bernard Doctor
AGE LEVEL / LENGTH: 5-8 years / 24 pages
PUBLISHER / COPYRIGHT DATE: Rourke Enterprises / 1987
FORMAT / ISBN: Hardcover / 0685581314; Library binding / 0865921733

Samantha Smith: Young Ambassador is part of Rourke Enterprise's young biography series called "Reaching Your Goal," which features famous Americans such as Beverly Cleary, Jesse Jackson, and Christa McAuliffe. The series profiles Americans who have set and reached admirable goals. Even though Maine's Samantha Smith died when she was only thirteen-years-old, the book states that Samantha reached her goals as a young ambassador: "She made people all around the world think about peace."

This biography makes a complex topic like international relations easily understandable for young children. *Samantha Smith: Young Ambassador* highlights specific details from Samantha Smith's childhood so that young readers can readily identify with her experiences. The book reveals that Samantha Smith was so shy before receiving publicity for her letter to the Soviet Leader Yuri Andropov that she wouldn't even try out for the school play. Details of her trip to the Soviet Union include swimming in the Black Sea, camping with a Young Pioneer group, placing flowers on monuments, and visiting the Moscow Circus. The book continues with information about Smith's pets (she hoped to become an animal doctor when she grew up). Smith's role on the TV series *Lime Street* and her relationship with actor Robert Wagner are also described. Finally, young readers learn about the plane crash that claimed the life of Samantha Smith, but they are once again reminded of the many accomplishments that she achieved during her short life. The final two pages of the book challenge young people to set goals for themselves and to develop a plan for reaching those goals just as Samantha Smith did.

LEARNING ACTIVITIES

1. Samantha Smith reached her goal of being a messenger for peace. What is a goal you want to reach? Use the guidelines on pages 22 and 23 of *Samantha Smith: Young Ambassador* to help you develop a plan for reaching your goal. Share your goal with a friend or relative and then report to that person on your progress as you work toward your goal.

2. Samantha Smith was a child many people admired. Select a child you know and admire. Interview that child and write a short story describing that child's qualities and experiences—what makes him or her so special.

3. Have a family or classroom discussion of how the Soviet Union has changed since Samantha Smith wrote to Yuri Andropov and since this book was published in 1987. Do you think Samantha Smith would have been pleased with the changes? Why or why not? What do you believe Samantha Smith would be doing if she were still alive today?

ABOUT THE AUTHOR

Author information on Patricia Stone Martin was unavailable.

THE REMARKABLE STANLEY BROTHERS

AUTHOR: Nancy Griffin / PHOTOGRAPHER: photographs from a variety of sources
AGE LEVEL / LENGTH: 10 years–adult / 56 pages
PUBLISHER / COPYRIGHT DATE: Gannett Books; available from Coastwise Press (listed in *Books in Print* under the title, *Famous Maine Stanley Brothers*) / 1987
FORMAT / ISBN: Paperback / 0930096762

Francis Edgar (F.E.) Stanley and Freelan Oscar (F.O.) Stanley were two fascinating twins from Kingfield, Maine. Although best known for their invention of the Stanley Steamer automobile, the brothers also invented dry photographic plates for cameras, the first X-ray equipment, and the artist's air brush. They also made world-famous violins.

The Remarkable Stanley Brothers tells a number of stories from the twin's childhood, including details of their first money-making businesses when they were seven and ten years of age. Their rivalry with George Eastman, founder of the Eastman Kodak camera company, and their tragic experiences with automobiles are all recounted. Author Nancy Griffin wonderfully portrays the Stanley Brothers as she includes detailed descriptions of their successes, their failures, and their practical jokes. A separate chapter describing how a steam car works and more than twenty black-and-white photographs and drawings help to add further interest to the biography.

LEARNING ACTIVITIES

1. Visit the Stanley Museum in Kingfield. Learn as many facts as possible about the Stanley Brothers. Drawing on that information, along with that provided in *The Remarkable Stanley Brothers*, create a trivia game about the Stanley Brothers. You might even make a gameboard in the shape of a Stanley Steamer.

2. Select one invention of the Stanley Brothers—the Stanley Steamer, X-ray equipment, air brush, dry photographic plates, etc.—and research it. How has the invention changed since it was first created? How has it stayed the same?

3. The Stanley Brothers earned money as kids with several business schemes. Interview people from different generations (from your generation, from your parents' generation, from your grandparents' generation) and learn how they earned money as children. How young were they when they first started working for money? How much were they paid? What did they spend their money on? After your interviews, look for similarities, differences, and trends that you found between generations.

ABOUT THE AUTHOR

Nancy Griffin moved to Maine's midcoast twenty-five years ago. She has worked as a news reporter and editor, which gave her the opportunity to pursue the writing of *The Remarkable Stanley Brothers* while working for the United Press International. She wrote a story about the current owners of Stanley Steamers living in Maine. In the process, she found a little background information on the inventors and was intrigued enough to research and write their story. She tested the working manuscript on her children.

Griffin says that she has been writing since she was a student in college, mostly for newspapers. She has been a freelance writer for the past ten years, covering fishery and health issues for magazines and newspapers. She also has started her own small publishing company, Coastwise Press.

The author lives in Thomaston. She is the mother of three grown daughters and has a house full of pets. Her hobbies include spinning, knitting, sewing, and ice skating.

HARRIET BEECHER STOWE
AND THE BEECHER PREACHERS

AUTHOR: Jean Fritz / PHOTOGRAPHER: photographs from a variety of sources

AGE LEVEL / LENGTH: 10-15 years / 144 pages

PUBLISHER / COPYRIGHT DATE: G.P. Putnam's Sons / 1994

FORMAT / ISBN: Hardcover / 0399226664

Harriet Beecher Stowe's Maine connections were brief, yet life-changing. While Stowe's husband was teaching at Bowdoin College, their family lived in a house in Brunswick where Longfellow had lived earlier when he was a student at Bowdoin. While in Maine in the early 1850s, Stowe wrote *Uncle Tom's Cabin*, which has been described as America's first protest novel. Stowe was adamantly opposed to slavery; and when the Fugitive Slave Law threatened to increase the rights of Southern slave owners, she did the most meaningful thing she knew how to do—she wrote. *Uncle Tom's Cabin* was a bestseller, with 10,000 copies sold each week during its peak sales period. The book made Stowe a celebrity not only in this country, but in Europe as well. She was in demand as a speaker, and thousands flocked to see her in person. During the Civil War, President Lincoln referred to her as "the little lady who made this big war."

Harriet Beecher Stowe and the Beecher Preachers traces Stowe's life beginning with her birth in Connecticut as the daughter of America's most famous preacher at that time, Lyman Beecher. The minister was a domineering figure, and he was disappointed each time his wife gave birth to a daughter instead of a son. After all, he wanted to fill the world with his "preacher" sons. Stowe worked hard to please her father; and into adulthood, she continued striving to please others. But no matter how hard Stowe worked at being the perfect mother, wife, and teacher, she often felt unfulfilled. It seemed that writing was her calling, and she was happiest when she could shut herself away and write. Stowe was first published at the age of twenty-four, when she won the $50 first prize in a story contest. She continued writing many stories and novels, including *The Pearl of Orr's Island* which was set on the Maine coast in the early 1800s.

Jean Fritz is one of the best biographers writing today. *Harriet Beecher Stowe and the Beecher Preachers* doesn't read like a biography full of dry facts and dates, but rather it reads like a novel which tells the spell-binding story of an extraordinary woman and writer. Fritz' book includes more than forty black-and-white photos and drawings, a family tree showing the Beecher Stowe family, and an afterword summarizing the lives of each member of the Beecher family, as well as a comprehensive bibliography and index.

LEARNING ACTIVITIES

1. Read all or part of *Uncle Tom's Cabin* and write a critique of it. Do you think the novel

was well-written? Was it melodramatic? Was it sentimental? Was it racist? Were the characters well-developed? Do you believe the novel had the power to change history? How so? Support your opinions with specific details and examples.

2. Discussion questions:

> —Do you think Harriet Beecher Stowe was happy as a child? Why or why not?
> —How would Stowe's life have been different if she had been born a male rather than a female?
> —Which members of Harriet Beecher Stowe's family do you think had the most influence upon her? Why?
> —Discuss the ways that death influenced Stowe's life. What about her mother's death? Her son's death?
> —If Stowe were alive today, what do you think she would be doing for work or what would she be writing about?

3. Write a picture book or short story about Harriet Beecher Stowe. What details will you include? How will you make her story understandable to younger readers? Share your story with some younger children and get their feedback on your story.

ABOUT THE AUTHOR

Jean Fritz was born in 1915. The daughter of missionary parents, she grew up in China. Fritz has been writing children's books for more than forty years. She is best known for her well-researched, humorous, and humanizing "question biographies": *And Then What Happened, Paul Revere?*, *Where Do You Think You're Going, Christopher Columbus?*, *What's the Big Idea, Ben Franklin?* She has also written fiction, including *The Cabin Faced West*, a pioneer story based on her great-great grandmother, and *Brady*, the story of a runaway slave. Fritz's autobiography, *Homesick: My Own Story*, was a Newbery Honor Book. In 1986, Fritz received the Laura Ingalls Wilder Award for her contribution to children's literature.

When referring to her Maine connections, Fritz says that her family summered in Gardiner, Maine, for many years. From there, she enjoyed exploring the rest of the state. She claims that Maine, along with Massachusetts, have always been her two favorite states to visit.

Fritz currently lives in Dobbs Ferry, New York, a small town on the Hudson River. She has two grown children and two grandsons. Her husband, who shared her frequent travels for researching books, recently passed away. Although she must use a walker now to get around, Fritz claims to "continue to be as active as possible."

HARRIET BEECHER STOWE: AUTHOR AND ABOLITIONIST

AUTHOR: Robert E. Jakoubek / PHOTOGRAPHER: photographs from a variety of sources
AGE LEVEL / LENGTH: 12 years–adult / 112 pages
PUBLISHER / COPYRIGHT DATE: Chelsea House Publishers / 1989
FORMAT / ISBN: Library Binding / 155546680X

The first chapter of *Harriet Beech Stowe: Author and Abolitionist* opens with Harriet Beecher Stowe (1811-1896) and her children being kicked out of a train station in Pennsylvania on their way to their new home in Brunswick, Maine. The station agent thought that the unkempt family were immigrants. Stowe gathered her children and complied, stepping out into the chilly late-night air to wait for their train. Of course, the station agent was wrong. The Stowes were not vagabonds—although they looked the part, since they had been traveling for days on their rough journey by train, boat, and stage coach from Ohio to Maine. Harriet Beech Stowe was on a journey that would lead her to fame. While living in Brunswick, where her husband was teaching at Bowdoin College, Stowe wrote her history-altering book, *Uncle Tom's Cabin.* Stowe had long been opposed to slavery, and she was determined to do her part to end it—by writing. On a Sunday in February 1851, Stowe was attending the First Parish Church in Brunswick when a story of an old black man being flogged to death suddenly "appeared" to her. She hurried home and began to write the scene onto paper. This scene grew into a forty-part magazine serial, which was published in 1852 as the book *Uncle Tom's Cabin.* Hundreds of thousands of copies of the book were quickly sold, making Stowe a famous and wealthy author.

The rest of Harriet Beecher Stowe's fascinating life is also richly detailed in *Harriet Beecher Stowe: Author and Abolitionist.* Her rigid upbringing with her minister father, her heartaches of dealing with the deaths of two sons and the disappearance of another one, her frustrations of trying to find the time to write in a hectic household, and her new-found public speaking career when she was in her sixties are all highlighted. This book is from the Chelsea House series, "American Women of Achievement," which showcases the lives of fifty American women who helped to shape the course of American history. Indeed, Harriet Beecher Stowe did alter American history, and the state of Maine played a small role in shaping Stowe's place in that history.

LEARNING ACTIVITIES

1. *Harriet Beecher Stowe: Author and Abolitionist* celebrates Stowe's life by telling her story. Find another way to celebrate Stowe's contribution to history without using written words. You might create a collage, a display, a dance, or a scrapbook. Strive to capture the essence of who Harriet Beecher Stowe was and what she stood for. Share your creation with others and answer their questions about Harrier Beecher Stowe.

2. Harriet Beecher Stowe struggled to find the time and energy for her writing. She was overwhelmed by caring for her home and family. Interview a writer in your community. How does that person balance their time for writing and their time for home and family? What writing schedule or routine does that person follow? Is the schedule or routine difficult to keep? Why or why not? What joys does a writing career bring? What headaches? What advice would that writer have for others trying to work as a fulltime writer?

3. Harriet Beecher Stowe was passionately opposed to slavery; so she wrote a book about slavery, one that she hoped would make a difference. Write a story or poem or essay on a subject that you are passionate about. Try to make your words reflect your passion.

ABOUT THE AUTHOR

Robert E. Jakoubek grew up in Iowa. He attended Indiana University and Columbia University. He is the co-author of *These United States*, a history textbook. He currently lives in New York City.

INTO THE DEEP FOREST WITH HENRY DAVID THOREAU

AUTHOR: Jim Murphy / ILLUSTRATOR: Kate Kiesler
AGE LEVEL / LENGTH: 8-14 years / 40 pages
PUBLISHER / COPYRIGHT DATE: Clarion Books (imprint of Houghton Mifflin Co.) / 1995
FORMAT / ISBN: Hardcover / 0395605229

Into the Deep Forest with Henry David Thoreau tells about Thoreau's trips to the Maine wilderness in the mid-1800s. Although information is pulled from three separate trips to Maine, the book reads as if it took place on a single trip to Mount Katahdin. Author Jim Murphy has done a skillful job of pulling quotes from Thoreau's own journals and tying the quotes together with a simple narrative describing Thoreau's experiences. As a result, the book reads like a cohesive whole and gives young readers a wonderful introduction to a great American writer, philosopher, and naturalist.

This book starts with a brief overview of Thoreau's life and then moves to the actual account of Thoreau's trip. Thoreau traveled with two companions, one a friend and the other a Native American guide. They begin their journey in a canoe on Moosehead Lake; then they travel down the Penobscot River. They must stop and "carryover" several times—that is, carry the canoe over land. They climb through a swampy area and a section of burned forest. Finally, they reach Mount Katahdin and begin their climb upward 5300 feet. The book ends as the fog lifts for a few seconds, and Thoreau catches a glimpse of "the country for hundreds of miles."

Thoreau's language is poetic as he describes the Maine wilderness. He describes two moose he encounters as "great frightened rabbits, with their long ears and half-inquisitive, half-frightened looks." When writing about Mount Katahdin, Thoreau says that it looks "as if it had rained rocks." And when Thoreau finally reaches the top of Katahdin and finds himself lost in thick clouds and mist, he writes "It is like sitting in a chimney and waiting for the smoke to blow away." The oil and pencil illustrations by Kate Kiesler are also poetic. Young readers of *Into the Deep Forest with Henry David Thoreau* will feel lucky to share a piece of Thoreau's journey, his journal, and his love affair with nature.

LEARNING ACTIVITIES

1. Learn more about Henry David Thoreau. Read nonfiction books about him and selections from some of Thoreau's own books (e.g., *Walden, The Maine Woods*). After your research write a summary of what you learned.

2. Keep your own nature journal. Plan a nature experience with an adult, such as a walk in the woods, a hike up a mountain, or a canoe trip on a river. Throughout your experiences, write journal entries describing what you see. Thoreau took the time to write in his journals no matter how "lost" he was in the Maine wilderness. As a result, his writings often make readers feel that they are sharing Thoreau's trip first-hand. Strive for the same personal effect with your writing.

3. Look back through the illustrations in *Into the Deep Forest with Henry David Thoreau*. Then visit a wooded area of Maine and try to find as many plants, birds, and animal tracks as you can that were included in the book. Can you find dwarf raspberries, belted kingfishers, or rabbit tracks? What else can you find? Do the items in nature look like those pictured in the book?

ABOUT THE AUTHOR

Before becoming a freelance writer, Jim Murphy worked as an editor of children's books for Clarion. He has been writing for the past nineteen years, and he has more than twenty-five books to his credit. His works range from picture books to young adult novels to nonfiction books. His books include *The Long Road to Gettysburg, The Boys' War*, and *The Great Fire*, a 1996 Newbery Honor Book.

Murphy has vacationed in Maine numerous times. He claims to love driving on Maine's "tiny back roads—it's like entering a different and more exciting era." In fact, one time while traveling in Maine on a rainy and foggy night, Murphy got lost. He says that five hours later, he finally found his way to the city of Bangor. His adventure reminded him of what it must have been like for early pioneers in this state. While writing *Into the Deep Forest*, Murphy hoped to capture for young readers "the experience of true wilderness through the eyes of Henry David Thoreau."

Murphy currently lives in New Jersey, with his wife and two sons. His wife, Alison Blank, is the executive producer of *The Magic School Bus* animated TV series on PBS and editor of *The Magic School Bus* magazine. Murphy enjoys cooking, gardening, and puttering around their 100-year-old Victorian house. His collections include old postcards of trains and ships, stereopticon cards, and odd farm implements.

ABOUT THE ILLUSTRATOR

See information about Kate Kiesler on page 72.

E.B. WHITE: SOME WRITER!

AUTHOR: Beverly Gherman / PHOTOGRAPHER: photographs from the E.B. White Collection at Cornell University Library
AGE LEVEL / LENGTH: 10 years–adult / 160 pages
PUBLISHER / COPYRIGHT DATE: Atheneum (div. of Simon & Schuster)(hardcover); Morrow (paperback) / 1992
FORMAT / ISBN: Library binding / 0689316720; Paperback / 0688128262

E.B. White: Some Writer! begins with White's birth, in 1899, and boyhood years in Mount Vernon, New York, and ends with his death, in 1985, at his North Brooklin, Maine, saltwater farm. Readers will learn about White's passions—writing, animals, Maine, farming, sailing—as well as his fears—not being able to write something important or to meet writing deadlines, speaking in public, getting sick, not being able to provide for his family.

Elwyn Brooks White's love for Maine and his Maine connections are stressed throughout the book. Starting as a boy, E.B. White visited Great Pond (one of the Belgrade Lakes) each August with his family. White continued visiting Maine until he bought a saltwater farm in North Brooklin, Maine, in 1933. Then White commuted between his work in New York City and the farm, spending more and more time in Maine, until he eventually moved there. White did much of his writing, including *Charlotte's Web*, in his small boat house. White treasured the words of Henry David Thoreau and carried *Walden* with him everywhere. In 1963, White was nominated for the Presidential Medal of Freedom by President Kennedy. After Kennedy's assassination, White actually was presented the medal, at Colby College in Waterville, by Maine Senator Edmund Muskie. White often felt ill and his hay fever was particularly bad on his farm, but White was quoted as saying, "I would really rather feel bad in Maine than good anywhere else."

E.B. White: Some Writer! is a highly readable and thoroughly enjoyable biography. After getting to know E.B. White the man and the writer, Mainers will be proud to claim "the father of *Charlotte's Web*" as one of their own.

LEARNING ACTIVITIES

1. Make two timelines—one of world events (e.g., World War I, the Great Depression, World War II) and one of E.B. White's life (using information from *E.B. White: Some Writer!*). Then compare the two timelines. How did world events seem to influence E.B. White's life and writings? Do you think White's writings had any influence on the world?

2. E.B. White was afraid to speak in public. He may have been an eloquent writer, but he never gave himself a chance to become an eloquent speaker. Write a persuasive essay trying to convince E.B. White that he should have given more speeches. Try to be specific, clear, and brief with your advice.

3. E.B. White loved Maine and the world loved E.B. White. Design a plan for a Maine memorial of E.B. White. Your memorial plans should highlight White's Maine connections. Where would your memorial be placed? How would you let E.B. White fans know about your memorial?

ABOUT THE AUTHOR

Beverly Gherman wrote her first biography when she was in fourth grade. At that time, if she didn't know any facts about her subject, then she just made them up. Later in life, Gherman returned to writing biographies, but this time she enjoyed diving into the research. Her biographies have featured Georgia O'Keefe, Agnes de Mille, Sandra Day O'Connor, Dr. Roentgen, and Robert Louis Stevenson.

Gherman made her first trip to Maine while doing her research for *E.B. White: Some Writer!* She visited White's saltwater farm and interviewed White's son, Joel, who was a boatbuilder. Gherman found Maine to be "an addictive place," just as E.B. White's books have always been to her.

Gherman has two grown children and two grandchildren. She lives with her husband in San Francisco.

TO THE POINT: A STORY ABOUT E.B. WHITE

AUTHOR: David R. Collins / ILLUSTRATOR: Amy Johnson
AGE LEVEL / LENGTH: 8-12 years / 54 pages
PUBLISHER / COPYRIGHT DATE: Carolrhoda Books / 1989
FORMAT / ISBN: Library binding / 0876143451; Paperback / 087614508X

To the Point: A Story About E.B. White traces the life of E.B. White from childhood to his death in 1985. This easy-to-read biography focuses on White, the writer. The opening chapter tells how "En" (his nickname as a child) snuck into his older brother's room to use his typewriter. As a child, he was fascinated by the dictionary, and he had his first story published in *St. Nicholas* magazine at the age of twelve. E.B. White's passion for writing is traced through his college days and early career as a journalist.

White's ties to Maine are brought forth as well, from his summers on Belgrade Lakes as a child to his move to a saltwater farm in Brooklin as an adult. An afterword to the book relates how White wrote *Charlotte's Web* in a small boathouse on his Maine farm.

LEARNING ACTIVITIES

1. In *To the Point*, we learn that E.B. White made a pig and a spider the heroes of *Charlotte's Web* because he thought that pigs and spiders were viewed unfairly and treated cruelly by most people. Select another animal that you feel is misunderstood. Write a short story with that animal as the hero.

2. It is said that writers write best about what they know, what they have experienced. E.B. White's life as a Maine farmer is strongly reflected in *Charlotte's Web*. Make a list of what you know, what your experiences include. Select one of these topics and write a story about it.

3. Why do you think author David R. Collins titled this book *To The Point?* The chapters in the biography are numbered, but not titled. Write an appropriate title for each chapter. How did you decide upon chapter titles?

ABOUT THE AUTHOR

As a high school English teacher, David R. Collins was challenged by one of his students to complete a writing assignment that he had given the class. Collins accepted that challenge, and sixty-three books later he is still writing. "Writing for young readers is exciting and exhausting," Collins states. "Every word must count. With everything I write, I try to entertain and educate." Since Collins still works as a fulltime English teacher, he does most of his writing during the summer. He currently lives in Moline, Illinois, and says that "people" are his hobbies.

Collins has written numerous biographies of famous people, including J.R.R. Tolkien, Charles Dickens, John Deere, Beatrix Potter, Lee Iacocca, and Christa McAuliffe. He has a special affection for E.B. White:

> *Charlotte's Web* is truly a literary classic. Notice, I do not label it a children's book, for this volume has love, life, death, hate, friendship—all the deepest emotions of people. E.B. White was an extraordinary man whose writing talents were endless.

Collins has no Maine connections other than time spent in the state researching *To the Point.* He says he discovered the "magic" of Maine that E.B. White had written about. "Maine offers a unique aura of being in a living and lively part of the world, yet being sheltered from the fast-paced but empty existence so many people find themselves in. The people are warm, friendly, and respectful of one's privacy."

ANDREW WYETH

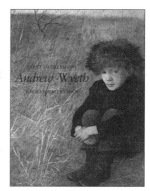

AUTHOR: Richard Meryman / PHOTOGRAPHER: photographs from a variety of sources, including many photographs of Wyeth's paintings

AGE LEVEL / LENGTH: 12 years–adult / 92 pages

PUBLISHER / COPYRIGHT DATE: Harry N. Abrams, Inc. Publishers / 1991

FORMAT / ISBN: Hardcover / 0810939568

Andrew Wyeth is part of the "First Impressions" series published by Harry N. Abrams Publishers. These biographies provide young readers with an in-depth profile of famous artists, along with a broad sample of their artwork. Author Richard Meryman gives readers a close view into Andrew Wyeth's motivation and inspirations. A friend of the artist for many years, Meryman was able to discover the story behind many of Wyeth's paintings.

Andrew Wyeth grew up in Chadds Ford, Pennsylvania, as the youngest son of N.C. Wyeth, a well-known and respected artist. Wyeth's father was a powerful force in his life. He both loved and feared his father. His father taught him volumes about life and about painting. Andrew Wyeth's artistic eye followed many passions, including soldiers and war, Halloween and the macabre, boats and the ocean. Wyeth's connections to the Maine towns of Port Clyde and Cushing are also featured, including the story behind Wyeth's numerous paintings of Christina Olson and the Olson clapboard house.

Andrew Wyeth includes more than 50 photos of the artist and his works. His childhood drawings, his early watercolors, and his tempera paintings are all featured. But the text is rich too, filled with many memorable quotes by Wyeth and his family. For example, when describing the artistic process involved when seeing an inspirational scene, Wyeth says, "You come on something in nature and you're excited. Maybe the weather is stormy and you have terrific feelings. If you can get them down before you begin to think, then you get something." This book is a wonderful introductory tour of Wyeth's work and a glimpse into the mind of an artistic genius.

LEARNING ACTIVITIES

1. Select two of Andrew Wyeth's works from this book and write a detailed comparison of the paintings. In what ways are they similar? Different? What do you think is the theme of each painting? What do you notice about colors, perspective, shadows, etc.? How does each painting make you feel? Which of the paintings do you like best? Why?

2. *Andrew Wyeth* shows what factors and incidents influenced this famous artist's work. The work of artistic people—whether they paint, write, sculpt, create music, make crafts, or work in another medium—is influenced by key factors and incidents in their lives. Select a local "artist" (person who creates) from your community and interview that person. Try to learn what has influenced that artist's work. Write a brief biographical summary of your selected artist.

3. *Andrew Wyeth* tells of Wyeth's life from his birth until the time he was 28-years-old and his father died. Learn more about Andrew Wyeth's life and works after that time. Read nonfiction books and magazine articles about him and view samples of his work. How did his work change? What influences affected his work? Using your new information, write a follow-up chapter to *Andrew Wyeth*.

ABOUT THE AUTHOR

Richard Meryman was born in Washington, D.C. He worked as a reporter and editor for *Life* magazine from 1949 to 1972. In fact, he first met and interviewed Andrew Wyeth in 1964 for an article in *Life*. The two became friends, and Wyeth selected Meryman as his eventual biographer; and so, Meryman gathered material during the next thirty years— notes from conversations and taped interviews. The result is Meryman's biography for adults, *Andrew Wyeth: A Secret Life*, published by HarperCollins in 1996.

Meryman currently lives in New York City with his wife, Elizabeth Burns, who is the art director of *Sciences* magazine. He works as a freelance writer, authoring both magazine articles and books. Meryman's hobbies include skiing, tennis, and squash.

MORE MAINE BIOGRAPHIES, AUTOBIOGRAPHIES, AND JOURNALS

Below is a list of quality Maine biographies, autobiographies, and journals that have recently gone out of print. You are likely to find them at your local library. They are listed alphabetically by the name of the person that is featured in the book.

THE CALL OF THE RUNNING TIDE: A PORTRAIT OF AN ISLAND FAMILY
written by Nancy Price Graff, photographed by Richard Howard, 8-12 years, 1992, Little Brown & Co., 80 pages. This photo-essay describes a year in the life of the Joyce family on Swans Island.

BOATBUILDER
written & photographed by Hope Herman Wurmfeld, 8 years–adult, 1988, Macmillan Publishing, 64 pages. This book focuses on Ralph Stanley who builds customized boats in Southwest Harbor, Maine.

CELIA'S ISLAND JOURNAL
written by Celia Thaxter, adapted & illustrated by Loretta Krupinski, 5-10 years, 1992, Little, Brown & Co., 32 pages. This picture book features selections from the childhood journal of Maine author and poet Celia Thaxter (1835-1894). Thaxter's journal describes her experiences while living on the Isles of Shoals where her father worked as a lighthouse keeper.

INFORMATIONAL BOOKS

SARAH'S BOAT: A YOUNG GIRL LEARNS
THE ART OF SAILING

AUTHOR / ILLUSTRATOR: Douglas Alvord
AGE LEVEL / LENGTH: 8-14 years / 48 pages
PUBLISHER / COPYRIGHT DATE: Tilbury House Publishers / 1994
FORMAT / ISBN: Hardcover / 0884481174

Sarah's Boat: A Young Girl Learns the Art of Sailing is an informational book disguised as a fictional story. It tells the story of a girl named Sarah who improves her sailing skills and enters a Labor Day sailing race off the coast of Maine. The story serves as a format for teaching young readers about sailing.

Douglas Alvord's detailed illustrations show the parts of sailboats, how to tack, and how to do an "S" jibe. The end of the book includes a glossary with names for parts of boats, sailing terms, and points of sail. This book serves as a good beginning guide for young people. Alvord's diagrams and directions are clear and easy to understand. One can't learn to sail simply by reading a book; but for those who are in the process of learning or want to learn, *Sarah's Boat* is the next-best-thing to being on the water.

LEARNING ACTIVITIES

1. If possible, learn to sail or try to improve your sailing skills with adult supervision. Reread *Sarah's Boat: A Young Girl Learns the Art of Sailing* several times. What new information or lessons does the book teach you? Each time you sail, keep a journal of your experiences—what happened, what you learned, how you felt, etc.

2. *Sarah's Boat* is a how-to book and a fictional story all in one. Select a skill that you are good at (e.g., building a campfire, grooming a pet, rollerblading). Then write a how-to book about that skill. Show a character learning the new skill and include diagrams with step-by-step directions. Then share your book with a friend who is interested in learning the skill your book teaches. Does your friend find the book helpful? Does he or she have suggestions on how you could improve the book?

3. Study the anatomy of two or more boats. Look at diagrams and photos of boats as well as actual boats, if possible. Then make a chart showing the ways the boats are similar and how they are different. What does each boat's characteristics tell you about its usage (e.g., who can use it, the amount of passengers or cargo it can hold, where the boat can be used, how the boat would be maintained)?

ABOUT THE AUTHOR/ILLUSTRATOR

Douglas Alvord has written and illustrated several boating books for adults, including

Water: The Romance and Lore of America's Small Boats and *Beach Cruising*. He also has illustrated two books by Maine author Sarah Orne Jewett: *A White Heron* and *The Country of the Pointed Firs*. He lives on the coast of North Carolina.

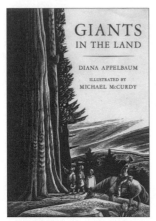

GIANTS IN THE LAND

AUTHOR: Diana Appelbaum / ILLUSTRATOR: Michael McCurdy
AGE LEVEL / LENGTH: 6-10 years / 32 pages
PUBLISHER / COPYRIGHT DATE: Houghton Mifflin Co. / 1993
FORMAT / ISBN: Hardcover / 0395647207

"There were giants living on this land once"–so begins this book which tells part of the history of the white pine, Maine's state tree. In the 1760s, King George the Third of England claimed all the large white pine trees of northern New England for his navy. He wanted them for masts for ships. Europe had no trees tall enough and straight enough for masts, but the white pines of New England grew more than 200 feet tall and four feet wide—they were perfect.

Giants in the Land chronicles the steps involved in harvesting such large trees and bringing them to the ocean, where a special mast ship waited to carry the pines to England. First, the best trees were selected and branded with the King's arrow symbol. Then, in winter, straight roads were cleared that led from the selected trees to the river. Before the trees were chopped down, their landings needed to be cushioned so that the giant trees wouldn't splinter into pieces. A bed of branches was laid down, a blanket of snow was hoped for, and smaller trees in the vicinity were studied to see which ones the large pine could hit so as to buffer its fall. Finally, the "giant" was felled with axes. Then the white pine was chained to giant wheels and axles and a team of twenty oxen. The oxen slowly dragged each tree uphill (hitched in front of the tree) and downhill (hitched behind the tree to slow the tree's downhill roll) until they came to the rivers—the Saco, the Androscoggin, and the Kennebec. There the pines were loaded onto the mast ships for the journey to England.

Giants in the Land is a unique book. Its tall format fits its tall subject. Plus Michael McCurdy's black-and-white scratchboard drawings add a rough, primitive feel to the book. Best of all, author Diana Appelbaum helps young readers to understand a specific and interesting piece of New England history—the harvesting of white pines during colonial times.

LEARNING ACTIVITIES

1. How big were the white pine trees of northern New England during the 1760s? First

of all, in a large open space mark off an *estimate* of what you believe would be the size of a white pine that is four feet wide and 200 feet tall. Then, actually measure a four feet by 200 feet space. How close was your estimate? Next, find an actual white pine tree growing today and measure its size as best you can (you will probably need to estimate its height). Compare the size of today's pine with the large pines of colonial times.

2. Write a short play for *Giants in the Land*. Add conversation to the text—what you believe the loggers would have said to each other throughout the process of harvesting a giant white pine tree. Then have some friends help you to perform your play. You may want to stage your play for an audience.

3. Research the Maine state tree, the white pine. What do white pines look like? How do they differ from other pine trees? How big can they grow? How fast do they grow? What are the best climate and surroundings for white pines? When did the white pine become the Maine state tree? Write the information you learn in a report.

ABOUT THE AUTHOR

See information about Diana Appelbaum on page 19.

ABOUT THE ILLUSTRATOR

Michael McCurdy has illustrated numerous children's books. His books are often about the history of the U.S. He lives with his wife and two children on a farm in Massachusetts.

PUFFIN'S HOMECOMING:
THE STORY OF AN ATLANTIC PUFFIN

AUTHOR: Darice Bailer / ILLUSTRATOR: Katie Lee
AGE LEVEL / LENGTH: 4-7 years / 32 pages
PUBLISHER / COPYRIGHT DATE: Soundprints / 1993
FORMAT / ISBN: Hardcover / 0924483903; Paperback / 156899141X; Paperback with stuffed toy puffin / 1568991479 (other formats with toys and audio tapes also available)

Puffin's Homecoming: The Story of an Atlantic Puffin is a science book from the Smithsonian Wild Heritage Collection. It tells the story of an Atlantic Puffin who arrives from the North Atlantic Ocean each spring to the same island where it was born. The puffin preens, dives for sand eels, and escapes from a black-backed gull. When the puffin returns to his burrow (the same burrow he uses every summer), he finds his mate waiting for him. They tap beaks in greeting. The puffins mate and then claw out their burrow, cleaning it and bringing new grass and seaweed to make a nest. In late April, the female puffin lays one large white egg. The two puffins take turns warming the egg. After forty days, a fuzzy chick is born. The chick eats sand eels and herring brought by its parents; and it grows very fast, eating half its weight in fish every day. When the chick is grown in July, it jumps into the sea and swims off—not returning to land for two years!

The simple text and authentic-looking illustrations in *Puffin's Homecoming* make it an interesting and informative book for young readers. Children will learn many puffin facts within the context of the story. The last page of the book includes a glossary and additional information about puffins.

LEARNING ACTIVITIES

1. Make a puffin fact list. After reading *Puffin's Homecoming: The Story of an Atlantic Puffin*, make a list of all the facts you learned about puffins (e.g., puffins return to the same burrow each year, adult puffins can carry up to twenty-two fish at a time, puffin chicks will not return to land for at least two years). Then take turns with a friend asking and answering questions such as: Do puffins find a different burrow each year? How many fish can a puffin carry at a time? How long will puffin chicks stay at sea?

2. Discuss *Puffin's Homecoming: The Story of an Atlantic Puffin*. For example, on pages 13 and 17, the book refers to puffins greeting each other by tapping their beaks together. What do you think this greeting means? On page 18, the book tells how puffins clean their burrows. Why do you think they clean their burrows? On page 20, the book says that younger puffins gather grass for nests but they must let it blow away since they have no burrows. Why don't they have burrows? As you review the end of the book, discuss why you think puffin chicks go out to sea for two years.

3. As a class or with a group of friends, work together to create your own "wild heritage" picture book about another Maine bird or animal (e.g., chickadee, loon, moose, lobster). Read information about your selected animal, write a simple story, and add illustrations to create your book. Divide the task into parts so that everyone in your group has a job for the book. Then share your book with another class.

ABOUT THE AUTHOR

Darice Bailer has worked as a journalist since 1989. She has had articles published in *The New York Times* and *The Washington Post*. *Puffin's Homecoming* was Bailer's first children's book. Since its publication, she has had three more children's books published, including *The Last Rail: The Building of the First Transcontinental Railroad*, *Head to Head: Football's Steve Young and Troy Aikman*, and a book about the Super Bowl. Bailer is currently working on two more children's books, one about the Pony Express, and another about hump-backed whales.

Bailer currently lives in Wilton, Connecticut, with her husband, daughter, and twin sons. Each summer, Bailer brings her family for a vacation in Maine, on Moose Pond in Bridgton, where they enjoy fishing, swimming, and canoeing.

ABOUT THE ILLUSTRATOR

Katie Lee was born in Kenya, Africa, and grew up in England. She has worked as an art instructor and has had exhibits of her botanical and zoological illustrations shown in England, Scotland, and throughout the United States. In addition to *Puffin's Homecoming*, Lee has illustrated a number of other children's books, including *Black Bear Cub*, *Orca Song*, and *Loggerhead Turtle*. She is also the author and illustrator of *A Visit to Galapagos*. Her illustrations are done with gouache. Lee is the mother of three grown children, and she currently lives in South Salem, New York.

MAINE LIFE AT THE TURN OF THE CENTURY THROUGH THE PHOTOGRAPHS OF NETTIE CUMMINGS MAXIM

AUTHORS: Diane & Jack Barnes / PHOTOGRAPHER: selections from Nettie Cummings Maxim's photographs
AGE LEVEL / LENGTH: 10 years–adult / 128 pages
PUBLISHER / COPYRIGHT DATE: Arcadia Publishing / 1995
FORMAT / ISBN: Paperback / 0752402404

Maine Life at the Turn of the Century Through the Photographs of Nettie Cummings Maxim celebrates an earlier and simpler time in Maine. From its adorable cover photo of watermelon-eating children, and through its almost two hundred black-and-white photos, this book shows farm life in Bethel, Maine, at the turn of the century, from the viewpoint of photographer Nettie Cummings Maxim. Maxim was born and bred on a farm on Bird Hill, in Bethel. In 1895, she acquired a camera and became a self-taught photographer. Photography was not easy back then. She had to develop her own glass negatives; she had to pose her subjects for extended periods of time since her camera's speed was slow and lighting was limited; and she had to create her own studio by tacking a backdrop to the side of the barn. The results were often magnificent, especially her portraits.

Authors Diane and Jack Barnes carefully researched Maxim's background, photos, and the history of the area. Photo captions are interesting and provide readers with an informative narrative for the photographs. The book is divided into eleven chapters, including "The Farm," "Berry Picking," "Summertime," and "Barn Cats." Readers will end the book wishing for more Maxim photos; unfortunately, her tragic death from diphtheria, at the age of thirty-three, cut short her career during its prime. *Maine Life at the Turn of the Century Through the Photographs of Nettie Cummings Maxim* is part of the "Images of America" series, published by Arcadia Publishing. All books in the series feature earlier photographs, some of specific regions of Maine, such as *Along the Kennebec: The Herman Bryant Collection* and *The Casco Bay Islands*, while others are about specific Maine towns such as Dexter, Augusta, and Rockland.

LEARNING ACTIVITIES

1. Arrange a visit to your nearest historical society and view earlier photographs from your own community. Study the photos carefully. Which people and families are featured? What work and leisure activities are shown? Which town buildings or landmarks are shown? After your visit, write an essay summarizing what you learned about the history of your community.

2. Collect old family photos. Have copies made or make photocopies. Interview older family members to learn as much as you can about who was in each photo, what was happening, and the location of each photo. Then combine the photos into a family booklet and write informative captions for each photo.

3. Research the history of photography and write a report describing how photography has changed over the years. How have cameras changed? How have developing procedures evolved? What can photographers do today that they could not do twenty, fifty, or one hundred years ago?

ABOUT THE AUTHORS

Diane and Jack Barnes are a wife-and-husband team. They operate a working farm in Hiram, Maine; teach courses at the University of Southern Maine; and have written books about the Oxford Hills and Sebago Lake Area for Arcadia Publishing's "Images of America" series. In addition, Jack Barnes is a literary columnist for the *Maine Sunday Telegram* and *The New Hampshire Sunday News*. He has also had poetry, essays, short stories, and articles published in many newspapers and magazines. A collection of his writings since 1979, called *The Best of Barnes*, has been published by the Nightshade Press.

SHAKER HOME

AUTHOR / PHOTOGRAPHER: Raymond Bial
AGE LEVEL / LENGTH: 8-12 years / 40 pages
PUBLISHER / COPYRIGHT DATE: Houghton Mifflin Co. / 1994
FORMAT / ISBN: Hardcover / 0395640474

Shaker Home tells about the history and heritage of Shakers, from their formation in England in the 1770s up to their present-day struggle to survive with only a handful of members. Sabbathday Lake, Maine, is one of only two remaining Shaker communities.

Sister Frances Carr, of Sabbathday Lake, is quoted in this book as she refers to the continued existence of Shakers: "We'll go away in time, as will everybody. But our ideas and our way of life will never go away."

Shaker Home is a testament to the never-ending appeal of the simplicity and beauty of Shaker life. Bial's color photographs were actually taken at the Shaker Village of Pleasant Hill, Kentucky; but visitors to the Sabbathday Lake Shaker Village in New Gloucester, Maine, will swear that many of the photos were taken there. Readers can glimpse the Shaker lifestyle through the perfectly-maintained white buildings, the Shaker inventions from the flat broom to ladderback chairs, and the meeting room with benches placed on one side for females and the other side for males. Bial's text is simple, yet informative, full of details and quotes. Reading *Shaker Home* is the next best thing to a visit to an actual Shaker Village.

LEARNING ACTIVITIES

1. Select one of the Shaker inventions (e.g., chair rail, washing machine, slotted spoon) named in *Shaker Home* and learn more about it. How was the invention made? What was it made out of? What need did it fill? How has that invention changed over the years? Give a written or oral report about your selected invention.

2. Visit the Shaker Village at Sabbathday Lake in New Gloucester, Maine. Take a tour of the museum, the buildings, and the grounds. Afterwards, write a story, poem, or song which summarizes your feelings about the visit.

3. Reread *Shaker Home* and notice how author/photographer Raymond Bial manages to capture the spirit and essence of Shaker life even though *no* people are shown in any of his photographs. Create your own photo-essay about another place (e.g., a kindergarten classroom, a library, a summer camp). Do not photograph any people in your selected place, but still try to capture the spirit of the place through your words and your photos (or drawings, if you prefer).

ABOUT THE AUTHOR/PHOTOGRAPHER

Raymond Bial has had more than twenty-five books, mostly photo essays, published for children and adults. Originally, he made artistic black-and-white photographs, including portraits of rural Mainers and beach scenes. Now he works primarily with color photographs. Some of his most recent children's books include *Portrait of a Farm Family*, *Frontier Home*, *Cajun Home*, and *Country Fair*. For *Shaker Home*, Bial visited and researched at Sabbathday Lake. Although the photos for the book were taken at the Shaker Village of Pleasant Hill, Kentucky, Bial says that Sabbathday Lake had an important role as "a significant Shaker community."

Bial currently lives in Urbana, Illinois, with his wife and three children. In addition to writing and photography, he enjoys gardening and traveling.

THE ABENAKI

AUTHOR: Colin G. Calloway / PHOTOGRAPHER: photographs from a variety of sources
AGE LEVEL / LENGTH: 12 years–adult / 112 pages
PUBLISHER / COPYRIGHT DATE: Chelsea House Publishers / 1989
FORMAT / ISBN: Library Binding / 1555466877

The Abenaki is part of the "Indians of North America" series, published by Chelsea House Publishers, a series of more than sixty books about Native American tribes across the continent. In six chapters, this book provides a vivid picture of the Abenaki Indians, both historically and in modern times. The chapters are: "The People of the Dawnland," "Society, Art, and Culture," "Traders, Diseases, and Missionaries," "Wars and Migrations," "The Survival of the People," and "The Abenaki Today."

Readers will learn many interesting facts about the Abenaki. They lived in two kinds of dwellings: wigwams, which were cone-shaped and could be easily dismantled and carried from one place to another; and longhouses, which were larger, sturdier, and more permanent homes where as many as sixty people could live. The Abenaki believed they were descended from animals and had special animal "totems" to symbolize their connection to particular animals. For recreation, the Abenaki played word games and lacrosse. A listing of Abenaki place names shows that "Katahdin" means "the principal mountain," "Kennebec" means "long water without rapids," and "Piscataqua" means "where the river divides."

The Abenaki includes numerous black and white photos, and an eight-page, full-color section showing close-ups of Abenaki baskets, crafts, and tools. A bibliography, glossary, and index are also included. Adults will also enjoy this well-written, comprehensive book which offers an eye-opening view of the Abenaki's struggles and survival.

LEARNING ACTIVITIES

1. *The Abenaki* was published in 1989. What has happened to Maine's Abenaki population since then? Do they still struggle with poverty? In what ways have they continued to invest their land claims settlement? Have the Penobscot found ways to better utilize the Sockalexis Memorial Ice Arena that they built on Indian Island? Do the Passamaquoddy continue to run a bilingual education program and radio station? Search for newspaper and magazine articles about the Penobscot and Passamaquoddy during the past ten years. What new information can you find? Contact officials at the Pleasant Point State Indian Reservation and the Penobscot Indian Reservation in Old Town to gather information

about the status of their tribes in the 1990s. Use all the information you gather to write a follow-up chapter to *The Abenaki*.

2. Look closely at the photos of baskets made by the Abenaki in the book. Try to view their actual baskets at the Maine State Museum in Augusta, the Hudson Museum in Orono, or the Penobscot National Historical Society in Old Town. Many adult education programs offer a course in basket-making. If possible, take such a course or invite a basket-making instructor to visit your classroom to give a demonstration. Write a story, poem, or descriptive passage about what you have learned about basket-making.

3. See the listing of "Abenaki Place Names" on page 86 of *The Abenaki*. Add to the list. What towns, rivers, lakes, etc. from your region have Native American names; and what are their meanings? Keep an ongoing list and add to it over several months, creating as long a list of "Abenaki Place Names" as possible.

ABOUT THE AUTHOR

Colin G. Calloway was born in England. After moving to the United States, he taught high school in Vermont, and later served as the editor and assistant director of the D'arcy McNickle Center for the History of the American Indian at the Newberry Library, in Chicago. He has written numerous articles on Indian history and has taught American Indian history courses at the university level.

LOBSTERS: GANGSTERS OF THE SEA

AUTHOR: Mary Cerullo / PHOTOGRAPHER: Jeffrey Rotman
AGE LEVEL / LENGTH: 8-14 years / 64 pages
PUBLISHER / COPYRIGHT DATE: Cobblehill Books (div. of Dutton & Penguin Books) / 1994
FORMAT / ISBN: Hardcover / 0525651535

This book is packed with information about the American (or "Maine") lobster. With its descriptive text and more than 35 full-color photographs, *Lobsters: Gangsters of the Sea* helps young readers to see lobsters and lobstering closely. The seven chapters include lobster lore, lobster courtship, aquaculture, and how people eat a lobster.

The overall theme of the book is one of interdependency. Lobstermen depend upon lobsters in order to make a living and support their families. But, similarly, lobsters are dependent upon lobstermen and their baited traps in order to eat and survive. A study done along the Maine coast found that when a group of 48 lobstermen voluntarily removed their traps for six weeks from a popular lobstering area, that the lobsters also left that area; they needed the food from the traps in order to survive. Contrary to what people may believe, all lobsters are not caught in traps. Many lobsters reach in and raid traps, smaller lobsters eat from traps and then escape, and lobstermen often throw old bait overboard as a "free" meal for lobsters.

Lobsters: Gangsters of the Sea presents information about lobstering laws; the book also explains why lobsters can be different colors, how the community of Monhegan Island observes Trap Day, and much more. A helpful index and bibliographies (one for adults and one for young readers) are included in the back of the book.

LEARNING ACTIVITIES

1. Before reading *Lobsters: Gangsters of the Sea,* write a summary of what you know about lobsters and any questions you have about lobsters. After reading the book, check the information you wrote down. Which of it is true? Not true? Write the answers to any of your questions that were answered by the book. Add any new information you learned, and create your own lobster fact list.

2. *Lobsters: Gangsters of the Sea* describes how lobstering works in Monhegan Island. Write to or interview lobstermen from another Maine lobstering community. What are the lobstering laws and traditions there? How are they similar and different from those on Monhegan Island?

3. Select one part of lobsters or lobstering and research it further. For example, you might learn more about how lobster traps are made and work, or you might learn more about lobster eggs and babies, or you might learn more about aquaculture. Give an oral presentation about your findings. Use demonstrations and photos to clarify your presentation.

ABOUT THE AUTHOR

For over twenty years, Mary Cerullo has been writing magazine articles, curriculum materials, nature trail guides, and brochures on science topics. Previously, she worked for the University of Maine Sea Grant Program, where she explained scientific research to the public, fishermen, and other marine interest groups. She calls herself "a science interpreter." In 1992, Cerullo was named the Outstanding Marine Educator of the year by the National Marine Educators Association.

For *Lobsters: Gangsters of the Sea,* Cerullo researched the Maine lobster and interviewed many Maine people. She also is the author of several other children's books, including *Sharks: Challengers of the Deep, Coral Reef: A City That Never Sleeps,* and *The Octopus: Phantom of the Sea.* She is also the author of a teacher's reference book, *Reading the Environment: Children's Literature in the Science Classroom.*

Cerullo has lived in Maine since 1981, and boasts that her two children are "natives." Cerullo and her family make their home in South Portland. They enjoy exploring tidepools, camping, and biking, especially in Acadia National Park.

ABOUT THE ILLUSTRATOR

Since 1974, Jeffrey Rotman has been diving and photographing marine life. He has worked as a wildlife photographer, underwater photographer, and journalistic photographer. He lives in Somerville, Massachusetts.

A YEAR ON MONHEGAN ISLAND

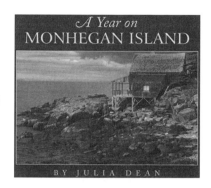

AUTHOR / PHOTOGRAPHER: Julia Dean
AGE LEVEL / LENGTH: 8 years–adult / 48 pages
PUBLISHER / COPYRIGHT DATE: Ticknor & Fields Books for Young Readers (a Houghton Mifflin Company) / 1995
FORMAT / ISBN: Hardcover / 0395664764
AWARDS: Lupine Award, 1995

A Year on Monhegan Island is a photographic essay about the seasonal changes found on an island located ten miles off the coast of Maine. The book begins in the winter as the six students from the island's one-room schoolhouse prepare for a Christmas celebration by cutting down and decorating a Christmas tree for the schoolhouse and by practicing a play for the community's Christmas celebration. Monhegan Island's most important winter event is Trap Day, on January 1, when the island's six-month lobstering season begins and lobstermen first set their traps. Residents of the island help to load the lobster traps by passing hundreds of them from the shore down the wharf and onto the lobster boats.

After a spring filled with fog and mud, summer arrives on Monhegan Island along with hundreds of tourists and summer residents. Shops, inns, and galleries greet the new arrivals. Since the early 1900s, Monhegan Island has been a friend and inspiration to artists, including Robert Henri, Rockwell Kent, and Jamie Wyeth. Tourists to Monhegan enjoy quiet pastimes, such as bird watching and hiking the seventeen miles of island trails. By Columbus Day, all the visitors are gone, and the year-rounders have a quiet fall to prepare for another isolated winter.

Through conversational text and people-centered photos, author/photographer Julia Dean shows the "real" Monhegan Island. She shares the island's challenges, such as having to leave home after eighth grade to attend high school on the mainland, and the controversies such as dealing with the island's growing deer population. Monhegan is a modern anomaly since it has only had private telephones since 1983 and electricity since 1984. This book gives readers of all ages a wonderful and rare glimpse at Maine island life.

LEARNING ACTIVITIES

1. After reading *A Year on Monhegan Island*, have a discussion with friends or family members about the book. Which season would be your favorite on the island? What do you think the residents of Monhegan should do about their deer population? Would you be able to live away from home after eighth grade in order to go to high school? Why or why not? What would you enjoy the most about island life? The least? What else would you like to know about life on Monhegan Island that was not included in the book?

2. Work with a group of peers to create a photo-essay about your own community. Interview longtime residents. Visit your local historical society to learn more about your community's history. Take photos of important buildings and people from your town. Plan how you will organize your book. Divide the jobs of interviewing, writing, photographing, editing, etc. among group members. Allow time for making several revisions of your book. Afterwards, you might wish to share your book with town groups or have it available to residents through your town or school library.

3. If possible, visit a Maine island. You may need to learn the ferry schedule. Write to your selected island's Chamber of Commerce ahead of time to learn about special events and places to visit on the island. Write a journal entry describing your Maine island visit.

ABOUT THE AUTHOR/PHOTOGRAPHER

Julia Dean is a photo-journalist. She received a degree in photography from the Rochester Institute of Technology and a degree in journalism from the University of Nebraska. She began her photographic career as an apprentice for the famed photographer, Berenice Abbott. After working as a photo editor for the Associated Press, she taught photography courses to high school and college students, including working as an instructor at the Maine Photo Workshops in Rockport. Dean first visited Monhegan Island in 1977. When a publisher suggested to Dean the possible topic for a children's book of how a coastal village changes throughout the seasons, Dean remembered her earlier trip to Monhegan Island and knew that it would make a perfect subject for a photo-essay children's book.

Dean lives in Venice, California, where she runs a photography business that focuses on issues of cultural, humanitarian, and social concerns around the world. Dean is also currently working on another children's book, one about life in a rural village in India.

THE PENOBSCOT

AUTHORS: Katherine & Craig Doherty / PHOTOGRAPHER: photographs from a variety of sources
AGE LEVEL / LENGTH: 8-12 years / 64 pages
PUBLISHER / COPYRIGHT DATE: Franklin Watts (a div. of Grolier Publishing) / 1995
FORMAT / ISBN: Hardcover / 0531202070; Paperback / 0531157644

The Penobscot, an informational book about the Penobscot Indians of Maine, tells intriguing stories of the Penobscots' culture, beliefs, and daily life. Authors Katherine and Craig Doherty weave a fascinating tale of how the Penobscots first lived along the Penobscot River and Bay 9,000 years ago. During the 1400s before Europeans visited the area, there were 10,000 Penobscots; but by 1800, the Penobscot population had been reduced to a few hundred. The Penobscots were killed primarily by diseases, such as small pox, which the Europeans carried with them and for which the Penobscot had no immunity. Many other Penobscots were killed during the course of eight wars.

A chapter called "Religion and Beliefs" describes the traditional Penobscot belief in a creator spirit called Glooskap, who made the first Penobscot people out of the bark of an ash tree, and the belief that animal spirits bring people success when they hunt. Detailed accounts of the Penobscots' daily life include how the Penobscots traditionally cared for their babies, boiled maple syrup, used six different fishing methods, built shaped shelters, and much more. A final chapter describes modern Penobscot life after the 1980 Maine Indian Settlement Act. *The Penobscot* packs lots of easily readable information into a few pages, and it will leave young readers ready to learn more about the culture and history of this group of Maine's Native Americans.

LEARNING ACTIVITIES

1. Select one Penobscot tradition or custom described in this book and elaborate on it by creating a short story about it. For example, you might write a story about a young hunter who disobeys the custom of giving away his first kill, or you might write a story about attracting moose with a birch bark horn, or you might tell a story using a corn husk doll. Try to make your story believable and interesting.

2. Organize a debate over whether the Maine Indian Settlement Act was fair to the Penobscots. Have a team represent each side of the argument (the settlement *was* fair; was *not* fair), carefully plan and practice your arguments, and then hold the actual debate in front of an audience. Afterwards, ask the audience which side presented a better case, and why?

3. Learn more about the Penobscot language. What are some Penobscot words? How are they pronounced? What do they mean? Does the Penobscot language have a structured

word order? A structured grammar? Is it an easy or difficult language to learn? Is it a written language or solely an oral one? Write a report about what you learn.

ABOUT THE AUTHORS

Katherine and Craig Doherty have written other children's books about Native Americans, including *The Iroquois* and *The Wampanoag*. They live in New Hampshire where Mrs. Doherty works as a librarian and Mr. Doherty works as a high school English teacher. For five years they lived with their daughter on the Zuni Indian Reservation and worked in the Zuni Public School District.

THE PENOBSCOT

When summer was almost over, the families loaded their canoes and paddled back up the river. It was time to harvest the crops they had planted.

AUTHOR: Jill Duvall / PHOTOGRAPHER: photographs from a variety of sources
AGE LEVEL / LENGTH: 6-10 years / 48 pages
PUBLISHER / COPYRIGHT DATE: Childrens Press / 1993
FORMAT / ISBN: Library binding / 0516011944; Paperback / 0516411942

This nonfiction book tells about the Penobscot Indians of Maine. Young readers will learn through the large format text and numerous photographs about the history, traditions, and modern life of the Penobscots. A chapter entitled "A Year of Penobscot Life" follows the Penobscots from spring, when they traditionally lived in wigwams along the Penobscot River and planted crops and harvested sap from maple trees; through summer, when they canoed down the river to the ocean to catch fish and seafood; into late summer and early fall, when they returned to harvest their crops. Finally, in late fall and winter, the Penobscots hunted further north for game, while camping in the woods and setting traps. Then the cycle of their seasonal lives was repeated.

Information about the Penobscots' friendship with the French and disagreements with the English are also featured. A chapter called "A Nation of Heroes" tells briefly of the famous Sockalexis cousins—Andrew who was a marathon racer in the 1912 Olympics and Louis who was a famous baseball player for the Cleveland Spiders (who were later renamed the Cleveland Indians in honor of Louis Sockalexis). Finally, young readers will learn about the modern land claim case which reimbursed the Penobscot and Passamaquoddy Indians for land which had been taken illegally from them in the past. A glossary and index complete *The Penobscot*, which is part of Childrens Press' "New True Book" series.

LEARNING ACTIVITIES

1. Locate the Penobscot River on a Maine map. Draw your own copy of that river and also draw symbols along the river to show the activities of the Penobscot Indians during each of the seasons as described in the chapter "A Year of Penobscot Life." For example, you might draw plants where Indian Island is located, fishing spears in Penobscot Bay, and so on.

2. Write a letter to school children who attend the Indian Island School on the Penobscot Reservation in Old Town (Box 566, Old Town, ME 04468). Ask what their school day is like. Do they have lessons which teach them the Penobscot language? Which Penobscot traditions do they continue to learn and practice? Who are other famous Penobscots in addition to the Sockalexis cousins?

3. Study the handmade crafts, tools, and clothing made by the Penobscots and pictured in this book. If possible, view actual Penobscot crafts, tools, and clothing at a Maine museum. What do you notice about their design? Their colors? Their patterns?

ABOUT THE AUTHOR

Jill Duvall is a political scientist. She has a degree from Georgetown University. She has researched and written frequently about many national and international issues, such as world hunger, human rights, and international relationships.

MAINE: HELLO USA

AUTHOR: LeeAnne Engfer / PHOTOGRAPHER: photographs from a variety of sources
AGE LEVEL / LENGTH: 6-12 years / 72 pages
PUBLISHER / COPYRIGHT DATE: Lerner Publications / 1991
FORMAT / ISBN: Library binding / 0822527014

Maine is part of Lerner's "Hello USA" series. This small book is a terrific beginning resource book for children. It is divided into five major sections. In the section entitled "Did You Know?" young readers are told some fun trivia about the state, such as the size of the world's largest lobster boiler and the name of the state's second most popular tourist attraction. The section called "A Trip Around the State" explains the different land regions, the types of wildlife and plants, and the types of weather found in Maine. The next section, "Maine's Story," tells about the history of the state, describing its Native American populations, the European explorers who visited, Maine's involvement in wars, its move to statehood, and the ways that its early settlers made a living. The fourth section, "Living and Working in Maine," explains modern business and recreation in the state. Finally, a section called "Protecting the Environment" discusses threats to Maine's natural resources and scenic beauty.

The end of *Maine* also includes helpful lists of Maine's famous people, facts-at-a-glance, a pronunciation guide, a glossary of terms, and a thorough index. Some of the book's information is routine and expected, such as the information on lobsters and lumbering; but the book also includes little-known information, such as the fact that the inventor of the microwave oven was born in Howland, Maine, and that board-game pioneer Milton Bradley came from Vienna, Maine. All in all, this book is an informative, fun, beginning Maine resource for young readers.

LEARNING ACTIVITIES

1. Create a Maine fact game using this book. Create question and answer cards with information found in the book. Then play the game with others, testing your knowledge of the state.

2. Select a fact from this book, such as the fact that 2.5 million people visit the L. L. Bean store every year, or that 4,000 Native Americans live in Maine, or that Maine lobstermen catch 22 million pounds of lobster each year. Try to verify or prove your selected fact. What sources should you check? Has the information changed since the book was published in 1991?

3. Select one of the "Famous People" listed in *Maine*. Research your selected Mainer. Then write a report of that person's life and career.

ABOUT THE AUTHOR

LeeAnne Engfer grew up in Iowa and Minnesota. After attending the University of Minnesota and receiving a journalism degree, she wrote for local newspapers in Minnesota. When she joined the staff of Lerner Publications as an editor, she was given the choice of a state to write about. Most of the books in the series were researched and written by staff editors at Lerner. Engfer did not hesitate on her choice. She selected Maine, which she describes as her "fantasy state." In fact, one night while working on the book, she had a very vivid dream about being in Maine. Engfer is also the author of two books from Lerner's "All About Pets" series: *My Pet Cat* and *My Pet Hamster and Gerbils*.

Engfer currently lives in St. Paul, Minnesota. Her hobbies include reading, yoga, swimming, and cooking.

BEACONS OF LIGHT: LIGHTHOUSES

AUTHOR / ILLUSTRATOR: Gail Gibbons
AGE LEVEL / LENGTH: 5-10 years / 32 pages
PUBLISHER / COPYRIGHT DATE: Morrow Junior Books (hardcover); Liguori Publications (paperback) / 1990
FORMAT / ISBN: Hardcover / 0688073794; Paperback / 0892437847

Beacons of Light: Lighthouses provides a look at lighthouses worldwide and includes history and information about their construction. Young readers will learn that the first lighthouses built in Egypt were stone towers with fires burning at the top and that the first U.S. lighthouse was built in 1716 in Boston. Readers wll also learn that lighthouses are visible for up to twenty miles due to a lens invented by Augustin Fresnel which uses prisms to increase the reflected light.

Gibbons's detailed illustrations of lighthouses are complemented by her simple, informative text. Eight of the twenty-one lighthouses in the book are located in Maine, including Matinicus Rock Lighthouse, Owls Head Lighthouse, Portland Head Light, and West Quoddy Head Lighthouse. Fun facts at the end of the book include trivia about several Maine lighthouses.

LEARNING ACTIVITIES

1. Cover up the names of the lighthouses and guess which ones are from Maine. Explain the rationale for your guesses. Do Maine lighthouses look alike? Do they have similar shapes, colorings, styles?

2. Maine has more than thirty-five lighthouses. Research and list as many Maine lighthouses as possible. The *Maine Atlas and Gazetteer,* published by DeLorme Mapping Company, will be helpful. Where is each located? How old is each one? In what color and pattern are the lighthouses painted?

3. Create a lighthouse photo album. Take photographs of Maine lighthouses, if possible, or collect postcards of Maine lighthouses or photographs of lighthouses from Maine magazines, such as *Down East.* Collect the photographs in a book, with facts about lighthouses and/or poems inspired by lighthouses.

4. Create a trivia game based on *Beacons of Light: Lighthouses.* Draw a gameboard in the shape of a lighthouse and make up question/answer cards, using information from the

book. Sample questions might be: What was the first lighthouse in North America? (Boston Light) What is a diaphone? (A foghorn that uses compressed air to give off two tones, a high and low one.) What is the name of the famous dog who used to ring the bell at the Owls Head Light? (Spot)

ABOUT THE AUTHOR/ILLUSTRATOR

See information about Gail Gibbons on page 39.

COUNTRY FAIR

AUTHOR / ILLUSTRATOR: Gail Gibbons
AGE LEVEL / LENGTH: 4-8 years / 28 pages
PUBLISHER / COPYRIGHT DATE: Little Brown and Company / 1994
FORMAT / ISBN: Hardcover / 0316309516 (recently out of print)

Country Fair is a celebration of fairs. Author/illustrator Gail Gibbons visited numerous fairs in her "home" states of Maine and Vermont in order to gather ideas for this book. Her brightly-colored illustrations are filled with details, and so is her text.

Gibbons begins the book with workers prepping the grounds and buildings. Then on opening day, the high school band plays, and fairgoers enjoy games of ring toss, darts, bingo, and more. They eat fair food: cotton candy, pizza, fried dough, etc. They go on rides, such as the Ferris wheel and merry-go-round. They visit exhibits of prized vegetables, flower arrangements, plus arts and crafts. They watch calf-judging, pig-calling, a fiddler's contest, horse racing, tractor pulling, and a country band. As night falls, fireworks burst into brilliant colors trying to match the colorful country fair.

Country Fair is a fine book to share with children before visiting a fair. It will inform them about what to expect and help them to focus their excitement and anticipation. But, perhaps, this book is best shared *after* a visit to an agricultural fair. *Country Fair* can serve as a way to relive the celebration and savor the memories until the fair returns next year.

LEARNING ACTIVITIES

1. Read *Country Fair* before and after visiting your local country fair. Then compare the book to your actual fair. How many days is your fair open? What foods, exhibits, and rides are at your fair? What parts of the fair did you find in the book but not at your local fair? Write a list of all the ways the fair in the book and your real fair were alike and different.

2. Select one part of your nearest agricultural fair and research it. For example, you might learn more about sheep-shearing, or about your local 4-H club, or about the history of your fair, or about ferris wheels. Create a report, oral or written, about the information you learn.

3. Create a booklet about a fair you visit. Take photographs or draw pictures of different parts of the fair. Then place the photos/drawings in book form and write a caption under each picture. Share your fair booklet with a friend.

ABOUT THE AUTHOR/ILLUSTRATOR

See information about Gail Gibbons on page 39.

GULLS . . . GULLS . . . GULLS

AUTHOR / ILLUSTRATOR: Gail Gibbons
AGE LEVEL / LENGTH: 5-10 years / 32 pages
PUBLISHER / COPYRIGHT DATE: Holiday House / 1997
FORMAT / ISBN: Hardcover / 0823413233

We call them seagulls, but the birds that dominate the Maine coastline are actually herring gulls. Herring gulls are the most common kind of gull found in North America. Matinicus Island resident Gail Gibbons describes the life cycle, behaviors, and habitat of herring gulls in her picture book, *Gulls . . . Gulls . . . Gulls*. Through the text and illustrations, young readers will learn specific bird vocabulary, such as preening, molting, roosting, egg tooth, and fledgling. Many interesting herring gull facts are included; for example: herring gulls get light brown streaks on the top of their heads during the wintertime, and gull chicks find food by pecking at the red mark on their parents' beaks.

Simple diagrams and maps in *Gulls . . . Gulls . . . Gulls* show the body parts of gulls, the migration patterns of herring gulls in North America, and pictures of other kinds of gulls found in North America. A final page includes a dozen additional gull facts.

LEARNING ACTIVITIES

1. Keep a gull-sighting journal with friends or classmates. Over the course of a month, write down all the places where you see herring gulls. Do you see them by the ocean? At lakes? By rivers? At dumps or landfills? At the end of the month, discuss your sightings. In which location did you see the most gulls? The least gulls? Was a source of food for the gulls available at each location? What was the food? Did you usually see one gull alone or a group of gulls?

2. In *Gulls . . . Gulls . . . Gulls*, Gail Gibbons tells us that herring gulls get light brown streaks on their heads during the winter. Arrange for a winter visit to a Maine coastal beach during the wintertime. Look for gulls. Do you see the brown streaks on their heads? What else do you notice about the winter beach? How is it different than a summer beach?

3. The final page of the book explains that terns are birds that are related to gulls. Terns are smaller than gulls, and they have deep forks on their tails. Research terns. What else can you learn about them? What do they eat? Do they migrate? Where do they make their nests? What sound do they make? Make a tern list with all the facts you learn. Try to find at least twenty facts about terns using nonfiction books and bird guides.

ABOUT THE AUTHOR / ILLUSTRATOR

See information about Gail Gibbons on page 39.

PAPER, PAPER EVERYWHERE

AUTHOR / ILLUSTRATOR: Gail Gibbons
AGE LEVEL / LENGTH: 4-8 years / 32 pages
PUBLISHER / COPYRIGHT DATE: Harcourt Brace / 1983
FORMAT / ISBN: Hardcover / 0152594884; Paperback / 0152014918

Paper, Paper Everywhere explains how trees are turned into paper. The book includes detailed illustrations of the inside of a paper mill and uses simple text so that even young readers can understand the papermaking process. Author/illustrator Gail Gibbons follows the process from the forest to the paper mill to the final shipping of the paper, which is used "to make books, streamers, napkins, kites, paper hats, masks," and other products.

This book also features "paper puzzler" pages, which challenge children to find all the objects in the picture that are made out of paper. They can check their answers using answer keys at the end of the book.

LEARNING ACTIVITIES

1. Have a paper hunt. See how many objects you can find made out of paper in a kitchen, in a bathroom, in a classroom, in the garage, at a grocery store, etc.

2. If possible, visit a paper mill. Arrange for a tour or interview a paper mill worker. Compare actual papermaking with the steps described in *Paper, Paper Everywhere*. Has

papermaking changed since this book was written in 1983? How so? What new technology do paper mills use?

3. Learn about paper recycling. Visit a recycling center and read nonfiction books about recycling. What types of paper can be recycled? How is paper treated so that it can be reused? How many times can paper be recycled? Is there a limit? What products are made of recycled paper? Make a poster showing some of the information you learned about paper recycling.

ABOUT THE AUTHOR/ILLUSTRATOR

See information about Gail Gibbons on page 39.

THE PUFFINS ARE BACK!

AUTHOR / ILLUSTRATOR: Gail Gibbons
AGE LEVEL / LENGTH: 5-10 years / 32 pages
PUBLISHER / COPYRIGHT DATE: HarperCollins / 1991
FORMAT / ISBN: Hardcover / 0060216034; Library binding / 0060216042

The Puffins Are Back! describes the puffins yearly return to a Maine island to mate and raise their chicks. It also provides an historical look at Maine's puffin population, from the time the species was nearly extirpated in the state up to the successful efforts of the National Audubon Society to reintroduce the puffin to Maine. Numerous facts about puffins are given, such as why they have two eyelids, how they make a burrow, and how many fish a baby puffin eats.

Gail Gibbons's puffin story is easy to read and understand, yet at the same time it is chock full of interesting facts about puffins. Gail Gibbons decided to write this book because she and her husband live on a farmhouse on Matinicus Island, off the coast of Maine, during part of each year. On Matinicus Rock, an island five miles from Matinicus, there is a colony of puffins. While Gibbons was on Matinicus Rock researching her book, *Beacons of Light: Lighthouses*, she met members of the Audubon Society who were working on the puffin project. Gibbons was excited to learn about their efforts: "We're always hearing about how we've hurt our planet. This book shows how mankind has repaired what he has damaged."

LEARNING ACTIVITIES

1. Research other Maine shore birds (e.g., herring gull, tern, cormorant). What do they eat? Where do they make their nests? How do they care for their young? Are they endangered? Who are their enemies? Write a report about the information you learn.

2. The puffin almost was extirpated in Maine. Learn about other endangered Maine animals. Arrange to interview or write to a state wildlife biologist or member of the National Audubon Society. Ask which animals are in danger and what people can do to protect them. Write a booklet about protecting Maine wildlife.

3. Using *The Puffins Are Back!* as a guide, give an informational talk about puffins. Show pictures, diagrams, and maps to explain where and how puffins live. Include information about the puffin restoration project and how puffin chicks are hatched and raised. Allow time for questions after your presentation.

ABOUT THE AUTHOR/ILLUSTRATOR

See information about Gail Gibbons on page 39.

ROUGH & READY LOGGERS

AUTHOR: A.S. Gintzler / PHOTOGRAPHER: photographs from a variety of sources
AGE LEVEL / LENGTH: 8-14 years / 48 pages
PUBLISHER / COPYRIGHT DATE: John Muir Publications / 1994
FORMAT / ISBN: Hardcover / 156261164X; Paperback / 1562612344

Rough & Ready Loggers tells about the history of lumbering in the United States from the 1600s through modern times. Although the book includes information for the entire country, it also includes many specific references to logging in Maine. Young readers will learn about river drivers from Maine called the Bangor Tigers; the first water-powered sawmill in the country built in 1631 on the Salmon Falls River in Maine; and the stories of some of Maine's famous loggers including John Ross, Logger Bradbury, and Jigger Jones. The history of logging white pines in New England is also detailed.

Numerous black and white photos and a comprehensive index are also included in *Rough & Ready Loggers*. Later chapters discuss the use of computers in today's lumber industry, and modern-day concerns about logging and the environment. This reference book is a fun, fact-filled guide to one of Maine's largest industries.

LEARNING ACTIVITIES

1. You have read tall tales about Paul Bunyan. Create your own tall tale about one of Maine's real loggers—John Ross, Logger Bradbury, or Jigger Jones (see pages 36-37 in *Rough & Ready Loggers*). Remember that it's all right to "stretch" the truth in a tall tale.

2. Interview someone who logs today and learn what their job is like. What equipment do they use? What hours do they work? Whom do they supply logs to? What are the greatest dangers in their work? In what ways do they protect the environment? Write a summary of your interview.

3. Write and illustrate a picture book entitled "Maine Logging." Use information you find in *Rough & Ready Loggers* that is specific to Maine as well as any information you can gather from other nonfiction books and from interviews. Share your picture book with a young friend.

ABOUT THE AUTHOR

A.S. Gintzler has worked as a writer and editor for periodicals, book publishers, corporate media, and network television research. While he was a college student in New England, Gintzler traveled the coast of Maine from Portland up into Canada. As a musician, Gintzler has performed songs of Shantymen. While researching *Rough & Ready Loggers*, Gintzler found that logging and lumbering have strong Maine roots, exemplified by rivermen like John Ross and woodsmen like Jigger Jones. He says their stories are stories of "raw endurance, determined survival, and hard living." In addition to *Rough & Ready Loggers*, Gintzler has also written five other books in the *Rough & Ready* series including ones about cowboys, homesteaders, railroaders, prospectors, and outlaws and lawmen.

Gintzler lives outside Santa Fe, New Mexico, with his wife and child. He says that his favorite hobbies are "observation and learning—what makes the world go round and what makes people tick." He regularly practices meditation and physical conditioning.

HEART DISEASE

AUTHOR: John Coopersmith Gold / PHOTOGRAPHER: photographs from a variety of sources
AGE LEVEL / LENGTH: 10-14 years / 64 pages
PUBLISHER / COPYRIGHT DATE: Crestwood House (div. of Simon & Schuster) / 1996
FORMAT / ISBN: Library binding / 0896868621 (recently out of print)

This nonfiction book tells all about heart disease, but it personalizes the subject and gains readers' attention by telling the story of one man's heart attack. That man is Dennis "Duke" Dutremble, a Maine teacher and politician from Biddeford. Dutremble suffered a heart attack when he was only thirty-nine years old. Although he was young for a heart attack, his family had a history of heart disease, and Dutremble had characteristics associated with heart disease—he was overweight, he smoked, and he was in a high stress job. After his heart attack, Dutremble underwent coronary bypass surgery. Dutremble went back to work, but three years later he had a mild stroke. Today, Dutremble takes heart medication and strives for a healthier lifestyle.

Heart Disease, part of Crestwood House's Healthwatch series, makes a complex subject accessible to young readers. The most difficult chapter tells how the heart works, explaining its anatomy and function. Other chapters are more easily understood; they explain the different types of heart disease, the causes of heart disease, how heart disease is diagnosed, and how to treat heart disease. The book also includes a helpful glossary, an index, and a listing of books and organizations with more information on heart disease.

LEARNING ACTIVITIES

1. Pretend you are a teacher and create a test about the book, *Heart Disease*. Try to include a variety of questions (e.g., true/false, matching, fill-in-the-blank, essay). Then try your test out. Ask a friend to read and study *Heart Disease*, and then take your test. How did your friend do on your test? What did your friend think of your test?

2. Learn your family's history of heart disease. Interview family members to see which, if any, relatives have had high blood pressure, angina, heart attacks, irregular heart rhythms, etc. How long did family members suffer from heart disease? What risk factors (e.g., smoking, being overweight) did they have for heart disease? What treatment did they receive, and did it seem to work? Summarize your information on your family's history of heart disease and give copies of it to family members so that they will have the information handy to review and to share with their doctors.

3. Create your own prevention plan for avoiding heart disease. What health habits can you start now which will reduce your risk of heart disease in the future? Use *Heart Disease* as a guide to help you make a list of "healthy heart habits." Then carry out your plan. Keep a log where each week you can write about your progress.

ABOUT THE AUTHOR

John Coopersmith Gold was born in Ohio and grew up in New Hampshire. He moved to Maine after college and has now lived in the state for more than a decade. He says that his "native" wife constantly reminds him that he is now and will always be a "transplant." Nevertheless, Gold claims that there is no where else he'd rather live—"except maybe during March!"

Gold has a degree in zoology, but when job prospects in that field seemed dim, he turned to journalism for a career. He has worked at the *Journal Tribune* in Biddeford for the past twelve years. In addition to his newspaper writing, Gold also writes freelance articles for business and fisheries publications. He has also written two other children's books: *Book Banning: Board of Education v. Pico* and *Cancer*. For his book *Heart Disease*, Gold was looking for a "real" patient to use as an example of how the disease can impact a person and family. He was pleased that Biddeford native and well-known politician, Dennis Dutremble, allowed Gold to share his story.

Gold currently lives in Saco with his wife, stepson, and their dog Oatmeal. Gold's wife Susan is also a writer (see page 257); together they operate a desktop publishing company. His interests include puttering around the house, hiking, canoeing, and surfing the Internet.

ALZHEIMER'S DISEASE

AUTHOR: Susan Dudley Gold / PHOTOGRAPHER: photographs from a variety of sources
AGE LEVEL / LENGTH: 10-14 years / 48 pages
PUBLISHER / COPYRIGHT DATE: Crestwood House (div. of Simon & Schuster) / 1996
FORMAT / ISBN: Library binding / 0896868575

Young readers of *Alzheimer's Disease* will not only learn about the disease, but they will also learn the story of one man's struggle with the disease. This book features Edward Dudley from Oakland, Maine, who is the author's father. The beginning of the book profiles Dudley as a younger man when he was a successful bookkeeper and salesman who was known for his great sense of humor. But Alzheimer's disease changes all that. In his sixties, Dudley begins to show more and more symptoms of Alzheimer's. He loses weight because he forgets to prepare meals for himself, he gets lost in familiar places, and he forgets routine tasks such as how to start a lawn mower. Author Susan Dudley Gold explains that there is no simple test for Alzheimer's Disease; her father was diagnosed as a result of his symptoms and after a battery of tests ruled out other problems with the brain.

The book continues by explaining how Alzheimer's patients are cared for and the different programs, residential facilities, and day-care centers that are available. Safety of Alzheimer's patients is of utmost importance because they are likely to act dangerously, e.g., becoming lost, or forgetting that they have turned on a stove. The "Safe Return Program" of the Alzheimer's Association is explained. Finally, current drug treatments and Alzheimer's research are explained. A glossary, index, and sources of further information are included at the end of the book.

Alzheimer's Disease, which is part of Crestwood House's Healthwatch series, tells the facts of the disease; but even more, it tells the "story" of the disease. Details of Edward Dudley's struggle with Alzheimer's disease show young readers that this disease cripples more than the patient; it devastates the patient's family as well. Dudley's grandson laments the loss of his grandfather's personality and the pastimes, such as fishing, that they can no longer share together. The grandson describes his grandfather: "He is a shell of the person he once was." Young readers of *Alzheimer's Disease* will gain a new-found knowledge of the disease and empathy for Alzheimer's patients and their families.

LEARNING ACTIVITIES

1. Write to one or more of the organizations listed on page 45 in the back of *Alzheimer's Disease*. Ask for additional information on the disease. Even though this book was recently published, there continue to be new developments in Alzheimer's research. In addition to the information you send for, have a reference librarian help you search for the most current information on the diagnosis, treatment, and prevention of Alzheimer's disease. Write a report about any new information you learn.

2. Get to know the personal side of Alzheimer's disease. Learn about what is involved to become a volunteer who can help an Alzheimer's patient. If appropriate for you, volunteer at a care program for Alzheimer's patients or volunteer to help family members of an Alzheimer's patient. If volunteering directly with patients, be sure to follow the specific instructions from care-givers. And if you have an idea you'd like to try (such as playing a simple game or performing with an instrument), make certain to get permission from care-givers before actually trying it. Keep a journal of your experiences.

3. Author Susan Dudley Gold wrote effectively about Alzheimer's disease because she did thorough research and saw first-hand the effects of the disease through her father's illness. Write a booklet about a different disease or illness. Select one that you are familiar with through your own experiences or those of family members. Does someone in your family suffer from asthma, diabetes, or migraine headaches? Research the disease, but also include personal experiences and knowledge in your booklet.

ABOUT THE AUTHOR

Susan Dudley Gold was born in Portland and raised in Scarborough. Not only has Gold lived in Maine for her entire life (except while attending college), but so have seven generations of her family. *Alzheimer's Disease* tells the story of one of those family members, her father. He was born in Oakland; and after suffering for many years from Alzheimer's disease, he died at the Maine Veteran's Home in Scarborough.

Gold graduated from college with a degree in English. She has worked as a reporter for the *Journal Tribune* in Biddeford, as a writer for a number of state and regional publications, and as an editor for a business magazine, a neighborhood newspaper, and a real estate newspaper. With her husband she owns a desktop publishing company in Saco. Gold has written more than twenty children's books. Her titles include *Multiple Sclerosis, Arthritis, Roe v. Wade: Abortion*, and *Miranda v. Arizona: Suspects' Rights*.

Gold lives in Saco with her husband (also a writer—see page 255) and her son. She leads a local pain support group for people who suffer from chronic pain; Gold has rheumatoid arthritis. Her hobbies include quilting, reading, canoeing, and camping.

MAINE: AMERICA THE BEAUTIFUL

AUTHOR: Ty Harrington / PHOTOGRAPHER: photographs from a variety of sources
AGE LEVEL / LENGTH: 10 years–adult / 144 pages
PUBLISHER / COPYRIGHT DATE: Childrens Press / 1992 (rev. ed.)
FORMAT / ISBN: Library binding / 0516004654; Vinyl bound Braille edition / 1569561575

Maine: America the Beautiful is a comprehensive reference book, a mini-encyclopedia of the state. If one wanted to know who was governor in 1902 (William Cobb), or about an historical landmark in Waldoboro (Old German Church), or the average yearly snowfall (70 inches on the coast and 100 inches inland), all that information plus lots more is included in this book.

The book's chapters include "The Land," "The People," "The Beginning," "Independence and Statehood," "The First Fifty Years," "Government and the Economy," and "Culture and Recreation." In addition, the book is filled with photographs and maps. At the back of the book, readers will find a comprehensive list of "Facts at a Glance" (including the words of the state song, census information, information about the state's museums, and more) and a thorough index.

LEARNING ACTIVITIES

1. In the manner of a science fair, organize a Maine fair. Encourage your fellow classmates to select a section of *Maine: America the Beautiful* that interests them. They can develop a project, display, or performance to demonstrate what they have learned. Open your Maine fair to the public, serve Maine refreshments (e.g., blueberry muffins, apple cider), and even award prizes if you'd like.

2. Use *Maine: America the Beautiful* to create a test of Maine. From the book, select 10-20 facts and create questions about them. Sample questions might be: What percentage of Mainers live within 20 miles of the coast? What is the population of Maine? What are the names of two major Indian tribes in Maine? Pose these questions to 15-30 people you know. Before you conduct the survey, predict how many people will be able to answer the questions correctly. Check your predictions and watch for patterns. Did one age group know more than others? Did students know more than adults?

3. *Maine: America the Beautiful* is a great reference work, but since it was published in 1992, some facts have changed. Look through the book for outdated information and write an addendum to the book with updated information.

ABOUT THE AUTHOR

Since Ty Harrington was nine years old, he has been coming to Maine to white-water canoe and mountain climb. He became a writer after he had applied to *National Geographic* for the job as a cook on a research vessel. The magazine gave him a test assignment, and he was hired as a writer instead. Harrington wrote *Maine: America the Beautiful* when Childrens Press asked him to write about a state he loved. He chose Maine.

HONEYBEES AT HOME

AUTHOR / ILLUSTRATOR: Lynne Harwood
AGE LEVEL / LENGTH: 6 years–adult / 40 pages
PUBLISHER / COPYRIGHT DATE: Tilbury House, Publishers; unbound copies available from Lynne Harwood / 1994
FORMAT / ISBN: Hardcover / 0884481190

Honeybees at Home is an unusual nonfiction book about Maine's state insect. From beginning to end, it packs in much interesting information about honeybees; but it does so in a conversational, down-to-earth way. Author/illustrator Lynne Harwood of Anson, Maine, retells her own experiences with bees; and as she does so, readers will feel as if they are simply having a chat with Harwood on her Anson farm.

Honeybees at Home includes details about how to start and move hives, about how protective clothing and smokers can protect humans from bee stings, about how hives need to be protected from mice and skunks, about how to tell resident bees from robber bees, about how bees stay warm in the winter, and much, much more. Young readers will learn the special vocabulary of beekeeping—brood, drone cells, fume board, honey supers, winter cluster, etc.

Harwood's colorful illustrations—oil paintings on different shapes of wood—further add to the hominess of the book. Adults as well as children will enjoy *Honeybees at Home* as much for its "feel" for beekeeping as for its facts about beekeeping.

LEARNING ACTIVITIES

1. Make a "bee" dictionary. Read through *Honeybees at Home* and write down all the vocabulary words about bees and beekeeping (e.g., honeycomb, bee venom, skep, brood, drone) and a definition for each word. Try to make your definitions clear and understandable. Double check your definitions by comparing them with definitions in a dictionary.

2. Even though *Honeybees at Home* is a nonfiction book, it reads like a fictional story due to the personal details and conversational style. Select a topic on which you know some information (e.g., caring for a pet, collecting baseball cards, cooking a favorite meal, jump-roping, playing soccer) and write a booklet about that topic. Try to include both facts and personal insights in your booklet. Share your booklet with a friend.

3. The illustrations for *Honeybees at Home* were actually painted onto different-shaped pieces of wood. Look back through the book and notice the different shapes for the illustrations. What do you think the illustrator was trying to show with the shape of each illustration? Try your hand at creating an unusually-shaped illustration. What were you trying to show with your shaped picture?

ABOUT THE AUTHOR/ILLUSTRATOR

In 1972, Lynne Harwood moved to Maine from New York City, with six other people who bought land together to form a commune. The group scattered, and Harwood is the only one who has stayed in Maine. She has worked as an artist, gardener, and beekeeper since coming to Maine. She learned about beekeeping from her neighbors.

Harwood originally illustrated *Honeybees at Home* with colored pencils, but her publisher asked her to try oil paints. Harwood was pleased with the brighter colors of the oil paints. She painted the illustrations on birch plywood and used the natural grain of the wood for the background of the text—after all, she says, "Honeybees are at home in wood." *Honeybees at Home* was her first book. She has since illustrated *Opening Our Wild Hearts to the Healing Herbs*, a medicinal herb book, authored by Gail Edwards.

Harwood lives in Anson with her two teenaged children. Her garden is ever expanding, and she continues to keep bees. She visits classrooms and gives talks on beekeeping and brings along an observation hive for children to see.

LOBSTER'S SECRET

AUTHOR: Kathleen M. Hollenbeck / ILLUSTRATOR: Jon Weiman
AGE LEVEL / LENGTH: 5-8 years / 32 pages
PUBLISHER / COPYRIGHT DATE: Soundprints / 1996
FORMAT / ISBN: Hardcover / 1568992785; Hardcover "Mini-book" / 1568992793; Hardcover with toy lobster / 1568992807; other editions with toys and audio tapes are also available

Lobster's Secret tells the story of an American lobster along the Maine coast. Lobsters are nocturnal animals which leave their dens at night. The lobster is shown using its antennae to help it sense danger and to find food. It escapes from two enemies: a codfish and a sculpin. It locates a red rock crab and a starfish for food. The lobster is also shown molting (shedding its shell). Afterwards, the lobster must stay in its den since its newly-forming shell is too soft to protect it from enemies. In a few weeks, the lobster's shell will be strong and hard once again.

As part of the Smithsonian Oceanic Collection, *Lobster's Secret* provides young readers with much factual information about lobsters packed into an entertaining story. The final page of the book includes additional lobster facts, a glossary, and a guide to other ocean plants and creatures found in the book.

LEARNING ACTIVITIES

1. This book is called *Lobster's Secret*. Why? What do lobsters have for a secret? How do they protect their secret? Can you think of any other animals that have secrets? What are they?

2. Pretend to be a teacher and create a lobster quiz based upon the information you learned from *Lobster's Secret*. Challenge a friend to read the book and then take your quiz.

3. If possible, plan a trip to the ocean for a seashore scavenger hunt. Before your trip, make a list of ocean plants and animals to look for. Use *Lobster's Secret* and nonfiction ocean books as guides to help you create a list of ocean animals and plants that you might expect to find (e.g., starfish, different sponges, sand dollars). On your trip, find as many items on your list as possible. Check off each item as you find it. Remember that you are trying to *see* each item, not keep it. Leave the ocean plants and animals where you find them so that they may keep living in their natural habitat and so that other people may enjoy the same seashore sights.

ABOUT THE AUTHOR

Author Kathleen M. Hollenbeck has two important Maine connections. Her first children's book, *Lobster's Secret*, is based on the Maine lobster; and, in 1987, she was married in Kennebunkport, Maine, because that's where her parents lived at the time.

Hollenbeck has been writing for publication since 1984. She has written numerous textbooks, drug education curriculums, literature programs, teacher resource books, and other educational products. She has also worked for *Weekly Reader*. Hollenbeck currently lives in Coventry, Rhode Island, with her husband and three young children.

ABOUT THE ILLUSTRATOR

Jon Weiman is from Philadelphia. He has a BFA degree in Graphic Design from Tyler School of Art. He is on the board of directors of the Society of Illustrators. He also works as an associate professor at Pratt Institute and an adjunct instructor at the Fashion Institute of Technology.

Weiman has illustrated more than 300 book covers. In addition to *Lobster's Secret,* he has illustrated another children's book, *Beluga Passage.* His illustrations for *Lobster's Secret* were done on strathmore illustration board with acrylics, gouache, and colored pencil. Weiman currently lives in Brooklyn, New York. His hobbies include martial arts and photography.

ROUND BUILDINGS, SQUARE BUILDINGS, & BUILDINGS THAT WIGGLE LIKE A FISH

AUTHOR / PHOTOGRAPHER: Philip M. Isaacson
AGE LEVEL / LENGTH: 10 years–adult / 122 pages
PUBLISHER / COPYRIGHT DATE: Alfred A. Knopf (div. of Random House) / 1988
FORMAT / ISBN: Hardcover / 0394893824; Paperback / 0-0679806490; Library Binding / 0394993829 (recently out of print)

Round Buildings, Square Buildings, & Buildings That Wiggle Like a Fish explains architecture to kids. Author/photographer Isaacson brings buildings to life, giving them a personality and spirit the reader may not have noticed before. Although *Round Buildings* features architecture from all over the world, it deserves a place as a Maine book. Fourteen sites in the book are in Maine, including the Grange Hall in East Hebron, buildings from the Shaker Village in New Gloucester, and the Continental Mill in Lewiston. These Maine buildings stand in good company with the Taj Mahal and the Parthenon.

Round Buildings is divided into a dozen chapters with titles such as "Light and Color," "Doorways," and "Shapes." The book has a large, easy-to-read text and plenty of white space on pages which helps young readers two ways: (1) it keeps them from feeling overwhelmed; and (2) it allows them to savor the beautiful photographs of buildings. At the end of the book there is also a listing of each building photographed, with additional historical and descriptive information.

LEARNING ACTIVITIES

1. Before reading the book, cover the text, look at all the photographs, and guess which buildings are from Maine. Why did you make the guesses you did? Check the text and the listings in the back of the book to see if you were correct.

2. Study the photographs of Maine buildings in this book. How are they similar? Do you notice any patterns in their architecture? Focus on a single aspect of Maine architecture: a particular period of time, a specific type of structure (e.g., churches, camps, town halls, libraries), the life of a Maine architect, etc. Research your selected topic and write a summary of what you learn.

3. After looking at the photographs in *Round Buildings*, then take your own photographs or make drawings of buildings in your town. Study the buildings. How can your photos/drawings show the concepts Philip Isaacson discussed in his book: light and color, doorways, ornaments, shapes, etc.? Arrange your pictures into a booklet and share it with others.

ABOUT THE AUTHOR/PHOTOGRAPHER

Philip Isaacson was born in Lewiston, Maine, and has lived there all his life. The chairperson of the Bates College English Department once told Isaacson that he had a knack for writing, but Isaacson was doubtful. In 1966, the features editor of the *Maine Sunday Telegram*, who knew that Isaacson was interested in art, asked him to write a piece for the newspaper. Isaacson remembered what his professor had said earlier, so he decided to try his hand at writing about art. He has been writing a weekly art column for the *Maine Sunday Telegram* for the past 30 years.

Round Buildings, Square Buildings, & Buildings That Wiggle Like a Fish grew from Isaacson's attempts to interest his own children in architecture when they were young. Isaacson proudly recalls the warm response the book has received from notable architects and writers, including John McPhee. Isaacson is also the author/photographer of two other books: *The American Eagle* and *A Short Walk Around the Pyramids and Through the World of Art*. Isaacson practices law and lives in Lewiston. He has three children and four grandchildren.

WHO BELONGS HERE? AN AMERICAN STORY

AUTHOR: Margy Burns Knight / ILLUSTRATOR: Anne Sibley O'Brien
AGE LEVEL / LENGTH: 8-14 years / 36 pages
PUBLISHER / COPYRIGHT DATE: Tilbury House, Publishers / 1993
FORMAT / ISBN: Hardcover / 0884481107; Paperback / 0884481697;
Paperback activity guide to accompany the book / 0884481115

Who Belongs Here? An American Story tells the story of a Cambodian refugee boy named Nary who emigrates to the U. S. Author Margy Burns Knight based the story on her experiences as an English as a Second Language teacher in Augusta schools. Nary had to leave Cambodia during a civil war in which many families starved and millions of people were killed, including Nary's parents. In the U. S., Nary lives with his grandmother and uncle. He loves his new-found freedom and the "abundance" of America, but he doesn't understand why some of his schoolmates call him "chink" and "gook" and tell him to go back where he belongs. Nary helps to plan a lesson on refugees for his social studies class so that they may better understand him. Nary continues working to fit in as an American by developing friendships and learning to play the drums, while striving to maintain his Cambodian heritage by drawing pictures of Cambodia and learning to write the Khmer language.

In addition to Nary's story as a Cambodian refugee, *Who Belongs Here?* also presents a parallel narrative about immigrants in general—how many have come to the United States, where they have come from, how they entered the U. S., the different words and foods that they brought with them, and more. Additional information on immigrants is included in the back of the book. For interested teachers, an activity guide for the book is also available.

Who Belongs Here? is a wonderful celebration of diversity. It tells simple truths with an eloquent story and interesting facts. Anne Sibley O'Brien's full-color pastel illustrations are rich, multi-layered, and thought-provoking.

LEARNING ACTIVITIES

1. Learn about immigrants in your area. Does your school have ESL (English as a Second Language) teachers? Which languages do their students speak? Which countries do the students come from? Visit an ESL class and write a summary of the visit—what you learned, how you felt, what surprised you.

2. In *Who Belongs Here?* author Margy Burns Knight presents some foreign words that are now used as English words, and some foods that were brought to the U. S. from other countries. Make a list of as many words or foods from other countries as you can find. Write each word, its meaning, what country it comes from, and facts about its origin. Can you come up with a list of 25, 50, 100, or more words?

3. The back flap of *Who Belongs Here?* tells about the heritage of the author and illustrator. What countries did your ancestors come from? How many years ago? Write a description of your own heritage.

ABOUT THE AUTHOR

Margy Burns Knight was born and raised in Pennsylvania. She has been a student in England, a teacher in Switzerland, and a Peace Corps volunteer in Benin, Africa. She moved to Maine in 1972 to attend Bowdoin College. She has worked as an ESL (English as a Second Language) teacher to Cambodian, Vietnamese, Chinese, Afghan, Polish, and Ugandan students.

In 1990, Knight heard Doug Rawlings read his poem called "The Wall," which inspired the idea for her first nonfiction book, *Talking Walls*. Since then, she has written other multicultural books, including *Welcoming Babies* and *Talking Walls, The Story Continues*. Knight frequently visits schools to share her multicultural message.

Knight lives in Winthrop, Maine, with her husband and two children. She volunteers in schools and enjoys her hobbies of biking, walking, reading, and baking banana bread.

ABOUT THE ILLUSTRATOR

Anne Sibley O'Brien lived as a young child in Illinois and New Hampshire and grew up in South Korea. She has traveled to Japan, Hong Kong, India, Nepal, Europe, Guatemala, and the Caribbean.

O'Brien was a studio art major at Mt. Holyoke College and studied Korean arts at Ewha Womans University in Seoul during her junior year. She illustrated her first children's books, a set of board books, in 1985. Since then she has illustrated numerous books including the *Jamaica* series, written by Juanita Havill, and four books written by Margy Burns Knight, including *Talking Walls* and *Welcoming Babies*. She is the author and illustrator of *The Princess and the Beggar*, a book based on a Korean folktale. O'Brien says that the models for the children in *Who Belongs Here?* are from Maine, mostly students from the Reiche School in Portland. She illustrated the book using water soluble pastels.

O'Brien lives on Peaks Island, Maine, with her husband and two children. Her hobbies include reading, singing, and acting in plays. She frequently serves as a consultant on diversity education in the greater Portland community.

PROJECT PUFFIN:
HOW WE BROUGHT PUFFINS BACK TO EGG ROCK

AUTHOR: Stephen W. Kress, as told to Pete Salmansohn / PHOTOGRAPHER:Stephen Kress
AGE LEVEL / LENGTH: 6-12 years / 40 pages
PUBLISHER / COPYRIGHT DATE: Tilbury House / 1997
FORMAT / ISBN: Hardcover / 0884481700; Teacher's Guide / 0884481727

Project Puffin: How We Brought Puffins Back to Egg Rock gives young readers a first-hand, close-up view of how puffins were successfully reinstated to Eastern Egg Rock, off the coast of Maine, in the 1970s and 1980s, after an absence of 100 years. This translocation project from Great Island, Newfoundland, Canada, to Eastern Egg Rock took eight years before it was considered successful and the puffins actually began laying eggs on the island. *Project Puffin* is told from the first-person perspective of Stephen Kress, a research biologist and seabird expert for the National Audubon Society. Writer Pete Salmansohn recounts Kress's story in a way that makes young readers feel part of the experience.

The text is packed with interesting puffin facts and terms. Puffins have barbs on the roofs of their mouths which allow them to hold a dozen or more small fish in their beaks at a time. Female puffins lay one egg a year, and that egg must be incubated by the parents for forty-two days. Brooding is when a hatched puffin chick must sit under a parent's wing to stay warm. Billing is the word for the affectionate beak tap between two puffins. Color photographs, charts, and maps add further details to the story.

Project Puffin, a National Audubon Society book, includes a glossary, details on puffin-watching boat trips off the coast of Maine, and information on how to adopt a puffin. A teacher's guide, called *Giving Back to the Earth: A Teacher's Guide to Project Puffin and Other Seabird Studies*, is available; targeted toward third to sixth graders, it includes over forty classroom activities: art projects, wildlife observation, and science demonstrations.

LEARNING ACTIVITIES

1. A glossary is a list of new vocabulary words found in a book. *Project Puffin* has a glossary in the back, but *don't* peek at it. While reading *Project Puffin*, write your own glossary for the book. Write down new words, their meanings, and arrange the words in alphabetical order. You may need to read the book more than once to find as many vocabulary words as possible. After completing your glossary, turn to the glossary on page 38 of *Project Puffin* and compare the two glossaries. Did your glossary include the same words as the book's glossary? Why or why not? What words did the book's glossary have that your glossary didn't have, and vice versa? How did your definitions compare with those in the book? Were your definitions or the book's definitions easier to understand? Why?

2. On pages 34 and 35 of *Project Puffin*, other seabirds are pictured and briefly described. Research one of those birds (Common Tern, Roseate Tern, Arctic Tern) or another seabird and write a report about your selected bird. Where does it live? How big is it? What does it eat? What are its enemies? Is it endangered? How is it being protected?

3. Make a large puffin time-line on newsprint or chart paper. Include important dates mentioned in *Project Puffin* on your time line (e.g., 1600s—pioneers kill seabirds for food; 1901—only one pair of puffins left south of the Canadian border; 1973—The Puffin Project on Eastern Egg Rock begins). Use your timeline as a guide to help you tell someone the story of the Puffin Project.

ABOUT THE AUTHORS

Stephen Kress is the National Audubon Society's seabird expert. He has directed the Puffin Project since 1973. He has appeared as a nature expert on television shows such as *Good Morning America* and on *National Geographic* films. He is the author of newspaper and magazine articles as well as several books, including *National Audubon Society's Bird Garden*.

Pete Salmansohn has worked with Stephen Kress since 1980. He is a certified teacher and has led hundreds of public boat cruises to see puffins on Eastern Egg Rock off the

Maine coast. He also published numerous articles about puffins in periodicals such as *The Boston Globe*, *Wildlife Conservation*, and *Birder's World*.

AN OUTWARD BOUND SCHOOL: LET'S TAKE A TRIP

AUTHOR: Alison Murray Kuller / PHOTOGRAPHER: Tom Stewart
AGE LEVEL / LENGTH: 8-12 years / 32 pages
PUBLISHER / COPYRIGHT DATE: Troll Associates / 1990
FORMAT / ISBN: Library Binding / 0816717311

An Outward Bound School: Let's Take a Trip takes readers to isolated Hurricane Island, off the coast of Maine near Rockland. A group of teens participate in an eighteen-day Outward Bound Wilderness course. Participants learn sailing, rock-climbing, first aid, trip-planning, and team-building as they try to survive in the rugged wilderness. Their final adventures are solo retreats in the wilderness and a six-mile run around the island.

Color photographs show the students' outdoor experiences and a variety of items from their immediate environment, such as starfish, mussels, urchins, and rosehips. New vocabulary words are clearly explained in the text—words like bouldering, mantle up, and relaying. This book provides an enjoyable inside look at an Outward Bound School.

LEARNING ACTIVITIES

1. Students at the Outward Bound School have to learn many new skills. Select one new skill that you'd be interested in learning—something you never tried before, but always wished you had. Use any necessary resources (books, people, etc.) in order to learn about your target skill. Keep a journal, complete with photographs or drawings, of your learning experience.

2. Write to the Hurricane Island Outward Bound School in Rockland, Maine. Ask for brochures about the school. What time of year do they operate? How do they select students for inclusion in their program? What skills do they teach? Combine this information into an advertisement for the school.

3. Research the history of Outward Bound. It has a number of schools in different regions of the United States. Learn when Outward Bound started, what its philosophy is, how it is financed, how it has grown.

ABOUT THE AUTHOR & PHOTOGRAPHER

Author information on Alison Murray Kuller and photographer information on Tom Stewart were unavailable.

THE ABENAKI

AUTHOR / PHOTOGRAPHER: Elaine Landau / photographs from a variety of sources
AGE LEVEL / LENGTH: 8-12 years / 64 pages
PUBLISHER / COPYRIGHT DATE: Franklin Watts / 1996
FORMAT / ISBN: Hardcover / 0531202275; Paperback / 0531157822

The opening chapter of *The Abenaki* tells about Azeban, a mischievous raccoon trickster who appears in Abenaki tales. Stories such as those about Azeban were used by the Abenaki to entertain their children as well as to teach them lessons. For example, one story of Azeban tells how he thought he could be louder and mightier than a waterfall, but while shouting he fell off a cliff into the waterfall. From this story, Abenaki children learn that they should not be too sure of themselves and that they must respect nature at all times.

In addition to Abenaki stories and legends, this nonfiction book tells about the food, clothing, religion, customs, and history of the Abenaki people. Information is included about the Eastern Abenaki from Maine and the Western Abenaki from New Hampshire, Vermont, and parts of Ontario and Quebec. Young readers will learn many interesting Abenaki facts and words, such as: totems (the animal symbols which represented Abenaki families), shaman (an Abenaki spiritual leader), and sagamore (the chief of an Abenaki village). The end of the book includes a brief glossary and reading list.

LEARNING ACTIVITIES

1. At the beginning of *The Abenaki*, you learn about the tales of Azeban, the raccoon trickster. Write your own short story about Azeban (or if you prefer, create a new trickster character). Your story should be entertaining, but also teach a lesson. You may want to draw illustrations for your story.

2. Read another informational book about a different Native American tribe, such as the Sioux, Hopi, Iroquois, Apache, or Navajos. Then make a chart comparing that tribe with the Abenaki. Compare their food, clothing, houses, customs, religion, transportation, tools, and other cultural information.

3. Make a Jeopardy-type game using information from *The Abenaki*. You might have categories such as Abenaki history, food, Abenaki words, family life, and Abenaki geography. Make certain that you create answers for which others can create appropriate questions. For example, if you had the answer "The name for a piece of tanned animal skin tied around the hips," then the question would be "What is a breechclout?" Or if you had the answer "The name for the potato-like wild plant that was a staple of the Eastern Abenaki's diet," then the question would be "What is the ground nut?" You may wish to work with a small group of peers to create this game. Then challenge other peers to play it.

ABOUT THE AUTHOR

Elaine Landau is the author of more than ninety nonfiction children's books, including others about Native Americans, such as: *The Ottawa, The Pomo, The Sioux, The Cherokees*, and *The Chilula*. Currently, she lives in New Jersey, and works as a full-time writer. Previously, she worked as a newspaper reporter, editor, and librarian. She has a bachelor's degree in English and journalism from New York University, and a master's degree in library and information science from Pratt Institute.

MONARCHS

AUTHOR: Kathryn Lasky / PHOTOGRAPHER: Christopher Knight
AGE LEVEL / LENGTH: 6-12 years / 64 pages
PUBLISHER / COPYRIGHT DATE: Harcourt Brace & Co. / 1993
FORMAT / ISBN: Hardcover / 0152552960; Paperback / 0152552979

Monarchs describes the development of a monarch butterfly from egg to larva to caterpillar to chrysalis, and finally to a butterfly. It also describes the journey of monarchs from North Haven Island, in Penobscot Bay, Maine, to their wintering grounds in Mexico.

The monarch's Maine connection features eighty-two-year old Clara Waterman, who every year gathers milkweeds covered with caterpillars and watches their transformation into butterflies. She never tires of this magic of nature, and frequently invites children to share the wonder of hatching butterflies.

Monarchs is an exceptional nonfiction book. Christopher Knight's photographs are beautiful, capturing all the details of a monarch's life from a tiny white egg "no bigger than the head of a pin" to the butterfly-filled trees of the towns of El Rosario and Valle de Bravo in Mexico. Likewise Katherine Lasky's text is intriguing. She has a fine narrative style that makes the book flow like a story. For example, when describing the early growth of the caterpillar, she says "After two weeks of eating, the caterpillar is now two inches long and is more than 2,700 times its original weight. If a six-pound human baby grew as fast as a caterpillar, it would weigh eight tons in twelve days." *Monarchs* is a book to be enjoyed and savored time and again, just as Clara Waterman of North Haven enjoys and savors butterflies hatching time and again.

LEARNING ACTIVITIES

1. Ask someone who has hatched butterflies to help you share that experience. Gather caterpillars and some of the plants they live on. Place them in jars and watch their transformation from caterpillar to chrysalis to butterfly. Be sure to free the butterfly when it is ready to fly. Record your observations with photographs, drawings, and/or a journal.

2. Create a monarch butterfly game. Make a gameboard in the shape of a butterfly and create question cards based on the information found in the book *Monarchs*. Develop a set of rules for your game and invite a friend to play with you.

3. On pages 48-53 of *Monarchs*, notice the colorful butterfly costumes of the children of Pacific Grove, California ("Butterfly Town, USA"). Design and make your own butterfly costume. Then visit a nursery school in your costume and tell youngsters an informational "story" about butterflies.

ABOUT THE AUTHOR

Kathryn Lasky was born in Indianapolis, Indiana, in 1944. She showed an interest in writing at an early age. In fact, Lasky says, "I think perhaps I always felt that this was my profession, announced or unannounced, proclaimed or unproclaimed, paid or unpaid. I have always been a writer."

Lasky is the author of more than thirty children's books. Her work includes picture books, historical young adult novels, and nonfiction. Lasky's recent picture book, *Marven of the Great North Woods*, tells the story of a boy befriending a lumberjack; the book was illustrated by Maine artist Kevin Hawkes (see page 303). Her most recent novels are *Beyond the Burning Time*, *True North: A Novel of the Underground Railroad*, and *A Journey to the New World: The Diary of Rember Patience Whipple*. Many of her nonfiction books have been a collaborative effort with her photographer husband, Christopher Knight, including *Monarchs*, *Days of the Dead*, and *Sugaring Time*, a Newbery Honor Book about maple sugaring.

Kathryn Lasky lives in Cambridge, Massachusetts, with her husband and two children. They also have a summer home on Deer Isle, Maine, where they return each year. Her book, *Monarchs*, grew from the experiences she and her husband had with monarch butterflies on Deer Isle and North Haven. Lasky also wrote *Fourth of July Bear* (see page 92), a picture book set on Deer Isle, with her daughter as the main character. Lasky says that her family looks forward to sailing, hiking, and biking each summer on Deer Isle.

ABOUT THE PHOTOGRAPHER

Christopher Knight's family originally came from Maine with "a liberal sprinkling of fishermen and sea captains." Knight and his wife, author Kathryn Lasky, were married on Deer Isle and continue to return to their summer home there each year.

Knight is the photographer of numerous nonfiction books, many written by his wife. His books include *The Weaver's Gift*, *Puppeteer*, *Sugaring Time*, and *Think Like an Eagle: At Work with a Wildlife Photographer*. Knight lives in Cambridge, Massachusetts, with his wife and two children.

A DUCK IN A TREE

AUTHOR / PHOTOGRAPHER: Jennifer A. Loomis
AGE LEVEL / LENGTH: 5 years–adult / 32 pages
PUBLISHER / COPYRIGHT DATE: Stemmer House / 1996
FORMAT / ISBN: Hardcover / 088045136X

A Duck in a Tree is a handsome photographic story. It tells about the wood duck, a duck which migrates to Maine each spring from Florida. The wood duck is unusual in that it lays its eggs inside the hollow of a tree.

This book's simple text and striking color photos follow a pair of wood ducks from their arrival at a Maine woodland pond in late April. Soon after arriving, the ducks select a nesting site. The hen inspects old tree hollows and abandoned woodpecker holes while the drake supervises. After the nesting cavity is readied, the hen proceeds to lay one creamy-white egg each day for a few weeks, creating a clutch of eggs. After the eggs are laid, the hen stays to incubate the eggs in the tree while the drake finds a protected area to molt. For a month while molting, the drake is unable to fly and can only whistle warnings to the hen if a predator is near. Just one day after the ducklings hatch, they leap from the nest high in the tree to the pond below. Swimming, feeding, and preening lessons follow until the ducklings can survive on their own. As autumn arrives and an unexpected snow falls, the wood ducks begin their thousand-mile migration to Florida.

In the back of *A Duck in a Tree*, readers will find a glossary, bibliography, as well as instructions on how to make and place a wood duck nesting box. Wood ducks are elusive. Readers will feel fortunate that award-winning photographer Jennifer A. Loomis sought out these secretive birds.

LEARNING ACTIVITIES

1. After reading *A Duck in a Tree* with a friend, take turns questioning each other about wood ducks. For example, one of you might ask, "What month does the wood duck arrive in Maine?" (April) or "How many hours a day does the wood duck hen incubate her eggs?" (20 hours or more) or "Why can't the raccoon in the book find the wood duck's eggs?" (because the nest is so well hidden). Your questions might refer to the glossary— "What does molt mean?" "What's the name for a male duck?" Ask questions back and forth. If one of you doesn't know the answer to a question, then check the book.

2. If possible, have an adult help you to make a wood duck nesting box. Follow the instructions carefully on pages 29 and 30 in *A Duck in a Tree*. But first, you will need to scout out an appropriate place for the nesting box. After creating the nesting box, check on it from a distance several times throughout spring, summer, and fall. Keep a journal or draw pictures of any wood duck sightings.

3. Using *A Duck in a Tree* as a model, select another Maine bird or animal and write a simple story about it. Don't worry about having photographs, but you may add drawings if you wish. You will need to research your bird or animal first. Select the most important information and write an interesting story using that information. Share your story with a friend.

ABOUT THE AUTHOR/PHOTOGRAPHER

Jennifer A. Loomis is a licensed wildlife rehabilitator for the state of Maine. She nurtures orphaned and injured wild animals until they are ready to be returned to the wild. She also has a federal permit which allows her to care for injured raptors (high-flying birds, such as hawks and eagles) and songbirds until they can be released back into the wild. Loomis is a wildlife photographer whose work has been published in magazines, college texts, and calendars. She is listed in *Who's Who in Photography*.

A Duck in a Tree is Loomis's first children's book. The photographs for it were taken over a period of several years with "a Nikon F4 camera, a 300 mm lens, a sturdy tripod, slide film, and many hours of patience." Loomis is a self-taught writer. She is currently working on two other children's books, one about an orphan raccoon and the other about a lost kestrel (a small hawk).

Loomis lives in Eliot, Maine, with her husband. She has three grown children. She frequently travels on "photographic and hiking" trips. Her hobbies include quilting, cross-stitch, folk art painting, gardening, and landscaping.

THE WABANAKIS OF MAINE AND THE MARITIMES

AUTHOR: Maine Indian Program / ILLUSTRATOR: drawings, maps, & photographs from a variety of sources
AGE LEVEL / LENGTH: 10-14 years / 512 pages
PUBLISHER / COPYRIGHT DATE: American Friends Service Committee / 1989
FORMAT / ISBN: Paperback / 0910082170

The Wabanakis of Maine and the Maritimes is a comprehensive resource book about the Penobscot, Passamaquoddy, Maliseet, Micmac, and Abenaki Indians. It is divided into four major sections: historical overview, lesson plans, readings, and fact sheets. The historical overview section gives background information about the history and culture of the Wabanaki. Lesson plans make up the largest section of the book, with specific activities to teach children about creating a Wabanaki timeline, interpreting English and Wabanaki treaties, understanding Columbus Day from a Native American perspective, and much, much more. The readings section includes written legends based upon

Wabanaki oral history, Wabanaki stories from 1400 to the 1920s, interviews with Wabanaki people today, and children's essays. The fact sheets section of the book includes brief entries on different aspects of Wabenaki history, culture, and way of life. For example, one fact sheet shows the Penobscot calendar where June is called "grubbing hoe moon" and January is called "moon that provided little food grudgingly." Another fact sheet shows a long list of plants and how they are used medicinally. And still another fact sheet shows how to make a cornhusk doll.

The Wabanakis of Maine and the Maritimes was written and compiled by the Curriculum Committee of the Wabanaki communities. It was a labor of love that took more than three years to complete. The result is a resource book which puts hundreds of years of Wabanaki facts and tradition at the fingertips of Maine children. The book also includes a phonograph record with Wabanaki words and songs, a list of resources (including museums to visit), a bibliography, and index.

LEARNING ACTIVITIES

1. Select one activity from the lesson plan section of *The Wabanakis of Maine and the Maritimes* and teach that activity to your classmates. Just as a teacher must do, read the lesson plan several times to prepare for the lesson. You may want to role-play how you will lead or teach the activity before actually doing it. When you are prepared, teach the activity to your class. Afterwards, ask them for feedback on the activity. Did they enjoy it? What did they learn? How could the activity have been improved?

2. Select parts of the readings section from *The Wabanakis of Maine and the Maritimes* to perform for an audience. Invite friends or classmates to join you. For example, you might turn one of the legends into a play to act out, or you might create a puppet show that follows one of the Wabanaki stories, or you might read selections from the Wabanaki interviews and children's essays as a readers-theater performance. After practicing your performance, present it to a real audience.

3. Select one of the craft, construction, or cooking projects from *The Wabanakis of Maine and the Maritimes*. You might make a wigwam, cornhusk doll, or hulled corn soup. Follow the directions carefully. Afterwards, write a journal entry about what you learned from the project. Was the project easy or difficult for you? Why? What did you learn from the project? How would you change the project if you were to try it again?

4. *The Wabanakis of Maine and the Maritimes* includes hundreds of facts about the Wabanaki. As you read parts of the book, compose questions about the information you have learned (e.g., What was the hardest time of year for the Wabanakis to survive?—February and March because food supplies might be gone and snow might be limited for tracking game; what was a medicinal use for yellow birch bark?—to treat rheumatism or diarrhea; what does Cobbosseecontee mean in Penobscot?—sturgeon gathering place).

ABOUT THE AUTHORS

The Wabanakis of Maine and the Maritimes was written and compiled over the course of three years by the Curriculum Committee representing a number of Wabanaki communities. The committee was sponsored by the Maine Indian Program, which is part of the New England Regional Office of the American Friends Service Committee. The book truly was a collaborative effort. The four-page acknowledgement section lists the members of the Curriculum Committee (Penobscot Carol Dana; Maliseet Peter Paul; Creek Roberto Mendoza; Micmacs Richard Silliboy, Cathy Murphy Francis, Marline Sanipass Morey, and Mary Shaw; Penobscot Vivian Massey; Passamaquoddies Mary Bassett, Wayne Newell, and Laura Dana; non-Indian Robert Leavitt), scores of other consultants, and teachers who field-tested the materials in their classrooms.

APPLES, HOW THEY GROW

AUTHOR / PHOTO-ILLUSTRATOR: Bruce McMillan
AGE LEVEL / LENGTH: 4-12 years / 48 pages
PUBLISHER / COPYRIGHT DATE: Houghton Mifflin Co. / 1979
FORMAT / ISBN: Hardcover / 0395278066

Apples, How They Grow describes in detail how apple trees and apples grow throughout the four seasons. The book begins in the wintertime, showing a barren-looking tree along with a close-up photo of bud scales which protect the flowering part of the tree. As spring comes, the flower buds swell and burst open. The transformation continues as the apple blossoms grow and are cross-pollinated by bees. With summer, fuzzy swollen bumps are transformed into smooth, shiny apples. In the fall, the apples finish growing to full-size and then are plucked and savored by two hungry youngsters.

The black-and-white photographs for *Apples, How They Grow* were taken at McDougal's Orchards in Springvale, Maine. This book, with its simple text accompanying the large-format photographs, can serve as a simple introduction to apple growing for younger readers. But it may also be enjoyed by older readers who can learn more detailed, scientific information about apples by reading the smaller italicized print. A helpful glossary in the back of the book includes the definitions of apple growing vocabulary (e.g., cross-pollinate, dormant, fruiting spur, sepal).

LEARNING ACTIVITIES

1. Photocopy five to eight of the large photos from *Apples, How They Grow* which show the apple tree at different stages of development. Then mix up the photos and challenge a friend to put them back in the correct order. If there are any errors, show your friend the correct order and explain the different stages of apple growing.

2. Arrange four visits to an apple orchard, one during each season of the year. Study the trees and compare them with Bruce McMillan's photos in *Apples, How They Grow*. Do the apple trees look the same as the ones in the book? Why or why not? Take a photo of the same tree during each season; then write your own description for the photos, telling how the tree changes during each season.

3. *Apples, How They Grow* is a how-to book. Create your own book explaining another process. For example, you might make a how-to book about growing a garden. Make certain to include all important steps in your how-to book and explain any special vocabulary words. Also include photos or drawings in your book. When you finish, share your book with friends and ask them if your information is clear.

ABOUT THE AUTHOR/PHOTO-ILLUSTRATOR

See information about Bruce McMillan on page 5.

A BEACH FOR THE BIRDS

AUTHOR / PHOTO-ILLUSTRATOR: Bruce McMillan
AGE LEVEL / LENGTH: 8-14 years / 32 pages
PUBLISHER / COPYRIGHT DATE: Houghton Mifflin Co. / 1993
FORMAT / ISBN: Hardcover / 0395640504

A Beach for the Birds tells about the least tern, an endangered species in Maine and the smallest of all terns. From 1989 to 1991, Bruce McMillan photographed and studied the least tern on a barrier beach in Kennebunk, Maine. McMillan follows the bird from its arrival in May, through its mating and hatching season, until its migration south in late August.

This book is packed with interesting facts and photographs. Young readers learn that bird bills are made from keratin (the same material that people's fingernails are made of); they see least terns diving for sand eels; they learn that least terns have brood patches (a small patch of bare skin that appears only during breeding season) on their breasts to keep their eggs warm; they see close-up photographs of speckled least tern eggs and chicks; and much more.

A Beach for the Birds can be read on several levels. For younger readers, the story of the least tern is more easily understood through McMillan's parallel story; he compares people's beach experiences of fishing, splashing in the waves, and being protected by lifeguards with the least tern's experiences of diving for fish, cleaning its feathers, and protecting its eggs on the beach. For older readers, the text offers many details (e.g., least terns can safely drink saltwater because they have a gland that filters out the salt; the incubation period for least tern's eggs is about twenty-one days; least tern parents learn to recognize their chicks' "peep" after they are only a day old.) and new vocabulary words (e.g., fovea, scrapes, fledgling). For readers who are bird lovers or have a real eye toward science (including adults), McMillan presents additional detailed facts about least terns at the back of the book, as well as a comprehensive index and bibliography.

LEARNING ACTIVITIES

1. Study another Maine bird. Select a bird and gather information about it from nonfiction books (including bird guides). Try to observe the bird and take notes about how it looks, how it moves, its habitat, etc. Take photos or make drawings of your selected bird, if you can. Finally, combine all your information into a report or a booklet. Try to make your information interesting to read and easy to understand, as Bruce McMillan did in *A Beach for the Birds*.

2. On the copyright page of *A Beach for the Birds*, Bruce McMillan offers information on the Wells National Estuarine Research Reserve and the Rachel Carson National Wildlife Refuge. If possible, arrange a visit to one of these places. Keep a log of what you learn.

3. Learn more about endangered species. How does an animal come to be listed as an endangered species? Does its listing as "endangered" depend upon the number of that kind of animals that still exist? Does it depend upon the threats (predators, environmental dangers) to the animal? Are endangered species identified and labeled at the state level, the national level, or both? Who actually labels an animal as endangered—biologists, environmentalists, politicians? Research nonfiction books about endangered species, write to wildlife organizations, such as the Audubon Society, and interview experts from the state Fisheries and Wildlife Department. Once you gather information about endangered species, you might create a pamphlet summarizing your findings or arrange to give a presentation before a local civic organization.

ABOUT THE AUTHOR/PHOTO-ILLUSTRATOR

See information about Bruce McMillan on page 5.

GOING ON A WHALE WATCH

AUTHOR / PHOTO-ILLUSTRATOR: Bruce McMillan
AGE LEVEL / LENGTH: 4-12 years / 40 pages
PUBLISHER / COPYRIGHT DATE: Scholastic / 1992
FORMAT / ISBN: Hardcover / 0590457683 (recently out of print)

Going on a Whale Watch follows two children on a whale watch. The reader witnesses the children's enjoyment at seeing live whales and watches them imitate different whale actions. But most of the book shows dolphins, minke whales, humpback whales, and fin whales as they are seen on a whale-watching trip to Jeffrey's Ledge in the Gulf of Maine.

Photo-illustrator Bruce McMillan captures the whales in action—spouting, breeching, feeding. He shows close-up photos of the whales' blowholes, flippers, and tails. Although the book appears to be one whale-watching trip, Bruce McMillan actually took twelve different day trips in order to complete all the photographs of the whales.

Although the photographed whale-watching trip will appeal to the youngest readers, perhaps the greatest strength of *Going on a Whale Watch* is its visual glossary filled with whale information and fun facts that older children and adults will appreciate. Readers learn that some whales can hold their breath for 90 minutes, that a fin whale inhales in one breath as much air as 3,000 people, that whales have finger bones, plus much more.

LEARNING ACTIVITIES

1. If possible, go on a whale watch yourself. If you can't, talk to someone who has. Compare your experiences or those of the person you talk to, with those found in the book *Going on a Whale Watch*. Did you or the other person see different kinds of whales? Which ones? Which actions did the whales do? Breach? Spout?

2. Play a whale trivia game with a partner, incorporating the information you learned in *Going on a Whale Watch*. Make question cards and challenge each other to answer and collect the most cards. You might ask questions, such as: how much does an adult fin whale weigh? (120,000 pounds); do humpback whales have a single or paired blowholes? (paired blowholes); what part of the whale's body has no bones? (the tail)

3. Bruce McMillan's book contains extensive information about whales. Select one kind of whale (e.g., minke, humpback, fin) and learn more about that specific whale. Read nonfiction books, interview a whale expert. Make a poster showing and summarizing the information you learned about your selected whale.

ABOUT THE AUTHOR/PHOTO-ILLUSTRATOR

See information about Bruce McMillan on page 5.

THE WEATHER SKY

AUTHOR / PHOTO-ILLUSTRATOR: Bruce McMillan
AGE LEVEL / LENGTH: 8 years–adult / 40 pages
PUBLISHER / COPYRIGHT DATE: Farrar Straus Giroux / 1991
FORMAT / ISBN: Hardcover / 0374382611; Paperback 0374482667

Weather is a favorite subject in Maine, perhaps because it is ever-changing. Mainers who want to talk knowledgeably about weather should read Bruce McMillan's *The Weather Sky*. Although the book represents temperate climates worldwide, it was photographed entirely in Shapleigh, Maine, near the author's home. This area of the state has been referred to as "thunderstorm alley" by the Portland office of the National Weather Service.

The Weather Sky uses charts, photographs, and diagrams to clarify weather words and patterns. Readers will learn the names of clouds, the Latin origins for weather words, and explanations for weather changes in each of the four seasons. The end of the book includes a helpful glossary and index. McMillan succeeds in making a complicated topic easily understandable to young readers.

LEARNING ACTIVITIES

1. Use *The Weather Sky* as a guide for skywatching. For a week or longer, study the sky several times a day. Try to determine what kinds of clouds there are. Does the weather have a weekly pattern? Keep a journal of your observations.

2. Maine is famous for its weather. As the Maine expression goes, if you don't like the weather, just wait ten minutes. Collect stories and sayings about Maine weather. Interview older Mainers to learn how they predict the weather. What signs in nature do they look for? Combine this information into a Maine weather booklet.

3. Arrange a visit to the National Weather Service office in Gray, Maine (call 207-688-3216) or invite a meteorologist from a local radio or TV station to speak at your school. Plan your questions ahead of time. For example, you might ask: "Shapleigh, Maine, where *The Weather Sky* is photographed, is known as thunderstorm alley. How did it get its name?" And you might ask: "Do any other Maine locations have weather nicknames?"

ABOUT THE AUTHOR

See information about Bruce McMillan on page 5.

A MOUNTAIN ADVENTURE: LET'S TAKE A TRIP

AUTHOR: Patricia Griffith Morgan / PHOTOGRAPHERS: Michael Plunkett & Tom Herde
AGE LEVEL / LENGTH: 8-12 years / 32 pages
PUBLISHER / COPYRIGHT DATE: Troll Associates / 1988
FORMAT / ISBN: Library binding / 0816711739

A Mountain Adventure: Let's Take a Trip follows a group of hikers as they climb Mt. Katahdin, Maine's highest peak. The adventure begins at Katahdin Stream Campground, where the hikers spend the night. Early the next morning, the hikers prepare their supplies and begin to ascend. They climb past Katahdin Falls, Katahdin Stream, Thoreau Spring, Knife Edge, to the peak, which is almost a mile high. Different hikers are shown in other parts of Baxter State Park—at Basin Pond, Chimney Pond, and Daicey Pond.

This book, with its striking color photographs, brings hiking on Mt. Katahdin to life. The book packs in lots of hiking vocabulary and information in its few pages. Young readers learn about a moose's bell, the timberline, blazes, cairns, cirques, and more. They also learn about the importance of hiking with a first-aid kit and packing plenty of drinking water. *A Mountain Adventure* is an adventure and learning experience all in one.

LEARNING ACTIVITIES

1. Baxter State Park, like other natural settings in Maine, offers many exciting outdoor activities, including hiking, camping, canoeing, fishing, and swimming. Visit a mountain, lake, or state park near you and participate in one or more of these activities. Chronicle your visit with photographs and a log.

3. This book explains how two places in Baxter State Park were named: Thoreau Spring (named in honor of the writer Henry David Thoreau, who visited the site in the mid 1800s); and the Knife Edge (which describes a section of Katahdin which features a formation of thin, jagged rocks). Research the names of streets, buildings, ponds, etc., in your community. How did they get their names?

3. *A Mountain Adventure* shows Baxter State Park during the fall season. During other seasons, the park remains beautiful, though different in appearance. Select a location with a good view near you. Observe that location during different seasons. Take photographs or draw pictures of your selected place. Then compare your photos/illustrations and discuss differences during the seasons.

ABOUT THE AUTHOR & PHOTOGRAPHERS

Author information on Patricia Griffith Morgan and photographer information on Michael Plunkett and Tom Herde were not available.

A RIVER ADVENTURE: LET'S TAKE A TRIP

AUTHOR: Patricia Griffith Morgan / PHOTOGRAPHER: Michael Plunkett
AGE LEVEL / LENGTH: 8-12 years / 32 pages
PUBLISHER / COPYRIGHT DATE: Troll Associates / 1988
FORMAT / ISBN: Library binding / 0816711712

In *A River Adventure: Let's Take a Trip*, a group of teenage canoeists and their guides journey through Maine's Allagash Wilderness Waterway. After learning proper paddling and safety techniques, the canoeists head down river for an inspiring and tiring adventure. They carry their canoes around dams, find wild mushrooms and berries, canoe through rapids, dive off high cliffs for a swim, and see wildlife such as moose and osprey.

This book educates readers about canoeing in a wilderness area. New vocabulary words are italicized, with their definitions conveyed in a meaningful context. Young readers will learn about a ground cloth, reflector oven, portage, poling, bunchberries, Indian pipe mushrooms, and more. The color photographs help make the adventure seem realistic.

LEARNING ACTIVITIES

1. Learn more about whitewater canoeing and rafting. Write to a company that guides whitewater trips, asking for brochures and information. Check nonfiction books for further information. What kind of equipment do you need? What safety precautions are necessary? Is the water flow regulated? If so, how? How many people can ride in a canoe or raft at a time? How are whitewater guides trained? Write a report about what you learn.

2. Use a map of northern Maine to trace the route of the canoeists down the Allagash Wilderness Waterway, as described in *A River Adventure*. Find Eagle Lake, Farm Island, Churchill Dam, Chase Rapids, Umsakis Lake, Long Lake, and Allagash Falls. What other places did the canoeists pass through?

3. Draw a map of the river that is nearest to you. Include the three or four nearby towns that the river passes through. Locate dams, bridges, scenic views, and other points of interest along the river. What industries are located on the river? Are they dependent on the river for their business? Share your map with a social studies class and explain the importance of the river.

ABOUT THE AUTHOR & PHOTOGRAPHER

Author information on Patricia Griffith Morgan and photographer information on Michael Plunkett were unavailable.

LUCKY MOUSE

AUTHOR: Elizabeth Ring / PHOTOGRAPHER: Dwight Kuhn
AGE LEVEL / LENGTH: 4-8 years / 32 pages
PUBLISHER / COPYRIGHT DATE: The Millbrook Press / 1995
FORMAT / ISBN: Library binding / 1562943448

Lucky Mouse is a photographic story about a baby deer mouse that falls off a logging truck and then is placed by some children into the nest of a white-footed mouse who is caring for her own babies. The white-footed mother mouse readily adopts the deer mouse, nursing and cleaning her as one of her own. The book follows the deer mouse until she is grown and has her own babies.

Lucky Mouse is a wonderful nonfiction book for young readers. Its simple story format is captivating, and author Elizabeth Ring weaves in many interesting facts, such as a mother mouse stops nursing when the babies are four weeks old, mice teeth continuously grow like people's fingernails, and a male mouse is called a buck. Dwight Kuhn's photographs are amazing; it's hard to imagine how he was able to witness such intimate scenes of a mouse's life. The final four pages of the book include numerous questions and answers about mice, providing information on how fast a mouse runs, what a mouse's best sense is, the number of litters a mouse has in a year, and much more.

LEARNING ACTIVITIES

1. Arrange to watch a real mouse. View a friend's pet mouse or observe one at a pet shop. If you see a mouse in the wild or in a barn, remember *not* to handle it (for their own sake, wild animals should remain "wild"; also, there is always the possibility that they can carry serious diseases). Then draw pictures or write a short story about what you see the mouse doing.

2. The mouse in the book was called "Lucky Mouse." Do you think the mouse was lucky? Why or why not? Do you believe wild animals survive because of luck or because of their skills? Why do you think so? Have you ever been lucky? If so, how? Some people say you *make* your own luck? Do you agree? Why or why not?

3. Create a mouse game. You might make a gameboard in the shape of a mouse or question cards with mouse prints on them. For your game, ask questions about mice based on the information you learned in *Lucky Mouse* (e.g., what are two enemies of mice?—owls and weasels; how does a mouse clean its nest?—it doesn't, it makes a new nest instead; what kind of sounds can mice hear that people can't?—high-pitched sounds).

ABOUT THE AUTHOR
See information about Elizabeth Ring on page 195.

ABOUT THE PHOTOGRAPHER

Dwight Kuhn has worked as a biology and chemistry teacher for eighteen years in Maine. He currently works fulltime as a photographer. He has had more than a dozen children's books published, and he is currently working on another dozen. Kuhn's books have been photographed primarily in the state of Maine and feature close-up photos of plants and animals. His books include *More Than Just a Vegetable Garden, Turtle's Day, Night Flier, My First Book of Nature,* and *Seeds and Seedlings* (see page 296). Kuhn lives in Dexter, Maine, with his wife, who works as an elementary school teacher. They have four children.

THE WHALE IN LOWELL'S COVE

AUTHOR / ILLUSTRATOR: Jane Robinson
AGE LEVEL / LENGTH: 6-10 years / 48 pages
PUBLISHER / COPYRIGHT DATE: Down East Books / 1992 (original edition-1990)
FORMAT / ISBN: Hardcover / 0892723084

This nonfiction book tells the story of a humpback whale that stayed for a month in Lowell's Cove in Harpswell, Maine, during the summer of 1990. Author Jane Robinson, who lives in Harpswell, gives a detailed account of the whale's visit. She includes many sidebars and diagrams with additional whale facts. Young readers will enjoy the entertaining story and the wealth of information contained in *The Whale in Lowell's Cove.*

The humpback whale suddenly appears in the cove and is trapped by a net which is used by fishermen to keep pogies (a kind of fish) in the cove. The whale may have entered the cove in order to eat the pogies. The whale appears to be content as she swims, plays, and eats in the cove. But, soon, word of the whale spreads; and townspeople and tourists flock to see it. Their boats crowd the whale, and some people even poke at the whale with oars. Whale experts are called in to evaluate the situation. They worry about the whale's safety, with the cove so crowded. Too many propellers could accidentally cut the whale. So, boaters, except for local fishermen, are temporarily banned from using the cove.

However, the whale is still in danger. First she gets caught in a lobster line. Then she gets tangled in the net and almost drowns. The whale experts and fishermen decide they must come up with a plan to free the whale from the cove without letting all the pogies escape (after all, the fishermen have to make a living). When the whale is near the net and the pogies are swimming nearer shore, a second net is laid across the cove between the whale and the pogies. Now that the pogies are still trapped, the outer net is lowered to free the whale. The whale swims quickly out to sea, breaching time and again, as if celebrating her freedom.

LEARNING ACTIVITIES

1. Share *The Whale in Lowell's Cove* with a friend and take turns challenging each other with whale questions about the book. For example, you might ask, "What do some whales have instead of teeth to help them eat fish but no water?" (baleen plates) Or a friend might ask, "What is the shape of a humpback's spout?" (V-shaped because it blows air out two blowholes) Continue taking turns asking each other whale questions.

2. Author/illustrator Jane Robinson, as a resident of Harpswell, actually lived through the experience of the whale being in Lowell's Cove. Select an interesting story from your own community, gather information from those who witnessed the experience, and then draw pictures or write a story about the experience. You might even ask to place your work in your school or town library for a time so others in your community can enjoy reliving the experience through your words or pictures.

3. Organize a fundraiser at your school and raise money so that your class or school can adopt a whale. Write to the International Wildlife Coalition for more information:

> Whale Adoption Project
> International Wildlife Coalition
> 634 North Falmouth Highway / P.O. Box 388
> North Falmouth, MA 02556-0338

ABOUT THE AUTHOR/ILLUSTRATOR

Jane Robinson first came to Maine when she attended second grade at Longfellow School in Brunswick. She left soon after arriving, but she returned to the state as an adult. Robinson has a BFA from Bennington College, and she has enjoyed drawing and painting with oils over the years. *The Whale in Lowell's Cove* is her only book to date. Robinson works as a teacher and spends her summers as a member of an archaeological field crew. She lives in Harpswell in a 1910 cottage surrounded by perennial gardens. Her hobbies include hiking, cross-country skiing, and jogging.

CHIPMUNK AT HOLLOW TREE LANE

AUTHOR: Victoria Sherrow / ILLUSTRATOR: Allen Davis
AGE LEVEL / LENGTH: 3-7 years / 32 pages
PUBLISHER / COPYRIGHT DATE: Soundprints / 1994
FORMAT / ISBN: Hardcover / 1568990286; Hardcover "Mini-book" / 1568990294; Mini-book and stuffed toy / 1568990448; other editions with toys and tapes are also available

Chipmunk at Hollow Tree Lane is an early science book and part of Smithsonian's Backyard series. With simple text and large realistic illustrations, this book introduces young readers to chipmunks. The story starts in the fall showing the chipmunk as it hurries to gather as many seeds and nuts as possible before winter arrives. The chipmunk in this story must compete for food with a crow and another chipmunk. The chipmunk's burrow, with its stash of hidden food, is also shown. Finally, as winter arrives, the chipmunk is shown nesting in its burrow as it sleeps and occasionally awakens to eat. The chipmunk remains in its burrow until spring arrives.

One would expect excellent quality from a book that has the Smithsonian name on it; readers of *Chipmunk at Hollow Tree Lane* will not be disappointed. This book helps to fill a real need—simple yet informative science books for young children. In addition to the interesting text, the last page of the book also includes a simple glossary, a guide to the names of other plants and animals which appear in the book (e.g., white pinecone, American toad, wild strawberry), and additional information about chipmunks (e.g., chipmunks stay in the same burrow all their lives, chipmunks can carry up to 3,000-4,000 seeds in their cheek pouches at a time). Best of all, the book is only one of a series of wildlife books illustrated with the drawings by Allen Davis, who lives in Scarborough, Maine; other books in the series feature a rabbit, woodchuck, and skunk.

LEARNING ACTIVITIES

1. Make a "Chipmunk Fact List." Write a list on chart paper of all the facts you learned about chipmunks from this book. Then check other nonfiction animal books; try to add at least three more chipmunk facts to your list.

2. *Chipmunk at Hollow Tree Lane* shows the chipmunk during the fall and winter seasons. Draw your own illustration of a chipmunk during springtime or summertime. What do you think the chipmunk will be doing in these different seasons? Write a few words to go along with your illustration, or tell a friend about your illustration.

3. Use *Chipmunk at Hollow Tree Lane* as a scavenger list. With an adult, search a yard, field or wooded area to try to find as many animals and plants as you can that are named or, pictured in this book. Keep a list of what you find.

ABOUT THE AUTHOR

Victoria Sherrow is from Ohio. She studied both law and children's literature. Working as a fulltime writer since 1979, she has had over 50 books published, including ten picture books and many short stories and articles. Many of her stories are about nature. In addition, she has worked as an editorial assistant for the Westport Publishing Group and as a faculty member for the Institute of Children's Literature. Sherrow currently lives in Westport, Connecticut, with her husband and three children. Her hobbies include painting, tennis, gardening, and birdwatching.

ABOUT THE ILLUSTRATOR

Allen Davis grew up in New York, where his nature studies were limited to looking at Audubon prints at the library. At an early age, he began drawing nature scenes. But, now as a resident of Scarborough, Maine, Davis enjoys having the subjects of his illustrations as close as his backyard. Other children's books he has illustrated include *Cottontail at Clover Crescent*, *Woodchuck at Blackberry Pond*, and *Skunk at Hemlock Circle*. His artwork has also appeared in educational textbooks and school anthologies. Davis lives with his wife and son in a colonial farmhouse.

MAINE: PORTRAIT OF AMERICA

AUTHOR: Kathleen Thompson / PHOTOGRAPHER: photographs from a variety of sources
AGE LEVEL / LENGTH: 8-14 years / 48 pages
PUBLISHER / COPYRIGHT DATE: Raintree Steck-Vaughn Publishers / 1996
FORMAT / ISBN: Library binding / 0811473392; Paperback / 0811474445

Maine: Portrait of America is based on the *Portrait of America* television series. This informational book packs much information into a few pages. The book is divided into four major sections: history, economy, culture, and the future. The history section details the Passamaquoddys, the Penobscots, the Vikings, and numerous European explorers. It describes Maine's first settlement (the Popham Colony in 1607), the influence of Father Sebastian Rale, Maine's involvement in the first naval battle of the Revolutionary War, and more historical information up through both World Wars and the Indian Land Claims Settlement. In addition, the history section includes a four-page profile of Senator Margaret Chase Smith and a two-page feature called "Keeping Acadia in Madawaska."

The economic section highlights Maine's businesses, industries, and natural resources. A feature of this section is "The Ships and Boats of Bath." The culture section includes information about Maine's museums, famous writers, and festivals, as well as a feature on the Portland String Quartet. The section on Maine's future describes the state's concerns as population grows and business declines in some areas of the state.

In addition, *Maine: Portrait of America* includes a map of the state, an historical timeline, a Maine almanac, a listing of places to visit in Maine, and a comprehensive index. Reading *Maine Portrait of America* is a bit dry at times, as it packs in fact upon fact, but it serves as a thorough resource (for its 48 pages) and a good springboard for further Maine studies.

LEARNING ACTIVITIES

1. Select one explorer from the history section of *Maine: Portrait of America*. Research that explorer, especially the explorer's Maine experiences, and give an oral report about what you learned.

2. Reread pages 40–41 of *Maine: Portrait of America* which feature the Portland String Quartet. Select a musical group or performer from your area of the state. Interview that group or performer and write a short feature article about your selected musician(s).

3. On page 47 of *Maine: Portrait of America*, a listing of eight annual Maine events and ten places to visit are named. These lists are far from comprehensive, so add to the lists. Write to the Chamber of Commerce in selected towns and cities throughout Maine and ask them to name important events and places in their town or city. Combine your new information with the book's to create a more comprehensive list of Maine events and places to visit.

4. Make up your own learning activity for *Maine: Portrait of America*. Use the book to design an activity. Then invite a friend to do your activity. How did your activity work out? Did it turn out the way you planned?

ABOUT THE AUTHOR

Author information on Kathleen Thompson was unavailable.

MORE MAINE INFORMATIONAL BOOKS

Below is a list of quality Maine informational books that have recently gone out of print. You are likely to find them at your local library. They are listed alphabetically by author.

FINESTKIND O' DAY: LOBSTERING IN MAINE
written & photo-illustrated by Bruce McMillan, 6-10 years, 1977, Lippincott, 48 pages. A boy's day spent lobstering is recorded with photos and with detailed text including many vocabulary words and facts about lobsters and lobstering.

ACADIA NATIONAL PARK
written by Ruth Radlauer, photographed by Ed Radlauer & Ruth Radlauer, 8-12 years, 1978 (original) & 1986 (revision), Childrens Press, 48 pages. This book is a close-up, photographed look at Acadia National Park, including its soil, flowers, trees, history, and special sites.

STERLING: THE RESCUE OF A BABY HARBOR SEAL
written by Sandra Verrill White & Michael Filisky, 5-10 years, 1989, Crown Publishers, 32 pages. An orphaned baby harbor seal is rescued by the Marine Mammal Stranding Network in Maine and raised at the New England Aquarium until it is strong enough to return to a colony of harbor seals off the Maine coast.

ACTIVITY BOOKS

THE BIRDS OF MAINE: A COLORING-LEARNING BOOK;
THE WILDLIFE OF MAINE: A COLORING-LEARNING BOOK

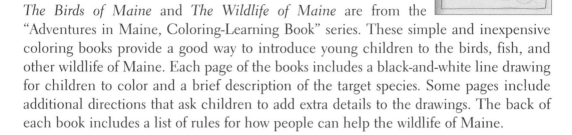

AUTHOR: John Crowder / ILLUSTRATOR: drawings from a variety of local artists

AGE LEVEL / LENGTH: 3-7 years / 32 pages

PUBLISHER / COPYRIGHT DATE: Escapade Games Inc. / 1995

FORMAT / ISBN: Paperback (Birds of Maine) / 1887487018; Paperback (Wildlife of Maine) / 188748700X

The Birds of Maine and *The Wildlife of Maine* are from the "Adventures in Maine, Coloring-Learning Book" series. These simple and inexpensive coloring books provide a good way to introduce young children to the birds, fish, and other wildlife of Maine. Each page of the books includes a black-and-white line drawing for children to color and a brief description of the target species. Some pages include additional directions that ask children to add extra details to the drawings. The back of each book includes a list of rules for how people can help the wildlife of Maine.

The Wildlife of Maine book includes lobsters, red fox, black bears, harbor seals, white-tailed deer, and twenty-five other Maine animals. Young readers will discover some interesting facts, such as "The black racer snake is Maine's largest snake and can grow to over six feet long" and "Raccoons are a distant cousin of the panda bear and can weigh as much as thirty pounds."

The Birds of Maine not only shows the birds on the black-and-white coloring pages; but the inside front and back covers also show a colored, detailed drawing of each bird. The thirty birds featured include the bald eagle, the loon, the ruffed grouse, and the red-winged blackbird. Young readers will enjoy coloring this book and learning fun facts about birds. For example, they'll learn that the only common hummingbird in Maine is the ruby-throated hummingbird, which beats its wings in a figure-eight pattern, and that ring-neck pheasants were first introduced to the U.S. in 1880 when 42 birds were brought from Shanghai, China.

LEARNING ACTIVITIES

1. Learn about the animals in *The Birds of Maine* and/or *The Wildlife of Maine*. After you feel you know the animals fairly well, play a guessing game with a partner. Take turns describing one of the animals to each other; for example: "The animal I'm thinking of is related to the squirrel. It carried seeds in its cheeks. It sleeps longer in the winter, but it doesn't actually hibernate. What animal am I thinking of?" (This is a chipmunk.) Or, "The bird I'm thinking of makes nests on islands off the coast of Maine. It lays its eggs in the same spot year after year unless that area has been disturbed. Then that bird will not lay eggs that year. What bird am I thinking of?" (This is a tern.)

2. Add your own coloring page to one of these books. Find a picture of a Maine bird or animal that is not included in *The Birds of Maine* or *The Wildlife of Maine*. Then make a line drawing of your selected animal and write a short description of the animal. Photocopy your drawing and share it with some friends for them to read and color.

3. Learn more about one of the Maine birds or animals included in these books. Select a bird or animal and read bird or animal guides. You also might write to the Maine Audubon Society or the Gray Farm Visitors Center for more information on your animal (the addresses for both places are included in the back of the coloring books).

ABOUT THE AUTHOR

John Crowder has long had an interest in writing for children. Three years ago he pursued that interest by starting a publication company with his wife, Dale. Crowder spent two "long" winters reading thirty-seven books about Maine. From these books, he created several hundred questions for the *Adventures in Maine Trivia Game*, now out of print. Crowder then worked on three Maine theme coloring books. He contacted the Maine Audubon Society for assistance and continued his own research. The results were *The Birds of Maine*, *The Wildlife of Maine*, and *Activities in Maine* coloring-learning books.

Crowder works as an adult education instructor for industries. He has taught first grade Sunday school for many years. Crowder moved to Maine from Massachusetts seven years ago. He lives in Wiscasset with his wife and their two teenage children.

SUNNY'S MITTENS

AUTHOR: Robin Hansen / ILLUSTRATOR: Lois Leonard Stock
AGE LEVEL / LENGTH: 9-12 years / 48 pages
PUBLISHER / COPYRIGHT DATE: Down East Books / 1990
FORMAT / ISBN: Spiralbound paperback / 0892722908

The first half of *Sunny's Mittens* tells the story of a girl named Sunny, who learns from her Nana how to knit her own mittens. Full-page color illustrations complement the story. Sunny's Nana shows her different knitting styles, how to select yarn, how to knit the mittens (including the thumbs), how to finish off the mittens, and how to embroider them. Sunny smiles with pride when she wears her finished mittens.

The second half of the book includes a how-to lesson for knitting mittens. The lesson is broken into numerous steps, such as: "How to Wind Yarn So It Pulls from the Center of the Ball," "Knitting a Purl Round without Purling," and "Finishing Your Mittens and Working in the Ends." Instructions are also provided for making a hat to match the mittens. The knitting lesson is clearly written, with many diagrams to clarify the instructions.

LEARNING ACTIVITIES

1. *Sunny's Mittens* teaches readers how to make mittens. Write your own how-to book, giving step-by-step directions for another activity. You might tell how to play a game, cook a food, or make a craft-object. Draw diagrams for your written directions. Then check to see how good your instructions are by giving them to someone else to follow.

2. Many senior citizens, such as Sunny's Nana, know skills or handicrafts which often are not taught to younger generations. Some people fear that when the older generation dies, we will lose such skills as tatting (making lace) or woodcarving. Select an older relative to teach you a skill or handicraft. If such a relative doesn't live nearby, arrange to visit a retirement community or nursing home to find a "teacher."

3. Think of a time when an older relative, such as a grandparent, taught you something. It may have been how to make something or it may have been a life-lesson, such as respect for nature or the value of saving money. Write a poem, story, or journal entry describing your learning experience.

ABOUT THE AUTHOR

Robin Hansen was born on Great Diamond Island, Maine. Since her father was in the military, she spent her childhood traveling around the country and the world. Hansen always felt close to Maine, even though she did not live here. She returned to the state in her late twenties and has lived here ever since, with her husband and four children. They live (and grow apples) on an old farm in Bath, with sheep, dogs, and cats.

"I was a closet writer as a child," Hansen reports, "writing enormous, long novels. When I was nine, six pages was long, but I was into 200-page wonders by high school. All this 'play' writing taught me to write and to love writing." *Sunny's Mittens* is based on Hansen's experiences while teaching her own daughter to knit. She has written several other knitting books.

ABOUT THE ILLUSTRATOR

Lois Leonard Stock vacationed in Maine as a child, visiting an aunt on Vinalhaven and spending time in the Damariscotta region. Later, she received an art degree from Colby College in Waterville. After obtaining a masters degree from the University of Wisconsin, Stock returned to Maine. Her paintings have been included in both business and private collections in Maine and Massachusetts. Her illustrations have also been included in educational publications and in local trade books. For her children's book, *Sunny's Mittens*, Stock used her mother and a friend's daughter for models. The illustrations for the book were done in color pencil and graphite. Stock currently lives in Portland, where she enjoys doing volunteer work and singing with the Portland Community Chorus.

MILKWEED AND WINKLES: A WILD CHILD'S COOKBOOK

AUTHOR / ILLUSTRATOR: Elizabeth McKey Hulbert
AGE LEVEL / LENGTH: 6 years (with adult supervision)–adult / 64 pages
PUBLISHER / COPYRIGHT DATE: Windswept House Publishers / 1995
FORMAT / ISBN: Spiralbound paperback / 1883650283

Milkweed and Winkles: A Wild Child's Cookbook is a unique cookbook in several ways. First of all, it is targeted toward youngsters. Secondly, its recipes all use wild Maine foods for ingredients. Finally, the book's format makes it read more like a journal than a cookbook. *Milkweed and Winkles* describes how author Elizabeth McKey Hulbert (also known as GrandBee) and her granddaughter forage for and cook wild foods that they find near Hulbert's Mt. Desert Island home.

Recipes include common ones such as blueberry muffins, blackberry pie, and clam chowder. More unusual recipes include rosehip jam, periwinkle dip, and candied violets. Detailed instructions are included for how to identify, gather, and clean the wild foods. Warnings are also included, such as avoiding wild mushrooms and not eating raw fiddleheads. Hulbert's line drawings add a whimsical touch to this fun book which adults will enjoy as much as children. *Milkweeds and Winkles* is a celebration of natural foods and a call for cooking side by side.

LEARNING ACTIVITIES

1. With adult supervision, select one recipe from the book and cook it. Follow the directions carefully. Afterwards enjoy the food you prepared. Then write a critique of it. How did you like the food? Was it easy or hard to prepare? Were the directions accurate? Would you make any changes in the recipe if you were to prepare it again? If so, what changes? How did the food rate in terms of taste, texture, appearance, etc.?

2. Invite an older relative or friend to teach you how to prepare a special recipe. After helping to cook the food, write an accurate recipe for it. Make sure that your recipe is easy to understand, with detailed directions.

3. Select one wild food from *Milkweeds and Winkles* and research it. Look in nonfiction books and cookbooks. Interview people who forage or cook with your selected wild ingredient. Learn as much as you can and prepare a written report about the food. Add drawings to your report to help clarify information about how the food looks, where it is located, and how best to harvest it.

ABOUT THE AUTHOR/ILLUSTRATOR

See information about Elizabeth McKey Hulbert on page 51.

OBSERVA-STORY: PORTLAND TO CUT AND COLOR

AUTHOR & PROJECT COORDINATOR: Nancy Lightbody / GRAPHIC DESIGNER:
Sarah Hatch Malley
AGE LEVEL / LENGTH: 6-10 years / 24 pages
PUBLISHER / COPYRIGHT DATE: Greater Portland Landmarks, Inc. / 1976
FORMAT / ISBN: Paperback / 0960061258

Observa-Story: Portland to Cut and Color is a wonderful activity book for children from Portland, or for anyone who wishes to learn more about the historical buildings of Maine's largest city. The book includes a variety of activities related to Portland's buildings—scale-sized buildings to cut, color, and assemble; dot-to-dots for drawing buildings; a mobile to assemble from Portland's statues; a fold-out map of Portland, and cut-out buildings to glue on the map. Many buildings are featured in the book, including the Portland Observatory, Portland Head Light, the Longfellow House, the Clapp Mansion, the Spring Street Firehouse, and Portland Public Library.

Each drawing is finely detailed with the building's date of construction and its architectural style listed. Also, historical facts are presented throughout the book (e.g., the granite walls of the First Parish Church survived the Fire of 1866; Fort Gorges was built during the Civil War). It is printed on durable, thick paper, and the publisher gives permission for teachers to reproduce up to 50 copies of pages for classroom use.

LEARNING ACTIVITIES

1. Select one building from *Observa-Story: Portland to Cut and Color* and learn more about it. Who built the building? How large is the building? What uses has it had? How has the building changed over the years? Write a report about your selected building.

2. Go on a tour of Portland with an adult. Use the map in *Observa-Story: Portland to Cut and Color* as a guide. Try to find as many buildings and statues as you can from the book. Do they look as you expected they would? In what ways do the illustrations differ from what you actually see?

3. With some friends, create an activity book about your own town. Select well-known buildings and sites to include. You may take photos of places first and use the photos as guides to help you draw cut-and-paste drawings, dot-to-dots, etc. If possible, make copies of your town book and share them with others.

ABOUT THE AUTHOR/PROJECT COORDINATOR

Nancy Lightbody currently works as an elementary school teacher and an instructor of graduate students in the special education department at the University of Southern

Maine. She worked with a small group from Greater Portland Landmarks to create *Observa-Story*. The group felt it was important to help young people to become more aware of the "many architectural treasures" in Portland. It was Lightbody's job to coordinate the project, select appropriate sites, develop activities in response to the individual buildings, select an artist and printer, and write the rhyming couplets for the booklet.

As a child, Lightbody vacationed in Camden, Maine, where she visited her grandparents. In 1974, she moved to Falmouth, where she continues to live with her husband and two teenage daughters. Her hobbies include jogging, gardening, stargazing, and canoeing.

ABOUT THE GRAPHIC DESIGNER

Sarah Hatch Malley grew up in Dexter, Maine, where she developed an early interest in monuments and the architectural heritage of old buildings. Her grandfather was the founder of a private boy's school which was located in stately, historic buildings. Malley majored in art education in college and had the opportunity to work on *Observa-Story* for Portland Landmarks. Malley searched the files of Portland Landmarks for photos of historic buildings. She then used these photos to create pen & ink drawings for the activity book. Portland Public Schools currently use portions of *Observa-Story* in their third grade curriculum. Malley's motivation behind her work on the project is her belief that all children should learn about "their historical, architectural heritage."

Malley has continued to work professionally in the areas of graphic production and book design. She also currently works as a substitute art and regular classroom teacher. In addition, she enjoys creating paper-mâché jewelry. Malley lives with her husband and daughter in South Portland.

SEEDS AND SEEDLINGS

AUTHOR: Elaine Pascoe / PHOTOGRAPHER: Dwight Kuhn
AGE LEVEL / LENGTH: 8-12 years / 48 pages
PUBLISHER / COPYRIGHT DATE: Blackbirch Press / 1997
FORMAT / ISBN: Library binding / 1567111785

Seeds and Seedlings is part of the Nature Close-up series, published by Blackbirch Press; other books in the series focus on earthworms, tadpoles, and butterflies/moths. The close-up color photos for this book were all taken in Maine by noted nature photographer Dwight Kuhn, of Dexter, Maine.

The book is divided into three chapters: "From Seeds to Flower," "Growing Plants from Seeds," and "Investigating Seeds and Seedlings." After the first chapter, which introduces how seeds grow, the book is filled with simple seed experiments. Young scientists can follow detailed photographic instructions that explain how to plant seeds in a garden or in containers, as well as how water, air, temperature, and light affect seed growth. Each experiment includes a list of required materials, the question to be answered by the experiment, a step-by-step procedure, questions about the results and conclusion of the experiment, and photographs showing how to do the experiment. The experiments are fun and informative. A glossary, bibliography, index, and listing of seed companies are included.

LEARNING ACTIVITIES

1. Have a seed scavenger hunt. Make a list of as many seeds as possible, such as acorns, corn kernels, apple seeds, dandelion seeds, and maple seeds (helicopters). Make several copies of your seed list and challenge friends to find as many seeds from the list as possible. You may prefer to search with partners or in small groups. After the search, see who found the most seeds and compare the seeds to each other.

2. Do one of the experiments from *Seeds and Seedlings*. Write a science paper about your experiment and prepare a display about it. Then share the results of the experiment and what you learned with your class. Invite classmates to try other experiments from the book so you can host your own seed science show.

3. Following the format for experiments in *Seeds and Seedlings*, create a new seed experiment. First of all, decide what question you want to answer about seeds; then design an experiment to answer that question. Make sure to include a list of materials, a step-by-step procedure, questions about the results and conclusion, and diagrams or photographs showing how to perform your experiment. Invite a friend to follow your directions and try your experiment. How did it turn out? Were your directions clear? Did the experiment answer the seed question you posed?

ABOUT THE AUTHOR

Elaine Pascoe has been writing for twenty years. She began working for newspapers, and then for magazines and reference books. She also has written nonfiction books for both children and adults. After working as an editor-in-chief of a children's book publishing company, Pascoe moved to full-time writing. In addition to *Seeds and Seedlings*, Pascoe collaborated with photographer Dwight Kuhn on three other books for Blackbirch Press' Nature Close-up series: *Earthworms*, *Tadpoles*, and *Butterflies and Moths*.

Pascoe lives in northwestern Connecticut. She is the mother of a grown daughter. Her hobbies include gardening and horseback riding.

ABOUT THE PHOTOGRAPHER

See information about Dwight Kuhn on page 282.

MORE MAINE ACTIVITY BOOKS

Below is a list of quality Maine activity books and games that have recently gone out of print. You are likely to find them at your local library. They are listed alphabetically by author.

A GIFT FROM MAINE
written by James Plummer's sixth grade class at Memorial School in New Gloucester, Maine, illustrated by students and a variety of Maine artists, 10-14 years, 1983, Gannett Publishing Co., 149 pages. This book is a compilation of hands-on project ideas for Maine children from Maine artists, writers, and craftspeople, including projects such as making a fishmobile, stenciling a Maine T-shirt, writing a true life story, making a picture map of Maine, etc.

SO YOU THINK YOU KNOW MAINE
written by Neil Rolde and WCBB, photographs from a variety of sources, 10 years–adult, 1984, Tilbury House Publishers, 215 pages. This game book about Maine is based upon the public television show by the same name which includes toss-up questions, category questions, pens-in-hand questions, visual questions, and essay questions on such topics as Maine history, the unorganized territories, and Maine folklore.

APPENDICES

MORE MAINE AUTHORS AND ILLUSTRATORS

Below is a listing of additional children's book authors and illustrators from Maine. These authors and illustrators have not been included in the main part of the book for a variety of reasons: their books are about non-Maine subjects, their books about Maine are currently out of print, or their books did not meet the standards we set for inclusion in *A Celebration of Maine Children's Books*. We recognize and thank these authors and illustrators for their valuable contributions to children's literature in the state of Maine.

NED ACKERMAN — Ackerman currently lives in Camden, Maine. His grandfather was adopted by a family from the Blackfoot Native American tribe in Montana in the 1890s. Ackerman has studied the culture of the Blackfoot tribe; and his first novel, *Spirit Horse*, features a Blackfoot boy who tries to tame a wild horse.

DAVID LEWIS ATWELL — This author of two picture books, *The Day Hans Got His Way* and *Sleeping Moon*, lives in Rockland, Maine.

DEBBY ATWELL — Atwell is the author and illustrator of *Barn*. She also illustrated *The Day Hans Got His Way* and *Sleeping Moon*. She lives in Rockland, Maine.

BETTY BATES — Bates is from Evanston, Illinois. Her husband's family owns an apple orchard in Turner, Maine, where they visit each August. In fact, she wrote a chapter book with that orchard as its setting, *Ask Me Tomorrow* (see page 151). Bates's fifteen published children's books — including the titles *Call Me Friday the Thirteenth* and *Thatcher Payne-in-the-Neck* — are all currently out of print. Bates continues to write stories for *Cricket* and *Highlights* magazines.

HOLLY BERRY — Berry lives in Waldoboro, Maine, on a blueberry farm. She works as a printmaker and illustrator. Her illustrations are featured in the picture books: *Old MacDonald Had a Farm*, *Busy Lizzie*, *The Gift of Christmas*, and *Market Day*.

ASHLEY BRYAN — Bryan currently lives on an island off the Maine coast. He is nationally known for his vibrant, colorful illustrations of African folktales and African spirituals. He also writes poetry. His children's books include *The Ox of the Wonderful Horns and Other African Tales*, *Beat the Story-Drum, Pum Pum*, *Sing to the Sun*, and *Ashley Bryan's ABC of African American Poetry*.

SHERRY BUNIN — Bunin is the author of two books: *Dear Great American Writers School* (a World War II novel set in Kentucky, in which a teenage girl enrolls in a correspondence writing course) and *Is That Your Sister?* (a true adoption story). Bunin grew up in Kentucky, but she has vacationed in Maine for over thirty years. She has lived on Vinalhaven for the past four years.

JOANNA CAMPBELL—Joanna Campbell is the pseudonym that Jo Ann Simon uses for her young adult novels. She is the author of the Thoroughbred series, including *The Wild Mustang*. She lives in Camden, Maine.

MIMI CARPENTER—Carpenter grew up in the central Maine area and currently lives and works from her studio in Oakland. She is known for her "sea" artwork–which includes shells, mermaids, and sea creatures–that has been featured in her three children's books: *Mermaid Tidal Pool, What the Sea Left Behind,* and *Of Lucky Pebbles & Mermaid's Tears.* Carpenter frequently visits schools throughout New England and inspires children to create their own sea creatures and stories.

MARY CHESLEY—Chesley moved to Maine as a child fifty years ago; she currently lives in Monmouth. She is the author of *Miss Purdy's Problems* and is currently working on more "Miss Purdy" books, as well as a children's gardening book.

EMILY CHETKOWSKI—Chetkowski lives in Westminster, Massachusetts, but she has summered in Islesboro for many years. She is the author of two children's books: *Mabel Takes a Ferry* and *Amasa Walker's Splendid Garment.* Chetkowski frequently visits schools and does book signings (along with her dog Mabel).

JANE COWEN-FLETCHER—Cowen-Fletcher lives in South Berwick. She is the author-illustrator of several children's books, including *Mama Zooms, It Takes a Village,* and *Baby Angels.*

MICHELLE DIONETTI—Dionetti has lived in York since 1978. She is the author of several children's books, including a picture book, *Coal Mine Peaches,* and a chapter book, *Mice to the Rescue.* Her most recent book is a picture book biography of Vincent van Gogh, called *Painting the Wind,* illustrated by Maine artist Kevin Hawkes (see next page).

ANNE WESCOTT DODD—Dodd graduated from Cony High School and the University of Maine. She has taught writing and education courses at the University of Maine and Bates College. She is the author of numerous books for adults and the children's book, *Footprints and Shadows,* which is illustrated by Henri Sorensen. Dodd currently lives on Mere Point in Brunswick. She enjoys beachcombing with her grandchildren and making suncatchers, lamps, and jewelry from the seaglass they find.

KATHY LYNN EMERSON—Emerson moved to Maine in 1965 to attend Bates College. She has lived in East Wilton since the mid 1970s. She is the author of adult historical novels and several children's books, including *Julia's Mending, Someday,* and *Making Headlines: A Biography of Nellie Bly.* Two of her children's books have been set in Maine; they are *The Mystery of Hilliard's Castle* (see page 151) and *The Mystery of the Missing Bagpipes.*

ROBERT ENSOR—Ensor has owned an old house in Port Clyde for forty years and has lived there fulltime since 1983. He is both an author and an illustrator. His books include *Nellie the Lighthouse Dog*, *Nellie The Flying Instructor*, and *Good Molly Miss Molly and the 4th of July Parade*.

WALTER GAFFNEY-KESSELL—Gaffney-Kessell lives in Kennebunkport. He has done numerous black-and-white illustrations for children's books. He recently illustrated in watercolors his first full-color picture book, *This Is Me Laughing*, which features one of his daughters. He is also the illustrator of *Daddy Will Be There* by Lois G. Grambling.

ROY GALLANT—Gallant was born in Portland and currently lives in Rangely. He is a respected and prolific science writer for young adults. His first books were published in the 1950s and were part of the Exploring series by Doubleday. Some of his other titles include *The Rise of Mammals*, *Ancient Indians: The First Americans*, *The Peopling of the Planet Earth*, and *Earth's Vanishing Forests*.

GEORGE GJELFRIEND—Gjelfriend has lived in an isolated log cabin in East Orland for the past ten years. He is the author of a chapter book for children, called *High Island Treasure*.

KEVIN HAWKES—Hawkes studied illustration at Utah State University. His first children's book, which he both wrote and illustrated, was *Then the Troll Heard the Squeak*. He has illustrated more than a fifteen books, including: *By the Light of the Halloween Moon* (by Caroline Stutson), *The Librarian Who Measured the Earth*, *Marven of the Greart North Woods* (both by Kathryn Lasky, page 270), *Painting the Wind* (by Michelle Dionetti, see previous page), *Boogie Bones* (by Elizabeth Loredo), *My Little Sister Ate One Hare* (by Bill Grossman), *The Poombah of Badoombah* (by Dee Lillegard), and *Imagine That! Poems of Never Was* (by Jack Prelutsky). Hawkes lives on Peaks Island, with his wife and three children, where he enjoys his hobbies of bicycling, gardening, reading, playing soccer, and flying kites.

JUDITH HEAD—Head moved with her husband to Maine in 1982. Her first children's chapter book was published in 1995. It is called *Culebra Cut* and tells the story of a family that moves from Maine to Panama in 1911 to work on the Panama Canal. Head is currently at work on another historical book.

NICHOLAS HELLER—Heller moved from New York to Maine in the early 1990s. He is the author and illustrator of more than fifteen picture books, including: *Peas*, *Goblins in Green*, *This Little Piggy*, and *The Giant*. He lives in Portland, with his wife and two children.

EMILY HERMAN—Herman has lived in Georgetown for the past twenty-five years. She is the author of two children's books: a ghost story called *Hubknuckles* (see page 91), which is currently out of print and an early chapter book called *The Missing Fossil Mystery*, which was published in the fall of 1996.

PHILIP HOOSE — This author of *It's Our World, Too! Stories of Young People Who Are Making a Difference* (a 1993 Lupine Honor Book) lives in Portland and works at the Nature Conservancy.

ANNE HUNTER — Hunter lived in Maine from 1990 to 1997; she currently lives in Vermont. She both wrote and illustrated her first children's picture book, *Possum's Harvest Moon*, which was published in the fall of 1996 and its spring 1998 follow-up book, *Possum and Peeper*, both published by Houghton Mifflin. She also is the illustrator of three other picture books: *On Grandpa's Farm*, by Vivian Sathre, *Nocturne*, by Jane Yolen, and a poetry anthology by Maine's own Paul Janeczko (see below).

CYNTHIA JABAR — Jabar lives in Portland, Maine. She is the illustrator of several picture books, including *Rain Song*, *Snow Dance*, and *Won't You Come and Play with Me?*

LISA JAHN-CLOUGH — Since she was born, Jahn-Clough has spent summers on Monhegan Island. She moved to Brunswick at the age of ten. She currently spends the school year in Boston, where she teaches children's literature courses at Emerson College and spends summers in Portland, where she does most of her "book work." Jahn-Clough is the author and illustrator of *Alicia Has a Bad Day*, *A Happy Birthday Book!*, *ABC*, *Yummy*, and *123 Yippee*.

PAUL JANECZKO — Janeczko, from Hebron, is a nationally-known editor of poetry anthologies. The poetry collections which he has edited include *Postcard Poems*, *Pocket Poems*, *The Place My Words Are Looking For*, and *Home on the Range: Cowboy Poetry*. He also has had two of his own poetry books published (both currently out of print), *Stardust Hotel* and *Brickyard Summer* (see page 180). Using the pen name J. N. Fox, Janeczko also wrote *Young Indiana Jones and the Pirates' Loot* which is set in Maine.

MARGARET KENDA — Kenda lived in the Bangor area and taught at the University of Maine for ten years. She is the co-author, along with Brewer resident Phyllis S. Williams, of a series of educational activity books for kids: *World Wizardry for Kids*, *Math Wizardry for Kids*, *Science Wizardy for Kids*, and *Cooking Wizardry for Kids*.

RUSS KENDALL — Kendall is an award-winning photojournalist who lives in Portland, Maine. He has collaborated with author Kate Waters on four books in the Plimouth Plantation series: *Sarah Morton's Day*, *Samuel Eaton's Day*, *Tapenum's Day*, and *On the Mayflower*. He is also the author and photographer for *Eskimo Boy* and *Russian Girl*.

STEVEN KROLL — Kroll, the author of more than seventy-five children's books, lived in North Yarmouth for four years from 1969 to 1973. At that time, he was just beginning his career as a writer. He taught creative writing at the University of Maine at Augusta for one year. Several of his children's books have been set in Maine, including *Multiple Choice* and *Big Jeremy*, which are both out of print, and an early chapter book, called *Patrick's Tree House*. Kroll's other children's books include *The Biggest Pumpkin Ever* and *The Boston Tea Party*.

JUDY LABRASCA — LaBrasca moved to Maine from Philadelphia in 1975. After making furniture and clocks which she sold at a store in Portland, she turned to illustrating for a career. She has illustrated two children's books: a chapter book, *The Secret of the Seal*, by Deborah Davis, and a book of poetry, *When Whales Exhale*, by Constance Levy. She is currently working on illustrations for a picture book and an alphabet book.

BERNIE MACKINNON — MacKinnon was born in Canada, attended the University of Maine, and has lived in Portland. He is the author of young adult novels, including *The Meantime* and a coming-of-age novel set in rural Maine, called *Song for a Shadow*.

KATHY MALLAT — Mallat is an elementary art teacher in Lebanon, Maine. She co-created her first picture book, *The Picture Than Mom Drew*, with Maine author and photo-illustrator, Bruce McMillan. Her second book, *Seven Stars More*, is a rhyming bedtime book to be published by Walker & Co. in spring of 1999.

STEPHEN MOOSER — Mooser grew up in California, but he now lives part of each year in Bar Harbor. He is the author of numerous chapter books for children, including both humorous ones and horror ones. His titles include *It's a Weird, Weird World, Elvis is Back! And He's in the 6th Grade, The Hitchhiking Vampire, The Headless Snowman*, and *The Thing Upstairs*. Mooser is also one of the founders and the current president of The Society of Children's Book Writers and Illustrators.

MARY PALMER — Palmer, a life-long resident of Maine, was born in West Baldwin and currently lives in South Paris. Palmer is best known for her poetry books, which include *Mother Moose Rhymes, More Mother Moose Rhymes, As Clean as a Whistle*, and *Sharing Secrets*.

PETER PARNALL — Parnall lives on a farm in Waldoboro. He has illustrated more than eighty books, including three Caldecott Honor Books. He also has authored more than ten books for children, including *Winter Barn, Water Pup, Quiet* (see page 92), and *Woodpile* (see page 92).

OLGA PASTUCHIV — Pastuchiv's family is Ukrainian. She moved to Maine about eight years ago because the state reminded her of Greece where she had lived for a short time. She currently lives in Richmond. She had her first children's book, *Minas and the Fish*, published in the spring of 1997 by Houghton Mifflin; she is both the book's author and its illustrator.

KATY PERRY — Perry is the author of several books for adults and two children's books, *My Grandmother Wears Crazy Hats* and *The Laughing Lighthouse*. Perry was born in Millinocket and currently lives in Hallowell, where she runs her own publishing company, Perry Publishing.

DAWN PETERSON — Peterson is an illustrator from the Portland area. She moved to Maine in 1978 and five years ago began illustrating children's books. Her books include two books by Kate Rowinski, *L. L. Bear's Island Adventure* and *Ellie Bear & the Fly-Away Fly*, and two books by Emily Chetkowski, *Mabel Takes a Ferry* and *Amasa Walker's Splendid Garment*.

RODMAN PHILBRICK — Philbrick's first novel for young readers, *Freak the Mighty*, has won numerous awards and has been made into a feature film, entitled *The Mighty*. He is also the author of *The Fire Pony* and *Max the Mighty* (a sequel to his first novel). Philbrick and his wife, novelist Lynn Harnett, divide their time between Marathon, Florida, and Kittery, Maine.

LAURA RANKIN — Rankin currently lives in York Harbor. She is the author and illustrator of the picture books *The Handmade Alphabet* and *Merl & Jasper's Supper Caper*.

ENRIQUE O. SANCHEZ — A resident of Bar Harbor, Sanchez has illustrated more than fifteen children's books, including *Amelio's Road, Lupe and Me, Saturday Market*, and *The Golden Flower: A Taino Myth from Puerto Rico*.

MARGARET SCHEID — Scheid is a graduate of the College of The Atlantic in Bar Harbor. For her senior thesis, she wrote and illustrated a children's book, *Discovering Acadia: A Guide for Young Naturalists*, which later was published by Acadia Publishing. She worked at Acadia National Park for ten years. She currently lives in Nova Scotia, Canada, where is working on several children's books.

LISA SHANO — Shano vacationed in Maine as a child and moved to the state fifteen years ago to attend the University of Southern Maine. She is the author and illustrator of one children's book, which she also published. The book is called *Creature Comforts*, and it has quilted illustrations.

LAURIE SPENCER — Spencer moved to Maine in the mid 1980s. She has been illustrating professionally for eight years, including commercial work and illustrations for children's magazines, such as *Cricket* and *Highlights for Children*. The first children's book she illustrated is *The Kwanzaa Contest*, by Marian Moore and Penny Taylor. She also illustrated the chapter books, *Alison's Puppy* and *Alison's Fierce and Ugly Halloween*, by Marion Dane Bauer.

SARAH STAPLER—Stapler has lived in Maine fulltime for the past ten years. She currently lives in Bowdoinham, where she designs gardens as well as writes and illustrates children's books. She has written and illustrated three books: *Trilby's Trumpet, Cordelia Dance!*, and *Spruce the Moose Cuts Loose* (see page 93). She also is the illustrator of several other children's books, including *Waiting-for-Papa Stories, Waiting-for-Christmas Stories*, and *The Bear Next Door.*

MARIA TESTA—Testa writes children's books in Portland. Her published works include *Dancing Pink Flamingos and Other Stories, Thumbs Up, Rico!*, the picture book *Nine Candles*, illustrated by Amanda Schaffer, and the picture book *Someplace to Go*, illustrated by Karen Ritz.

WILLIAM WEGMAN—Wegman, a resident of Rangeley, Maine, is famous for his children's books featuring photographs of his Weimaraner dogs. Some of his titles are *Puppies, Cinderella (Fay's Fairy Tales)*, and *Little Red Riding Hood (Fay's Fairy Tales).*

JANE WEINBERGER—Weinberger was born in Milford and graduated from Old Town High School. She currently lives in Mount Desert, where she runs her own publishing company, Windswept House Publishers. She is the author of ten children's books, including *Wee Peter Puffin; Cory, the Cormorant; Mrs. Witherspoon's Eagles*; and *Stormy.*

PHYLLIS S. WILLIAMS—Williams' actual last name is Sawyer. She is a lifetime resident of Brewer. She is the co-author, along with Margaret Kenda, of a series of educational activity books for children, including *World Wizardry for Kids, Math Wizardry for Kids, Science Wizardry for Kids*, and *Cooking Wizardry for Kids.*

BARBARA WINSLOW—Winslow has lived on a small farm in rural Maine for more than twenty years. Before that, she lived and taught in Alaska, an experience which led to her first published picture book called *Dance on a Sealskin* (published by Alaska Northwest Books and illustrated by her friend Teri Sloat).

JAMIE WYETH—Monhegan Island resident and a member of the world-renowned Wyeth art family (his grandfather–N.C. Wyeth, his father–Andrew Wyeth) has illustrated a picture book called *Cabbages and Kings*, written by Elizabeth Seabrook.

AUTHOR AND ILLUSTRATOR ADDRESSES

Below is a list of author and illustrator addresses. Addresses are included only for those who have asked to be listed. A special thanks to those authors and illustrators for being willing to be available to their fans. Young people wishing to write to any of these authors and illustrators should be considerate and practical. Keep your letters short and to the point. Also, if you would like a response, enclose a self-addressed, stamped envelope for a reply. Be patient. Authors and illustrators have busy schedules; sometimes they are traveling and doing presentations at schools and conferences, and they have deadlines to meet for publishers--so it may take awhile to get a response to your letter. But don't be shy about writing. Children's book authors and illustrators write in hopes that their work will resonate with young people; and so if a children's book has made you laugh, cry, think, or cheer, then let the author or illustrator know how their book has "touched" you.

A

Charlotte Agell
c/o Tilbury House Publishers
132 Water St.
Gardiner, ME 04345

Josephine Haskell Aldridge
c/o Simon & Schuster Books
for Young Readers
1230 Ave. of the Americas
New York, NY 10020
(note: Due to ill health, author
not able to write back; but she
still enjoys receiving letters)

Diana Appelbaum
100 Berkshire Rd.
Newton, MA 02160

B

Darice Bailer
3 Salem Rd.
Wilton, CT 06897
e-mail: dbailer420@aol.com

Diane & Jack Barnes
Brookfield Farm
Hiram, ME 04041

Betty Bates
55 Knox Circle
Evanston, IL 60201

Raymond Bial
First Light Photography
P.O. Box 593
Urbana, IL 61801

David F. Birchman
2196 Greenpark Ct.
Thousand Oaks, CA 91362

Kelly Paul Briggs
RR1 Box 4163B
Camden, ME 04843

Ron Brown
784 Essex St.
Bangor, ME 04401

Joseph Bruchac
P.O. Box 308
Greenfield Center, NY 12833

Sherry Bunin
RR1 Box 586
Vinalhaven, ME 04863

Nancy Butts
420 Zebulon St.
Barnesville, GA 30204
e-mail:
nanbutts@mindspring.com

C

Mimi Carpenter
RR3 Box 2220
Belgrade Road
Oakland, ME 04963

Abby Carter
c/o Little Brown & Co.
34 Beacon St.
Boston, MA 02108

Mary Cerullo
101 Highland Rd.
South Portland, ME 04106

Mary Chesley
P.O. Box 105
Monmouth, ME 04259

Emily Chetkowski
P.O. Box 588
Westminster, MA 01473

David R. Collins
3403 45th St.
Moline, IL 61265

Nantz Comyns
P.O. Box 2042
West Scarborough, ME 04070-
2042

John Crowder
RR4 Box 1595
Wiscasset, ME 04578

D

Allen Davis
2 Vale St.
Scarborough, ME 04074

Maggie Steincrohn Davis
P.O. Box 370
Blue Hill, ME 04614-0370

Julie Dean
1231 Electric Ave.
Venice, CA 90291

Sis Boulos Deans
260 Gray Rd.
Gorham, ME 04038

Michelle Dionetti
P.O. Box 660
York Harbor, ME 03911

Anne Wescott Dodd
39 Windmere Road
Brunswick, ME 04011

Mrs. Driver & 93-94 Class
Woolwich Central School
Box 1595
Woolwich, ME 04579

E

LeeAnne Engfer
c/o Lerner Publications
241 First Ave. North
Minneapolis, MN 55401

Robert Ensor
Marshall Point Road
P.O. Box 269
Port Clyde, ME 04855

F

Paula Fox
c/o Robert Lescher, Ltd. (agent)
67 Irving Place
New York, NY 10003

Lisa Rowe Fraustino
P.O. Box 67
Sebec, ME 04481
e-mail: lisafrau@aol.com

Jean Fritz
50 Bellewood Ave.
Dobbs Ferry, NY 10522

G

Jean Craighead George
20 William St.
Chappaqua, NY 10514

Gail Gibbons
Goose Green
Corinth, VT 05039
or
P.O. Box 218
Matinicus, ME 04851

A.S. Gintzler
c/o John Muir Publications
P.O. Box 613
Santa Fe, NM 87504

George Gjelfriend
Box 31
East Orland, ME 04431

John Coopersmith Gold
92 Franklin St.
Saco, ME 04072

Susan Dudley Gold
92 Franklin St.
Saco, ME 04072

Alberta Gould
c/o Heritage Publishing Co.
P.O. Box 792
Farmington, ME 04938

Nancy Griffin
c/o Coastwise Press
27 Green St.
Thomaston, ME 04861

Brenda Guiberson
20130 8th Ave. NW
Shoreline, WA 98177

H

Robin Hansen
RFD 1 Box 796
Bath, ME 04530

Bob Hartman
127 Monitor Ave.
Ben Avon, PA 15202

Lynne Harwood
RFD Box 2060
Anson, ME 04911

John & Ann Hassett
Box 272
Waldoboro, ME 04572

Judith Head
c/o Lerner Publications
241 First Ave. N.
Minneapolis, MN 55401

Nicholas Heller
47 Tyng Street
Portland, ME 04102

Emily Herman
P.O. Box 336
Georgetown, ME 04548

Kathleen M. Hollenbeck
c/o Soundprints
165 Water St.
Norwalk, CT 06854-3700

Deborah Hopkinson
P.O. Box 1052
Walla Walla, WA 99362
e-mail: hopkind@whitman.ed

Jean Howard
P.O. Box 160
Cranberry Isles, ME 04625

Elizabeth McKey Hulbert
457 Seawall Rd.
Manset, ME 04679

Anne Hunter
c/o Houghton Mifflin
Children's Trade Books
222 Berkeley St.
Boston, MA 02116

I

Dahlov Ipcar
HC 33 Box 1432
Georgetown, ME 04548

Philip Isaacson
P.O. Box 891
Lewiston, ME 04240

J

Lisa Jahn-Clough
c/o Houghton-Mifflin
Children's Book Dept.
222 Berkeley St.
Boston, MA 02116

K

Margaret Kenda
P.O. Box 79
Sudbury, MA 01776

Liza Ketchum
(formerly Liza Ketchum
Murrow)
521 Bankside Hollow
Acton, MA 01718

Kate Kiesler
c/o Clarion Books
215 Park Ave. South
New York, NY 10003

Margy Burns Knight
11 Pleasant St.
Winthrop, ME 04364

Jackie French Koller
c/o Atheneum Books
1230 Ave. of the Americas
New York, NY 10020
website:
http://members.aol.com/jackiek/i
ndex.htm

Steven Kroll
64 West 11th Street
New York, NY 10011

Dwight Kuhn
P.O. Box 152
Dexter, ME 04930

L

LaBrasca, Judy
7 Walcott Ave.
Falmouth, ME 04105

Glenna Lang
43 Stearns St.
Cambridge, MA 02138

Katie Lee
34 Bittersweet
South Salem, NY 10590

Betty Levin
16 Old Winter St.
Lincoln, MA 01773

Nancy Lightbody
210 Falmouth Rd.
Falmouth, ME 04105

Megan Lloyd
c/o Henry Holt & Co.
115 West 18th St.
New York, NY 10011-4195

Jennifer A. Loomis
c/o Stemmer House
2627 Caves Rd.
Owings Mills, MD 21117-2998

M

Kathy Mallat
RR1 Box 480
West Lebanon, ME 04027

David Mallett
P.O. Box 94
Sebec, ME 04481

Sarah Malley
89 Grandview Ave.
South Portland, ME 04106

Jacqueline Briggs Martin
312 Second Ave. N.
Mount Vernon, IA 52314

Cherie Mason
Goose Cove Rd.
Sunset, ME 04683

Petra Mathers
Rt. 2 Box 456
Astoria, OR 97103

Bruce McMillan
P.O. Box 85
Shapleigh, ME 04076-0085
(note: Author may not be
able to write back)

Wesley McNair
1 Chicken St.
Mercer, ME 04957

Catherine Frey Murphy
R.D. 1 Box 38
Earlville, NY 13332

O

Elizabeth Ogilvie
General Delivery
Cushing, ME 04563

Stella Ormai
26 East Manning Street
Providence, RI 02906-4048

P

Mary Palmer
138 High St.
So. Paris, ME 04281

Nancy Winslow Parker
51 East 74th St.-3R
New York, NY 10021

Olga Pastuchiv
114 Main St.
Richmond, ME 04357

Katy Perry
Perry Publishing
9 Middle St.
Hallowell, ME 04347

Dawn Peterson
P.O. Box 10334
Portland, ME 04104

Sanford Phippen
160 Main St. #C
Orono, ME 04473

Lynn Plourde
P.O. Box 362
Winthrop, ME 04364

Ethel Pochocki
RR1 Box 110
Brooks, ME 04921

R

Pat Davidson Reef
55 Foreside Common Dr.
Falmouth Foreside, ME 04105

Elizabeth Ring
397 Old Sherman Hill Rd.
Woodbury, CT 06798

Jane Robinson
Box 323
South Harpswell, ME 04079

Peter & Connie Roop
2601 N. Union St.
Appleton, WI 54911-2141

Kate Rowinski
21 Sisquisic Trail
Yarmouth, ME 04096

Joanne Ryder
244 Crocker Ave.
Pacific Grove, CA 93950

S

Steve Sanfield
22000 Lost River Rd.
Nevada City, CA 95959

Ruth Sargent
136 Island Ave.
Peaks Island, ME 04108

Meg Scheid
c/o Acadia Publishing Co.
P.O. Box 170
Bar Harbor, ME 04609

Lisa Shano
102 Portland St.
Yarmouth, ME 04096

Victoria Sherrow
3 Cardinal Lane
Westport, CT 06880

Christine Nyburg Shrader
P.O. Box 845
Langley, WA 98260

Dorothy Simpson
General Delivery
Cushing, ME 04563

Jan Slepian
212 Summit Ave.
Summit, NJ 07901

Harry Smith
Studios of Harry Smith
50 Harden Ave.
Camden, ME 04843-1609

Maggie Smith
c/o Orchard Books
95 Madison Ave.
New York, NY 10016

Liz Soares
c/o Windswept House Publishers
P.O. Box 159
Mt. Desert, ME 04660-0159

Daniel San Souci
694 Calmar Avenue
Oakland, CA 94610

Laurie Spencer
140 Providence Ave.
South Portland, ME 04106

Sarah Stapler
P.O. Box 48
Bowdoinham, ME 04008

Lois Leonard Stock
The Studio
3 Stratton Place
Portland, ME 04101

Melissa Sweet
29 West St.
Portland, ME 04102

T

Jeanne Titherington
c/o Greenwillow Books
William Morrow & Co.
1350 Ave. of the Americas
New York, NY 10019

V

Cynthia Voigt
Deer Isle, ME 04627

W

Jon Weiman
88 Wyckoff Street (3C)
Brooklyn, NY 11201

Jane Weinberger
Windswept House Publishers
P.O. Box 159
Mount Desert, ME 04660

Barbara Winslow
RR 1 Box 2570
Norridgewock, ME 04957

Jeanette Winter
c/o Philomel Books
Putnam & Grosset
200 Madison Ave.
New York, NY 10016

PUBLISHER ADDRESSES

Below is a listing of publishers of Maine children's books along with their addresses and phone numbers. To find a book included in A *Celebration of Maine Children's Books*, you will first want to check at your local library or bookstore. If they do not have a particular book that you want, you might ask them to order it for you or you may wish to contact the publisher directly.

A

Abrams, Inc.
100 Fifth Ave.
New York, NY 10011
800-345-1359

Amereon Ltd.
P.O. Box 1200
Mattituck, NY 11952
516-298-5100

American Friends Service
Committee
1501 Cherry St.
Philadelphia, PA 19102
888-588-2372

Apple Island Books
P.O. Box 190
Shapleigh, ME 04076-0190
207-324-9453

Arcadia Publishing
1 Washington Center
Suite 305
Dover, NH 03820
603-743-4266

Audio Bookshelf
174 Prescott Hill Rd.
Northport, ME 04849
800-234-1713

Avon Books
1350 Avenue of the Americas
New York, NY 10019
800-223-0690

B

Bantam Doubleday Dell
Publishing Group Inc.
1540 Broadway
New York, NY 10036-4094
800-223-6834

Belle Grove Pub. Co.
P.O. Box 483
Kearny, NJ 07032
201-991-8749

Biddle Publishing
P.O. Box 1305 No. 103
Brunswick, ME 04011
207-833-5016

Blackberry Books
617 East Neck Rd.
Nobleboro, ME 04555
207-729-5083

Blackbirch Press
260 Amity Rd.
Woodbridge, CT 06525
800-831-9183

C

Carolrhoda Books
241 First Avenue North
Minneapolis, MN 55401
800-328-4929

Candlewick Press
2067 Massachusetts Ave.
Cambridge, MA 02140
800-331-4624

Chelsea House Publishers
P.O. Box 914
Broomall, PA 19008-0914
610-353-5166

Childrens Press
Div. of Grolier Inc.
Sherman Turnpike
Danbury, CT 06816
800-621-1115

Clarion Books
a Houghton Mifflin Co.
215 Park Ave. South
New York, NY 10003
800-225-3362

Coastwise Press
27 Green St.
Thomaston, ME 04861-1530
207-354-0955

Cricketfield Press
P.O. Box 250
Rockport, ME 04856-0250
800-742-8667

D

Dell/Delacorte
1540 Broadway
New York, NY 10036
800-223-6834

Dickinson Family Publications
9 Deering St.
Portland, ME 04101
207-774-2263

DK Ink
95 Madison Ave.
New York, NY 10016
888-342-5357

Down East Books
P.O. Box 679
Camden, ME 04843
800-766-1670

Dutton Children's Books
375 Hudson St.
New York, NY 10014
800-331-4624

E

Escapade Games
34 Gorham Rd.
Wiscasset, ME 04578
800-200-9717

F

Farrar, Straus & Giroux
19 Union Square West
New York, NY 10003
800-788-6262

Fawcett Books
201 E. 50 St.
New York, NY 10022
800-726-0600

Firefly Books Ltd.
P.O. Box 1338
Buffalo, NY 14205
800-387-5085

Franklin Watts
Div. of Grolier Inc.
Sherman Turnpike
Danbury, CT 06816
203-797-3500

Front Street Books, Inc.
P.O. Box 280
Arden, NC 28704
800-788-3123

G

David R. Godine Publisher
P.O. Box 9103
Lincoln, MA 01773
800-344-4771

Greater Portland Landmarks
165 State St.
Portland, ME 04101
207-774-5561

Greenfield Review
P.O. Box 308
Greenfield Center, NY 12833
518-584-1728

Greenwillow Books
1350 Ave. of the Americas
New York, NY 10019
800-843-9389

H

Harcourt Brace & Co.
Children's Book Division
525 B Street, Suite 1900
San Diego, CA 92101
800-831-7799

HarperCollins Children's Books
10E 53rd St.
New York, NY 10022-5299
800-331-3761

Lynne Harwood
RFD Box 2060
Anson, ME 04911
207-696-5733

Heartsong Books
P.O. Box 370
Blue Hill, ME 04614-0370
207-288-4019

Heritage Publishing Co.
P.O. Box 792
Farmington, ME 04938
207-778-3581

Holiday House
425 Madison Ave.
New York, NY 10017
212-688-0085

Henry Holt &Co.
115 West 18th St.
New York, NY 10011
800-488-5233

Houghton Mifflin
222 Berkeley St.
Boston, MA 02116
617-351-5000

L

Landmark Editions
P.O. Box 270169
1402 Kansas Ave.
Kansas City, MO 64127
800-653-2665

Lerner & Carolrhoda
Publications
241 First Ave. North
Minneapolis, MN 55401
800-328-4929

Lighthouse Depot
c/o Kathy Finnegan
P.O. Box 1690
Route #1
Wells, ME 04090
207-646-0515

Little, Brown & Co.
34 Beacon St.
Boston, MA 02108
800-343-9204

Lothrop, Lee & Shepard
1350 Avenue of the Americas
New York, NY 10019
800-843-9389

M

Magazine Incorporated
1135 Hammond St.
Bangor, ME 04401
207-942-8237

Maine Writers & Publishers
Alliance
12 Pleasant St.
Brunswick, ME 04011-2201
207-729-6333

Millbrook Press Inc.
2 Old New Milford Rd.
Brookfield, CT 06804
800-462-4703

William Morrow & Co.
1350 Ave. of the Americas
New York, NY 10019
800-843-9389

John Muir Pub.
P.O. Box 613
Santa Fe, NM 87504-0613
800-888-7504

Mulberry
1350 Ave. of the Americas
New York, NY 10019
800-843-9389

Catherine Frey Murphy
R.D. 1 Box 38
Earlville, NY 13332
315-691-3481

O

Orchard Books / Div. of Grolier
95 Madison Ave.
New York, NY 10016
800-621-1115

P

Penguin USA
375 Hudson St.
New York, NY 10014-3657
800-331-4624

Puffin Books
375 Hudson St.
New York, NY 10014
800-331-4624

Putnam & Grosset Group
Children's Books
200 Madison Ave.
New York, NY 10016
800-631-8571

R

Raintree Steck Vaughn Pub.
466 Southern Blvd.
Chatham, NJ 07928
800-531-5015

Random House
201 East 50th St.
New York, NY 10022
800-726-0600

Rizzoli International Pub.
300 Park Ave. S.
New York, NY 10010
800-221-7945

Rourke Enterprises Inc.
108 Springvale Dr.
Vero Beach, FL 32964-2939
407-465-3132

Rutledge Hill Press
211 7th Ave. North
Nashville, TN 37219-1823
800-234-4234

S

Scholastic Inc.
555 Broadway
New York, NY 10012-3999
800-526-0275

Silver Burdett Press
299 Jefferson Rd.
Parsippany, NJ 07054-0480
201-739-8000

Simon & Schuster Books for
Young Readers
1230 Ave. of the Americas
New York, NY 10020
800-223-2348

Soundprints
165 Water St.
Norwalk, CT 06854-3700
800-228-7839

Stemmer House Pub. Inc.
2627 Caves Rd.
Owings Mills, MD 21117-2998
800-676-7511

T

The Tidal Press
P.O. Box 160
Cranberry Isles, ME 04625
207-244-3090 (May-Nov.)
        or
129 Mount Vernon St.
Boston, MA 02108
617-523-7995 (Nov.-May)

Tilbury House Publishers
132 Water St.
Gardiner, ME 04345
800-582-1899

Troll Associates
100 Corporate Drive
Mahwaa, NJ 07430
800-929-8765

U

University Press of New England
23 S. Main St.
Hanover, NH 03755-2048
800-421-1561

V

Viking Children's Books
375 Hudson St.
New York, NY 10014
800-331-4624

W

Albert Whitman & Co.
6340 Oakton St.
Morton Grove, IL 60053-2723
800-255-7675

Windswept House Publishers
P.O. Box 159
Mount Desert, ME 04660-0159
207-244-7149

OF INTEREST

Below is a listing of organizations, exhibits, collections, and conferences that are of interest to readers of Maine children's books:

MAINE WRITERS & PUBLISHERS ALLIANCE

This non-profit organization supports and promotes Maine literature–children's books as well as books for adults. MWPA publishes *Maine In Print*, Maine's only statewide literary newspaper, which includes booknotes on the latest Maine children's books. This organization also offers numerous writing and publishing workshops throughout the state and sells close to 2,000 Maine titles at a discount to its membership. MWPA sponsors several book signing events which feature Maine children's book authors and illustrators. Two of these events are the Maine Festival, held at Thomas Point Beach in Brunswick each August, and the MWPA Holiday Open House, held early in December at their Brunswick office. MWPA also sponsors an annual Chapbook competition. For the first time in 1998, this contest is targeted toward children's literature. Children's literature will continue to be the focus of the contest once every four years. For more information, contact:

Maine Writers & Publishers Alliance
12 Pleasant Street
Brunswick, ME 04011
207-729-6333

IN CELEBRATION OF CHILDREN'S LITERATURE CONFERENCE

This University of Southern Maine event celebrates its seventeenth conference in July 1998. This three-day institute held in mid-July at the USM Gorham campus features workshops by nationally-known authors, illustrators, critics, poets, storytellers, librarians, and teachers. In addition, this annual conference includes a Maine segment that features Maine children's books, their authors and illustrators. For more information, contact:

In Celebration of Children's Literature
Professional Development Center
University of Southern Maine
305 Bailey Hall
Gorham, ME 04038
207-780-5326

MAINE BOOK COLLECTIONS

Maine book collections, including Maine children's books, are available at several libraries in the state. These collections are generally available for viewing in the collection rooms. Some collections include older Maine children's books from the 1800s and early 1900s. Maine book collections may be found at the following libraries:

Maine State Library
Maine Author Collection
64 State House Station
Augusta, ME 04333
207-287-5600
(a collection of books by Maine authors; not
available for circulation)

Bangor Public Library
Maine Collection
145 Harlow Street
Bangor, ME 04401
207-947-8336
(Maine children's books are located in a section of
the children's room and are available for circulation
if multiple copies of a book are available)

University of Maine Fogler Library
The Maine Juvenile Collection
Special Collections Department
University of Maine
Orono, ME 04469-5729
207-581-1688
(Maine children's books; available for very limited
circulation–ask Special Collections librarian)

MAINE CHILDREN'S BOOK ILLUSTRATORS GALLERY

A permanent collection of original artwork from Maine children's book illustrators is on display at the Maine Children's Book Illustrators Gallery at the Kennebunk Free Library. This gallery displays close to thirty pieces of artwork by a variety of Maine illustrators, including: Dahlov Ipcar, Barbara Cooney, Gail Gibbons, Mary Beth Owens, Ruth Sargent, Peter Parnall, Charlotte Agell, and Kevin Hawkes. The collection is located in the lower lobby of the library at the entryway to the children's room. Accompanying the exhibit is a notebook in which featured illustrators have included biographical information and details about their artwork. For more information, contact:

Kennebunk Free Library
112 Main Street
Kennebunk, ME 04043
207-985-2173

CAMDEN PUBLIC LIBRARY-THE CHILDREN'S GARDEN

In Camden Public Library's new children's garden, young readers may escape to a "secret garden" and read on circular reading benches which are supported by sculpted stone books which represent 79 different children's books by Maine authors and illustrators. The garden area is screened by spruce and fir trees and includes a variety of flowers found in Maine children's books–lupine, wild strawberries, violets, chamomile, lavender, and more. The featured books include early classics, such as *A White Heron*, by Sarah Orne Jewett and *Rebecca of Sunnybrook Farm*, by Kate Douglas Wiggin as well as modern Lupine Award winners, such as *A Year on Monhegan*, by Julia Dean and *Grandmother Bryant's Pocket*, by Jacqueline Briggs Martin. The center of the garden features books by Camden authors and illustrators. A 20-page booklet is available at the library which gives an overview of the garden's landscape and detailed descriptions of each featured book, including biographical information on the authors and illustrators. For more information, contact:

Camden Public Library
55 Main Street
Camden, ME 04843
207-236-3440

MAINE ARTS COMMISSION

The Maine Arts Commission is an independent state agency funded by the Maine State Legislature and the National Endowment for the Arts. This commission publishes the Maine Artist Roster & Resource Guide which includes listings of Maine children's book authors and illustrators who provide educational programs for schools. The Maine Arts Commission also sponsors an annual Arts in Education program, which has in the past included a Maine Children's Literature Day. For more information, contact:

Maine Arts Commission
State House Station 25
55 Capitol Street
Augusta, ME 04333
207-287-2724

INDEXES

TITLE INDEX

Below is an alphabetical listing of all books included in *A Celebration of Maine Children's Books.*

AUTHOR INDEX

Below is an alphabetical listing of all authors and editors of books included in *A Celebration of Maine Children's Books.* Note that biographical information for authors is found in the entries marked with (bio) after their page numbers.

ILLUSTRATOR INDEX

Below is an alphabetical listing of all illustrators, photographers, and photo-illustrators for books included in *A Celebration of Maine Children's Books*. Note that biographical information for illustrators is found in the entries marked with (bio) after their page numbers.

SUBJECT INDEX

A

Abenaki Indians, 26, 33, 155, 268, 272-3, 285
Acadia National Park, 287
activity books, 291–8
adoption, 119, 125
alcoholism, 110-1, 131
Allagash Wilderness Waterway, 280
alphabet books, 3–5, 8–10
Alzheimer's Disease, 255-6
animals
  endangered species, 275, 282
  farm, 75, 147, 169
  tracks of, 80–1
  See also specific names
anthologies, 155–63
antiques, 105
apples, 40, 90, 274, 301
architecture, 79, 262, 295
Aroostook County, 77
artists, 106, 200, 201, 204, 225-6
artists, youth, 32, 83, 210
asthma, 110
authors/writing. *See* Author Index; *specific author's name*
autobiographies, 198-9, 211-2, 227

B

Bangor, Maine, 45
basketball, 186
Baxter, Percival P., 184-5
Baxter School for the Deaf, 185
Baxter State Park, 184, 198, 279
beaches, 53, 73, 275
Beals Island, 132
bears, 65
beavers, 55–6
bees, 259
Bethel, Maine, 235
Biddeford, Maine, 254
biographies, 183–97, 200-10, 213-27
birds, 249, 271, 275-6, 291
  herons, 156
  puffins, 233–4, 251, 265-6
Blodgett, Cindy, 186
blueberries, 65
boats/boating, 53, 69, 83, 231, 280
  building, 227, 232
  See also lobsters/lobstering
Boothbay Harbor, Maine, 84
Boston, Massachusetts, 79

Bowdoin College, 197, 217
Brewer, Maine, 197
Brown, Margaret Wise, 188–9
Brunswick, Maine, 197, 217, 219
buildings, 79, 262
Bunyan, Paul, 36–7
Burgess, Abbie, 46, 189-91
butterflies, 269

C

Camden, Maine, 102, 106, 205
camping, 70
cancer, 118
canoeing, 280
caribou (animal), 8
cars, Stanley Steamer, 215-6
Carson, Rachel, 193–6
cats, 176–8
Chamberlain, Joshua, 197
chapter books, 97–152
chipmunks, 284
Christmas, 16–7, 22, 38-9, 70-1, 77-8, 172-3
Civil War, 161, 197, 217, 219
clams/clamming, 93, 132
colors, learning, 7
cooking, 78, 294
counting books, 6, 10–11, 172
Cranberry Isles, 48
Criehaven Island, 140
Cushing Island, 204, 225
Cystic Fibrosis, 118

D

Dead River, 100
death, 28, 50, 98, 106, 126-7, 147-8
Deer Isle, 63
diaries, 46, 48
disabilities/special needs, 22, 48, 98-9, 122, 144
dogs, 70, 163, 175
dolls, 105
dreams/dreaming, 175
drugs/substance abuse, 108
ducks, wood, 271
Dudley, Edward, 255-6
Dutremble, Dennis, 254

E

Eastern Egg Rock, 265
East Union, Maine, 102

ACKNOWLEDGEMENTS

Grateful acknowledgments are due to the following publishers for permission to reproduce covers or interior illustrations as follows:

To Down East Books for *Island Alphabet: An ABC of Maine Islands*, copyright © 1995 by Kelly Paul Briggs; *ABC's of Maine*, © 1980 by Harry Smith; *Lobster for Lunch*, illustrations copyright © 1992 by JoEllen McAllister Stammen; *The Story of Andre*, copyright © 1979 by Lew Dietz and Harry Goodridge; *The Whale in Lowell's Cove*, copyright © 1992 by Jane W. Robinson; *Sunny's Mittens*, illustrations copyright © 1990 by Lois Leonard Stock; *The Best Maine Stories*, cover illustration copyright © 1994 by Sarah Knock. To Harry N. Abrams, Inc., Publishers for *Andrew Wyeth*, copyright © 1991 by Harry N. Abrams, Inc. To Apple Island Books for *The Alphabet Symphony*, copyright © 1977 by Bruce A. McMillan. To Arcadia Publishing for *Maine Life at the Turn of the Century*, through the Photographs of Nettie Cummings Maxim copyright © 1995 by Diance and Jack Barnes. To Doubleday, a division of Bantam Doubleday Dell Publishing Group, Inc. for *The Little Island*, copyright 1946, renewed 1973 by Mrs. Roberta B. Rauch, as executrix. To Biddle Publishing Co. for *Highlights of Margaret Chase Smith's Life*, copyright © 1994 by Woolwich Central School. To Blackbirch Press, Inc. for *Seeds and Seedlings*, copyright © 1997 by Dwight Kuhn. To Candlewick Press for *Grandfather's Trolley* copyright © 1995 by Bruce McMillan. To Chelsea House Publishers for *Edan St. Vincent Millay: Poet*, copyright © 1989 by Lisa Desimini, Chelsea House Publishers. To Clarion Books, a division of Houghton Mifflin Co. for *Into the Deep Forest with Henry David Thoreau*, copyright © 1995 by Kate Kiesler. To Mary Dickinson Wood Publisher for *Dahlov Ipcar, Artist*, copyright © 1987 by Pat Davidson Reef; *Bernard Langlais, Sculptor* copyright © 1985 by Pat Davidson Reef. To Escapade Games, Inc. for *The Wildlife of Maine: Coloring–Learning Book*, copyright © 1995 by Escapade Games, Inc. To Front Street Books, Inc. for *Chesire Moon*, copyright © 1996 by Dan Burr. To David R. Godine, Publisher, Inc. for *The Town that got out of Town*, copyright © 1989 by Robert Priest. To Childrens Press for *Maine: America the Beautiful*, copyright © 1989 by Childrens Press; *The Penobscot*, copyright © 1993 by Childrens Press; *Margaret Wise Brown: Author of* Goodnight Moon, copyright © 1993 by hildrens Press. To Harcout Brace & Co. for *The Seasons of Arnold's Apple Tree*, copyright © 1984 by Gail Gibbons; *I Swam with a Seal* copyright © 1995 by Charlotte Agell; *A Mouse's Tale*, copyright © 1991 by Pamela Johnson. To HarperCollins Children's Books for *Big Red Barn*, illustrations copyright © 1989 by Felicia Bond; *Charlotte's Web*, illustrations copyright © 1952, 1980 by Garth Williams; *The Puffins are Back!*, copyright © 1991 by Gail Gibbins; *The Fire Bug Connection: An Ecological Mystery*, copyright © 1993 by Dan Brown, HarperCollins Children's Books; *Inch by Inch: The Garden Song*, copyright © 1995 by Ora Eitan. To Holiday House, Inc. for *The Ghost of Lost Island*, copyright © 1991 by Trina Schart Hyman. To Houghton Mifflin Co. for *A Beach for the Birds*, copyright © 1993 by Bruce McMillan.; *Hugh Pine*, illustrations copyright © 1980 by Lynn Munsinger; *A Summer to Die*, copyright © 1977 by Lois Lowry; *Giants in the Land*, copyright © 1993 by Michael McCurdy; *Grandmother Bryant's Pocket*, illustrations copyright © 1996 by Petra Mathers; *Cousin Ruth's Tooth*, copyright © 1996 by Marjorie Priceman; *A Year on Monhegan Island*, copyright © 1995 by Julia Dean. To Dahlov Ipcar for *My Wonderful Christmas Tree*, copyright © 1986 by Dahlov Ipcar. To Landmark Editions, Inc. for *Fogbound*, copyright © 1993 by Steven Shepard. To Carolrhoda Books, Inc. for *Keep the Lights Burning, Abbie*, copyright © 1985 by Carolrhoda Books. To Little, Brown & Co. for *A Prize in the Snow*, illustrations copyright © 1994 by Mary Beth Owens. To Maine Writers and Publishers Alliance for *Maine Speaks: An Anthology of Maine Literature*, copyright © 1989 by Maine Writers and Publishers Alliance. To Millbrook Press, Inc. for *Rachel Carsen: Caring for the Earth*, copyright © 1992 by Elizabeth Ring. To William Morrow & Co., Inc. for *Beacons of Light: Lighthouses* copyright © 1990 by Gail Gibbins; *Pumpkin Pumpkin*, copyright © 1986 by Jeanne Titherington; *Where are You Going, Emma* copyright © 1988 by Jeanne Titherington; *Fire in the Wind*, jacket art copyright © 1995 by Jos. A. Smith; *A House by the Sea*, illustrations copyright © 1994 by Melissa Sweet; *Jigsaw Jackson*, illustrations copyright © 1996 by Daniel San Souci. To John Muir Publications for *Rough & Ready Loggers*, copyright © 1994 by John Muir Publications. To Orchard Books for *ASH: A Novel*, jacket art copyright © 1995 by Julie Granahan. To Penguin Books USA, Inc. for *Blueberries for Sal*, copyright 1948, © 1976 by Robert McCloskey, *Time of Wonder*, copyright 1957, © 1985 by Robert McCloskey; *Miss Rumphius*, copyright © 1982 by Barbara Cooney Porter. To Philomel Books for *Snow*, illustrations copyright © 1995 by Jeanette Winter. To G. P. Putnam's Sons for *Harriet Beecher Stowe and the Beecher Preachers*, cover illustration copyright © 1994 by Ellen Thompson. To Rissoli International Publications, Inc. for *A Weekend with Winslow Homer*, copyright © 1993, 1996 by Rissoli International Publications, Inc. To Scolastic, Inc. for *Emergency Rescue! Nightmare* at Norton's Mills copyright © 1993 by James and Lois Cowean; *Pigs in the Mud in the Middle of the Rud*, illustrations copyright © 1997 by John Schoenherr. To Silver Burdett Press for *Samantha Smith: A Journey for Peace*, copyright © 1987 by Dillon Press (Silver Burdett Press). To Soundprints for *Chipmunk on Hollow Tree Land*, copyright © 1994 by Trudy Management Corporation and the Smithsonian Institution. To Stemmer House Publishers, Inc. for *A Duck in a Tree*, copyright © 1996 by Jennifer A. Loomis. To Tidal Press for *Bound by the Sea*, copyright © 1986 by Jean G. Howard. To Tilbury House, Publishers for *A Caribou Alphabet*, copyright © 1988 by Mary Beth Owens; *I Slide into the White of Winter*, copyright © 1994 by Charlotte Agell; *Who Belongs Here? An American Story*, illustrations copyright © 1993 by Anne Sibley O'Brien. To Windswept House Publishers for *The Liberty Pole*, copyright © 1987 by Maynard R. Hatcher. To Blackberry Books for *Island in the Bay* copyright © 1993 by Dorothy Simpson. To University Press of New England for *The Quotable Moose: A Contemporary Maine Reader*, copyright © 1994 by Wesley McNair.

Authors' note: As *A Celebration of Maine Children's Books* was going to press, we learned about some upcoming children's books by Maine authors and illustrators. Although it was too late to include these books in the main body of our book, we did want to briefly note these books in this At Presstime listing so that readers may look for them as they become available. In most cases we were not able to preview advance copies of these books, but we gathered information about them from their authors and publishers. Therefore, we cannot speak directly to the exact content or quality of these books; but, as Maine children's book connoisseurs, we anxiously await the arrival of these new books. We thought you might too.

EXPLORING THE DEEP DARK SEA
written and illustrated by Gail Gibbons, ages 5-10, 32 pages, Little, Brown & Co., April 1999, hardcover, ISBN 0316309451. This nonfiction picture book follows a deep-sea diving adventure in a submersible as it collects plants and animals found at different levels of the ocean in the north Atlantic.

MARSHES AND SWAMPS
written and illustrated by Gail Gibbons, ages 5-10, 32 pages, Holiday House, March 1998, hardcover, ISBN 0823413470. This nonfiction picture book tells how marshes and swamps differ, their importance in the balance of nature, and the different kinds of animal and plant life found in marshes and swamps. Information is included about northern salt marshes.

SOARING WITH THE WIND: THE BALD EAGLES
written and illustrated by Gail Gibbons, ages 5-10, 32 pages, William Morrow Junior Books, March 1998, hardcover, ISBN 068813730X. This nonfiction picture book about bald eagles includes information about the Indian lore of bald eagles, how eaglets learn to fly, and how bald eagles have been reintroduced into their natural environment.

A NET OF STARS
written by Jennifer Richard Jacobson, illustrated by Greg Shed, ages 4-8, 32 pages, Dial Books for Young Readers, June 1998, hardcover, ISBN 0803720874. In this picture book, Cumberland author Jennifer Richard Jacobson tells the story of a little girl named Etta who longs to ride the ferris wheel when the county fair comes to town, but first she must overcome her fear of heights.

THAT SWEET DIAMOND: BASEBALL POEMS
written by Paul B. Janeczko, illustrated by Carole Katchen, ages 8-12, 40 pages, Atheneum Books for Young Readers, April 1998, hardcover, ISBN 068980735X. Hebron, Maine, poet Paul Janeczko shares his passion for baseball with these poems about umpires, vendors, double plays, rain delays, and more.

MARVEN OF THE GREAT NORTH WOODS

written by Kathryn Lasky, illustrated by Kevin Hawkes, ages 6-10, 48 pages, Harcourt Brace & Company, 1997, hardcover, ISBN 0152001042, 1997 Lupine Award winner. This picture book shares the story of Marven who is sent by his parents in 1918 to a logging camp in order to save him from the city's influenza epidemic; Marven keeps books for the camp and befriends a gigantic French-Canadian lumberjack.

EVERYBODY'S SOMEBODY'S LUNCH

written by Cherie Mason, illustrated by Gustav Moore, ages 8-12, 40 pages, Tilbury House, Publishers, September 1998, hardcover, ISBN 0884481980. In this picture book set on the Maine coast, a young girl learns about predators and prey after her cat is killed by a coyote. An accompanying teacher's guide written by Cherie Mason and Judy Kellogg Markowsky (80 pages, paperback, ISBN 0-88448-199-9) provides educators with information and learning activities about the importance of predators and prey in the balance of nature.

CAPTAIN'S CASTAWAY

written by Angeli Perrow, illustrated by Emily Harris, ages 4-8, 32 pages, Down East Books, October 1998, hardcover, ISBN 0892-724196. This four-color picture book, based upon a true story and set in Maine, tells the story of a castaway dog that is washed up on a lighthouse island and is befriended by a little girl.

WILD CHILD

written by Lynn Plourde, illustrated by Greg Couch, ages 4-8, 32 pages, Simon & Schuster Books for young Readers, October, 1999, hardcover, ISBN 0689815522. This poetic picture book personifies the season of Autumn as a "wild child" who will not go to bed without a song, a snack, pajamas, and a kiss from Mother Earth.

ELEVEN SECONDS: A STORY OF TRAGEDY, COURAGE, & TRIUMPH

written by Travis Roy with E.M. Swift, ages 12-adult, 226 pages, Warner Books, January 1998, hardcover, ISBN 0446521884. In this autobiography, Yarmouth-Maine-native Travis Roy recounts becoming paralyzed while playing in his first Boston University hockey game and his struggles to rebuild a new life after his spinal-cord injury.

STONE WALL SECRETS

written by Kristine and Robert Thorson, illustrated by Gustav Moore, ages 8-12, 40 pages, Tilbury House, Publishers, June 1998, hardcover, ISBN 0884881956. In this picture book, as a boy and his grandfather repair the family farm's old stone walls, the boy learns about the geology of the New England coast. An accompanying teacher's guide by geologist Ruth Deike (80 pages, paperback, ISBN 0884481964) provides hands-on classroom activities that illustrate basic earth science concepts.

HITTY, HER FIRST HUNDRED YEARS WITH NEW ADVENTURES
written by Rosemary Wells and Rachel Field, illustrated by Susan Jeffers, ages 8-12, 80
pages, Simon & Schuster Books for Young Readers, October 1999, hardcover, ISBN
0689817169. This new version of the 1930 Newbery Medal winner about a hundred
years in the life of a doll named Hitty appeals to younger readers with its shorter format,
full-color illustrations, rewritten text, and new adventures.